Bonds of Blood?

Bonds of Blood?

*State-building and Clanship in
Chechnya and Ingushetia*

Ekaterina Sokirianskaia

BLOOMSBURY ACADEMIC
LONDON • NEW YORK • OXFORD • NEW DELHI • SYDNEY

BLOOMSBURY ACADEMIC
Bloomsbury Publishing Plc
50 Bedford Square, London, WC1B 3DP, UK
1385 Broadway, New York, NY 10018, USA
29 Earlsfort Terrace, Dublin 2, Ireland

BLOOMSBURY, BLOOMSBURY ACADEMIC and the Diana logo
are trademarks of Bloomsbury Publishing Plc

First published in Great Britain 2023
Paperback edition published 2024

Copyright © Ekaterina Sokirianskaia, 2023

Ekaterina Sokirianskaia has asserted her right under the Copyright,
Designs and Patents Act, 1988, to be identified as Author of this work.

For legal purposes the Acknowledgements on p. xi constitute
an extension of this copyright page.

Series design by Adriana Brioso
Cover image: Elder Akhmet Barakhoev addresses protesters during 2018 mass
rallies in Ingushetia, 27 November 2018. (© Yakub Gogiev)

All rights reserved. No part of this publication may be reproduced or transmitted
in any form or by any means, electronic or mechanical, including photocopying,
recording, or any information storage or retrieval system, without prior
permission in writing from the publishers.

Bloomsbury Publishing Plc does not have any control over, or responsibility for,
any third-party websites referred to or in this book. All internet addresses given in this
book were correct at the time of going to press. The author and publisher regret any
inconvenience caused if addresses have changed or sites have ceased to exist,
but can accept no responsibility for any such changes.

A catalogue record for this book is available from the British Library.

Library of Congress Cataloging-in-Publication Data
Names: Sokirianskaia, E. L., author.
Title: Bonds of blood? : state-building and clanship in Chechnya and
Ingushetia / Ekaterina Sokirianskaia.
Description: London ; New York : Bloomsbury Academic, 2023. |
Includes bibliographical references and index.
Identifiers: LCCN 2022038652 (print) | LCCN 2022038653 (ebook) |
ISBN 9781350271692 (hardback) | ISBN 9781350271739 | ISBN 9781350271708 (epub) |
ISBN 9781350271715 (pdf) | ISBN 9781350271722
Subjects: LCSH: Nation-building–Russia (Federation)–Chechnia. |
Nation-building–Russia (Federation)–Ingushetia. | Authoritarianism–Russia
(Federation)–Chechnia. | Authoritarianism–Russia (Federation)–Ingushetia. |
Clans–Russia (Federation)–Chechnia. | Clans–Russia (Federation)–Ingushetia. |
Chechnia (Russia)–Relations–Russia (Federation) | Russia (Federation)–Relations–Russia
(Federation)–Chechnia. | Ingushetia (Russia)–Relations–Russia (Federation) |
Russia (Federation)–Relations–Russia (Federation)–Ingushetia.
Classification: LCC DK511.C37 S634 2023 (print) | LCC DK511.C37 (ebook) |
DDC 327.47–dc23/eng/20220926
LC record available at https://lccn.loc.gov/2022038652
LC ebook record available at https://lccn.loc.gov/2022038653

ISBN:	PB:	978-1-3502-7173-9
	ePDF:	978-1-3502-7171-5
	eBook:	978-1-3502-7170-8

Typeset by Integra Software Services Pvt. Ltd.

To find out more about our authors and books visit www.bloomsbury.com
and sign up for our newsletters.

Contents

List of Figures	ix
List of Tables	x
Acknowledgements	xi
Acronyms	xii
General Maps	xiii
Introduction	1

1 Theory: Approaches to State and Society … 5
   Concepts and hypothesis … 5
   The state … 7
   Modern state-building: state-centred perspectives … 9
   'State-in-society' approaches … 11
   'Clan politics' theories … 12
   Descent and kinship in anthropological theory … 15
   Trust networks, the 'economy of favours' and neopatrimonialism … 18

2 Political Order and Social Integration prior to, during and after the Caucasian War … 25
   Political order and social institutions prior to the Caucasian War (pre-1817) … 25
   Debates on Nakh feudalism and *teip* structures … 27
   Proto-national political institutions and law: *Mekhk-Khel, tukhum* and *adat* … 31
   Social integration and social change during the Caucasian War … 33
      The stirrings of war … 33
      Shamil's imamate … 35
      Political structures and social institutions during and after the Caucasus War … 37
   The Russian state and Chechen and Ingush social institutions after the Caucasian War … 39
      In the Imperial state: social change after the Caucasian War … 39
      New institutions and laws. New sectors of the economy … 40

3	State-Building, Informal Institutions and Social Integration under the Soviet Union (1921–1991)	43
	Social change and the early Bolshevik state (1922–1940)	43
	Deportation, social change and social institutions (1944–1957)	46
	Social change after exile (1957–1991)	51
	Collective memory as a political resource	55
4	Social Integration in Ingushetia and Chechnya	61
	Fieldwork methodology and challenges	61
	Descent groups in Ingushetia and Chechnya	63
	Is the *teip* a social organization? Mechanisms of maintaining *teip* unity	68
	Common residence	68
	Common ownership of land/property	71
	Common defence	72
	Rule of the Elders	74
	Religious rituals (funerals, weddings, mold*)*	77
	Kinship	78
	Categories of kinship and relations between them	78
	Kinship relations and kin solidarity	80
	Co-habitation: kinship enclaves	80
	Kinship and blood feud	82
	Regionalism	82
	Religious institutions	83
	Tariqas *and* virds	83
	Murid *groups and local religious authorities*	85
	Fundamentalists	86
	Mechanisms of recruitment to office	87
	Kinship and jobs	87
	*Role of neighbours/*zemlyaks, *religious, professional and ideological networks*	88
5	State-Building Project in Chechnya under Dzhokhar Dudaev (1991–1994)	91
	State-building policies (1991–1994)	94
	The economy	95
	Law enforcement, justice and the military	99
	Political crisis: the Parliament vs. the President	101
	State-building and informal social institutions	106
	Teips	106
	Neo-traditionalism: the Mekhk-Khel *and Elders in politics*	110

	Kinship	112
	Religion	113
	Political elite formation: ideology, merit and loyalty	114
	The mountains vs. lowland divide?	114
	Regionalism	115
	Slipping towards war	118
6	State-Building in Chechnya under Aslan Maskhadov (1997–1999)	123
	Elections and the early elite	125
	Challengers to the Maskhadov regime	127
	State-building policies	132
	The economy	132
	Industry	133
	Agriculture	135
	Education and healthcare	135
	The armed forces	137
	Law enforcement and criminality	137
	Judicial system	139
	Political crises and government response	140
	State-building: informal institutions and practices	145
	Paramilitary groups	145
	Religion and ideology	146
	Regional opposition	146
	Teips and Elders	147
	Descent, kinship and personal networks in Maskhadov's elite	148
7	State-Building in Ingushetia under Ruslan Aushev (1992–2001)	153
	National movements, founding of the Republic	153
	Creation and consolidation of institutions	156
	State-building, 1992–2001	157
	The economy	157
	Agriculture	159
	Law enforcement	161
	Education and healthcare	162
	Political discord, and the Chechen Wars	164
	State-building and informal social institutions	166
	Teips *and* familias	166
	Kinship, personal networks, ideology in the Ingush elite	172

8	In the Authoritarian State: Ingushetia under Murat Zyazikov (2002–2008)	177
	Conflict spillover	178
	Corruption and 'clanship'	180
9	Ingushetia under Yunus-Bek Yevkurov (2008–2019)	185
	Intra-confessional schism	188
	Economy and governance	191
	The Yevkurov 'clan'	193
	Opposition and protests	195
	The border agreement and massive protests of 2018	197
	2019 protests and clashes: Russia's biggest politically motivated criminal case	203
	Teips in Ingushetia under Yevkurov	206
	Religious groups (*virds*, Salafi communities)	208
10	Chechnya under the Kadyrovs (2000–)	211
	The birth of 'kadyrovtsy'	212
	Establishing control (2004–2008)	215
	Crushing or submerging competitors and insurgency	215
	Silencing the critics	217
	Pseudo-legitimacy	218
	Trust and betrayal	220
	The Chechen elite today	223
	Social reactions	226
Conclusions		231
Bibliography		238
Index		257

List of Figures

2.1	Chechen *teip* structure, nineteenth century (M. Kosven's theory)	29
2.2	Chechen *teip* structure, nineteenth century (M. Mamakaev's theory)	30
2.3	State and society during the Imamate of Shamil (1840–1858)	38
11.1	The model of elite composition and nature of ties within government in Chechen and Ingush societies	236

List of Tables

3.1　Ethnic composition of urban and rural population in Chechen-Ingush Soviet Socialist Republic (ChIASSR) in 1959 and 1970 (in thousands) (Grebenshikov 1977)　52
4.1　Territorial segments of Chechen and Ingush lineages and *teips*　70
7.1　*Teip* representation in Ingush political elite 1992–2001 (four representatives or more)　174

Acknowledgements

I would like to thank Professor Zsolt Enyedi, my PhD supervisor at the Central European University, without whom my return to academia after five years of living and working in the North Caucasus would not have been possible. It is due to his pedagogical wisdom, flexibility and strong faith in me that eventually this book project could be realized. Further, I am very grateful to Doctor Julie Wilhelmsen at the Norwegian Institute of International Affairs (NUPI), for believing in my research and supporting my continued work, as well as for being a thorough, thoughtful and stimulating reader and critic. I also wish to thank Professor James Hughes for his excellent comments and advice on several chapters of this book, and to Susan Høivik and Bryon McWilliams for their edits and comments.

I am deeply indebted to friends and colleagues in Ingushetia and Chechnya, who helped me in my fieldwork, spent hours trying to explain to me the logic of Chechen and Ingush politics and informal social institutions, and drove me all around Ingushetia and Chechnya for interviews. I wish to thank them for being frank and open about the many sensitive issues that we discussed, and for keeping me warm and safe throughout my time in the region. My special thanks go to my interviewees, for entrusting me with their memories and stories, for sharing their views – and for their hospitality.

At least 90 per cent of the credit for this work goes to my mother and to my husband, whose faith and care have kept me going. And here let me add a note of thanks to my cat Kuzya, who shared sleepless nights with me, always staying next to – sometimes on – my laptop computer.

Acronyms

ChIASSR	Chechen-Ingush Autonomous Soviet Socialist Republic
ChRI	Chechen Republic Ichkeria
FSB	Federal Security Service
FSK	Federal Counter-Intelligence Service
HRC	Human Rights Center
ICNU	The Ingush Committee of National Unity
KoUNKh	Committee for Management of National
MVD	Ministry of Internal Affairs
NO ASSR	North Ossetian Autonomous Soviet Socialist Republic
OKChN	United Congress of the Chechen People
OSCE	Organization for Security and Cooperation in Europe
RI	Republic Ingushetia
RSFSR	Russian Soviet Socialist Republic
SB /*Sluzhba Bezopasnosti*	Security Service (of Akhmad Kadyrov)
SIZO	Preliminary detainment facility
SNB	National Security Service
UNHCR	United Nations High Commissioner for Refugees
USSR	Union of Soviet Socialist Republics
WDP	Wainakh Democratic Party

General Maps

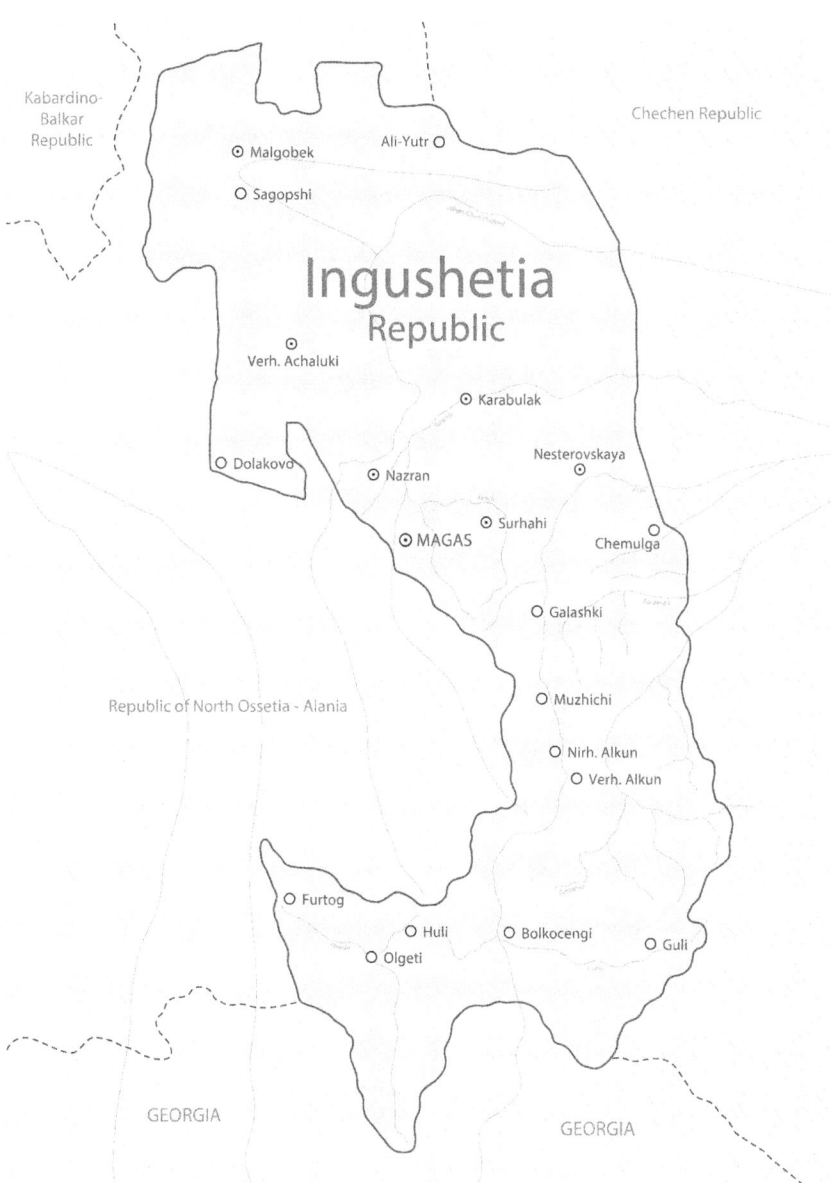

Map 1 Map of Ingush Republic (licensed via Shutterstock).

Map 2 Map of Chechen Republic (licensed via Shutterstock).

Introduction

Since the 1990s, the North Caucasus has been the scene of one of the deadliest and most protracted armed conflicts in Europe, a source of regional and global insurgency and an area of massive violations of human rights. After collapse of the USSR, several regions challenged the integrity of the Russian Federation, but Chechnya was the only republic where the separatist movement resulted in two full-scale wars with Moscow, followed by over a decade of lower-intensity armed conflict between the separatist-Islamist insurgency and the security forces. Ingushetia became caught up in an intense struggle over a territorial dispute with North Ossetia that resulted in a short but ferocious armed conflict in 1992, the only such ethnic clash in post-Soviet Russia.

In recent years, violence in the North Caucasus has abated significantly, but political conflicts linger on. Chechnya has become an enclave of lawlessness within now fully dictatorial Russia while Ingushetia lives in chronic political crisis caused by an ineffective authoritarian government, corruption and, since October 2018, new conflict over the demarcation of its de facto administrative borders with Chechnya.[1]

This book is intended as a response to the widely accepted analytical claim that stability, quality of governance and challenges of democratization and consolidation in the North Caucasus hinge on the politics of pre-existing informal structures – primarily clans, or *teips*. Indeed, Chechen and Ingush *teips* and their leaders seem to feature prominently in the public space. The Ingush protests that broke out in 2018 in response to the border dispute with Chechnya showcased the Elders presiding over the rally in their picturesque, traditional tall woollen hats and speaking in the name of their clans. In 2020, the Ingush clan leaders announced that their members would not support the amendments to the Russian Constitution proposed by the Kremlin. The Chechen elite is often cited as a classic example of a political-military clan tightly integrated on the basis of kinship.

This book is the first attempt since the nineteenth century at systematic analysis of the role of descent groups (*teips* or *taips*) and kinship in contemporary subnational state-building in Chechen and Ingush societies. It is based on over 300 interviews, five years of participant observation and altogether 20 years of work on the region.

---

[1] On 26 September 2018, Ramzan Kadyrov and Yunus-Bek Yevkurov, the heads of Chechnya and Ingushetia, respectively, concluded an administrative boundary delimitation deal. In Ingushetia, this was widely perceived as violating the territorial interests of the Ingush, and resulted in mass protests against the government, schism in the elite and a visible deterioration of ethnic relations with the Chechens. The protests were eventually crushed, the leaders were imprisoned or fled the country, and Yunus-Bek Yevkurov was forced to resign.

I first became aware of the 'clan politics' argument with regard to Ingushetia and Chechnya as a graduate student at St Petersburg State University. But it was not until 2003, when I moved from St Petersburg to the North Caucasus, that I started to analyse this issue seriously – and realized that these widely held assumptions as to the role of *teips* were crude, simplistic and often directly false, and that the phenomena of kinship and clans remained poorly understood.

However, a few weeks in the field showed me that learning about clans from interviews and surveys would be no easy task. Matters related to kinship and family were often seen as private affairs, preferably not to be discussed. Some local intellectuals and the representatives of the political elite were reluctant to discuss the political relevance of *teips*, seeing my interest in this issue as indicating a colonial mindset on the part of this outsider. Other, more traditionalist respondents, were happy to speak but reproduced idealized, romanticized discourse about the institutions of kinship. Respondents with little formal education generally had scant understanding or experience of being interviewed about political matters for academic purposes. They were often suspicious of the interviewer, which in turn tended to make them a poor source of information.

To deal with these challenges I opted for the ethnographic method of participant observation. I settled in the region, took up positions at a human rights NGO in Ingushetia, and became a lecturer at the history department of the Chechen State University, with a local salary and lifestyle. I shared housing with refugees in Nazran and stayed with Chechen families in Grozny, commuted by public transport (a noteworthy setting for political debates), did my shopping at local markets and had my hair cut at local salons. Everywhere I talked to people.

My position at the human rights group Memorial involved working with victims of rights abuse in Chechnya, Ingushetia and North Ossetia. This meant considerable travel, sometimes to distant high mountain settlements, and enabled me to observe certain families, villages and individuals in different situations over extended periods of time. I spent altogether five years in the region, and some of what I learnt about 'how things work' is reflected in this book.

In compliance with the principle outlined by the American anthropologist David Schneider (Schneider 1984), for the first four years I simply observed, without asking structured questions. Then, having gained some familiarity with local societies, having analysed kinship terms and mapped kinship systems, I started my interviews.

First, I selected 20 *teips*/lineages (10 Chechen, 10 Ingush) from various areas of Ingushetia and Chechnya for in-depth analysis. I interviewed several members of each *teip*, from different settlements, of various ages and, when possible, both males and females.

Second, I studied several settlements (Achaluki, Ekazhevo, Gamurzievo, Kantyshevo, in Ingushetia; Gekhi-Chu, Samashki, Shatoy, Zamaj-Yurt, Zumsoi in Chechnya) and tried to map clanship and kinship relations there and see the role of traditional institutions at the local level. I then spoke with representatives of various *teips* in each village, to get their accounts of the settlement and relationships within the village.

Third, I analysed the personal networks that were used for gaining access to jobs and public office, by interviewing professionally active Chechens and Ingush.

Between 2008 and 2010 I conducted more than 200 in-depth interviews with *teip* leaders or activists, politicians, experts, scholars, NGO workers, lawyers, former combatants, students at Islamic universities, journalists, Sufi and fundamentalist religious leaders, and Elders, supplemented with a new round of interviews in 2019 and 2020. In addition, between 2017 and 2018, I interviewed 22 Chechen exile politicians in Europe and USA, former fighters and activists.

For reasons of personal security, many of my interviewees agreed to speak only on condition of anonymity, so I have withheld or changed their names. It proved particularly difficult to do fieldwork in Chechnya in recent years: the climate of fear is massive, and none of my sources agreed to have their names mentioned.

I also had many opportunities to discuss kinship-related issues with groups, often spontaneous conversations at tea or during lunch break, or during long trips around Ingushetia or Chechnya – or around the table of a hospitable Chechen family in Europe. I found such talks particularly rewarding because my interlocutors would argue with each other and contribute arguments to the discussion, brainstorming for examples, trying to explain things to me. This proved preferable to conducting formal focus groups, as I had a relationship of trust with these people, and they were ready to offer important insider views. I think it was particularly helpful to have started my structured fieldwork only after several years in the field. I could then ask informed questions, which in turn helped the respondents to open up.

Although the main focus of this book is on the immediate past, I devote considerable space to prior historical analysis as well. Here the aim has been to check the degree of historical tenacity of primordial institutions; to refute the arguments of primordialists on their own ground; and to indicate the plausibility of certain theories on the nature of the political processes and who the real decision-makers are.

Further, this research builds on a set of explanatory case studies of the post-Soviet state-building projects pursued by individual political leaders (presidents Dudaev, Maskhadov, Aushev, Zyazikov, and heads of republics – Kadyrov and Yevkurov) that sought to provide theory-informed propositions about the interaction of informal patterns of social integration and state-building in the Northern Caucasus.

In this book I speak of subnational 'state-building', notwithstanding the fact that in Ingushetia since 1992 and in Chechnya since 2003 the post-Soviet state-building projects have been carried out de facto and *de jure* within the formal framework of the Russian Federation.

Many experts on federalism hold that, after the collapse of the USSR, Russia had no choice but to adopt a federal system: its vast territories, the multinational population, pre-existing territorial divisions, and – most importantly – centrifugal forces and ethnic separatism were simply too strong at that time (Busygina 2018; Zubarevich 2018; Isakova and Jalilova 2018). Russian federalism is asymmetric and complex, reflecting the unique features of the country: its constituent entities differ greatly in size, population, degree of urbanization, the volume of gross national product, budget revenues and birth rates.

Under the Constitution of 1993, national republics received the status of subnational states: they have their own constitutions, parliaments, presidents (subsequently renamed heads) and supreme courts. Each region could introduce local features in institutional design, to accommodate regional needs. I use the term 'state' in the purely sociological sense: other usages – especially those common in international relations studies – are not considered.

My analysis of these state-building case studies and elite profiles draws on interviews, the academic literature, newspapers, statistical data and memoirs. I have consulted a broad array of documents and statistics produced by governments, parliaments, courts and NGOs, as well as monitoring periodicals issued in the two republics.

And what did I find? Basically, that Chechen and Ingush societies are *not* clan-based. Informal social structures did play a role in subnational state-building, but there were much stronger factors that influenced the outcomes, and the trajectories of these republics were not determined by any 'primordial' social constructs. Until quite recently, elite formation and political processes in the North Caucasus were not shaped by any pre-existing informal identities or structures, but by regional leaders on the basis of ideology, political programmes, religion and/or economic interests. The current prominence of trust groups in politics is in fact the outcome of the subnational authoritarianism brought about by political changes in Russia under Vladimir Putin. I argue that the strength of ties in the government is directly influenced by existence of effective systems of checks and balances and the factor of risk to its members – such as physical elimination or prosecution for economic crimes. The greater the personal risks to elites, the stronger are the ties which hold them together – as exemplified by the incumbent regime in Chechnya.

This book is meant as a contribution to theory debates about informal social structures in unevenly modernized societies and subnational state-building in post-communist Russia. What is the relationship between state and society? What is the role of history, leadership, ideas? How do they play out at the subnational level, in a region with a complex history of colonialism, Soviet authoritarian modernization and post-Soviet decades of war and trauma? Have the post-Soviet state-building processes in the North Caucasus been driven by primordial structures and ties – or do they reflect the great winds of change of 1989–1991, as has been the case in Moscow, Berlin, Warsaw? Has the failure to build consolidated pluralist polities been predetermined by the traditional structures of the society?

These are the basic questions I seek to answer in the following chapters of this book.

1

Theory: Approaches to State and Society

This study emerged as a reaction to the mainstream claim that the degree of consolidation, conflict, stability and quality of governance of political regimes in Ingushetia and Chechnya are primarily a function of the interplay between the subnational state-building projects and pre-existing informal structures, mainly clans (*teips*). The fragmentation and social complexity of Chechen and Ingush societies, as well as their late and uneven modernization, are also cited as factors that destabilize politics in the two republics and impede effective state-building (Naimark 2001; Tishkov 2004; Lieven 1998; Collins 2006).

Such explanations may sound convincing, but little research has enquired into precisely what these 'primordial' social structures are, whether they have changed over time, how they function and interact with the state, and what other patterns of social interaction have played important roles in post-Soviet state-building in Ingushetia and Chechnya.

This book draws on several disciplinary strands that are rarely brought together in a sustained examination of the questions in focus here. I combine historical, anthropological, sociological and political science approaches in order to shed light on the macro- and micro-level social dynamics of descent and kinship in Chechen and Ingush politics.

Concepts and hypothesis

My analysis builds on the concept of *pattern of social integration:* a set of identities, practices and power structures that dominate the behaviour of social organizations, creating special social subsystems within a society. Such a pattern of social integration requires an informally institutionalized power structure and a common identification among its social group.

I have found this concept useful because I needed a fairly broad, non-normative term to indicate a range of heterogeneous informal subsystems in a given society. Terms such as 'integrative mechanism' or 'network' would be too narrow and specific, whereas 'social organization' indicates a higher degree of formal institutionalization, while a 'pattern of social integration' is a rather generic concept that serves my purposes well.

My initial hypothesis was in line with the 'clan politics' claim: I had hypothesized that subnational state-building in Chechnya and Ingushetia was determined by interactions with clans. However, extensive fieldwork, interviews with experts, analysis of historical data and of modern political processes showed that this hypothesis would have to be dropped. Instead, I argue that, as a result of demographic growth and social change brought about by colonization, Soviet modernization and forced resettlements, *teips* are no longer important in political integration. However, I find that informal patterns of integration still play a role in society, and therefore I provide detailed bottom-up analyses of five patterns of social integration that are prominent in Chechen and Ingush societies today: *descent, kinship, religion, regionalism* and *ideology*. Thereby I hope to clarify much of the confusion surrounding the interplay of informal institutions and practices and their interactions with the state.

The challenges associated with doing research on informal institutions start with defining what such institutions are, and how to distinguish them from formal institutions. As Helmke and Levitsky note, the term 'informal institution' has been applied to 'a dizzying array of phenomena, including personal networks, clientelism, corruption, clans and mafias, civil society, traditional culture and a variety of legislative, judicial and bureaucratic norms'; they define informal institutions as 'socially shared rules, usually unwritten, that are created, communicated, and enforced outside of officially sanctioned channels' (Helmke and Levitsky 2004: 727). Yaroslav Startsev, another scholar of informal institutions, holds that the social science literature uses the term 'informal institution' in a highly normative fashion that presupposes binary oppositions like 'transparent/shadowy', 'official/unofficial', 'written/unwritten', and designates the *absence* of a quality – and he asks: why is the formal so important as the reference point for the study of political institutions (Startsev 2005: 333–4)?

Indeed, informal institutions can obstruct the functioning of formal institutions and create problems. It is widely recognized that, in matters of politics, primordial informal institutions and patterns of social integration clash with the integrative logic of the state.

According to the renowned American anthropologist Clifford Geertz, this holds true especially for patterns of political integration that are based on primordial ties: 'one is bound to one's kinsman, one's neighbor, one's fellow believer, *ipso facto*, as the result not merely of personal affection, practical necessity, common interest, or incurred obligation, but at least in great part by virtue of some unaccountable absolute import attributed to the very tie itself' (Geertz 1973: 259). The primordial patterns of political integration are of the same order as state power: as 'self-sustaining, maximal social units, as candidates for nationhood' (Geertz 1994: 32).

Informal institutions may also enhance the effectiveness of state institutions by providing solutions to problems that cannot be remedied within the formal state framework. Indeed, they can reinforce or even substitute for the formal institutions they appear to undermine (Helmke and Levitsky 2004: 728). Thus, according to Startsev (2005: 333), the interaction between the two should be a key focus of research.

Helmke and Levitsky (2004: 728) proposed a now widely recognized typology of interactions between formal and informal institutions, including complimentary, accommodating, substitutive and competing relations. I have adopted a modified version in which the various informal patterns of social integration and the state are seen as interacting in five main ways: *accommodation/cooperation, compartmentalization, competition/challenge, marginalization* and *capture*. *Accommodation* implies peaceful and constructive interaction for mutual benefit. *Compartmentalization* results in the parallel existence of state and informal actors within closed subsystems, each following their own logic. *Competition* implies rivalry between and among various informal identities and institutions, including direct challenge. *Marginalization* pushes an actor to the periphery, whereas *capture* results in informal institutions partly or fully taking over the state. This typology is applied in the subsequent chapters.

Helmke and Levitsky note another gap in research on informal institutions: much of the empirical literature has neglected questions of why and how such institutions emerge: 'They are frequently taken as historical givens. As a result, they often understate the degree to which informal institutions are modified, adapted or even reinvented over time' (2004: 730). With this book I aim to fill the gap as regards informal institutions and identities related to descent and kinship in the two North Caucasian republics of Ingushetia and Chechnya. I examine how the state and informal organizations have accommodated, blended with, marginalized and subjugated each other, noting the resultant effects on state-building and political unification.

The state

'The state is undeniably a messy concept', begins Michael Mann's sweeping 1988 study, *States, War and Capitalism*. Thousands of pages have been written on the state, yet scholars still barely agree on its definition. However, they do agree on what it is *not*: 'The state is not an eternal and unchanging element in human affairs. For most part of its history, humanity got by [...] without a state' (Pierson 1996: 35).

Societies had power structures well before the emergence of states. These early power structures were defined according to traditional rules and were obeyed because of the sacredness of their status (Weber 1995: 42). The rule of gerontocracy (the power of elders, understood literally as the oldest in years, and the most familiar with traditions) and primary patriarchalism (the rule of a given individual in an extended family, or kin group) are clear examples of political power structures that came before the rise of the state (Weber 1995: 43)

The authority of gerontocracies and primary patriarchies were cemented by legal codes: diverse sets of social norms, social pressure, customary law and judicial procedure. The power structures and legal codes of pre-modern societies were never cohesive. As noted by Joel Migdal, 'Through most of human history territories have hosted a diversity of rules of the game – one set for this tribe and another for a neighbouring tribe, one for this region and another for that ... Social control has not been of a piece, but it has frequently been highly fragmented through a territory' (1988: 275). In the case of Chechnya in pre-colonial times, the rule of Elders was supported by a blend of two often competing systems of law – *adat* and *Sharia*.

In order to become states, societies must undergo tremendous change – not merely reconstructing their social relationships, but conceptualizing them anew (Durkheim 1964). The power structures of stateless societies were first threatened by the emergence of the traditional state, which sought to subjugate them under its own control. Nevertheless, in the pre-modern state the penetration remained low, and the degree of local autonomy high. The pre-modern state was more of a 'unified symbol of an actual disunity' than a general factor of cohesion (Abrams 1988).

This was also true of Russia, which like most multinational empires, left the social structures of conquered or annexed peoples and territories relatively intact. Still, it brought about social change, through land reforms and fiscal policies that economically institutionalized individual extended families, and changed employment patterns – also among the Chechens and Ingush. In the context of colonial wars, new social integrative structures like Sufi Muslim brotherhoods emerged and were strengthened. Although the colonial wars shattered the traditional economic systems, and multiple relocations and mass extermination had a heavy impact on public order and social institutions, it was only the modern state that managed to achieve a high degree of penetration into society.

The modern state introduced routine, formalized, rationalized institutions that spread throughout the territories of the state (Weber 1978: 54–6). The state gradually expanded its power through regular taxation, a permanent bureaucracy, law creation and enforcement, and monopolies on mobilization and violence (Mann 1995: 325). In order to carry out these functions, the modern state attempted to subjugate all competing power centres, so as to establish a monopoly on rule-making.

The process of crystallizing the power of the modern state was never smooth. Historically, emerging states were sprawling organizations within societies that coexisted with many other formal and informal social organizations, ranging from kin groups to tribes and religious organizations (Migdal 1987: 396). The state elites now sought to dominate these social organizations and fought fiercely to monopolize the creation and enforcement of binding rules (Migdal 1987: 397).

State-building is a non-linear process: brief periods of sweeping change are followed by longer periods of adaptation and absorption, during which adjustments to these changes can be made (Khoury and Kostiner 1991: 17). In the North Caucasus, the Bolsheviks were the first Russian government that set about building a modern statehood, seeking to penetrate deep into the social structure, even in the domain of family life, in order to integrate various social segments into a cohesive political unit. In their early years, the Bolsheviks achieved impressive progress in terms of modernization and development. Later, the ensuing forced collectivization, with *de-kulakization*, anti-Islamic campaigns and the repression of the Muslim clergy, undermined much of this effort, strengthening traditional mechanisms of self-government instead.

In this book I understand state-building as a process of creating effective government that entails gaining a monopoly on binding rule-making, and the enforcement of those rules within the territory of the state, by force if necessary. I adopt Michael Mann's definition of the *modern state*:

> (1) A differentiated set of institutions and personnel embodying (2) centrality in the sense that political relations radiate outwards from a center to cover (3) a territorially demarcated area over which it exercises (4) a monopoly of authoritative binding rule-making, backed up by a monopoly of the means of violence'.
>
> (1993: 4)

A 'state' is not necessarily the same as a *modern* state. Young states often fail as regards one or more of Mann's defining attributes because they operate in weakly homogenized, loosely integrated societies with strong informal patterns of social integration that follow their own binding rules, and do not recognize the state's monopoly on justice and violence. I will use the Mannian definition as a benchmark in analysing Chechnya during its de facto independence. Further, Migdal sees the modern state as the culmination of a process transcending these localized patterns of social integration in societies that had previously made the rules (Migdal, Kohli and Shue 1994: 12). Chechnya and Ingushetia are still in the midst of this process.

Modern state-building: state-centred perspectives

The classic founding fathers of social science – Emil Durkheim, Karl Marx and Max Weber – treated the state as a holistic, autonomous structure existing above societies. They linked the emergence of the modern state to the diversification of labour, industrialization and capitalism which had led to the unprecedented centralization of modern societies. As the historical chapters of this book will show, for Chechen and Ingush societies the first Imamate of Shamil and the Russian colonial state were by definition autonomous – imposed and alien. However, the modernization processes that they enforced resulted in social change as described by the classics. These transformations eroded or destroyed the traditional structures, gradually creating some of the preconditions for effective local participation in governance.

Durkheim argues that the state must provide moral guidance to society. As society develops, the significance of the state's functions expands. The division of labour and social differentiation result in a society with a high level of interdependence. Solidarity through commonalities is replaced by solidarity through differences and the strengthening of social bonds. In turn, this new solidarity is maintained through the strong moral authority of the state – which proved extremely complicated in the context of violent colonial history such as of Ingushetia or Chechnya.

For Marx, the modern state is a class state governed by egoism of private property in the interests of the bourgeoisie. In this theory, capitalism destroys the personal ties of the pre-industrial means of dominance, leaving only naked self-interest as the bond between individuals. In his analysis of Bonapartism, Marx (1852) sought to portray the state not as a simple reflection of social forces, but as an example of the separation between the state and society through which the state seems 'to have made itself completely independent' of all classes and soars 'high above society'. Ironically, this Bonapartist state, soaring high above and completely detached from society, is a very precise description of Chechnya under Ramzan Kadyrov today. The Chechnya's elites (its modern bourgeoisie), installed, protected and guaranteed impunity by Moscow, are highly autonomous from society. They rule through coercion and money, intimidating opponents and buying supporters, while the social abyss between the privileged and the rest is unprecedented as will be shown in Chapter 10.

Weber's fundamental contribution to state theory is the concept of rational-legal bureaucracy, the result of centralizing trends in modern industrial society. The highly specialized division of labour in capitalist and socialist economies, says Weber, must inevitably lead to greater top-down bureaucracy – technically superior administration, and larger-scale planning and resources management. Employees of modern states live freely as individuals, constrained occupationally only by impersonal bureaucratic obligations. The legal rationale underlying this bureaucracy eliminates personal, irrational and emotional elements from the administration of the state, Weber argues. The state and its bureaucracy become increasingly autonomous of society and play a crucial role in moulding its institutions (Weber 1954, 1964). Weberian bureaucracy has been scarce in modern Russia, but – as shown in Chapter 3 – in the late Soviet period, the country (including some Chechens and Ingush who in the 1970s and 1980s were finally granted access to regional government jobs and higher management positions) developed certain elements and values of Weberian bureaucracy. That was probably the only such period in the history of the North Caucasus.

Classical social theorists saw their analyses of states as identifying universal qualities. They predicted that within recently modernized, post-colonial societies the processes of modernization and state-building would be similar to those observed in Western European countries. Such modernization involved major social reconstruction: traditional societies had to shelve their archaic customs and agrarian lifestyles, and embrace technology, education and open systems of government. Much of this is valid for today's Chechen and Ingush societies; however, their modernization has proved to be non-linear, uneven and dependent on the metropolis – resulting in different outcomes compared to the West.

Subsequent studies of modernization which further developed the classical theories have provided useful insights into social transformation from the pre-modern realities to modern, urban, secular, socially mobile and democratically governed societies. They underscore various aspects of modernization, from economic growth and social development (Rostow 1960: 4–16) to modernization on the level of individual consciousness (Inkels and Smith 1974), including by the internalization of certain values, such as achievement, success, spirit of invention and innovation (McClelland 1961).

Although some authors, like Daniel Lerner (1958), acknowledge that 'societies-in-a-hurry' do not always follow the Western path of development, the overall premises of modernization theory build on Western Europe as the norm. My analysis of Chechens and Ingush exemplifies the main premise of modernization theorists, which holds that social institutions transform with the advent of a modern economy fuelled by urbanization and education. At the same time, it shows that catch-up and dependent modernization often results in the uneven transformation of economies and technology (which can modernize rapidly), and of social institutions, practices and identities (which generally transform at a much slower pace). Moreover, pre-existing social identities and structures tend to be intentionally preserved and developed as distinct markers of cultural identity.

The world-wide wave of democratization after 1972 – during which, over a 20-year period, the number of countries with democratically elected governments increased from 44 to 107 – inspired another body of research that departed from the single uniform perspective on democracy, and explored different ways in which societies, even the poorer and less modernized ones, could build democratic states (Rustow 1970: 346). Did Chechens and Ingush have a chance to build a democracy? – or was their path predetermined by their history and traditional social structures? I hold that they had such an opportunity – but that the elites missed their chance to preserve democratic institutions (as in de facto independent Chechnya), or the conditions of increasingly authoritarian Russia did not allow subnational democratic governance to survive (as in Ingushetia under Ruslan Aushev).

The democratic transition literature sees the role of political elites in preserving democratic institutions, and the dynamics of relations between elites and constituencies, as crucial. Samuel Huntington (1984) claimed that democratic regimes brought about through mass protest seldom lasted; Juan Linz (1990) emphasized the importance of leadership in successful democratization, and the commitment of elites to democratic principles, as well as their ability to convince their societies of the value of democracy. Authors like Dankwart Rustow underscored the importance of a pre-existing sense of community for the success of democracy, 'preferably … quietly taken for granted that is above mere opinion and mere agreement', adding that 'the hardest struggles in a democracy are those against the birth defects of the political community' (Rustow 1970: 363).

In post-Soviet Ingushetia and Chechnya, leadership has played a very prominent role in regime transformation. However, in Chechnya, Rustowian lack of agreement over the basic framework of the political community – should it be separatist, Islamist or Russian? – and the high degree of political uncertainty were serious weaknesses of the de facto independent republic's state-building experiment. Moreover, democratic consolidation of the regimes has been a major problem in both republics.

'State-in-society' approaches

Three decades after the collapse of the USSR it is clear that most of the post-Soviet states have *not* transitioned to democracy – on the contrary, they have moved towards new forms of authoritarianism. In Russian regions, this shift was Moscow-imposed, but there was strong buy-in of this model from local elites. Explaining such processes requires a shift of focus on social dynamics and social practices that are conducive to authoritarianism based on informal politics and that create acute problems in quality of governance.

Scholars of the Middle East who emphasized that the state is not always a single monolithic entity with an ultimate monopoly of power offered models that would provide a promising framework for the analysis of relations between states, and society in Ingushetia and Chechnya (Khoury and Kostiner 1991; Migdal 1988; Migdal, Kohli and Shue 1994). The 'state-in society' approach developed by Joel Migdal and scholars like Atul Kohli and Vivien Shue, offered important directions in comparative politics. According to the 'state-in-society' approach, states may help to mould the societies of which they are a part, but also are continuously shaped by the societies in which they are embedded (Migdal, Kohli and Shue 1994: 2).

Migdal depicts society as a mélange of social organizations in which the groups exercising control can be heterogeneous in form, and in their rules. Social control may be concentrated among the groups, rather than largely in the state (Migdal 1988: 28).

Moreover, the state is not a fixed ideological entity. Rather, it embodies an ongoing dynamic, a changing set of goals in respect to its engagement with other social organizations (Migdal, Kohli and Shue 1994: 12). Such organization provides opportunities for individuals: 'social control rests on the organizational ability to deliver key components for individual's strategies of survival' (Migdal 1988: 27). This merging of social forces also presupposes a combination of rational strategies and emotional attachments. 'In stitching together strategies for survival, people use myths or symbols to help explain their place and prospects in an otherwise bewildering world', adds Migdal (1988: 29). In this mélange the state is one organization among many – which, as we will see in the following sections, very neatly describes the situation in post-Soviet Ingushetia and Chechnya.

In such societies, values are not centralized (Migdal 1988: 39). Thus, three systems of justice operate simultaneously in post-Soviet Ingushetia and Chechnya: customary law (*adat*), Islamic law (*Sharia*) and Russian law. When social organizations are in conflict, and each proposes a different vision of society, individuals must choose from among competing components in determining their strategies of survival or in maximizing their benefit. 'These are difficult choices when people also face the possibility of competing sanctions. The state becomes part of such an environment of conflict', notes Migdal (1988: 29).

The 'state-in-society' approach developed by Joel Migdal provides a very useful lens for the analysis of my case studies in the following chapters – with some limitations. Although post-colonial, and low-ranking in scale of economic development, the polities in the North Caucasus cases I have studied were nevertheless moderately industrialized; they did not suffer from extreme poverty and have been mostly literate. Partly for this reason, and partly because the state had been initially colonial and ethnically distinct, the idea of 'autonomy of the state' had already been internalized by the population, resulting in stable boundaries between the state and social forces, with basically unfluctuating distinctions between the state, and society. Migdal's model will play out differently in different periods of Chechen and Ingush state-building periods and be particularly accurate for Chechnya in its period of de facto independence 1997–1999.

'Clan politics' theories

Noteworthy among attempts to situate the state within the web of social organizations is the academic literature on clan politics that has emerged in early 2000s. This approach derives largely from regional studies of Central Asia, among the most outstanding contributions of which are *Clan Politics and Regime Transition in Central Asia*, and *Modern Clan Politics: The Power of 'Blood' in Kazakhstan and Beyond* (Collins 2006; Schatz 2004). Due to high relevance of the clan politics approach to my arguments, and because Kathleen Collins argues that her theory holds also for Chechnya, I examine these books in some detail here.

In her thorough comparative study of post-communist Central Asia, Collins asserts that clans played a predominant role in the process of regime transition, transformation and state-building and were 'the dominant social actors and political players' in political development (Collins 2006: 3, 7). She defines a clan as 'an informal organization comprising a network of individuals linked by kin and fictive kin identities' (2006: 17). Further, clans are seen as organizations that predate the modern state (2006: 43) and persist from pre-modern times (2006: 44) because of their capacity to adapt and resist repressive modern states (2006: 67).

Collins' terminology of clans is very broad. She speaks of a 'Samarkand clan', or the 'more narrow Tashkent clan', as well as 'Ferghana Valley Elites', 'Ajtmatov networks' or the Karimov 'Family' in Uzbekistan (Collins 2006). In her view, clans may be 'families', 'cliques', 'networks', 'oblasts' and 'regions', all of which Collins sees as variations on the theme. Collins explains their tenacity by the fact that Russian colonial and Soviet governance was either indirect, or limited and weak – which allowed local populations to continue live their daily lives in their own traditional ways (2006: 64). These institutions have clearly changed over time, and this transformation is relevant for the analysis of their current condition – which, however, is not taken into consideration.

Further: in both pre-modern and modern times in Central Asia, 'clans, tribes and localist networks have generally defined their groups according to kinship identity ties, even though actual blood ties do not always exist, more important than the objective reality of kinship is the subjective sense of identity and the use of norms of kinship – such as in-group reciprocity and loyalty – to bind the group and protect its members' (Collins 2006: 17). While admitting that clans can include representatives of a shared locality, village or regional network, as well as colleagues from school and business, she integrates them into her theory by gathering them into a network of fictive kinship (2006: 26).

The clan bond forms 'strong ties' based on predominantly ascriptive relationships and norms that make clan boundaries, although not fixed and unchanging, difficult to permeate (Collins 2006: 23). For Collins, 'clan constitutes the identity and social universe of its members'; it holds an intrinsic meaning and legitimacy and cannot merely change its social constituency (2006: 29, 58).

Collins extrapolates her analysis of Central Asia clans to Chechnya, taking the extreme violence in Chechnya as a vivid illustration of how 'interclan tensions may lead to group mobilization and violence' (2006: 41). However, without careful anthropological scrutiny of 'clans', or research into descent and kinship patterns in a given community, or analysis of the links between political elites and their communities, one cannot convincingly argue that pre-modern structures have truly persisted and have shaped current political realities. My research bolsters the argument for studying informal politics on a highly case-specific basis, because knowledge of the informal social and political forces in one geographic area should be critically tested before applying it, as facts, to another geographic area. Knowledge of Central Asia does not automatically apply to Chechnya.

Edward Schatz builds on Collins's argument that clans – which he sees as pre-existing kinship identities where precise genealogical knowledge defines membership – have managed to persist, avoiding the often brutal methods of modernization, because of their inherent concealed nature (Schatz 2004: 26). Further, he argues that by the 1990s clan politics no longer centred on relatively homogeneous groups but represented flexible kin-based networks that were a resource for individuals in their political and economic affairs (2006: 45).

He sees clan as the emotional building blocks of identity (Schatz 2004: 12). However, his observation that, when accessing power, Russians living in Kazakhstan behave much like the 'Fourth Umbrella Clan' seems to indicate the climate under a non-transparent, authoritarian, semi-legal government, and not pre-existing emotional identities.

Schatz asserts that his theory applies to most of the post-Soviet South, most clearly in Chechnya, where 'sub-ethnic teips became enshrined in Moscow's decision to launch a bloody invasion in 1994; some groups were most closely allied with Russia and others more staunch supporters of independence' (2004: xvi).

My research shows that the role of kin affiliations at the micro-level does not indicate a similar role for clan-based politics at the macro-level. I find that modern political clans in Chechnya are not organic kinship identity organizations, but interest groups motivated by the instinct for self-preservation and self-centred economic agendas. That can also explain why clans played no role in escalating Russian–Chechen relations to war in 1994.

Some scholars have gone further than Collins and Schatz and have based their arguments of Chechen clans on the findings of nineteenth-century ethnographic analyses or common orientalist stereotypes. The most notable example is Maria Sultan (2003), who holds that Chechen society is 'tribal and egalitarian in nature' and divided into 'nine Tukhums (tribes) subdivided into Teips (or clans), then village-level units and then into individual households' (Sultan 2003: 441). Moreover, according to Sultan, Chechen society is acephalous, or without a head, thereby 'bordering on anarchic, given the emphasis on equality' and 'very close to the archetype of democracy, given that it is councils of elders that are the only decision-making authority with any legitimacy in society' (2003: 442). She further argues that the Council of Elders, or Mekhk-Khel, is 'the main decision-making mechanism, entrusted with the power to adjudicate disputes, to decide on matters of war and peace' (2003: 442)

Sultan contends that there exists in Chechnya a 'fundamental incompatibility between the modern nation-state and a tribal social structure' (Sultan 2003: 443). At the root of this disconnect, she writes, is the dynamic 'at a deeper societal level' in Chechnya, and especially in the mountainous regions of Chechnya, 'of a traditional (though modernizing) tribal society in conflict with the alien modern nation-state, which for decades has been trying to incorporate tribal areas into itself, thereby flouting the social and legal codes of tribal societies and hence wittingly or unwittingly seeking to undermine the very foundations of society among the tribal peoples' (2003: 443).

Based on these arguments, Sultan makes policy recommendations: she prescribes the division of Chechnya into lowland and mountainous areas, in the hope that people living in the lowland territories would accept some kind of union with Russia. The mountain regions would then be organized into a 'Tribal Area' governed by a 'Political Agent' who would enforce the law through community councils. 'Should the perpetrator be absent, his property can be confiscated; should this fail, the Political Agent can hold the individual Teip responsible for the actions of its member and force the payment of a … stipulated fine for the offense. There can then be an entire series of actions in case of refusal, involving blockade of a certain Teip, etc.' (Sultan 2003: 456–457) Sultan's piece is a rare example of academic literature fully detached from the empirical reality.

A clan/tribal approach to explaining post-Soviet politics in Chechnya is also advocated by such distinguished analysts as Anatol Lieven, who defines Chechen society as a clan-based 'ordered anarchy' (1998: 331). The Russian scholar Valeriy Tishkov (2004) also found clans to be highly relevant in tipping Chechen society toward war.

Security-studies scholars Emil Souleimanov and Khuseyn Aliyev (2017) have argued that the traditional Chechen social structure, including the *teips*, and the socio-cultural codes that also included retaliation, and hospitality facilitated violent mobilization and pro-insurgent support. By contrast, in her study of clans and democratization, Charlotte Hille (2020), has focused on the prospects of democratization and state-building in 'clan-based societies', taking Chechnya as one of her cases, without providing convincing evidence as to why she considers Chechen society as being clan-based.

My book will test those claims.

Descent and kinship in anthropological theory

As clans are held to be embedded in the traditional kinship structures, much of this book is dedicated to the analysis of descent and kinship groups in Ingushetia and Chechnya. In what follows I review academic debates on descent and kinship that are relevant for my argument.

Throughout the history of anthropological thought, kinship has been viewed as a social structure characteristic of any society. Larger social structures based on kinship exist in many parts of the world; they are typically called 'descent groups', and are conceived as long chains of parent–child ties stretching back for generations (Parkin and Stone 2004).

The first influential theory of kinship was outlined by Henry Maine in his *Ancient Law* (1861). According to Maine, the origins of human societies were individual families held together by the authority of the eldest male patriarch. When the patriarch died, his children and families stayed together.

Extended families, organized unilineally, eventually formed the first primitive polities, according to Maine. These ensured continuity, and became subjects of primitive jurisprudence. It was only later that extended families integrated along kinship lines, transforming into societies bound by territorial attachment. Maine held that the development of human societies could be traced from families, to large descent groups, then to states: as polities grew, families became smaller and less patrilineal (Maine 1861).

Lewis Morgan, another founding father of the anthropology of kinship, drew distinctions – between kinship and descent, and the domestic and political uses of kinship – that later became central to the field (Morgan [1871] 1997). Morgan held that the family cannot be a basic unit of a social organization, because families consist of spouses of both sexes, and if ties through both sexes are recognized, then kinship cannot provide a basis for the establishment of exclusive groups (in: Harris 1990: 14, 15). Exclusive groups must be based on the principle of unilineal descent, claims Morgan.

Bronislaw Malinowski (Malinowski 1930) claimed that clan bonds develop much later as an extension of the primary family sentiment (Kuper 2004). He considered the family to be based on kinship, and of a bilateral nature that consisted of the totality of a person's entire array of kin relations. Descent, however, he saw as both unilineal and political.

Also, Meyer Fortes sees kinship as being bilateral, whereas descent is related to the allocation of individuals to corporate groups whose significance is jural and political (Fortes 1969: 10). According to Fortes, both the family and the descent group possess politico-jural and kin aspects because lineage is reproduced via the family, and perpetuation and segmentation of the lineage results from cleavages between family members, or generations of family. Basically: kinship relations are between individuals; clan relations are between groups (Fortes 1953: 33).

Meyer Fortes considered bilateral kinship relations important for binding together the major groups through marriage. Fortes used the term 'complementary filiation' to refer to the recognition of ties through which descent is not traced (Harris 1990: 25).

In his seminal work *Elementary Structures of Kinship* (1969; first published in 1949) Lévi-Strauss claimed that the ultimate origin of social solidarity was not filiation, but exchange. In his view, the incest taboo, common in most societies, encourages individuals to look for mates outside their kin group. In turn, the underlying demand for the continued circulation of women keeps various clans peacefully related. This produces a society consisting of a number of exclusive groups which exchange mates – this being almost the only reason why such descent groups need each other. Thus, the most primitive form of social solidarity is that of exchange, understood in terms of reciprocity.

Other important debates in social anthropology relevant for my study concern the degree to which kinship is biological or social or even 'fictive' in certain ways. A famous discussion on this matter took place between Rodney Needham and Ernest Gellner; as I find Gellner's argument more persuasive and relevant for my analysis, I will discuss it at some length.

According to Needham, the defining character of descent systems is social; in support of his argument examples of adoptions and leviratic marriage, when a brother marries his brother's widow, and raises his brother's children. 'Biology is one matter and descent is quite another, of a different order' (Needham 1960: 97) For Gellner, both adoption and leviratic marriage imitate biological kinship relations, therefore, the 'very possibility of classifying offspring as adoptive depends on the observer's knowledge of the disparity between the social and the physical relationship, and it is this disparity which gives the term its meaning' (Gellner 1987: 165).

According to Gellner, biological and social kinship systems overlap. To deny this, he says, is to deprive kinship theory of any explanatory power whatsoever (1987: 165). Gellner stresses that social kinship systems are not identical to physical kinship, and that it is important not to equate kinship beliefs with kinship realities. There are frequent situations, he writes, when genealogies became untrue, or after the fourth-generation men will name correctly their grandfather and perhaps his father, but beyond that his forefathers are 'arranged' in order to express, symbolize sub-groups existing in the tribe now (Gellner 1987: 169). However, Gellner also asserts that the reason why clans are even discussed as kinship structures is because the relationships inherent to clan membership satisfy the early criterion for classifying a social relationship under the rubric of kinship structure – not because clan members subscribe to the myth of common ancestry.

Clan is a concept related to other concepts – such as 'sub-clan', or 'lineage' or 'extended family' – that, in turn, denote groups for whom some social reality has a reasonable and systematic congruence with some kinship affinity (Gellner 1987: 168).

In short, Gellner holds that social kinship relationships are superimposed on social structures that are moulded exclusively by patterns of mating, as human biology is universal. It is the social recognition of physical kinship – the kinds of physical relationships utilized for recruitment by groups, and that vary from society to society – that should be researched and explained (Gellner 1987: 176).

My fieldwork in Ingushetia and Chechnya lends support to Gellner's position, as the biological aspects of kinship are taken very seriously in these societies. His assertion that fictive patterns (primarily adoptions) imitate biological kinship also follows the same logic, and does not distort the overall structure in the *teips* of the North Caucasus. However, my research shows – unlike the work of Collins, whose concept of fictive kinship in Central Asian societies includes neighbours and friends – that fictive kinship in Chechen and Ingush societies cannot be stretched too far: my interviewees were always very cognizant of who was a relative, and who was not, who belonged to the kinship group, and who belonged to a more broadly defined inner circle. Non-relatives and members of a more broadly defined inner circle were treated differently from relatives and kin; corresponding relationships involved a different set of rights and obligations. The argument that neighbours and friends should not be analytically differentiated from kinship is not applicable in the North Caucasus context.

Descent in Chechnya and Ingushetia is generally described in kinship terms. However, *teips* have become too big and fragmented to be truly called biological. My research shows that *teips*, indeed, have become social: they use kinship as an idiom, rather than a set of rights, obligations and duties. This I take as further proof of the disintegration of the clan as a social structure: the core idea of biological links has been lost, and even the social function of the kinship structure has become irrelevant. All that remains is a vague clan identity, and even that is fading away.

Lineages, however, are more tightly knit than *teips,* and share the underlay of biological connectedness. In fact, lineages are the remaining splinters of the once-powerful *teips*. As Harris (1990) correctly points out, genealogical distance causes kin ties to fade and relationships to become weaker, while the likelihood of shirking kinship duties becomes stronger. In more distant relationships, while kinship ties are equally ascribed, they may, paradoxically, be chosen on the basis of personal likings – transforming them into relationships of a different kind (Harris 1990: 62). During my interviews in Ingushetia and Chechnya, some respondents described exactly this mechanism, thus supporting Harris' observation. Some of these interviews are quoted in Chapter 4.

Still, the notion of kinship retains a distinctive normative content that determines the moral character of kinship – a morality that cannot be reduced to self-interest (Harris 1990: 42). According to Harris, kinship relations, more than any other, imply a set of obligations and duties.

To perform such a duty is not necessarily an act of amity, or altruism. As empirical evidence shows, kinship often involves rivalry and conflict. Kinship obligations are unspecified in nature and provide opportunities for negotiation and bargaining – but kinship presupposes a kind of relationship that excludes egoistic calculation (Harris 1990: 60). Moreover, kinship is based on a high degree of trust – the longer the period of interaction, the deeper the trust (p. 61).

Dividends of Kinship (2000), edited by Peter Schweitzer, explores the instrumental value of kinship in specific instances, mainly pertaining to the economy. Schweitzer likens his understanding of kinship as a 'dividend' to Bourdieu's usage of cultural, social, symbolic 'capital'. For Schweitzer, economic benefits are among the most visible dividends of kinship. Still, kinship cannot be reduced to the rational pursuit of economic interests, as they constitute 'part of a much larger package that also includes emotions, mental health, group cohesion … ' (Schweitzer 2000: 16)

This understanding of the dual nature of kinship as an ascriptive bond based on trust, as well as a social resource, underlies much of my empirical research. In both Ingushetia and Chechnya, kinship solidarity is a primary mechanism for finding jobs and getting access to public office and public goods, a mechanism for physical and economic protection, and to a significant extent a kind of life insurance, as in crisis situations families try not to leave their members without support.

Trust networks, the 'economy of favours' and neopatrimonialism

Both classic and contemporary studies emphasize the fundamental importance of trust in social relations. Various aspects of the institutional order tend to exacerbate the problems of trust. The flow of resources may be structured according to market or institutional relationships, or exchange based on rules of reciprocity. In all societies, institutionalized exchange is to some degree supported by more informal, pervasive networks of trust.

Economists assert that trust networks are particularly relevant to risk, as they provide a cheap sense of security in situations where enforcement of contracts is uncertain (Landa 1994: 101). It is typically assumed that such trust networks are kin-based, which in turn means that solidarity exists prior to entering into economic or public relationships. My research shows that, indeed, informal networks are prominent in many aspects of social life, as well as politics, in Chechen and Ingush societies. However, in these communities, trust networks are not descent- or kinship-based, even in instances when kinship is a prominent means of recruitment. Nor are such networks organic and pre-existing in any particular trust groups.

My analysis follows the framework set out in Charles Tilly's theory of trust networks in his 2005 book, *Trust and Rule*, and in Mark Granovetter's theory (Granovetter 1973) of strong and weak ties.

According to Tilly, trust networks extend into every corner of social life, including 'communication, mutual recognition, shared participation in some activity, flows of goods or services ... and other forms of consequential interaction and include any set of similar connections among three or more social sites' (Tilly 2005: 5, 7). Such trust networks consist of 'ramified interpersonal connections, consisting mainly of strong ties, within which people set valued, consequential, long-term resources and enterprises at risk to the malfeasance, mistakes or failures of others' (Tilly 2005: 12). Such networks place significant value on common enterprise, *inter alia* protection of personal secrets, high-risk politics. They build controls over malfeasance, and safeguards against the consequences of mistakes and failures. They regularly insert themselves in non-contentious politics, often with greater consequence than in contentious politics (Tilly 2005: 6).

Tilly further claims that groups which are linked not by kinship, but by religion, political commitment or trade may acquire and maintain very strong, even kin-like, solidarity. Moreover, trust can develop over time (Tilly 2005: 9).

I draw on Tilly's concept of trust networks as a risk management strategy in arguing that political networks are not necessarily derived from a common identity, but political and economic interests in a high-risk environment. Such relationships – of access, mutual economic dependence and risk-sharing – I call 'strong ties'.

The concepts of 'strong' and 'weak' ties have been explored by sociologists since the 1960s. The most comprehensive theory has been developed by Mark Granovetter, who defined the strength of ties as a (linear) combination of time, emotional intensity, intimacy (mutual confiding), and reciprocal services that characterize the ties themselves (Granovetter 1973: 1361) The strength of ties can be roughly established on an intuitive basis, according to Granovetter, who holds that ties can be multi- or uni-dimensional, and further distinguishes among strong, weak and absent (or negligible) ties.

For Granovetter, strong ties include relatives and close friends. Weak ties encompass acquaintances of various kinds. The importance of weak ties grows with the evolution of social systems, especially in relation to the division of labour – as increasing specialization and interdependence generate a wide range of specialized-role relationships in which each individual knows only a small part of the other's personality. Several studies have concluded that levels of education, income and mobility have an impact on the significance of one's weak ties, which, according to Granovetter, play a prominent role as bridges from one's inner circle to various other social circles (see Granovetter 1973; Lin et al. 1981; Lomnitz 1977).

I draw on Granovetter's distinction between strong and weak ties in my analysis of the formation of governments and political elites in Chechnya and Ingushetia. In the realm of politics, strong ties in the North Caucasus can be traced to mutual exposure to risks, reciprocal services and strong interdependence (when enterprises are at risk of malfeasance, mistakes and failures). Weak ties are loose connections that are predominantly formal, professional or procedural, and do not derive from interdependence or mutual risk.

The function of informal trust networks in the Russian context has been well described by Alena Ledeneva (Ledeneva 1998) in her *Nelzya, no mozhno* (Prohibited, But Possible), a Russian expression that sums up the distribution of public goods under the Soviet economy. Ledeneva characterizes the overweening dynamic as 'an all-embracing restriction and the labyrinth of possibilities around them' (1998: 1). She also investigates in great detail the culture of *blat*, which refers to a set of personal connections that can be mobilized for acquiring commodities outside the official system. *Blat* is a form of nepotism, an exchange of favours, usually quid pro quo.

Blat networks emerged in Soviet times in response to the structural constraints of the Soviet system, and then smoothly navigated the transition into the post-Soviet era – evolving into networks of trust, and a relatively new institution of *svoi lyudi*: a circle of trusted people. *Blat* is a form of exchange that is not monetary, a sort of barter based on personal relationships. The objective of *blat* is not direct exchange, but the exchange of favours over a prolonged period – usually at the public expense. Further, *blat* is often underlain by a rhetoric of friendship, of mutual support, of mutual self-interest (Ledeneva 1998: 37).

Ledeneva sees *blat* as the consequence of a controlling Soviet state, a response to the structural constraints of the system of distribution, and shortages: most *blat* practices withered after the shortage economy was followed by a shortage of money (1998: 3). Many elements of *blat* are gone now, but its principles – the ways people acquire scarce resources, or services, or evade the law – remain.

An extreme form of *blat* is clientelism, which presupposes asymmetric power relations based on discretionary allocation of public goods, titles and favours in return for political support. The delivery of a good or service on the part of patron or client comes as a direct response to the delivery of a reciprocal benefit by the other part. A politician will provide benefits only to individuals or groups that support or promise to support that politician; similarly, the client will support only the politician who delivers – or promises to deliver (Hicken 2011). Chechnya under Ramzan Kadyrov is a clear example of clientelist relations, as detailed in Chapter 10.

In post-Soviet Russia, patrons and clients or members of the same networks are bound together by *krugovaya poruka* (joint responsibility/mutual guarantees: one hand washing the other) – scheming between business and law enforcement that includes, but is not limited to, bribery and machinations in bookkeeping, privatization deals and corporate governance. Ledeneva sees such post-Soviet practices as being more exclusive than the widespread practice of *blat*: they are limited to closed circles of professional elites, and individuals who share a high degree of mutual understanding (Ledeneva 2006: 4).

Informal practices exist in every society, but are found predominately in environments where 'formal rules and informal norms are not synchronized and where rules of the game are consequently incoherent, where laws are applied unevenly and arbitrarily, where executive power dominates prosecutors, police, and often courts' (Ledeneva 2006: 90). Stability is preserved by an informal order buttressed by mutual control that is exercised within informal networks, such as the ties propagated by *krugovaya poruka*.

Such informal networks, networks of interests and networks of control – ensuring trust and reducing risks – have become indispensable in post-Soviet Russia (Ledeneva 2006: 211a). They are indispensable, too, in post-Soviet Ingushetia and Chechnya. As Henry Hale has noted, writing on patronal politics, people in such societies are caught in a vicious cycle. 'Not expecting others to behave according to formal rules, few risk working together when cheating is possible and the stakes are high without a side payment, a tight personal bond, or some kind of guarantee backed by force, the kind of force that can be supplied by a patron in high office or a criminal organization' (2014: 19). This, he holds, creates a social *equilibrium*: as everyone expects everyone else to behave that way, it makes no sense for individuals to do anything differently since this can only harm their own interests, and possibly severely.

The various individual mechanisms described by Ledeneva fall under the broader definition of neopatrimonialism, a term that gained traction within African studies after the 1960s and was then broadly applied to analysis of some of the post-Soviet states. Neopatrimonialism refers to the informal interaction of state interests with private interests, and is often used as a synonym for corruption, clientelism, patronage, cronyism, nepotism or *blat* (Laruelle 2012: 304).

If patrimonialism refers to regimes where most power relationships are personal relationships, neopatrimonialism is its modern variant. Here, legitimization is also based on law, international order, ideology and other socio-political mechanisms. Neo-patrimonialism combines the two logics of personal and legal-rational bureaucratic, whereby the distinction between the public and the private formally exits and is accepted, albeit not respected (Laruelle 2012: 303). According to Vladimir Gelman, neo-patrimonial institutions represent a kind of symbiosis, where the legal-rational shell of formal rules of the game conceal a neo-patrimonial 'core' of informal institutions that have a subversive influence on institutional performance. (Gelman 2016: 458)

The term 'neo-patrimonialism' has been criticized for overly broad application and poor definition of the diverse phenomena that it aims to denote; however, it does have analytical utility. In the post-Soviet context, neo-patrimonialism – understood as a political order dominated by a ruling elite that controls access to public resources and uses this for private purposes including for buying political loyalty – is an apt description of some regimes, especially in Central Asia and Russia.

As Gelman has noted, since the neo-patrimonial politico-economic order is associated with elements of traditional authority, its most widespread explanations are related to the effects of legacies of the past. 'Neopatrimonialism is often perceived as a rudiment of traditional societies that was so deeply embedded in the social and political organization that it either cannot be eliminated in the process of modernization or becomes a kind of traditionalist reaction to modernization's failures (…) in post-Soviet Russia scholars look for sources of neo-patrimonialism in virtually all stages of Russian and Soviet history' (Gelman 2016: 458). This is certainly true of many researchers focusing on Ingushetia and Chechnya who explain modern processes through the prism of path-dependency and historical determinism.

However, Gelman adds:

without denying the importance of various "legacies", one should take into account that the rise of post-Soviet neopatrimonialism in Russia and some other post-Soviet states, to a large degree, was a consequence of the purposeful actions of political and economic actors who aimed to maximize benefits to themselves during the process of redistribution of power and resources in the turbulent post-Soviet environment.

(2016: 458)

This 'legacy argument', contested by Gelman, is also contested in this book.

In his comprehensive study of post-Soviet states *Patronal Politics: Eurasian Regime Dynamics in Comparative Perspective* (2014), Henry Hale introduced the new term, 'patronal politics', to denote informal politics based on trust networks, intended to cover the many concepts and mechanisms related to post-Soviet informal politics. As defined by Hale, the term refers to 'politics in societies where individuals organize their political and economic pursuits primarily around the personalized exchange of concrete rewards and punishments through chains of actual acquaintance, and not primarily around abstract, impersonal principles such as ideological belief or categorizations like economic class that include many people one has not actually met in person. In this politics of individual reward and punishment, power goes to those who can mete these out, those who can position themselves as patrons with a large and dependent base of clients' (Hale 2014: 10)

Hale claims that his term 'patronalistic society' encompasses the notions of patrimonial/neo-patrimonialism, clientelism and 'corruption', as well as the dominance of informal politics over formal politics (Hale 2014: 20). He argues that in many post-Soviet countries power represents hierarchical networks 'through which resources are distributed and coercion applied' (Hale 2014: 10). These pyramids usually exist outside formal institutions, and the regimes differ as to whether these patronal networks are arranged in one pyramid or multiple competing pyramids (Hale 2014: 10).

Hale's theory has a strong emphasis on what he calls 'the great power of expectations' to explain the tenacity and strength of bond in patronal networks. Unlike other theories that emphasize coercion, resources and organization, Hale holds that 'clients obey patrons when they expect other clients to do so' (... while) 'individuals join the networks that they expect to give them the greatest payoffs once they have taken into account networks' various capacities to reward and punish' (Hale 2014: 36).

Much of it, he concludes, is self-fulfilling prophecy: when clients believe their network is strong, it becomes strong (Hale 2014: 36).

I test Hale's theory in the final chapter of this book, in analysing the Moscow-installed authoritarian regimes in Ingushetia and Chechnya between 2003 and 2020. Other empirical chapters explain how the mechanisms of political networking during the state-building experiments in post-Soviet Chechnya and Ingushetia can be understood largely through the concepts and mechanisms of trust networks, *krugovaya poruka*, corporatism and access networks, as discussed by Tilly, Ledeneva and Gelman. However, instead of Hale's 'great power of expectations', I emphasize the factor of *risk* – of physical elimination and prosecution for economic crimes – as the strongest binding force of informal networks in Ingushetia and Chechnya. I will argue that another two internal factors constrain the nature of ties within governments: an institutional system of checks and balances that helps to limit nepotism; and organized opposition that acts as a watchdog, guarding against nepotist practices.

2

Political Order and Social Integration prior to, during and after the Caucasian War

Informal institutions are often seen as highly resistant to change, as well as highly capable of survival. Yet such institutions and patterns of social integration *do* change – often quite quickly (Helmke and Levitsky 2004: 732). Chapters 2 and 3 provide the historical context to this book, this chapter offering analysis of the traditional political, legal and social institutions and structures of Chechens and Ingush and the process of their transformation before, during and after the Caucasian War.

Drawing on historical sources, I show how ethnographers, historians and travelogue writers have proven that Chechen and Ingush *teips* were fragmented and weakened already by the end of the nineteenth century, and indigenous supra-*teip* political structures had been pushed outside the political system by the state structures and refigured under the strong influence of Sufi Islam.

Political order and social institutions prior to the Caucasian War (pre-1817)

Proto-Chechen and Ingush tribes have inhabited the North Caucasus since at least the first century BC (Krupnov 1960; 1971; Vinogradov and Chokaev 1966; Akhmadov 2001; Martirosian 1933). They settled at the base of the main Caucasian range which kept them protected, as well as isolated.

However, two major passages connecting the Great Steppe with Transcaucasia and the Middle East were in close proximity to these lands. Peoples who travelled through these passages brought with them new cultural influences: novel forms of political and social organization, as well as more advanced crafts, weapons, and luxury and everyday household items (Krupnov 1960: 45). Archaeologists note the proximity of the tribes to great civilizations with superior knowledge of weapons, engineering and various forms of government.

According to Chechen historian Yavus Akhmadov, the Nakh population (which includes forefathers of today's Chechens and Ingush as well as Kists and Batsbijtsy) migrated high into the mountains late in 1262, where they remained until the 1390s, for protection from the Mongol invasions and the Mongol troops in the area of the Daryal Gorge (Akhmadov 2001: 227). As a result, the Nakhs remained relatively unaffected by the Mongols until 1395, when they suffered a major defeat at the hands of the legendary Timur, whose hordes scaled the mountains and wiped out hundreds of Nakh villages – killing, burning pastures, destroying churches and pagan sanctuaries, and enslaving the survivors (Akhmadov 2001: 234).

Some Chechen historians hold that the *teips* emerged at that time. The Chechen tribes, destroyed by Timur, fragmented into smaller social units and dispersed in the mountains, split temporarily, to reunite in better times. 'The people had to save their lives and instinctively develop mechanisms of self-preservation in such conditions', explained Magomed Muzaev, a Chechen historian who for nearly 30 years directed the State Department of Archives of the Government of the Chechen Republic in an interview.

After Timur abandoned the plains, they were settled by the Kabarday, a subgroup of the Circassian people. Chechens migrated back to the plains in the sixteenth century. The Ingush came down from the mountains in the late seventeenth century, after overcoming heavy Kabarday resistance (Akhmadov 2001; Kodzoev 2002: 148). Leaders of the Crimean Khanate, allies and vassals of the increasingly powerful Ottoman Empire sought to annex the North Caucasus in the early sixteenth century. So did the Safavid Empire, which in 1519 conquered Georgia (southern Nakhs fought on the Georgian side) and from 1524 to 1574 tried to advance on the North Caucasus. The Russian Empire, too, turned to the Caucasus after its conquest of the Astrakhan Khanate in 1556. During the second half of the sixteenth century, Russian Cossacks [*an ethnic group comprising mostly of Eastern Slavs, famed for their role in Russian military and colonization efforts –E.S.*] settled on the banks of the Terek River (Shnirelman 2007: 264).

Thus, from the sixteenth century, the North Caucasus came under the simultaneous influence of three regional powers – the Ottoman, Safavid and Russian Empires. Each of the three sought to strengthen its position in the region, and each had its supporters and vassals among local Nakh societies. By the eighteenth century, however, lowland Chechnya was becoming increasingly oriented toward Russia (Akhmadov 2001: 328). Ingush historian Nurdin Kodzoev notes a similar shift among the Ingush: in 1758 a delegation of nine elders in the town of Kyzlyar became the first Ingush to pledge allegiance to Russia. By 1771 most Ingush communities had followed suit (Kodzoev 2002: 153).

Allegiance to Russia accelerated the descent of the Ingush from the mountains to the plains. By the end of the eighteenth century, trade with Russian towns had encouraged other Nakh societies to look favourably on Russia, marking the beginning of the process of their integration with the Russian state. In 1781, several Chechen societies swore their allegiance to the Russian state – a gesture later represented by the Soviet Union as an act of voluntary incorporation into Russia by the Chechen and Ingush peoples. 'Of course, this had no basis in historical truth', claims Chechen historian Yavus Akhmadov, however (2001: 332). In his view, which is shared by several regional scholars, the initial period of Russian colonization of the North Caucasus was both peaceful and successful: many lowland and mountain peoples sought political alliances and protection from Russia in the seventeenth and eighteenth centuries, especially against the powerful Kabarday (Gakaev 1999: 10; Kodzoev 2002: 153; Akhmadov 2001).

Nonetheless, according to these scholars, such alliances cannot be regarded as *voluntary* accession to the Russian state. The Russian ethnologist Victor Shnirelman agrees: 'Declarations of citizenship were perceived as protectorates and alliances that at any moment could be broken, and, in a few years, again restored. Moreover, such declarations could be made simultaneously to representatives of two competing powers' (Shnirelman 2007: 269).

After defeating the Ottoman Empire in 1774, Russia intensified its colonization efforts: it built fortifications, founded 36 Cossack settlements, and distributed North Caucasian lands to Russian nobles. Nakh pastures were expropriated, and the Chechen and Ingush tribes were cut off from natural resources, such as salt deposits. Not only was their trade restricted, so were their movements.

In response to Russian colonization efforts, Mansur Usurma – the son of a shepherd, and a self-proclaimed *sheikh* – declared *gazavat* (holy war) against infidels. In parallel, he strove to force Chechen Muslims to abandon their semi-pagan traditions, to abolish *adat* customary law based on tradition and replace it with *Sharia* Islamic law (Dunlop 1998: 10). By 1785, Mansur's rebellion was backed by a force of 12,000 men. Over the course of the next six years Russia made repeated attempts to suppress the rebellion, and finally succeeded in arresting Mansur, who was subsequently sentenced to life in prison (Dunlop 1998: 11, 13). In 1807 and, again in 1810, Nakh societies were forced to declare their loyalty to Russia (Shnirelman 2007: 270).

Debates on Nakh feudalism and *teip* structures

The political organization of Nakh societies varied in the sixteenth and eighteenth centuries. Records from the 1500s mentioned several Nakh 'societies' (*teips*, or groups of *teips*).[1] Some societies were formally dependent on neighbouring polities, or other regional power centres (Kabardine, Circassian or Dagestani princes), whereas others remained independent (Bagrationi, in Martirosian 1933; Ajtberov and Akhmadov 1982; Zubov 1835: 32; Isaeva 1977: 40).

Powerful indigenous Nakh feudal polities emerged in the 1640s, including the Chechen princes Turlovs and the princedom of Braguny. Strong Ingush *teips* also distinguished themselves around this time, including Targim, Khamkho and Egi, the three of which joined forces to form the Galgai tribal union that controlled the strategic Assa River basin (Akhmadov 2001). Later, the Galgai applied their name to the entire Ingush people (Skitsky 1959; Martirosian 1933). The nature of feudalism in Nakh societies differed from the classical European model, as individuals were not personally dependent on their feudal lords. The princes who governed Nakh societies served as foremen, or a sort of contracted protectorate (Laudaev 1872; Bronevsky 1823; Akhmadov 2001). Moreover, any male member of the community could raise an issue for public discussion if it was relevant to the community at large. Decisions

---

[1] Nakh-Mokh, Michich, Chemberloi, Shatoy, Myalkhi, Majsty, Nashkhoi, Chianti, Merzhoi, Akki, Glalgal, Dzeirakh.

were made either during a *yu'rtan gulam* (public gathering of the men in a village), or before Councils of Elders.

The first person to record the features of what he described as 'mountain feudalism' was Johan Herber, a Russian traveller of German origin, who in 1728 wrote of the Kabarday:

> The owners [*princes – E.S.*] ... divided themselves among several small fiefdoms ... But it is not possible to call those who live in such fiefdoms [their] subjects. More frequently they are called comrades, since they live freely in the company of the prince and can leave the prince to join another one if there is a quarrel. Also, without the advice and consent of those who live with him ... [a prince] can do nothing. However, princes and their comrades do not leave each other's sides in times of need and stand together.
>
> (cited in Kosven and Khashaeva 1958: 68)

In the eighteenth century the Nakh societies underwent what contemporary Chechen historians call a 'democratization of society'. Feudal lords were expelled from Ingushetia and Chechnya (Laudaev 1872; Martirosian 1933; Bliev and Degoev 1994; Isaeva 1977; Akhmadov 2001; Dettmering 2005), as well as from the Black Sea region around which the Shapsugs, an Adyghe people, had settled (Kazharov 1992: 125, in Dettmering 2005: 475).

Scholars interpret this period of de-feudalization variously. Yavus Akhmadov (2001) holds that the princes were expelled because, in trying to establish authority, they attempted to limit the personal freedoms of the Chechens. Said Akhmet Isaev (1998) saw the advance of the military of the Russian Empire as the decisive factor: the princes left because they could no longer fulfil their main function of protecting the safety of their communities. According to the nineteenth-century Chechen ethnographer Umalat Laudaev (1872), the princes left because Chechens refused to comply with their orders, and the princes had no mechanisms to force them to obey. Whatever the reason, 'Chechen' princes disappeared 'well before the dawn of the nineteenth century', writes German historian Christian Dettmering (2005: 475).

An understanding of the degree to which Nakh communities were feudal is important for the analysis of their current social institutions. Feudalism of the traditional European type would have destroyed the egalitarian structure of *teips*, and undercut the rule of Elders and the *adat*, or customary law. However, according to some scholars, feudalism as practised among Nakhs actually reinforced *teip* identity, particularly in Ingushetia, where it followed family lines. Illustrative here is the case of the Ingush *teip* of Salgiev, as recounted by a scholar of North Caucasus societies:

> Fifteen generations ago [...] the Salgiev *teip* moved out of Tsorinsky territory because of overpopulation, and occupied [...] the territory where its members currently live, Salgi. When they needed to build a tower to protect their land, they rented out, then sold part of their territory to the Gu *teip*. Despite the fact that the latter bought their land, the Salgi teip considered the *Gu* to be their [vassals].
>
> (Khristianovich, in Martirosian 1933: 30)

According to the early twentieth-century historian Nikolay Ivanenkov, property rights in Chechnya were based on the principle of 'first come, first served' (1910: 16, 48). Thus, those who developed and cultivated virgin land held the personal and hereditary rights to it (Zelkina 2000: 22). Having occupied or cultivated land, a *teip* could then lease or sell it to other *teips* – regarding them as their dependents.

Social differentiation could be found within the *teip* itself. According to Magomed Mamakaev, the most influential Soviet scholar of *teips*, by the sixteenth and seventeenth centuries the *teip* had already ceased to be that 'wonderful organization where everyone was equal, and disputes were resolved by the popular collective' (Mamakaev 1973: 7). As a Soviet historian, Mamakaev explains transformation of *teips* in terms of Marxist methodology. The main means of production of the tribes was land, which was owned collectively. As agriculture developed, collective property gradually impeded production, and land came to be owned by extended families. The tribes fragmented into extended families that, in turn, gradually divided into individual families. In this way, the tribal community was replaced by the village community, where arable land was privately owned, but forests and pastures remained part of the collective (quoted in Martirosian 1933: 26).

This process had run its course in Chechnya by the seventeenth and eighteenth centuries, according to Mamakaev. Although the expansionism of feudal families encountered resistance from the remaining mountain peoples, 'their historical development occurred steadily along the lines of increasing feudal property at the expense of community lands' (Mamakaev 1973: 7). Two other scholars also note two parallel processes unfolding inside Chechen and Ingush communities at that time: a strengthening of the rich *teips* against the weak ones, and social differentiation within the *teip* – i.e. the emergence of *teip* elites (Kusheva and Usmanov 1978: 110).

In 1931 the Soviet researcher Mark Kosven put forth the theory of *patronymia*, which he later developed into an influential Soviet methodology widely used for analysing the kinship structures of the North Caucasus. Kosven defined *patronymia* as a group of families which emerged because of segmentation of family community and which to some degree retained their economic, public and ideological unity (Kosven 1964: 1). *Patronymia* emerged in tribal conditions but survived subsequent changes; with the

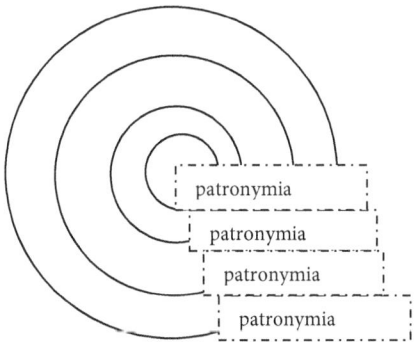

Figure 2.1 Chechen *teip* structure, nineteenth century (M. Kosven's theory).

further development of society, it underwent deep transformations, from the archaic tribal form to the state of disintegration and, finally, to the 'remnant' condition (Kosven 1964: 2). *Patronymia* grows and divides, giving birth to a complicated structure of small and large forms resembling concentric circles, or groupings, see figure 2.1. (Kosven 1964: 2).

By the nineteenth century, *patronymia* was disintegrating as a result of gradual and inevitable development of private property while retaining some degree of collectivism (Kosven 1964: 5). The ideological dimension of *patronymia*, however, was kept alive through the continued participation of *teips* in community celebrations and major family events like weddings, births and funerals (Kosven 1964: 7). Chechen and Ingush *teips* have been seen as particularly clear examples of *patronymia* at work Kosven (1964: 38, 45).

However, Magomed Mamakaev disagrees with Kosven, arguing that *patronymia* represents a rather small group of close kin, whereas *teips* are numerous and complex structures consisting of *gaars*, or different branches, that – unlike the greater *teip* – always know the names of their actual forefathers. In turn, writes Mamakaev, the *gaar* is divided further into even smaller groups, or *nek*, further divided into several even smaller *tsa*. Moreover, the *tsa* may be divided in several *dozal* (Mamakaev 1973: 12). A *dozal* is a nuclear family, new branches of which can be added only along male kinship lines. Overall, Mamakaev has held that Chechen *gaar*, not *teips*, fit Kosven's definition of *patronymia* in the nineteenth century, see figure 2.2.

Aleksey Robakidze (1973), who has researched Chechen and Ingush family structures using Kosven's methodology, explains that in the process of growth the *patronymia* and its territorial unity were disintegrating, as were other types of ties binding on the members. Thus, a *patronymia* of the first order produced a *patronymia* of the second order. Concentric circles of kin were created, characterized by reduced intensity of kinship as the number of relatives multiplied (Robakidze 1973: 3). According to this view, *dozal* (nuclear family) in the process of segmentation created *patronymia* of the first-circle, *nek*, and second-circle, *gaar*. *Gaars* made up the *teip* – a group of people united by real or imaginary kinship (Robakidze 1973: 4).

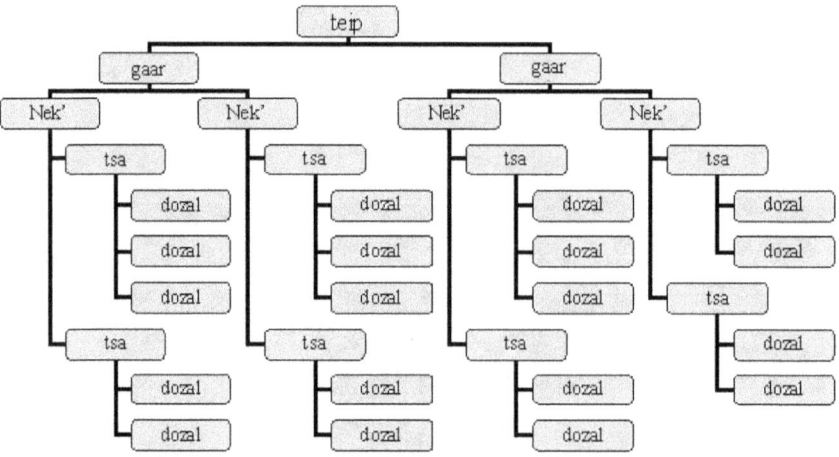

Figure 2.2 Chechen *teip* structure, nineteenth century (M. Mamakaev's theory).

In his essay, *The Chechen Tribe*, written in the early 1870s, Umalat Laudaev, a Chechen-origin officer of the Russian army and ethnographer, explains the division of *teips* into *gaars* and *neks* as a consequence of simple demographics: families kept growing:

> In the old times, when the clans were not yet numerous, they were not divided into parts and had one name, constituting something like one family. But as the number of family members grew [*teips*] fragmented into *gaars* and *neks*, i.e. what we now call branches and lineages. When the family members multiplied to such an extent that it was difficult for them to live on the land of their forefathers, they looked for other places to live, and began to fragment, and became unknown to each other.
> (Laudaev 1872)

Consequently, kin ties were weakened, according to Laudaev.

Kosven hypothesizes that the transformation of *patronymias* could have been a result of shared residence with other *patronymias*. In the past, *patronymias* were located in separate distinct settlements. As they grew in size, however, they took over more space, and in several villages. Finally, *patronymias* grew into neighbourhoods in large complex settlements (Kosven 1964: 3), where several *patronymias* lived together, and a community of neighbours (*sosedskaya obshina*) emerged. By then, the main principle of integration had become territorial (Kosven 1964: 9).

Laudaev also wrote that Chechens, after expelling the princes from the plains in the 1500s and 1600s, established large settlements in which several *teips* lived together. However, according to Kodzoev, it was not until the 1700s that the first significant Ingush multi-*teip* settlements emerged (Kodzoev 2002: 148). These settlements encouraged the territorial principle of integration.

This brief review of scholarly debates on the historical transformations of Chechen and Ingush social structures makes it clear that, even prior to the colonial war that caused major social upheaval, *teips* had become heterogeneous social structures whose members were united in complex networks of kinship – some real, others imaginary. The *teips* underwent a process of feudalization, expanded in numbers, resettled and branched out over territories, mingled in big villages with other *teips*, in this way losing their initial structure. According to Mamakaev (1973: 22), although the *teip* system had been disintegrating since the sixteenth century, its unity was maintained by the lack of statehood and by conflicts with the neighbours.

Proto-national political institutions and law: *Mekhk-Khel, tukhum* and *adat*

In his 1858 essay on Chechnya and the Chechens, historian Adolf Berge wrote:

> In the old days, say the Ichkerian Elders, when the Chechen people were not yet numerous and lived in the mountains […] all disputes were resolved by the Elders. At that time the Elders were clever. They lived long, and knew many

things, and always resolved disputes fairly, in accordance with their wisdom, and without guidance or any law.

(Berge 1859: 72, 73)

But by the end of the 1600s, following a long period of internal wars among Chechen *teips*, the authority of the elders was no longer respected. Their decisions – made without executive authority to enforce them – were not always implemented and were sometimes arbitrarily neglected (Berge 1859: 73). Moreover, their decisions were likely to be heeded only by weak families, whereas stronger families could reject their authority as they saw fit (Laudaev 1872).

To this day, Chechen legend holds that, in the midst of a particularly discordant period, a congress was convened in the mountainous area of Nashkhoy, and agreements were reached governing relations among Chechen *teips*. The *Mekhk-Khel* (Council of Land) was formed, and was convened regularly – among other things, to elect military leaders, who were granted almost unlimited power in times of war. Ultimately the *Mekhk-Khel* came to possess judiciary, legislative and executive authority: 'The Council of Land determined the customs and laws of various provinces that, depending on their economic and legal utility, were generalized and later spread in the rest of the country' (Mamakaev 1973: 44).

Further, Mamakaev writes that the *Mekhk-Khel* was elected according to a pyramid system comprising representatives of various *teips* and villages. Several of the elders I interviewed recall their grandparents telling them that the *Mekhk-Khel* was elected according to both *teip* and territory.

> My grandmother was more than a hundred years old when she died in 1984, and she told me that twelve people from Ingushetia were selected for the *Mekhk-Khel*. First, each *teip* in a given village named its strongest representative. Then, from among those candidates, the best was selected to represent the village. And then, from among the village candidates, one was chosen to represent the region. No incidental people turned up [in the *Mekhk-Khel*]. They were the best of the best, and the most respected.
>
> (Author's interview with Idris Chapanov, elder from Achaluki village, Ingushetia)

Two-thirds of the *teips* were united into nine *tukhums* – military–political units.[2] The remaining one-third of the Chechen *teips* each formed their own *tukhum* (Mamakaev 1973).[3] *Teips* referred to as Ingush formed five more *tukhums*, the most numerous being *Ghalgaj* (Zelkina 2000: 17). The *tukhum* was a territorial organization, ruled by a group of elders – representatives of all *teips* – who were to solve common

---

[2] Akkiy, Melkhiy, Nohchimakhoy, Terloy, Chantiy, Cheberloy, Shaory and Shoatoy; the Ortskhoy (or Qarabulaq) occupied a position midway between the Chechen and the Ingush, and was regarded as a separate group.

[3] Zurzuqoy, Maistoy, Peshkhoy, Sadoy and others.

issues of security and economic exchange, and resolve disputes among *teips* on the basis of customary law – *adat* (Mamakaev 1973: 16).

In Chechnya justice was also partly based on Islamic *Sharia* law. The two systems of law – *adat* and *Sharia* – often competed. '*Adat* spread and strengthened each time *Sharia* was in decline, and in turn *adat* was abolished each time *Sharia* found zealous proponents and followers' (Berge 1859: 74).

Social integration and social change during the Caucasian War

In 1801 Eastern Georgia was annexed by Russia, resulting in a situation that lent itself to the often-quoted metaphor by Karl Marx: 'the legs of the gigantic empire were cut off from its body'. To connect these 'legs' with the 'body', Russia needed to subjugate the North Caucasus, and St Petersburg took a hard-line approach.

The stirrings of war

The beginning of the Caucasian War is forever linked with the name of Alexei Yermolov (1777–1861), a Russian general who, in a report to the Emperor Alexander I, characterized the Chechens as 'a bold and dangerous people', the conquest of whom required a special tactical approach (Dunlop 1998: 15).

Yermolov's 'special approach' entailed the first anti-guerrilla military tactics in Russian history: in order to eliminate combatants, target the people who support them (Zubov 1835: 1). In May 1818, Yermolov provided the succeeding tsar, Nicholas I, with a detailed plan for a military campaign that called for a 'military-economic siege' intended to force the Chechens from the fertile plains back into the mountains (Gammer 1998: 58; Bliev and Degoev 1994). According to this plan, Russia would build a series of forts along the lower reaches of Sunzha River. The plan also called for the construction of settlements for the Cossacks in the territory between the Sunzha and Terek Rivers.

'Having lost their pastures and arable land […] the Chechens will be squeezed into the mountains', wrote Yermolov. 'Without farmland and pastures where their cattle can spend the winters during periods of severe cold, they will be left with nothing to do but reconcile themselves to the rule of Russia' (quoted in Zubov 1835: 4; Gammer 1998: 58).

Yermolov was given the go-ahead by Nicholas I. From 1817 to 1819, a string of Cossack settlements that occupied some 50 km of territory were built, as well as several military redoubts – including Nazran in Ingushetia, and the fortress of Groznaya in Chechnya (Bliev and Degoev 1994: 174). Every autumn Yermolov, seeking to starve the Chechen population into submission, had the Chechen corn fields destroyed just as the crops were ready to be harvested (Baddeley 1908). He also pursued a policy of collective punishment: if a Russian commander alleged that a given Chechen had taken part in an attack on Russian soldiers, or Cossacks, that Chechen's village was required to deliver 'the bandit' and his family to Russian authorities. If the villagers refused, Russian forces levelled the village (Dunlop 1998: 16).

'Villages that protested were ravaged and burned, and orchards and vineyards were destroyed all the way to their roots', wrote Yermolov. 'We investigated whether the people [*guerrillas – E.S.*] resisted, and whether among them people were killed in battle, or whether they allowed the swindlers to pass without hindrance. In the case of the latter the entire village was exterminated, and wives and children were slaughtered' (quoted in Bliev and Degoev 1994: 152).

Eventually, Chechens stopped trying to defend their villages when Russian soldiers approached. They abandoned their homes and fled into the forests with their families and cattle (Gammer 1998: 65; Bliev and Degoev 1994: 178). Ingush villagers were considered more 'peaceful' and were not directly engaged in the war. However, also in Ingushetia there were uprisings – and the Russian response was similar to that employed in Chechnya.

Yermolov's tactics had a massive impact on the political and social order of Chechens. According to Moshe Gammer, historian of the Caucasus War, 'The siege of some mountain communities, the expropriation of land from some, and the expulsion of others from the pastures in pre-mountainous regions destroyed the traditional forms of trade [...] Those living in the mountains could not meet all their needs, and were largely dependent on such economic ties, and the existing systems of production' (Gammer 1998: 71).

Furthermore, the state of perpetual crisis, combined with frequent resettlement, disrupted the normal functioning of traditional Chechen institutions – especially trials under *adat* law, and public meetings (*yurtan gulam*) held for discussing village affairs. In parallel, the war strengthened the supra-*teip* institutions, such as the *Mekhk-Khel* and *tukhums*, which, prior to the arrival in 1840 of Imam Shamil, were summoned frequently in response to rapidly changing conditions. In addition, the crises and forced migration served to strengthen kin solidarity.

By 1839 the mountain resistance appeared to have been suppressed.[4] The Russian administration in the Caucasus appointed police officers to villages, mainly from loyal locals, collected taxes and duties (Gammer 1998: 163). However, abuse of power by the state representatives was frequent, and Chechen resentment was growing.

In 1840, Chechen leaders asked Shamil – perhaps the most outstanding political and military leader ever to emerge from the North Caucasus – to lead their uprising against Russia (Dunlop 1998: 24). 'Unlike previous leaders, he not only defied the Russians, but held the resistance together for almost three decades of unbroken warfare against the army that defeated Napoleon', writes Sebastian Smith, the author of a best-selling book on Chechnya (1998: 45).

Shamil was a tough leader who offered the mountain people a stern life, strict rules of the Islamic law and constant war against the invader (Smith 1998: 46). In Chechnya, Shamil strove to eradicate the customary *adat* law, so as to erase clan distinctions. His primary goal as an *imam* was to enforce the *Sharia* rule. According to Smith, he

---

[4] In September 1839, Shamil suffered a major defeat at Akhulgo (Dagestan), where he had to surrender his older son Dzhamalaltdin to General Grabbe as a hostage. After that Shamil's prospects in Dagestan looked rather bleak.

'used Islam and personal ruthlessness, to reach across the deep tribal divides and create an alliance of Moslem highlanders' (1998: 45). Shamil's military strategy entailed containing Russian forces on the territory, which he knew well. He exhausted the enemy by compelling them to give chase for long distances, then leading them into the mountains – where he would attack.

In the 1840s Shamil also used resettlement and 'scorched earth' tactics. Described by Gammer as 'demographic war', this involved the mass resettlement of people from areas bordering Russia-controlled regions to lands under his control, then burning the territory in-between. The result was a no-man's land, with burned terrain that seriously inhibited Russian manoeuvres (Gammer 1998). Thus, both sides of the conflict employed forced migration as a tactic.

The historian Martirosian quotes a Russian military officer who reported to the chief of staff of the headquarters of the Caucasus army corps: 'in the whole of Chechnya there is no village, no household left that has not have been resettled several times from one place to another' (Martirosian 1933: 68).

In the Ingush lands, following a major popular uprising in Nazran in 1858, Russia enacted a policy of 'settlement enlargement' whereby small Ingush villages were destroyed and the residents resettled in larger villages of at least 300 households. By regrouping the Ingush, Russia hoped to be able to monitor the population more closely. Police forces were stationed in the larger settlements, and roads linking them to territory controlled by Shamil were destroyed (Gammer 1998: 253; Martirosian 1933: 68). Moreover, in central Ingushetia, the entire population was forcefully resettled between 1859 and 1861, and 13 Cossack settlements, each with 200 families, were founded on former Ingush lands.

The Ingush found themselves trapped between the mountains and the Cossacks, artificially divided into lowland and mountain populations. This pulverized Ingush unity, destroying the previous, mutually reinforcing lowland and mountain.

'This was when the [Ingush] *teip* system was broken', I was told by the Ingush historian Kodzoev. 'Before that, we lived in individual households, tilled the land, and maintained traditional self-rule. In the process of "settlement enlargement" we were all merged together. Later, demography played a role: the *teips* were growing, and some of them branched out, becoming more distant and, finally, intermarrying.'

The resettled Ingush were isolated even farther from Chechens, further distancing the two ethnically similar groups and accelerating their divergent paths of development.

Shamil's imamate

Shamil, as *imam*, was the head of the theocratic state, or imamate, he established from 1840 to 1859. He was the commander-in-chief – and the chief executive, and the legislature (Martirosian 1933: 63; Gammer 1998: 306).

Shamil collected taxes and fees and put great effort into imposing *Sharia*, which he intended to replace the local *adat*. He issued a set of laws governing war and the interpretation of *Sharia* norms, known as *Nizam*, where mutilating punishments for crimes were replaced by fees and threatening punishments (Berge 1859: 85, 87). His imamate was divided into provinces, or *naibstva* (initially, Chechnya and Dagestan were made up of 17 *naibstvas*, later 32), each of which was governed by a *naib* – one of Shamil's deputies. *Naibs* held executive as well as military power. They collected taxes, enforced the rulings of *Sharia* courts, and monitored compliance with Shamil's orders and recommendations (Gammer 1998: 306; Bliev and Degoev 1994: 384). *Naibs* also were responsible for military training and commanded the people of their provinces in times of war.

During war each *naib* commanded between 100 and 300 warriors, or *murids*, as well as 500 cavalrymen, or *murtazeks* drafted from the villagers (Berge 1859: 86).

Each *naibstvo* was divided into sub-regions, with a *mazum* in charge of each region (Berge 1859: 87). A *mazum* usually commanded a hundred warriors and monitored the village elders. In the late 1840s, the position of *mudir* was introduced. The *mudir*, positioned above several (three to five) *naibs*, reported on them to Shamil and commanded them in the battlefield (Bliev and Degoev 1994: 385).

The religious authority in every *naibstvo* was the *mufti* and several *qadis*. The *qadi*, a *Sharia* judge, was responsible for the maintenance of the mosque; he led the prayers, including the Friday sermon (*hutba*); resolved disputes and controlled implementation of *Sharia* law (Gammer 1998: 308). The *mufti* was the highest religious authority in a given *naibstvo*. In sub-regions, disputes were resolved by *mullahs* (Berge 1859: 87). The *mufti* eradicated any digressions from *Sharia* law, either himself or with the help of the *naib* (Gammer 1998: 308).

To monitor the *naibs* and *mudirs* and for collecting parallel information, Shamil established *mukhtasibs*: inspectors for proper implementation of *Sharia* (Gammer 1998: 307). In 1842, he also established a Privy Council, the *Divan*, consisting of his most trusted associates, which he convened when particularly important decisions had to be made (Gammer 1998: 306).

Shamil's imamate was dictatorial, but his authority was tempered by norms of *Sharia*. As a Sufi, he was accountable to his spiritual leader (*murshid*), the Dagestani cleric Jamaladin al-Ghazi-ghuzikumuqi. However, by the end of Shamil's rule, Chechens had wearied of his despotic order, and were disappointed: the stronger the Russian pressure, the tighter was Shamil's grip (Berge 1859: 89). Then, on 25 August 1859, Shamil and his close associates were besieged by Imperial troops in the Dagestani village of Gunib. There was no escape, and Shamil surrendered. He eventually accepted Russian citizenship and was granted the title of a Russian noble. He died in Medina, in 1871.

The state built by Shamil tried to reshape the social structures of mountain societies. Fragmented tribes and peoples were united by the centralized state, which aimed to enforce common legal norms, a complex government apparatus, a unified military-financial administration and, to some extent, a regular defence system. For Chechens, the imamate was their first experience of enforced statehood. It served as a model for a forward-moving Islamic state, something toward which segments of the population would then aspire. Ingushetia, however, was not part of the imamate, and therefore lacks such experience in its history.

Political structures and social institutions during and after the Caucasus War

Despite its transformations, the *teip* remained the main political unit among Chechen and Ingush societies in the nineteenth century, according to the previously mentioned Soviet scholar of *teip* Magomed Mamakaev, who counted 135 tightly knit, strictly exogamous groups. In his view, they shared 23 main characteristics – much like those that the famed anthropologist Lewis H. Morgan identified while studying the Iroquois in the United States – such as a common ancestor, common ownership of land and a tribal or familial cemetery (Mamakaev 1973: 33).

However, Mamakaev's claim has been challenged on several points. Firstly, other scholars have shown that, by the nineteenth century, Chechen *teips* were no longer exogamous; sometimes *gaars* (lineages) were not, either. Secondly, historians have shown that, during the same time period, collective property rights were already held by the *gaar*, not the *teip* (Dettmering 2005; Gantemirova 1981: 8–10; Isaev 1998). Thirdly, during the Caucasian War, the monolithic political structure of the *teips* was destroyed after their members were dispersed among far-flung non-contiguous settlements, which were increasingly mixed – even, reportedly, in the mountains (Dettmering 2005: 474).

According to historian Georgi Martirosian (1933), the process of intra-*teip* differentiation continued along economic lines. Both Shamil and Russian commanders 'bought' the loyalty of local elites. In return for their loyalty, such people received land, payments, gifts and trophies of war. The Caucasian War also generated intra-*teip* ideological divides: some members were supportive of Shamil's stern Muslim order and *Sharia*, whereas others sought to preserve Chechen traditions, such as *adat* and individual freedoms.

The *Mekhk-Khel* reportedly continued to function in Chechnya during the early years of the Caucasian War; documents reveal instances of Chechen leaders asking for the consent of the *Mekhk-Khel* to begin, and continue, the war with Russia before the uprising (Musrailov 1998). However, once Shamil was empowered, the *Mekhk-Khel* was pushed underground, according to Chechen historian Magomed Muzaev. Later, it co-existed along with Russian administrations, as a parallel authority. As a consequence of the Islamization of Chechnya during the war, the *Mekhk-Khel* gradually became more of a religious institution; its leaders were often well-known *mullahs* and *sheikhs*.

After Shamil, the *Mekhk-Khel* became an institution that evolved in response to the momentum, typically functioning as 'an organ of underground resistance', according to Magomed Muzaev. These changes reflect the process of differentiation between the imposed state and society, and how the traditional Chechen *teips* and the *adat* were relegated to the domain of local, private affairs under the imamate (see Figure 2.3).

> Already in the time of Shamil, the *teip* ceased being a social organism in the society. It lost its social functions and obligations. Many factors contributed to this, including the spread of Islam and disagreement within *teips*, and within society. Shamil finally broke the backbone of the *teip* order. His Islamic leaders

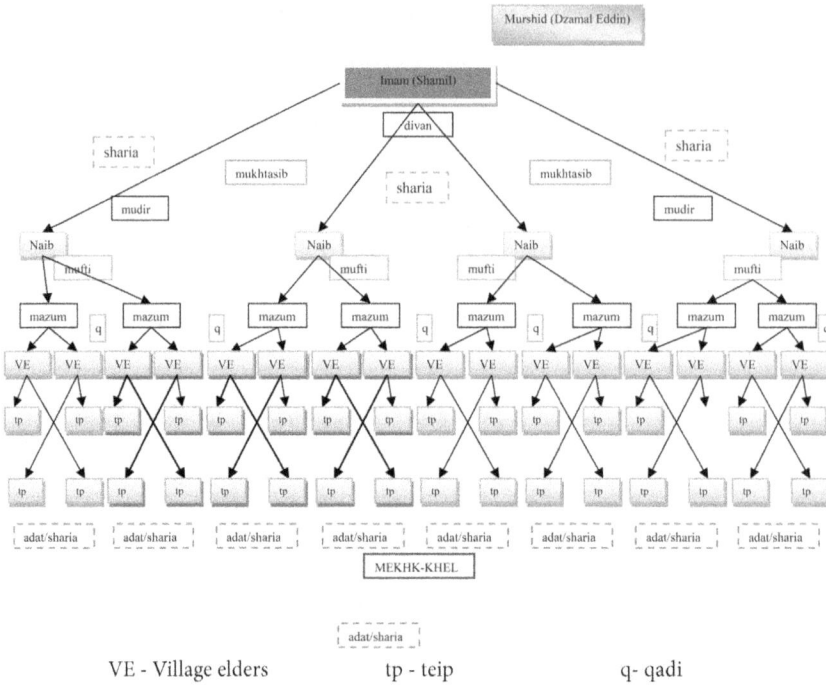

VE - Village elders   tp - teip   q- qadi

Figure 2.3 State and society during the Imamate of Shamil (1840–1858).

were people who had no status in *teip*-based society. They were nothings who became everythings, and they transformed the system of social relations.

(author's interview with the Chechen ethnologist Said-Magomed-Khasiev)

The *teip* was no longer the main pattern of social integration shaping the political order and social institutions of nineteenth-century Chechens and Ingush. After the war, *tariqas* and *virds* – Sufi Muslim brotherhoods – gained important political and social influence. A *tariqa* offers a mystical path to Allah that the Sufi Muslim believer (*murid*) follows under the guidance of his spiritual teacher (*murshid*), with whom he is expected to maintain a constant spiritual connection (Akaev 2004: 10). The leader of the *tariqa*, a *sheikh*, normally appoints a successor before he dies; this successor has official permission (*idzhaza*) to either continue the *tariqa* or found his own sub-order of the *tariqa* (Akaev 2004: 11). Two of the world's main Sufi *tariqas* are represented in Ingushetia and Chechnya.

Sheikh Mansur, who in the eighteenth century led the first major uprising against Russia in the North Caucasus, is seen as the first leader of the Naqshbandi *tariqa* in Chechnya. Subsequently, Imam Shamil led this *tariqa*. Another Chechen *sheikh*, Kunta-Khadzhi Kishiev, began preaching throughout the North Caucasus in the 1850s, as the great Caucasian War was nearing its end. Kishiev called for peace, humility, social justice and non-violent resistance to evil – the last of which particularly appealed to mountain peoples, who were exhausted by war. His ideological programme of survival with dignity, embodied in the Qadyriya, was effectively a form of passive resistance:

> If they tell you to go to church, do so: churches are only buildings, and in our souls we are Muslims. If they make you wear crosses, wear them: they are only pieces of iron, and in your soul you remain Muslim. But! If your women are used or abused, if you are forced to forget your language, culture and custom, rise and fight to death, till the last man!
>
> (quoted in Kodzoev 2002: 167)

A distinctive feature of this *tariqa* was *zikr* – a devotional act, in which words and prayers are repeated while believers move in circles and perform a devotional dance. The followers of Kunta-Khadzhi are still frequently referred to as *zikrists*.

In the 1860s, war-weary Chechens abandoned Naqshbandi and joined the new *tariqa*. The Ingush, who had converted to Islam in the late 1850s, also embraced Kishiev as a clear reaction to colonial expansion and protracted war. To this day. the Ingush like to say that Shamil was unable to convert them to Islam 'with his sword', whereas Kishiev succeeded 'with his words'.

In the 1860s the *zikrists* formed a religious structure that was headed by an *imam* and two sheikhs, who commanded *naibs* and *murids* (executive authority). From the latter the village foremen were elected (Akaev 1994). 'Soon all Chechnya, Nazran and a great portion of upper mountain societies were covered with this clandestine teaching as under a tight net' (Ippolitov 1836: 37, cited in Akaev 1994).

Zikrism became politicized, partly reproducing the organizational structure of Shamil's Imamate – which indicates that some of Shamil's institutions had taken root in Chechen and Ingush societies. *Tariqas* and *virds* cut across *teips*, becoming powerful patterns of social integration themselves. Both were especially relevant to nineteenth-century politics. As might be expected, the emergence of *tariqas*, *virds* and even larger settlements further divided the *teips*, making the structure of Chechen and Ingush societies more complex.

The Russian state and Chechen and Ingush social institutions after the Caucasian War

In the Imperial state: social change after the Caucasian War

The interference of the Russian Imperial state in community life had been limited. However, several decades later, the Caucasian War brought visible social change to Chechen and Ingush societies. This was due primarily to the *land famine*.

After the Caucasian War, the Russian administration began to redistribute land to loyal families, in an attempt to create a regional nobility (Mamakaev 1973: 59). This process led to a dramatic 'land famine' among local peasant communities. Already prior to this, several local landowners had owned more than 500 *dessiatins* of land each.[5] In addition to the Cossack settlements founded earlier, this took most of the best fertile land in Ingushetia and Chechnya (Gritsenko 1971: 14, 19).

Between 1863 and 1868, the government implemented its land distribution reform. A special estate-land commission (*Soslovno-Pozemelnaya Komissiya*) divided land according to *dyms*, or households, defined as an extended nuclear family, living as one household – usually the head of the family (father) and sons who lived with their wives and children as separate families together with him. In fact, this arrangement was negotiated with the community leaders, who thought that it would be easier to deal with the head of the extended family, rather than with many individuals. Land was allocated to each *dym*, which was expected to share it among its members (Gritsenko 1971).

Eventually, however, community leaders realized their mistake: as families grew, the sizes of individual plots of land decreased – often dramatically, because families grew quickly and constantly subdivided the land. Whereas a *dym* had consisted of five to eight people in the 1860s, by 1880 the figure had increased by 30 per cent. As a result of population growth, the distribution of arable land in 1873 was as follows (in *dessiatins* per person): Cossacks 21.3; Ossetians 5.3; Ingush 4.3, mountain Ingush 1.6 (in Kodzoev 2002: 171); Chechens 1.2 (in Mamakaev 1973: 59).

The land reform and fiscal policies elevated and economically institutionalized the extended nuclear family – the individual household or *dym* was now the main economic and fiscal unit. This accelerated the fragmentation of *gaar* and *nek* into individual two- or three-generation households (father and sons, with wives and children).

New institutions and laws. New sectors of the economy

In 1852 Russia established a 'Chechen court' (*Mekhkme-Chachani*). Based in Grozny, it consisted of a *qadi*, who resolved disputes according to *Sharia*, and three elders, who dispensed justice according to *adat*. The court was presided over by a Russian (Berge 1859: 80). Murder, illegal division of property, divorce were adjudicated according to *Sharia*, whereas offences like theft, arson, physical assault and insults to women were adjudicated according to *adat* (Berge 1859: 81). After 1858, however, new Regulations on the Governance of the Caucasian army reduced the application of *Sharia* to issues of faith and conscience (Berge 1859: 82).

The Russian policy of land reform, and the resultant land famine, brought changes in employment patterns among the Chechens and the Ingush. In order to cope with the deficit of arable land, mountain dwellers either rented farmland and pastures from Cossacks, or found work in the vineyards of Kyzlyar, or as builders and labourers in large plains settlements.

After 1893, with the opening of the Starye Promysla well in Grozny, locals also found work in oil refineries, and Grozny became a major industrial centre. Oil extraction and processing industries, as well as mechanical engineering and transport enterprises, mushroomed with the inflow of Russian and foreign capital. European

---

[5] One dessiatina = approx. 1.1 hectares (2.75 acres).

oil companies, especially those based in Great Britain, bought shares in Grozny oil companies, and invested in technological advances in oil production. Most workers at these refineries were Russian, but Chechens gradually joined in – first as unskilled labour, then increasingly as skilled labour. In 1914, Chechen entrepreneurs founded the Staroyurtovskaya Neft Oil Company, a joint stock enterprise that, for the times, was both modern and efficiently run (Kolosov 1964: 45).

Employment opportunities outside immediate Chechen and Ingush society gradually opened up isolated communities. Chechens and Ingush learned other languages, acquired new skills, and – at least temporarily – moved beyond the confines of traditional social structures. Gender roles were changing in communities where many men worked at seasonal jobs elsewhere. Women began to play more prominent roles in managing households.

This chapter has shown that the process of feudalization, loose as it was in Ingushetia and Chechnya, facilitated social changes within and between *teips*, while economic differentiation created new asymmetries of power. Nonetheless, before the colonial wars both societies remained stateless.

Imam Shamil was the first to draw a line between the state and traditional religious, political, legal and social structures. His Imamate aimed to submerge competing traditional institutions, replace traditional law by Islamic law, build a superstructure on top of traditional governing structure, thereby pushing traditional institutions into the domain of local issues, limited to village communities. However, his state-building efforts were only partly successful, and his governmental structures remained rather autonomous from Chechen and Ingush societies, which maintained their own self-government.

The 1818–1864 Caucasus War produced major social change: the traditional economic systems were destroyed, much of the male population was decimated, and many families were forced to resettle again and again. Sufi Islam took hold, bringing important changes to the public order and traditional social institutions. By the end of the nineteenth century, well before the 1917 Bolshevik Revolution, Chechen and Ingush social institutions – the *teips* in particular – had been gradually transformed, through colonization and state-building efforts, into informal social structures that functioned mostly outside the formal system of government.

3

State-Building, Informal Institutions and Social Integration under the Soviet Union (1921–1991)

The Bolsheviks were the first government to set out to build a modern state in the North Caucasus. The Soviet administration sought to penetrate deep into the social structure of the Chechen and Ingush peoples, even into the domain of family life, and integrate the various elements into a cohesive political unit. This chapter analyses the sweeping social changes brought about by the Soviet modernization programmes, which hastened the erosion of long-established traditional structures; and Soviet repression – from Stalinist exile to post-deportation restrictions on settlement, employment and religion – which also served to preserve certain informal institutions and practices. Further, this chapter deals with three types of memories which Chechens and Ingush share regarding their past within the Russian state, and which have had a profound impact on the political processes in the period 1991 to 2001.

Social change and the early Bolshevik state (1922–1940)

On 17 November 1920, Josef Stalin, as the people's commissar for nationalities affairs, acting in the name of the Bolshevik government, proposed to the North Caucasian peoples the establishment of a new mountain republic (Dunlop 1998: 42). The Congress of Terek *oblast* (administrative district) invited over 500 delegates from across the region to discuss the future of the region. Muslim delegates demanded the creation of a legal system based on *Sharia* and *adat*, without central government interference on the affairs of the mountain peoples, and the return of the lands expropriated during Imperial rule. Stalin accepted both conditions, and the Congress formally acknowledged Soviet rule (Avtorkhanov 2005).

Initially, the Bolsheviks made swift and impressive progress. From the 1920s through the 1930s the central government developed public healthcare and mechanized agriculture in the North Caucasus, as well as a formal secular education system in national languages. The Chechens and Ingush benefited in particular from *korenizatsiya* – literally 'rootification', or indigenization – a programme launched in 1923 aimed at promoting national languages, helping to shape a national elite and increasing government employment among representatives of the non-Russian nationalities.[1]

---

[1] For an excellent analysis of the logic and essence of this policy, see Terry Martin, *The Affirmative Action Empire* (2001).

The scale of the early Soviet affirmative action initiatives was quite unprecedented. Both Chechens and Ingush were on the list of the country's 97 'culturally backward nationalities', and thus eligible for preferential treatment in various class- and gender-based affirmative-action programmes. However, a major obstacle to *korenizatsiya* efforts among the Chechens and Ingush was the very low level of literacy, as minimum reading standards were a prerequisite for promotion to managerial and leadership positions. In 1926, the literacy rate among the Ingush stood at 9.1 per cent; among Chechens it was only 2.9 per cent. By comparison, some 45 and 78.1 per cent of Russians and Estonians (respectively) were literate, according to Terry Martin, author of the seminal work, *The Affirmative Action Empire* (2001).

During the First Five-Year Plan, tens of thousands of mountain people were steered into short-term courses that trained them for work such as accountancy (Martin 2001: 171). According to historian Gerhard Simon, the pace of education across the Soviet Union was unprecedented in the modern world, dwarfing the efforts of many European countries, let alone other Third World countries (Simon 1991: 266).

The rapid mechanization of labour required employees with higher education. Many Muslims were encouraged to send their children to school, where instruction in their native tongue had a profound effect on the development of the education system. Primary school teachers were largely non-Russian, as instruction was almost entirely in the language native to the area in which schools were situated. By 1939 the rate of *korenizatsiya* in the Chechen-Ingush Republic was higher than that in the Soviet republics of Ukraine or Belorussia.

The broadening of educational opportunities under the Soviet Union soon produced the first layer of Soviet intelligentsia, whose members generally displayed loyalty and attachment to the regime from which they had benefited. *Korenizatsiya* created a demand for teachers, journalists, writers, historians and, of course, bureaucrats. Chechens and Ingush gravitated to those spheres (Martin 2001: 382), establishing new networks as the rural, family-based economy started to reshape. New patterns of social integration emerged, such as worker's teams, professional unions and membership in the Communist Party or Komsomol, the Soviet youth organization.

According to the Russian historian Pavel Polian, the unrest following the defeat of the Russian Empire by the Bolsheviks resulted in a five- to sixfold decrease in oil production. By 1920, however, the Bolsheviks had managed to get oil production back to pre-revolutionary levels, and in 1922 some 18,000 people were employed in the oil industry in Chechnya – a considerable concentration of workers in that otherwise predominately agrarian region (Polian 2003). In 1928, another Soviet five-year plan targeted the North Caucasus for recruitment of one thousand mountain people annually to work at factories in Rostov-on-Don and major North Caucasian cities (Martin 2001: 152).

The Soviet programme of *korenizatsiya* was also aimed at changing the legal consciousness of the populace: local judges were trained and employed in the new Soviet courts, and special educational programmes were set up at workplaces, to acquaint the people with the new system and its laws (Babich 2000: 36). However, this project was not very successful among Chechen and Ingush communities. They saw the Soviet legal system as unfair, largely because it mandated strict penalties for minor offences but, in their eyes, was lenient on murderers. As a result, Chechens and Ingush rarely reported minor offences, and sought retribution for murder through blood feud – regardless of Soviet courts. Chechen and Ingush societies continued with a plurality of legal systems: Soviet laws simply joined *Sharia* and *adat*.

The political sovereignty of the mountain peoples of the North Caucasus proved short-lived: in October 1922 Moscow began to carve up the Soviet Mountain Republic, by first creating the autonomous *oblast* of Chechnya, and in July 1924 the autonomous *oblast* of Ingushetia. In December 1936, the two were merged into the Chechen-Ingush Autonomous Soviet Socialist Republic. In the process the Ingush lost their capital, the right bank of the Terek River in Vladikavkaz, which became part of North Ossetia. In 1930s a new ethnonym was introduced – 'the Wainakhs', literally 'our people', referring to both Chechens and Ingush, and emphasizing their unity. The legitimacy of this term has been disputed by some historians and public figures.

The real Soviet offensive started in 1929 with collectivization. The policy of *de-kulakization* targeted not only the better-off peasants, but often rural middle-class families – and even labourers opposed to farm collectivization. De-kulakization was often used as a pretext for settling the score with personal enemies, or rivals, and to target religious leaders. Local authorities were required to report regularly on the success of the de-kulakization campaign. In practice, families were often randomly selected and deported to Siberia in order 'to produce statistics'.

The goodwill that had been generated among the Wainakhs through modernization and development was eventually erased by forced collectivization, expropriation of property, mass arrests and deportations, and produced mass protests in Ingushetia and Chechnya (Polian 2003). Eventually, *kolkhoz* (collective farm) policies were adapted to Chechen and Ingush realities. The authorities turned a blind eye to the fact that the Chechens organized collective farms which were 'not simply small, but dwarfish' – tantamount to family-based (Polian 2003). For example, 87 collective farms were formally registered in the large Chechen village of Shali – but the situation was 'a parody of collectivization' (Polian 2003).

By the end of the 1930s, Chechen-Ingushetia had 412 collective farms, but output was very low. Many collective enterprises defrauded the government, and falsified documents. In 1939 alone, according to Polian, about 10 per cent of all farmland that produced grain was reported to have been destroyed by hail, pests and diseases. Subsequent investigation showed that the grain harvest had been lost as a result of neglect, and weeds. Moreover, collective farms in Chechnya and Ingushetia invested few resources in cattle, whereas horses reportedly confiscated from private households were discovered to still be living in the stables of their previous owners (Polian 2003).

In the 1930s – on top of collectivization, de-kulakization and the anti-religion campaign – the Soviet government launched a campaign against 'bourgeois nationalism' that wiped out nearly the entire stratum of North Caucasus intelligentsia, through exile or death. In 1937 yet another wave of repression resulted in the arrests of nearly 300 religious leaders in the Chechen-Ingush republic – or almost everyone who could read the Qur'an (Akaev 1994). Moreover, anti-Soviet uprisings – at least 12 had been recorded since the founding of the Mountain Republic, with from 500 to 5,000 armed combatants – continued until 1941, or the onset of the Second World War (Polian 2003).

Thus, early Soviet policies involved assertive affirmative-action programmes. These brought impressive development of the Chechen and Ingush social-professional structure, increased literacy and educational levels, changed employment patterns and promoted the emancipation of women. However, the subsequent collectivization of agriculture destroyed the economic basis of Chechen and Ingush extended families. Even the nuclear family household could no longer be the main source of income, due to limits on private economic production. Family members had to sell their labour to the *kolkhoz* or join industrial enterprises. This development disrupted family employment patterns, accelerating the erosion of strong extended family units embedded in a common economy. However, dissolving the traditional extended family structures of the Chechens and Ingush was not easy; moreover, many simply adapted the new *kolkhoz* regime to their habitual forms of economic activity.

From 1937 through 1941, mass repression against religious leaders and Chechen and Ingush intellectuals sought to destroy all alternative power centres in the republic. By eliminating the educated strata, Stalin undermined the achievements of *korenizatsiya*, and sabotaged the future cultural and professional development of both peoples.

Deportation, social change and social institutions (1944–1957)

In 1944 the Chechen-Ingush autonomous Soviet Socialist Republic was abolished, and the entire population was charged with 'collaborating with the Nazi occupants'. In the heart of winter, the people were rounded up and deported by train to Central Asia – primarily to Kazakhstan and to Kirgiziya, but also to Tajikistan and Uzbekistan. Many died from disease, cold and hunger while being transported. Many more perished upon arrival. According to Russian ethnologist Valery Tishkov, more than one-third of the Chechen population died between the North Caucasus and Central Asia (Tishkov 2001: 82).

Many of my respondents recalled how the deportees were collected from neighbourhoods and small villages in US-made Studebaker trucks and delivered to train stations, where they were jammed tightly into railway carriages. Declassified documents confirmed that, on average, 240 people were transported in each carriage (Kozlov and Kozlova 2004). Sometimes these would be filled with people from the same village, or neighbourhood – which at least meant that the deportees had a greater chance of reuniting in Kazakhstan or Kirgiziya.

After interviewing more than 50 deportees about their experiences in exile, I have come to the conclusion that deportation inflicted considerably greater suffering and losses on the residents of mountain villages. As their settlements were inaccessible to road vehicles, villagers were forced to proceed on foot – usually between 15 and 25 kilometres – to more centralized locations, where they were picked up and delivered to train stations. Those who walked could not take more luggage than they were able to carry in their hands; as families often had many small children, they were able to take only the basics.

As a result, many mountain people died of hunger on the way to Central Asia, or shortly after arrival. Elderly or seriously ill mountain dwellers who could not walk were simply shot. In the Chechen village of Khaibakh, in the high mountains of the Galanchozhsky region, some 705 people – mostly the elderly, as well as women and children from surrounding villages who could not walk on their own – were burned alive in the stables of a collective farm.

Khabisat Khasbulatova, born in 1910, from the high mountain village of K'orgi, recalled in an interview:

> On the day of deportation, all men were told to go to the village administration building, and women were ordered to pack. My daughter was four years old, and she was bedridden with a fever. When we were ready to go my husband said, 'Leave her at home, we'll come back tonight.' We left, and then I turned back and saw tears running down her cheeks. I rushed back and took her with me, tied her to my back with a woollen shawl.
>
> All day long they kept us outside, in the snow. The girl didn't make a single sound, she was so happy that she would be going with us. They let us take hardly anything. The next day they made us go to Yalkhoroy [*the regional centre – E.S.*] on foot. Many of the ill and elderly were left behind. Two of the Saidaev brothers, Israil and Mikail, had carried their elderly mother on their backs. Then the soldiers shot her dead in front of them.
>
> From Yalkhoroy we had to walk on foot to Alkun, in Ingushetia, and from there they picked us up in cars and took us to the Grozny railway station. No food was provided on the trains. We had only what we could take with us. Several days later, my daughter died. People hid their dead children because, when the soldiers noticed corpses, they threw them out the window. My brother Yakub performed a funeral rite, pronounced a prayer, and we wrapped her in cloth. At a train stop in Kizlyar he asked a local shepherd for a spade and buried my daughter.

In Kazakhstan, the train convoys stopped at every station. Each time, three to four families were called out, then the train continued on. At the stations, deportees were met by local residents in carts yoked to oxen, or cows, and led to small villages. Members of the same *teip*, *gaar* and *nek* were scattered across in the vast territories of Central Asia.

Many nuclear families were split up, too, because people were deported on the basis of where they were on the night of deportation, and many had been spending the night with relatives or parents (as is still common in the North Caucasus). I documented numerous cases of people who spent weeks and months wandering from village to village in Kazakhstan, trying to find their family members – despite harsh punishment for leaving one's specified place of exile without permission.

Some freedom of movement was permitted until 1946, after which it was forbidden. The system of exile, or 'special settlement', was enforced by a system of *komendaturas* (command centres) manned by officers of the NKVD, the predecessor of the KGB. Every ten days, all exiled Chechens and Ingush above the age of 10 were required to register at the local command centre. Leaving one's assigned place of exile meant risking a lengthy prison term.

'Our *teip* was fragmented into individual families all over Kazakhstan. In the village where my family lived, there was not a single Ingush, and certainly no one from the Aushevs' said Mussa Aushev, Elder of the Aushev *teip*. 'It took us a long time to find out where our relatives lived. People wrote letters, asking about each other. In the course of about three to five years, many found their kin through such correspondence, but were forbidden from visiting them until Stalin's death.'

However, Chechen and Ingush settlements after deportation were more compact than those of other deported peoples. The overwhelming majority of Chechens and Ingush, more than 400,000 individuals, had been moved to northern Kazakhstan and Kyrgyziya (now Kyrgyzstan). 'The separation of families … in the deportation of Chechens and Ingush did not have the same catastrophic consequences compared to other peoples. It did not have an impact on their linguistic situation, or ethnic self-awareness', writes Russian historian of deportation, Anna Kuznetsova (2005).

Still, the first two to three years of exile were a genocidal experience. Those who had managed to take money, corn or dried meat from home survived longer; others died of starvation and disease. According to official statistics of the Department of Special Settlements of the NKVD of the USSR, the number of Chechens and Ingush in exile fell by 90,560 within the 20 months after deportation. That period had the highest death rates (around 15 per cent) of the entire period 1944–1948, during which at least 144,704 Chechens and Ingush died.

By the third and fourth years, life in exile became easier, as people had begun to plant vegetable gardens, and the more productive collective farms donated cows to the exiles. The more entrepreneurial and hard-working Chechens and Ingush doggedly set about trying to find work in the existing labour market and grasped every opportunity to earn money or otherwise find goods for their households. The tradition of bearing responsibility for one's relatives bred shrewd survival strategies that yielded real results: those who survived the first few years usually survived to return to the North Caucasus.

'We were settled in a German village near the town of Kustanai, in Kazakhstan', Adam, a Chechen Elder from Goragorsk, told me. 'In the spring I collected potato peelings, and we planted them. The peelings yielded a good crop, much better than that of the Germans who had planted whole potatoes! The chairman of the local collective farm held us up as an example. "You see", he said, "they cultivated the land by hand, planted peelings, and got such a harvest!"'

Adam continued: 'In subsequent years there was famine in Chelyabinsk [*industrial city in the Ural Mountains of Russia – E.S.*], and people came from there and bought potatoes from us. With this money we bought a cow, two sheep and clothing.'

Following the death of Stalin in 1953, restrictions on movement were abolished for exiles. Many extended families reunited, or moved to urban centres. 'Our family was scattered around the entire steppe. [After 1953] we tried to move closer to each other. One would find a job, and others would then join him, move closer', explained Osman Khadziev, who had been deported from Khadziev Khutor, in the Prigorodny Region of North Ossetia.

Many respondents told me that they moved in with their matrilineal relatives, or in-laws. Previously, it had been unusual for Wainakhs to reside with their matrilineal kin. But during the period of deportation, kinship overtook descent as the primarily basis for solidarity. Alikhan Dozariev, at the time of interview the director of the Ingush Museum Memorial complex for victims of deportation, believes that this reshuffling increased national solidarity and erased *teip* and family frontiers:

> During deportation many people lost their families and had to survive with other families. And when a person lives with another family, he becomes part of that family. Grief united people. They had to share what they had with those who were surviving next to them, without dividing people into kin and non-kin. Everyone was a brother. The Ingush national consciousness was greatly strengthened during that period.

In 1955 Chechens and Ingush were granted domestic passports, and young people were able to gain university entry. Hard-working and entrepreneurial, many Wainakh families were well-off by the end of their years in exile. As Bersnak Gandarov, a lawyer from Karabulak in Ingushetia, told me:

> By the end of the deportation, we were living marvellously well. My older brother worked in an automobile shop, another brother was a driver, and third brother also was a driver. I studied at school. In 1957 we moved to Almaty [*then capital of Kazakhstan – E.S.*], and I continued my studies. In fact, we lived better then than now. Life had taught us to find a way. We are a very entrepreneurial and hardworking people. Many families became wealthy.

On 16 July 1956, the Supreme Soviet of the USSR issued the decree 'On abolishing limitations for special settlement of Chechens, Ingush, Karachay and their family members'. This paved the way for the mass resettlement of the Chechens and Ingush back to the North Caucasus. By 1961, the overwhelming majority had returned.

Remarkably, while in exile, the Chechen and Ingush peoples managed to retain their culture, language and informal social structures – not to mention their spirit of opposition, and silent resistance, to the Soviet regime. The dire conditions promoted greater solidarity among ethnic groups and individual families, and strengthened traditional institutions of self-government, customary law, etiquette and ritual. By virtue of these institutions, they were able to live 'parallel lives' that the authoritarian state was unable to penetrate. The influence of Elders, which had waned to almost symbolic levels prior to deportation, again gained ground during exile, particularly during the harsh years from 1944 to 1946. The Wainakh peoples consciously strove to preserve not only their traditions, but a national identity. It was in exile that the Elders enforced the strict endogamy that is still largely observed to this day.

At the same time, young Chechens and Ingush living in Kazakhstan assimilated more easily, and eschewed traditional ways. 'During the first years [*of exile – E.S.*] we did not perform *sakh* [*religious ritual, usually distributing meat or food in memory of a deceased person – E.S.*]. If a person died, and others had enough energy to bury him, this was already considered good', said Said-Ali, a Chechen who was born in 1911, and had been deported from the village of Khal-Keloy. 'Then, when life became better, we started to perform all our rituals in strict adherence to the rules. There were around 200 Chechens in the place where we lived, so we observed everything ... But young people were under the strong influence of their environment. Some started to smoke and drink.'

Not surprisingly, perhaps, during the initial years of exile, the Soviet special services reported an unprecedented increase in religious observance among Wainakh peoples. The Ministry of Internal Affairs determined that, by the end of 1946, there were 1,003 *mullahs* and other religious authorities among the deportees from the North Caucasus – almost twice as many as the number of members of the Communist Party among Chechens and Ingush, which stood at 593. 'Religious life was bustling, and the authorities could not understand what was happening within the community', write historians Vladimir and Marina Kozlov (Kozlov and Kozlova 2004).

During the 1950s a group of *zikrists* in the Akmolinsk region of Kazakhstan, headed by Vis-Khadzhi Zangiev, founded a new *vird* they called the 'white hats', or *beloshapochniki*. Vis-Khadzhi had altered some of the Wainakh customs and rituals, and established a low, fixed price for dowries, reducing the burden on many families struggling in exile.

Historian Anna Kuznetsova concludes that the 13 years of exile 'deepened ... the ethno-cultural strategy of the Chechens and Ingush, the inclination toward self-isolation and resistance to any minor pressure by the authorities ... National self-consciousness of the Chechens and Ingush was traumatized by the stigma of being a "nation of traitors"'. And although none of the Chechens or Ingush believed in the fairness of such accusations, 'public opinion' in Kazakhstan and, subsequently, upon return to the [Chechen-Ingush Autonomous Soviet Socialist Republic], was conducive to depressive moods and insularity" (Kuznetsova 2005).

I would argue that deportation taught the Chechens and Ingush not to resist minor pressures by the state, but to adapt to, or find ways around, or otherwise counteract totalitarian pressures by manoeuvring within a distinct social space that featured an alternative ideology. This space was carefully safeguarded by elders, religious leaders – and adults in general.

On the other hand, deportation undoubtedly stalled the economic and cultural development of Chechens and Ingush alike. While other Soviet nations were writing their Soviet versions of histories, developing literatures, industry and science, the Wainakhs were fighting for survival, struggling to make their way to a local factory, to establish themselves there, to bring relatives over, so that all could stay close and warm. That being said, scholars differ in their evaluations of the social progress of Wainakh societies during the 13 years in exile. Some emphasize the opening up of Chechen and Ingush societies, as a result of education in a multi-ethnic environment and the integration of mainly young people into a different cultural milieu. It was during exile that the influence of Russian – or Soviet – culture truly had an impact on young people. They began to go to the cinema, and young Wainakh men began dating Russian girls. '[Wainakh] youth started to learn many things that went beyond the framework of the customs and traditions of their people. A window to the big world was open to them' (Kozlov and Kozlova 2004).

Kuznetsova believes the period of exile had a freezing effect on the social and professional lives of Chechens and Ingush, not least because job opportunities were restricted to agriculture and unskilled labour. Such conditions, she notes, were not conducive to the creation of a Chechen or Ingush intelligentsia (Kuznetsova 2005).

Deportation finalized the processes that had begun during collectivization – destroying the traditional Chechen and Ingush economies of self-employment, with family-based agricultural and cattle-breeding households, and made most Wainakhs state-employed. It also fully undermined the territorial basis of Chechen kinship: the *teip* villages, kin-based neighbourhoods, traditional mechanisms of maintaining contact by attending funerals and weddings. Nonetheless, by the end of the deportation, the Chechens and Ingush managed to consolidate their families (usually extended families, up to second cousins), revive religious brotherhoods and establish regular Islamic practice. Moreover, *vird* leaders continued to play a prominent role. The process of creation of new *virds* continued, exemplified by the emergence of the new *vird* of Vis-Khadzhi Zangiev, part of the Qadyriya *tariqa*.

Social change after exile (1957–1991)

The 1956 decree of the Supreme Soviet that lifted the exile of Wainakh peoples was followed on 9 January 1957, by Decree № 721/4, which restored the Chechen-Ingush Republic, with the declared aim of creating the 'necessary conditions for national development of the Chechen and Ingush peoples'. The decree, however, did not return the Prigorodny Region from North Ossetia to Ingushetia. By way of compensation, the Supreme Soviet shifted into the Chechen-Ingush Republic the regions of Naursky, Nadterechny and Shelkovskoy, which were formerly part of Russia's Stavropol *krai*.

The Soviet government created a special organizing committee (*Orgkomitet*) to arrange for the resettlement of Wainakhs in an orderly fashion. However, thousands of Chechens and Ingush had already begun returning to the North Caucasus, and within a month following the issuance of the decree some 11,000 people had returned home (Kuznetsova 2005).

Over the next three years, the disorganized, spontaneous return of Chechens and Ingush to their homelands dashed all government plans and timeframes. By early 1958, instead of the planned return of 100,000 people, at least double that number, or 201,746, had returned (Kuznetsova 2005). And all of them needed to find accommodation in a republic into which some 540,000 other people had moved after the deportations of the Wainakhs. Attempts by police in 1957 to stem the tide, by detaining those who did not have permission from the *Orgkomitet*, were unsuccessful (Kozlov and Kozlova 2004).

On returning from deportation, many Chechens and Ingush found their houses occupied by others. Jobs were scarce, and the capacity of the republic's infrastructure (schools, kindergartens, hospitals) was limited. Moreover, the return to Chechen high mountain villages – in the Itum-Kalinsky, Sharoysky, Galanchozhsky, Chemberloysky and Shatoysky regions – was forbidden probably to prevent the emergence of new insurgences in the hills. Some villages and cemeteries had been destroyed. All returnees were forced to weave themselves into the existing social texture of the mainly rural lowland areas. The percentage of indigenous urban dwellers remained low until the 1980s, see table 3.1.

Government measures for the resettlement of Chechens and Ingush included the provision of loans for building houses and buying cattle. However, only 5 per cent of the returnees actually benefited from these loans; and, as of 1957, only one-fifth of the returnees had housing, while the rest lived on industrial premises or in dugouts (Kuznetsova 2005). Some returnees tried to reclaim their former houses by force. Some pressured the new occupants to leave. Others bought their former houses.

The labour market in the Chechen-Ingush Republic was unable to absorb so many new arrivals: most positions were already filled by the non-Wainakh population. Moreover, the economy of the region had become more developed. The modern oil, chemical industries and mechanical engineering required new skills that returnees did not possess, and had few opportunities to acquire.

As a result, the republic's economy became divided along ethnic lines. The 'Russian sector' comprised the oil industry, heavy-machinery manufacturing, infrastructure and other services, while the 'national sector' comprised agriculture and trade. 'National' cadres, like Chechens and Ingush, did not have equal access to the more prestigious, better-paid industrial jobs (Tishkov 2001: 116). Even in the late 1980s, the largest industrial enterprises in Chechnya, such as Grozneft and Orgsintez, employed more than 50,000 people each – yet allocated only a few hundred positions to Chechens and Ingush (Tishkov 2001).

Table 3.1 Ethnic composition of urban and rural population in Chechen-Ingush Soviet Socialist Republic (ChIASSR) in 1959 and 1970 (in thousands) (Grebenshikov 1977)

	Urban population		Rural population	
	1959	**1970**	**1959**	**1970**
Total in ChIASSR	293.7	444.1	416.7	620.4
whereof:				
– Chechens	22.3	90.8	221.6	418.1
– Ingush	4.2	35.6	44.0	78.1
– Russians	227.7	269.9	120.7	97.0
– Ukrainians	9.1	9.7	4.6	2.9
– Armenians	11.8	13.7	1.4	0.9
– peoples of Dagestan	2.4	3.7	14.6	15.9
– Tatars	3.9	4.3	–	–
– Jews	5.0	4.9	–	–
–Ossetians	1.2	1.4	1.9	1.2
Other nationalities and peoples	6.1	10.1	7.91	6.3

Source: P. Grebenshikov (ed.), *Checheno-Ingush ASSR 1917–1977* (Checheno-Ingush ASSR 1917–1977, Collection of Statistics) (Grozny: Chechen-Ingush Publishing House, 1977).

This concentration of Chechens and Ingush in the agricultural, light industry and food sectors was the result of deliberate Soviet policy, according to Kuznetsova (2005). Unemployment compelled more than 30, 000 Wainakhs to leave the republic annually for seasonal work in Russia. However, beginning in the mid-1970s, Chechens and Ingush slowly but steadily began to become more integrated into the sectors of the economy in the republic, which already ranked among the most industrialized in Russia. The numbers of people who were pursing higher education increased.

By 1977 the republic had two institutions of higher education: the Grozny Oil Institute, renowned throughout the Soviet Union, and the Chechen-Ingush Pedagogical Institute. Twelve specialized secondary educational institutions, and 566 schools, rounded out the republic's educational profile (Grebenshikov 1977). However, tables included in a 1967 collection of statistics, *Chechen-Ingush Autonomous Soviet Socialist Republic over 50 Years*, indicate that, despite representing nearly 60 per cent of the population of the republic Wainakhs were severely under-represented in educational institutions when compared to ethnic Russians.[2]

This situation was the result of the constrained economic situation of their families, who could not afford to send a teenager to higher schools and had to have him employed, and the general lower value that Wainakhs at that time attributed to higher education. Many young males joined their older relatives in seasonal jobs, mainly as construction workers in Russia, Ukraine and Kazakhstan.

Shamil, a businessman from Grozny, explained:

I remember, as we got older, on the first of September, the beginning of the school year, many Wainakh guys in our class would be missing. They came back to school only by the end of October or so, because their parents had taken them along while doing seasonal work, which finished up in late autumn.

The relative containment of Wainakhs to rural territories, and traditional sectors of the economy, and lower levels of education contributed to the tenacity of informal social structures. *Virds* and religious leaders continued to play prominent roles in society, according to Kuznetsova (2005), who reports around 500 *mullahs* in the republic in the 1970s. Customary and Islamic law, the *adat* and *Sharia*, played roles in both the Soviet law-enforcement and judicial systems; incidents of blood feud were often resolved, not via the legal system, but by obtaining the consent of both sides. Marriages were registered in accordance with *Sharia* norms; and, in cases of divorce, children typically stayed with the father – in keeping with *adat*, but contrary to the Soviet Family Code.

At the same time, the legal pluralism in the Chechen-Ingush Republic provided Wainakhs with some space for manoeuvre. For example, a divorced woman who sought custody of her children had Soviet law on her side – as long as she was prepared

---

[2] According to the 1970 census, Chechens comprised 47.8% of the republic's population (508,900), Ingush 10.7% (113,700), and Russians 34.5% (366,900). P. Grebenshikov (ed.), *Checheno-Ingushskaya ASSR 1917–1977* (Checheno-Ingush ASSR 1917–1977, Collection of Statistics). (Grozny: Chechen-Ingush Publishing House, 1977).

to confront social pressures. Similarly, families whose daughters were abducted as brides could turn to Soviet courts in a bid to punish the perpetrators, who faced up to ten years in jail.

Moreover, the Soviet identity started to catch up. Most of my respondents from Grozny claimed that in the 1980s *teip* and *vird* identity was not important at all. Many of them knew almost nothing about their *teips*, nor did they know the *teip* affiliations of other Wainakhs around them. In the multinational environment, the important thing was that they were 'Wainakhs', then 'Chechens' or 'Ingush' – further sub-divisions were not relevant.

The return from exile was another shake-up for the remnants of the *teip* system. Structurally the *teips* and lineages were yet once again territorially fragmented. Mountain villages – the centrepieces of *teip* culture – were now closed for residence; houses and cemeteries had been destroyed; and the traditional regular rituals linked to the cemeteries and villages were impossible. Moreover, the very nucleus of the *teip* structure – the residents of *teip* villages – were now scattered all around Chechen-Ingushetia.

At the level of identity, the return from exile brought the Chechens and Ingush into strong ethnic tensions with members of other nationalities in the republic. Disputes over property, competition for land and scarce employment often acquired ethnic overtones. This resulted in the strengthening of Chechen and Ingush national identities against other ethnic groups – enhancing internal group cohesion, but also reducing the significance of internal subnational divisions. However, *teip* identity continued to matter to some degree in connection with match-making for marriages.

In residential areas of Grozny, extended families lived apart, usually in neighbourhoods with multiple apartment blocks. In rural areas, however, kin-based Wainakh neighbourhoods were more common: conditions of high unemployment fostered solidarity among households that relied on livestock and vegetable gardens to survive. Such households usually were made up of nuclear families, but sometimes included adult brothers and cousins who lived next door. Despite the dramatic break-up of Wainakh family structures during exile and upon return, high birth rates, the predominantly rural lifestyle and the tradition of attending family ceremonies (funerals and weddings) in large numbers, taken up again after the return from exile, all served to galvanize kinship ties.

At the same time, Soviet modernization, industrialization and social change produced new patterns of social integration. Educational opportunities and urbanization bolstered these new patterns of integration (as with student groups, Communist Party membership, the *komsomol*, workplace teams and professional unions), not to mention new allegiance to the modern state, with Soviet citizenship. The intelligentsia, national *nomenklatura* and workers were new strata created by the Soviet state, which now operated in a more individualistic fashion.

However, the titular nationalities were under-represented in government positions. In 1979 and 1989, only 0.2 per cent of the adult Chechen population held governing positions (Kozlov 1999: 134, 141). Thus, Chechen networks did not establish themselves strongly at the republic-level government and administration.

Collective memory as a political resource

All beginnings contain an element of recollection. This is particularly so when a social group makes a concerted effort to begin with a wholly new start.
– Paul Connerton, How Societies Remember

The following chapters analyse Chechens and Ingush statehood projects launched in the early 1990s. New political identities, new social movements as well as the unprecedented political mobilization of the late 1980s were all focused on and deeply embedded in the collective social memory. Almost all my interviewees found in their ethnic group's history justification for the separatist cause in Chechnya, or the national movement in Ingushetia. Therefore, before analysing post-Soviet developments, I will briefly discuss relevant issues related to collective memories prior to the collapse of the USSR, as the national leaders drew heavily on these throughout the 1990s. Today, Chechen memories of grievances centre on the tragedies of the two wars, whereas the Ingush collectively remember the 1992 Ingush–Ossetian conflict. I return to some of these memories in subsequent chapters as well.

As explained by Ruslan, a Chechen who fought in the first Russo-Chechen War as a 17-year-old and, later, in the second war as an adult:

> For me, it all began in school. I had known ever since I was a child what had been done to our people. In school I scoured all the textbooks, but there was no mention of Chechens. There were wild tribes, indigenous peoples, but no Chechens. We had a history teacher, Nadezhda Nikolaevna. I asked her in class why there were stories of these other peoples … but nothing about us, a whole ethnic republic? I got only her angry glance as a response.
>
> Her husband was a local policeman, and a few days later he came up to my father and said, 'Your son is asking too many questions. He doesn't need to know those things. But I *did* need to know. I knew my grandfather was deported and died – a *kulak*, because he had two flour mills here, in the village. His three brothers were shot dead. My father was nine when he was deported to Kazakhstan with his grandmother. She died of hunger a month later. My father was raised in orphanages. I had always known that I would fight when the time came. I was a ready-made revolutionary.

Ruslan is now involved in private security business in a southern Russian town.

Issa Kodzoev, an Ingush writer, and leader of the Ingush national movement, Niiskho, explained to me in similar terms how the national struggle for statehood had begun for him:

> It started when we were students at the Pedagogical institute, all because we had been deported and we wanted to know the truth. In 1944, my family had numbered eleven people. I buried everyone who had been deported, and returned home alone. After my arrest, in 1962, I said in court that I would fight Soviet power till the end of my days.

The phenomenon of social or collective memories has been the subject of extensive theoretical and empirical research since Maurice Halbwachs introduced the topic into social science theory (see Halbwachs [1926] 1950). Drawing on Durkheim's belief that the function of remembering is to promote commitment to the group by emphasizing its values and aspirations, Halbwachs went further: he held that every group develops a memory of its own past that highlights its unique identity, and that collective memory is in fact a manifestation of this identity. He saw memory as a crucial condition of social order, solidarity and political action; moreover, it becomes reorganized and restructured when members of a given society remember together.

Scholars following 'the presentist' memory approach showed that nationalist movements create a master narrative that highlights a society's common past and legitimizes the aspiration for a shared destiny (Luke 1996 and Collini 1999, both cited in Misztal 2003: 56, 61). Nations who have lived through genocidal experiences, and been deprived of parts of their history, develop popular counter-memories that are particularly stable with regard to certain core elements. Political leaders build on these memories.

During my five years living among the Ingush and Chechens I heard hundreds of family histories and was present on dozens of occasions when people collectively remembered their pasts. Such occasions arose at the workplace, during tea with neighbours in the evenings and in villages where I spent the night. Storytelling often was a way of passing the time whenever a group of people got together. If an elder happened to be in the house, and he or she was inclined toward storytelling, everyone would gather around, and make themselves comfortable. Then someone would ask a question like, 'Vashi,[3] how did we live in the past?' And then the story would pour out.

I identify three types of social memories that Chechens and Ingush share about their experiences in Imperial Russia and the Soviet Union prior to 1990: memories of grievance, memories of success and memories of multiculturalism and inter-ethnic solidarity. Depending on the circumstances and the personal perspectives, one cluster of memories, or another, is actualized.

Memories of grievance are prominent in Chechen as well as Ingush self-identification. Deportation and exile under Stalin remain *the* central building block of such memories related to events before the outbreak of the recent Chechen wars. Collective memories preserve detailed accounts of the day of deportation, the train journey into exile in Central Asia, the struggle for survival during the early years and the loss of the dear ones. The pain associated with being labelled 'enemy of the people' remains acute, especially among those whose relatives fought on the front lines during the Second World War.

Thousands of Chechens and Ingush fought on the side of the Soviets during the war, including Islaj, an elder born in 1922, a resident of the Chechen town of Sernovodsk. He fought throughout the entire war, from Kiev to Stalingrad, where he was wounded during the legendary battle.

> The Battle of Stalingrad was the worst thing I've even seen. Not only people, but each and every dog in Stalingrad should have been declared a Hero of the Soviet

---

[3] Lit. 'Uncle', a respectful address to older man.

Union. I defended my Motherland, my blood was spilt – and then my family were deported as 'enemies of the people'. My father, four brothers and two sisters died in exile. Only my mother and I returned.

State-sponsored oblivion intensified the trauma. There was no mention of 'deportation' in the official press or history books. Wartime acts of heroism by Chechens and Ingush were silenced. Indeed, when Chechen writer Khalid Oshaev found many Chechen and Ingush names among those who had died during the defence of the Russian fortress at Brest-Litovsk, he was prohibited from publishing a book about the discovery, and his manuscript was stolen from the desk of an editor (Shnirelman 2007: 276).

Ilina Sajdullaeva, a literary editor in Grozny, explained:

I worked in LITO, the republic department of literary censorship. We were censoring periodicals and books in Russian, and in the national languages. Until the 1980s you couldn't use the words *deportation*, or *exile*, in the official press. Our instructions said, 'forbidden until special permission'.

In addition to Stalin-era deportation and the earlier Caucasian War (1817–1864), the Chechens and Ingush harbour powerful memories of collectivization, and the subsequent repression of the *mullahs*, as well as the discrimination they encountered upon return from exile, and the widespread lack of respect of their native languages and culture.

As the Chechen poet, bard and philologist Khussejn Betelgireev told me:

At the entrance to the university, it was written in huge letters: 'Great and Powerful Russian Language'. I was close to my students, and they told me about incidents of chauvinism from Russian-speakers. I remember, in the history department, there was a public lecture by Professor Katsin on 'One language of Communism'. His main point was that, under communism, there would be only one language – Russian.
   Students asked him, 'And what about our national poets and intellectuals?'
   'They are rotten intellectuals', he replied.

Chechen and Ingush youth in the 1980s became increasingly displeased at symbols of colonial domination. Repeated attempts were made to blow up the Grozny monument to Alexei Yermolov, the notorious Russian general during the Caucasian War, and red paint was poured over the statue (Shnirelman 2007: 278).

Memories of grievances affected people differently. In some families, grievances were often discussed; strong negative sentiments toward the Kremlin, and Russians in general, were even cultivated. Other families tried not to focus on negative associations. The ex-Chechen fighter Salambek, now living in Grozny, said in an interview:

As a child I spent most of my time with my grandfather. He told me a lot about the deportation, about two cousins who died [in exile] of disease. Ever since childhood I have been ready to fight for independence. I knew that it didn't start just yesterday, or today.

Memories of success mainly concern the periods of greater freedom, from the late nineteenth century through the Bolshevik Revolution, and ending with the death of Lenin – and then later, during the final years of Soviet rule. After incorporation into the Russian Empire, Chechens and Ingush fought in almost all of Russia's wars. The fact that Wainakh fighters were praised by the Russian tsars, and some were highly decorated by the Russian and Soviet militaries, holds a prominent place in the collective memory.

Khussain Akhmadov, head of the Chechen Parliament under Dzhokhar Dudaev 1991–1993, explained:

> We have a common fate with Russia. We participated actively in all the wars on the Russian side – the Russo-Turkish wars, the Russo-Japanese war of 1904–05, World Wars I and II, and in the civil war on the side of the Bolsheviks. We were the foundation of Soviet power in the Caucasus. We are accused of not fighting during World War II, but 400 Chechens were killed during the battle of Brest fortress alone. More than a thousand people were nominated as Heroes of Russia, but only 380 were subsequently decorated.

Many interviewees had positive recollections of educational opportunities, especially for young women. Workers remembered upward mobility and the possibility of free movement during the three last decades of the USSR.

Contrary to widespread belief, there is no innate hatred of Russians among Chechens. In fact, the overwhelming majority of Chechens and Ingush with whom I spoke recall *memories of multiculturalism and solidarity* under communism with nostalgia. In particular, many harbour warm memories of multicultural life in Grozny.

As Zina, from Grozny, explained:

> Life was much more interesting back then. On my street there were five Chechen families, and four Ingush households. Across the street was a very nice Armenian couple. Next to us lived a Russian man with his wife. We all celebrated each other's holidays: Ramadan, your Orthodox Easter. Everybody tried to cook the best of their ethnic cuisine, and invited their neighbours. Everybody really tried to display the best of their culture. I remember how I always liked Orthodox Easter. We painted eggs, too. It was fun.

Timur, an Ingush from Grozny, recalled:

> My friend Tima Islamov was really keen on the Beatles, and if he met another Beatles fan he couldn't have cared less about his nationality. We used to play hide-and-seek around the Drama theatre. And we courted girls. Fighting over a girl was a normal thing. No one cared what nationality you were. You just had to be a cool guy.

The focus of strong positive memories were memories about inter-ethnic solidarity during the times of deportation. Many of my respondents noted the assistance Russians provided to Wainakhs during the early years of Stalinist exile. 'The Russians planted vegetable gardens, and they always stored up pickles, potatoes and canned vegetables for the winter. They gave us some, and hand-me-down clothes for the kids. And the Russians in roles of authority were always nicer than the locals, and were eager to help', said Marika, a resident of Alkhan-Kala, Chechnya, who was born in 1936.

Another prominent cluster of memories revolves around the non-Wainakh teachers who invested much of themselves in educating non-Russian children. 'We were lucky with teachers', said Akhmet, and ethnic Ingush from Nazran. 'Our school was next to the local KGB headquarters. So, our teachers were Russians – the wives of KGB officers. It was amazing! They usually taught for only one year, but they put so much effort into trying to teach us!'

Ruslan, the Chechen combatant quoted earlier, told me that his most memorable schoolteacher was Russian. 'My favourite teacher was Marta Timofeevna. She taught Russian language and literature. She had a heart of gold … She was shot and killed in April 1995. I will never forget her.'

Thus, by the 1980s Chechen and Ingush social memory was deeply projected into the history of past grievances. However, the Soviet state was also connected with positive experiences of modernization, social change, inter-ethnic solidarity and multiculturalism, preserved in the public consciousness as cherished memories. True, in the early 1990s the Russian federal elite found itself having to deal with frustrated and traumatized nations – but, as shown here, memories of multicultural existence and memories of success left enough room for responsible policymakers to strengthen Chechen and Ingush common identity with the new Russia, to find compromise and avoid wars.

4

Social Integration in Ingushetia and Chechnya

The academic literature on Chechnya and Ingushetia identifies clans, or *teips*, as a key structure that shapes social integration in Chechen and Ingush societies. This chapter analyses the main patterns of social integration in Ingushetia and Chechnya today. It is based on five years of participant observation in the region and over a hundred structured interviews between 2003 and 2008, as well as additional fieldwork in 2008–2009 and 2017–2020. In the interviews quoted below, I provide the full names and settlements of those who agreed, and only the first name if the interviewee preferred to remain anonymous.

Fieldwork methodology and challenges

Not only are the structures called *teips* less significant than they used to be in communities across Chechnya and Ingushetia, the very word, *teip* – which came into Chechen from Arabic – no longer has the exactly same meaning.

After several weeks in the field, I noticed that people often used the term *teip*, but seemed to attribute different meanings to it: in daily conversations they could use the word '*teip*' (historical clan) when they were actually referring to '*gaar*' (lineage of that clan), to '*nek* (segment of lineage) or even '*tsijna naakh*' (immediate close kinsmen). 'Nowadays many people call their *familia* [*lineage* – E.S.] their *teip* and only sometimes do they remember that they belong to a larger *teip*', the Ingush historian Nurdin Kodzoev told me.

When speaking of *teip* in their daily affairs, many interviewees actually meant some smaller group of relatives.

> We do have *teips* … But within the *teips* there is something like a clan. A clan is smaller than a *teip*. Each *teip* will have different clans. This clan is very closely integrated. These are up to third cousins, may be further.
> – Muhammad Gazdiev, Ingush historian, member of national movement

> My *teip* – the Mutsolgovs – is just too big. It's impossible to know all the heads of the families. They originate from different settlements and belong to different Muslim *tariqa* … But *teip* also includes close relatives, brothers, cousins …
> – Magomed Mutsolgov, leader of Ingush NGO 'Mashr'

Later I realized that this lexical confusion might not be all that important in daily life, but it can be misleading for researchers as well as their respondents. The following fragment from a field interview I conducted with Khusein from the village of Dzhalka in Chechnya is illustrative of this confusion:

> I am responsible for my *teip* members. For example, when war started in 1999, I left with my family for Dagestan. My nephews, aged 18 and 19, had no parents or closer kin, so I took them with me. Somebody had to take them, otherwise I would later be blamed for saving myself and leaving them behind.
> – But they were your close kin, your nephews. Did you have responsibility for your closest relatives, or for all teip members?
> – Of course, my own kin.

Similar confusions sometimes occur with the term *Khel* ('Council' or 'Court'), which can be used to denote:

- the historical Council of the Land *(Mekhk-Khel)*;
- village Councils of Elders, local government *(Yurt-Khel)*
- people's court *(Khel)*, a group of seniors who assemble on a specific occasion to adjudicate a dispute.

Often when I asked, 'Do you have a Council of Elders in your village?' (meaning *Yurt-Khel*), I would get the answer 'yes' – and the person would start telling me about people's courts *(Khel)* instead. That made me realize the importance of clarifying exactly what meanings local speakers may attribute to a specific word.

I encountered similar contradictions when inquiring about the deterioration of tradition in Chechen and Ingush societies. Interviewees often spoke of how things ought to be, and not how they really were today. Most regretted that traditional institutions, such as *teips*, were losing influence. Respondents would begin by reproducing internalized stereotypical explanations about their societies; then, upon further questioning, they would give clearer, less romantic descriptions of societal changes.

Consider the following two exchanges:

> – Did Elders play a role in the Chechen revolution of 1991?
> – Of course! But the word of an Elder did not mean anything at the [*pro-independence* – E.S.] rallies. Everyone marched under one slogan. If even the most respected Elder of a *teip* had delivered a speech against independence, he would have been attacked right away.
>
> —
>
> – Does the *teip* still wield disciplinary capacity?
> – Of course!
> – But why did criminality skyrocket before and between the wars?
> – Who would listen to the *teip* then?

Thus, I learnt not to take all evidence at face value, to double-check the information to ask specific questions and often to summarize the argument of my respondents in order to make sure that I had understood correctly. With local scholars and participants in the political process I tried to discuss and brainstorm together, or I shared my findings with them, asking them to confirm or refute my hypotheses.

Some respondents were reluctant or afraid to speak about the role of clans and kin in the recent political processes. But mostly they spoke to me with great sincerity, for which I am deeply grateful.

Descent groups in Ingushetia and Chechnya

As is the case with any social identity, different people attach different significances to the *teip*. Some respondents were adamant in defending the strength, and meaning, of *teips*:

Chechen social structure is *teip*-based, everybody should know this. Whoever does not know this doesn't understand anything.
 – Israil Murtazov, history teacher, Sernovodsk Agricultural College, Chechnya

A *teip* has territorial, ethnocultural particularities. Now many Chechens think that, without *teip* structure, you would lose your identity, you would fall under the influence of others and be offended or humiliated by other members of society. The *teip* is a microcosm. It's a blood-kinship tie, a linguistic, psychological union, a union of souls. In this world people live.
 – Khussain Akhmadov, head of Chechen Parliament, 1992–1993

For me any Kodzoeva is a sister, I am obliged to protect her.
 – Issa Kodzoev, leader of Ingush national movement Nijskho, Kantyshevo, Ingushetia

Others, however, asserted that *teips* have withered to nothing:

Clans have disappeared. Only a formal identity remains as an attribute of traditionalism. Youth is not even taking this identity seriously anymore. *Teips* that are in conflict can now intermarry. Young men will just abduct a bride and that's it – hostile *teips* become relatives
 – Yakub Patiev, Ingush ethnologist

I think that the *teip* will gradually disappear completely, because everyone has already understood that the *teip* does not matter. The main thing is that we are Chechens.
 – Narkom Dadashev, elder of the Biltoy *teip*, Nozhaj-Yurt district of Chechnya

> For me a *teip* is just one's geographic area of origin.
> – Usam Baysaev, journalist/ activist, Chechnya

Regardless, two of the first questions people often ask when they first meet someone are '*Хьнег ву хьо?*' (Whose are you?), or '*Малага тейпа ву хьо?*' (Which *teip* are you?).

In Chechnya, learning the name of another person's *teip* gives information about that person's place of origin as well as the current residence of members of his extended family. The *teip* name can be used to identify common links and acquaintances that are important in establishing trust.

According to Chechen ethnologists, there are some 135 to 164 *teips* in Chechnya today (Garsaev Vakha, interview, June 2009). Most *teips* consist of patrilineal lineages (*gaars*), subdivided into branches (*neki*) consisting of nuclear families (*dozal*). A *teip* originates from one geographic area (one or several villages) and its members sometimes speak a distinctive dialect. Some *teips* have reached very significant numbers – for example, the Ingush *Ozdoy teip* allegedly has over 70,000 members; the Chechen *Benoy teip* counts 15 per cent of the Chechen population. The *teips* have myths of common descent, a historical motherland and their 'architectural heirlooms' – battle-towers in the mountains.[1]

Currently most Chechens bear surnames that stem from the Muslim names of their fathers/grandfathers. Members of one Chechen *teip* may have hundreds of different surnames. Also, members of *nek* (sub-lineage of *gaar*) will usually have several different surnames. That is why analysing kinship profiles of Chechen politicians by their surnames is impossible.

Teips in Chechnya operate with myths of common descent. All Chechens are thought to be the descendants of the legendary hero, Turpal Nokhcho, who lived in the mountainous area of Nashkho (later called Ichkeria), the cradle of the Chechen nation from which all indigenous Chechen *teips* originated.

The ancient Chechen capital, Motsar, is said to have been located in Nashkho. The *Mekhk-Khel*, or Council of Land, gathered there. According to legend, a huge copper pot in Motsar was decorated with plates bearing the names of all indigenous Chechen *teips*. The pot symbolized the unity of the Chechen clans, and anyone could eat the food cooked in that pot whenever the *Mekhk-Khel* was convened.

Older Chechens say that the original copper pot was destroyed by Imam Shamil, who tried to eradicate the deeply *teip*-oriented identity among Chechens. Others say that the pot, stamps and founding documents of the *Mekhk-Khel* were destroyed by Soviet soldiers in the wake of the mass deportations of Chechens by Joseph Stalin in 1944. A replica of the pot was cast at the *Krasnyi Molot* plant in Grozny during the early presidency of Dzhokhar Dudaev in the 1990s, and ceremonially placed in the village of Starye Atagi on Independence Day, 6 September 1994.

Individual Chechen *teips* are often traced to legendary figures' *teips*.

---

[1] Such towers are traditional military-architectural constructions, which families used for protection from enemies and for residence.

Generations of my forefathers lived in Rigahoi, I am the 10th generation. The forefathers say that our origin is Arabic. At the beginning of Islamization, a religious leader, Ibn Abbas, came from Samarkand. He arrived at Derbent [*Dagestan–E.S.*] by the Caspian Sea. From there he went to the Dagestani village of Zhal and from there founded our village. Ibn-Abbas had 12 sons and he sent them all to spread the word of Islam.
> – Adam, Elder from the Rigkhoi *teip*, resident of Goragorsk, Chechnya

Abdul-Rashid, an Elder in the Chechen *teip*, Zumsoi, told me that the *teip*'s original forefather, Beshto, left Georgia with his older son, Zumso, middle son Tumso and youngest son, Chianti, to settle in the mountains of Nashkho.

They lived there for a long time and, when the sons buried their father, they went to the mountains of Zumsoi. At that time not one person lived there. Tumso founded the village of Tumsoi-Yurt, and Chianti – Chianti-Yurt. The oldest son went to the very top of the mountain and founded our village, Zumsoi. We are now three brotherly *teips*: *Zumso*, *Tumso* and *Chianti*.

Some *teips* have alternative stories of their origin linked to a common craft, and can trace the etymology of their *teip* name to a common economic activity. Thus, the name of the Zumsoi *teip* is also thought to come from the word '*zum*', basket, because people of the Zumsoi were once skilled basket weavers. A senior of the village of Rigahoi reported that his *teip* had produced sables and other weapons: 'we originated as a village of craftsmen'. Both *teips* also have their myth of a common ancestor, as seen in the accounts quoted above. Such legends may have emerged later, to bring the *teip*'s history in line with similar stories of other *teips*.

Local scholars agree that a Chechen *teip* is a social identity based on a myth of kinship, while sociologically it is either a kin-territorial unit, or a socio-economic entity. 'Previously, it was believed that a *teip* is simply kin. That's a great misperception', said Magomed Muzaev, at the time head of the State Department for the Archives of the Chechen Republic. The Chechen *teip* has persevered through great shocks and has reconfigured. Some *teips* were more of a socio-economic phenomenon: they arose from craft guilds. Other *teips* originated from *nek* or *gaar* lineages and are divided into families. There also are new *teips* that have emerged from incoming populations: the Kabardine *teip*, Cherkzi, the Cossack *teip*, Gunoi, and the *teip* of the mountain Jews, Djukti.

Said-Magomed Khasiev, a Chechen ethnologist, explained: 'A *teip* is a community of neighbours that is constructed in terms of kinship. When the institution of the *teip* emerged, it was necessary to consecrate it. That is how the sacralization of the teip as an organ of kinship occurred. Without an ideology, it would not have been possible to create such an institution.' In his opinion, *teips* also emerged, in part, to counteract efforts to establish a feudal system in Chechnya.

Individuals, families and whole lineages could be integrated into an existing *teip*, even in quite recent history. For example, the Khadzhiev family from the village of Zumsoi is regarded as one of the most prominent families among the Zumsoi *teip* because their Elder and *mullah* Mukhadi Khadzhiev, who was an *alim* [*Islamic scholar*], was well-known and respected for his wisdom and mediation skills. Mukhadi died at the age of 105 in 2007; I had the privilege of speaking with him about his life and the history of the Zums (here he was an invaluable source) on several occasions, as I was a friend of his daughter and would stay in their house whenever I visited the village. After five years of being friends with the family, when I started analysing Zumsoi lineages, I discovered that the Khadzhievs were in fact not indigenous to this *teip*. They had found refuge among Zums in the nineteenth century after the fourth forefather of Mukhadi fled from the village of Shatoy because of a blood feud. 'Four of our ancestors are buried in Zumsoi, so we are Zums', Mukhadi's daughter told me.

Although none of the Zumsoi members I interviewed appeared to care that the Khadzhievs were not direct descendants of the legendary Zumso, Mukhadi's daughter recounted an episode during which one villager accused one of her brothers of not being a 'real' Zumsoi:

> My brother was so offended that he decided to get all the young men together and tell them that at least four of his forefathers had died in Zumsoi, and if they did not consider him a zums, they should say so while looking him straight in the face. But then the war started, and he left this world with this pain.

This account, combined with information gleaned from other interviews, shows that even if clan members know that they are not biological relatives, the myth of common origin has continued significance among *teip* members. If a family has fully integrated into a *teip* – but has done so relatively recently – some *teip* members might remind them of their 'alien' origin, especially in moments of conflict or tension. In short, kinship still plays a role in the descent idiom, particularly in villages of origin.

In Ingushetia I was told similar stories of whole lineages being incorporated into a *teip*:

> You know how many aliens we have in our *familia*? In the past we would incorporate entire lineages – slaughter a bull, or sheep, and consider them brothers. This way they merged with us, and some of them are not the best people!
> – Magomed-Sali Kotiev, of the Barkinkhoy *teip*

Incorporation of entire lineages into large descent groups is an interesting anthropological phenomenon, which seems to confirm Rodney Needham's point on the social nature of descent. As described in Chapter 2, in his argument with Gellner, Needham cited examples of adoption to prove his point. However, the fact that, in Ingushetia as well as in Chechnya, adopted lineages and families have always been perceived and remembered as 'non-kin' and thus to an extent alien, supports Gellner's position that biological kinship idiom in descent is highly relevant. That some Chechen *teips* are themselves aware that they originate from villages of craftsmen, but still adhere to a clearly created myth of one common ancestor, adds an interesting illustration to the theoretical argument of the two great anthropologists.

Ingush *teips* originated in the mountain areas of what is now Ingushetia. The Ingush believe that their common forefather was the legendary hero, *Ga*. The Ingush *teips* are often referred to as *'familia'* (lit. surname), because many members of Ingush *teips* have the same surnames. Sometimes lineages would spring out from the *teip*, which then took their own surname and established a new *familia* within a *teip* – but these are numbered in tens, not hundreds (as the case in Chechnya) and usually have Ingush linguistic roots, not Muslim ones.

Lineages of Ingush *teips* are also called *'familias'*. Thus, some *'familias'* are *teips* and have sub-lineages, while others are just lineages. For example, the 'Ozdoy' *teip* has 21 sub-*teips* and 47 *familias* – and at the same time the Ozdoevs are themselves a *'familia'*. Sometimes the same Ingush *familia* [here in the sense of surname] can appear in more than one *teip* (e.g. Tochiev, Sampiev, Keligov), but this is quite rare. In the Ingush case, knowing the place of origin, one can pinpoint *teip* belongingness with almost full certainty, so analysing clanship profiles of Ingush politicians is easy.

A family can opt to start a new lineage for various reasons, often to distinguish themselves from the larger *teip*. Abukar Gudiev, a member of the Ozdoy *teip*, told me that his father had changed his family name in the 1920s when he was sent to St Petersburg to study at the financial-economic college there. He already had a career as a Bolshevik, had intermingled with famous revolutionaries, and now wanted to differentiate himself from the rest of the Ozdoy *teip*. He took his father's name Gudi, and used a new family name, Gudiev, as part of the Odzoi *teip*.

The Ingush *teip* still tends to be exogamous, unlike its Chechen counterpart. Members of the Chechen Galay *teip* told me that they now prefer to marry within their *teip*, but into a different lineage, or with *teips* from the same region.

The Chechen *teip* seems to have been exogamous for quite a while: 99-year-old Khabisat Khasbulatova, from the village of Yandi-Kotar, told me that she and her husband both belonged to the Galay *teip*, but different lineages; her parents were also both *Galay* (*korchkhoy* lineage), and she said intermarriage was normal already then.

Moreover, I personally know quite a few Chechens whose parents are both from the same *teip*. This holds true, too, among Ingush from large *teips* – the parents are typically from different *familias* (lineages).

Chechens and Ingush share the belief that a 'common gene' remains in one's blood through the seventh generation of descendants – after seven generations, young people can intermarry. Therefore, it is especially important for a Chechen or Ingush man know his seven male forefathers. Many Chechens and Ingush, in fact, can trace their family genealogies back to 16, even 17, forefathers.

Full Chechen *teip* genealogies, however, are non-existent, because the numbers of members in Chechen *teips* have reached such enormous proportions. Still, some lineages (*gaars*) diligently record their family trees. In 2008, senior members of the Keloy *teip* gathered in the village of Chiri-Yurt to show me their family tree of *Bogur-gaar*. The tree – consisting of more than a dozen pages depicting various *gaars* arising from one ancestor, *Bogur*, who hailed from their mountain village of Khal-Keloy – was recorded in Arabic prior to the Bolshevik Revolution.

The comparatively small size of Ingush *teips* in relation to their Chechen counterparts (except for a few major *teips*, such as the Ozdoy and Evloy) has enabled members to reconstruct their genealogies all the way back to a common ancestor.

I found that there would often be one, perhaps several, members of a *familia* who had taken a special interest in their shared history and had begun collecting documents and other information in an effort to reconstruct their lineages – thereby also gaining clout among other members of the *teip*. Nearly every time I began to research a specific Ingush *familia* I would be referred to such people: they had studied the *teip*'s history meticulously, and were able to provide me with detailed, professional accounts of the *familia*'s past, backed up by relevant documents.

Other *familia* members would usually know the basics of their history: various myths, or legends, or anecdotes associated with their *teip*, their common forefather, the location of their battle-tower in the mountains, and (at least) seven patrilineal ancestors. Many older respondents carry handwritten lists of their ancestors in a money purse.

After the collapse of the Soviet Union, this interest in clan genealogy expanded as part of the rediscovery of roots. Today many lineages can show impressive achievements in rebuilding and reconstructing their histories. The large Ingush *teip*, Malsagov, even published a thick, colourful book on the history of their *teip*.

Not all *teip* researchers have grand ambitions. Magomed Gazdiev, a successful professional in his mid-thirties who reconstructed the tree of the Gazdievs and collected rare documents and photographs related to his *teip*, said that he was not interested in writing a book. 'This is just my hobby, what is there so special about *teip* to write a book about it? I'm just curious about my family history.'

Thus, Chechen and Ingush *teips* were once 'classic' descent groups characterized by patriliniality and a shared mythology of descent. The kinship idiom has remained important for their integrity, but members of a *teip* realize that their blood relatedness is a construction – especially among Chechen *teips*, whose size and blurred histories linked to an ancient past have prompted some members to abandon the kinship idea altogether. As members of the Galay *teip* explained to me, 'We are not relatives: we originate from the same area.'

Is the *teip* a social organization? Mechanisms of maintaining *teip* unity

We now turn to the *teip* as a social organization, to establish whether the mechanisms that maintained *teip* unity in the past are still working today. On the basis of interviews and analyses of historical sources, I identified five such mechanisms that used to maintain unity of a Chechen or Ingush *teip:* (1) common residence, (2) common ownership of land/property, (3) common defence/justice, (4) rule of Elders, (5) religious rituals (funerals, weddings, *mold* and *sakh*).

Common residence

As shown in the previous sections, not only have large *teips* fragmented into lineages (*gaars*) and sub-lineages (*neki*) across Chechnya and Ingushetia – their members have dispersed across the mountains, the plains and various settlements. Many resettled to low-lying areas, around their villages of origin. When possible, they resettled in places where their relatives already lived or had established economic ties. Differing segments of various *teips* resettled at different times, beginning as early as the sixteenth and seventeenth centuries and continuing until today. Because one settlement could generally not accommodate entire groups of relatives, *teips* split up into various territorial segments. Over the centuries, *teips* have become so widely scattered that they are no longer characterized by territorial unity and common habitation.

Some lineages fragmented as a result of blood feud:

Three or four generations ago, we lived in a place called Dlinnaya Dolina in the Prigorodny Region [*currently North Ossetia – E.S.*] Then we had blood feud there. A brother of my great-grandfather was then a teenager, a shepherd, and one night when thieves attacked his herd he fired and accidentally killed a man. Because of the blood feud that followed, our entire *familia* had to leave. We divided among the villages of Mochkhoy, Kantyshevo, Plievo and Barsuki, where most of us still live.

– Mohmad-Sali Kotiev, Kotiev *familia* senior (Barkinkhoy *teip*)

The process of descending from the mountains to the plains continues today. During the Second Chechen War more than a dozen mountain villages were fully or partially abandoned. Usually those who came down from the mountains attempted to settle as a compact group, among members of the same family, because residing among family members provides not only social support while becoming established in a new place, but protection and greater weight in the local community.

As a result, today a *teip* that has fragmented into numerous *gaars* and *neki* might be settled in significant numbers in anywhere from four to ten or even more villages. There, *teip* members are likely to be neighbours to members of some of the region's especially large *teips*, such as the Chechen *Benoy*, *Alleroy* and *Biltoy*, and the Ingush *Ozdoy* and *Yovloy*, who live in nearly all settlements. Territorial ties are stronger in Ingushetia than in Chechnya. For example, members of Ingush *teip* X who are living in Ingush village Y would call themselves X's Y (i.e. Surkhakhi's *Aushevs*, Barsuki's *Kotievs*, etc.).

Table 4.1 shows the fragmentation of the 20 *teips*/lineages studied, according to settlements.

The list of settlements is not exhaustive, but includes those with significant concentrations of descent groups. Members of all Chechen *teips* reside in Grozny; members of 40 to 50 *teips* reside in the Chechen towns of Urus-Martan, Argun and Gudermes. The same applies to the towns of Nazran, Karabulak, Malgobek and Magas in Ingushetia and to many large villages. However, urban centres are not included in Table 4.1.

Thus, territorial unity and common habitation no longer characterize *teips* or lineages in Chechnya and Ingushetia today.

Table 4.1 Territorial segments of Chechen and Ingush lineages and *teips*

Teip, region of origin	Settlements
Biltoy (Nozhaj-Yurt Region of Chechnya)	Mountains: *Bel'ty, Khochi-Ara, Rogun-Kozha, Nozhaj-Yurt, Aki-Mokh, Balansu, Zamaj-Yurt, Churchi-Irzu*
	Plains: *Novie Bilty, Argun, all villages of Gudermes/ Kurchaloy districts*
Zumso (Itum-Kali Region of Chechnya)	Mountains: *Zums*
	Plains: *Samashki, Roshni-Chu, Prigorodnoye, Gikalo, Alkhan-Yurt, Alkhazurovo*
Pamyatoy (Shatoy district of Chechnya)	Mountains: *Pamyatoy, Bekum-Kali, Vyardi, Gush-kert*
	Plains: *Starye Atagi, Goyty, Urus-Martan, stanitsa Ermolovskaya*
Bosoy (Cheberloy district of Chechnya)	Mountains: *closed for settlement*
	Plains: *Samaski, Starye Atagi*
Keloy (Shatoy district of Chechnya)	Mountains: *Keloy (Khal-Keloy)*
	Plains: *Duba-Yurt, Chiri-Yurt, Gikalo, Goyty*
Galay (Galanchozh district of Chechnya)	Mountains: *closed to settlement*
	Plains: *Yandi-Kotar, Roshni-Chu, Achkhoy-Martan*
Nashkhoy (Galanchozh district of Chechnya)	Mountains: *closed to settlement*
	Plains: *Samashki, Gekhi-Chu, Roshni-Chu, Alkhan-Kala, Valerik, Shalazhi, Achkhoy-Martan*
Rigkhoy (Vedeno Region of Chechnya)	Mountains: *Rigkhoy*
	Plains: *Goragorsk, Zakan-Yurt, Alkhan-Kala, stanitsa Petropavlovskaya, stanitsa Ermolovskaya*
Key (Galanchozh district of Chechnya)	Mountains: *closed to settlement*
	Plains: *Samashki, Achkhoy-Martan, Nadterechny*
Khakhkhoy (Shatoy district of Chechnya)	Mountains: *Shatoy*
	Plains: *Starye Atagi, Khambi-Irzi, Gekhi, Baba-Yurt (Dagestan)*
Ozdoevy (tower settlement Targhim, mountainous Ingushetia)	*All Ingush settlements*
Evloevy (tower settlement Nij, mountainous Ingushetia)	Major concentrations in *Nasyr-Kort, Ekazhevo, Ali-Yurt + Dolakovo, Gamurzievo, Altievo, Nasyr-Kort + all Ingush settlements* (except for v. Barsuki)
Aushevy (tower settlement Egikal, mountainous Ingushetia)	Mountains: *closed to settlement*
	Plains: *Karabulak, Ali-Yurt, Achaluki, Surkhakhi, Ekazhevo, Kantyshevo, Sleptsovsk,*
Chapanovy/lineage of Gorbakov *teip* (tower settlement Targhim, mountainous Ingushetia)	Mountains: *closed to settlement*
	Plains: *Achaluki,Majski, Nazran, Karabulak*
Gazdievy (tower settlement Egikal, mountainous Ingushetia)	Mountains: *closed to settlement*
	Plains: *Nazran, Chermen (Prigorodny Region)*

Kotievy/lineage of Barkinkhoevy teip (tower settlement Ozdig, mountainous Ingushetia)	Mountains: *closed to settlement* Plains: *Kantyshevo, Plievo, Barsuki*
Kodzoevy	Mountains: *closed to settlement*
	Plains: *Plievo, Tarskoye (Prigorodny Region), Kantyshevo, Yandyrka, Nasyr-Kort*
Merzhoevy	*Barsuki, Nazran, Altievo, Gamurzievo, Sagopshi, Achaluki, Akhi-Yurt, Ekazhevo, Galashki (Ingushetia), Bamut, Achkhoy-Martan (Chechnya)*
Khadzievy	*Srednee Dachnoye (Prigorodny Region), Karabulak, Nazran*
Uzhakhovy (Egikal, mountainous Ingushetia)	*Chermen (Prigorodny Region), Barsuki, Plievo, Stanitsa Troitskaya*

Common ownership of land/property

While travelling in the mountainous regions I often heard the remark 'Every plot of land belongs to someone'. Even though the Russian government does not recognize *teip* ownership of land, it is generally accepted among Chechens and Ingush that certain *teips* 'own' certain mountain territories. In fact, in the early 1990s, many disputes broke out over nominal *teip* ownership in Chechnya during the presidency of Dzhokhar Dudaev.

However, close examination of these conflicts shows that the parties involved almost always resided in the immediate areas in dispute. One such episode was recounted to me by Ruslan Tsokuev, a member of the Biltoy *teip*, and the administrative head of the village of Zamaj-Yurt, in the Nozhaj-Yurt district of Chechnya:

> We have a land dispute with the neighbouring village of Meskhety. Our youth are fighting with each other, provoking each other. Before 1933 we lived a bit further from here, but because of landslides, the authorities decided to resettle us here. Originally this was the land of Meskhety, the Alleroy *teip*. And our land was given to them for pastures and the like. They think that the land on which we now live is better, and that it belongs to them. In 1993 we had a massive fight over it, village against village – thank God, without fatalities. That was sheer luck.

None of the Ingush with whom I spoke could recall ever hearing of *teip*-against-*teip* disputes over land. Certain families, however, occasionally argued over the division of common pastures, or hayfields, according to interviews.

Even within the *teip* village of origin, the territory is divided and 'owned' by individual extended families. Thus, the reconstruction in Chechnya of the village of Zumsoi, abandoned by its residents as a result of insecurity and bombing in 2005, was scuttled in 2008 over issues of ownership. The authorities had pledged to reconstruct the village but insisted on reconfiguring it: the village, which had previously consisted of individual households scattered over a vast area, some 2 to 3 kilometres apart, was to become a compact settlement, with ten houses built in close proximity. Plans also called for construction of a school and administrative buildings.

Negotiations stalemated, however, because those who earlier had fled Zumsoi, and would be returning, to some of the new houses allocated to them, for free, argued that the land on which the houses were to be built belonged to other families. 'Why would I move into a house that doesn't belong to me? One day the owners will come and claim this land from me. I want my own house, on my familial land', one of the villagers told me.

Thus, Chechen and Ingush *teips*' ownership of land is purely symbolic today. When disputes emerge, this is usually among territorial segments of *teips* of the immediately affected settlements. Within the *teip* in the mountains, the land is also divided between individual extended families, and these distinctions are respected. The only property owned in common by the *teip* are architectural heirlooms – the family battle-towers that traditionally housed and protected families from marauding enemies. However, the state has now designated them as cultural monuments. *Teips* and *familias* cannot even repair the roof of a tower without consulting professional architects and obtaining permission from the Ministry of Culture of the republic.

Common defence

Chechen and Ingush consider every newborn child as belonging to the father's descent group, which assumes responsibility for his/her protection. In case of divorce, children are usually transferred to their father's family, who raise them. Can the *teips* protect their members as before?

Many with whom I spoke say that the *teips* are no longer able to protect their members as they once did. Said-Magomed Elsanov, an elderly member of the Bosoy *teip* living in Samashki, Chechnya, said that mutual respect, and defence, disappeared after his mountain community had been ripped apart by Soviet-era deportations. 'The *teip* at that time would not abandon its men in trouble', he said. 'There were many thieves who could steal cattle, property, even people – but a strong *teip* would protect its members.'

An Ingush respondent, Batarbek Akiev, who used to run the Dolakovo collective farm, explained that the loss of protection has led to a loss of respect. 'Ingush were respected when we had a *teip*-based society. The *teip* protected each person, down to the smallest boy. And now we do not have *teips*. If there were *teips*, would the authorities have dared to use violence to disperse demonstrations?'

Almost all my respondents emphasized that blood feud and defence in the face of humiliation fall in the domain of the descent groups and remain a working mechanism for their mobilization, indeed, almost the only one. In Ingushetia, the whole *familia* (lineage) or *teip* (if it is a small or average-sized one) may mobilize in case of blood feud:

> The whole *familia* will rise up, but the mortal blow should be inflicted by the immediate relative. Usually, all the work is done by youth in the *teip*, and the last shot should be fired by those who were offended.
> – Nurdin Kodzoev, Ingush historian

This, however, is not always true now, and assassins can be even hired.

In Chechnya, it is not the *teip*, but the lineage (*gaar*) or more often the sub-lineage (*nek*), that supports the blood feud:

> It's a big misperception that blood feuds are *teip*-based. Take our *teip* 'Alleroy'; it is one of the largest Chechen *teips*, and then take 'Benoy', another large *teip*. We can put forward 30–40 thousand mature fighters, so can they. It would be a civil war if we announced blood feud on each other!
> – Said-Magomed Khasiev, Chechen ethnologist

What the descent group does is to 'express solidarity' with the offended family (its members stop talking and intermarrying with representatives of the enemy *teip* (lineage), or leave public events demonstratively if their enemies turn up there, or even start fighting with them once they see them in the street). It supports revenge financially, with connections to sort things out with the authorities once vendetta has been fulfilled. Killing or humiliating a *teip* lineage member is still considered to be an offence that injures the dignity of the entire group. Adequate response is important for pre-empting attacks in the future.

All my respondents characterized blood feud as the heaviest burden a family can bear, irrespective of its side in the conflict. Consequently, some 99 per cent of accidental deaths (such as car accidents, or the mishandling of a weapon) are forgiven following a special ceremony of reconciliation called *maslat* – but premeditated murder is rarely forgiven.

During the Soviet period, reconciliation of blood feuds served as an inexhaustible source of easy money for the corrupt police. 'Sometimes a person was killed in a car accident. In such a case family usually settle the issue peacefully. Of course, after the settlement no one would go file a complaint to the police', said Mussa Aushev, Aushev *teip* Elder. 'Sometimes there would be a car accident with, say, five fatalities, but no one was punished. In the Soviet times, the investigating authorities would take bribes to close the case. They would dash about from family to family, trying to sniff out whether they had reconciled. And if they had, the police would immediately show up to claim their juicy bribes.'

Historically, the risk of punishment by the state has not been an obstacle to blood feud. Under the Soviet Union, if an arrest was made, the victim's family would often not testify against the suspect, thereby averting his imprisonment – which would only postpone, for years, the opportunities for revenge. Sometimes members of a *teip* would help to arrange a resolution with the authorities, and even collect the money to pay bribes. Today, according to my respondents, if blood feud is proportional and not political, the authorities do not intervene:

> There was a case when one of the President's guards hit a Kozdoev. The Kodzoevs responded, then the others started shooting and shot this Kodzoev dead. Kodzoevs in return killed this officer of the Presidential Guard ... The President came up to the site, one of the men explained what had happened, and that the one who got killed was guilty and so no one had interfered – and the President left and let the families settle the issue.
> – Nurdin Kodzoev, Ingush historian

Among 'common' Chechens and Ingush, matters of blood feud and humiliation are resolved in accordance with traditional mechanisms of customary law, the *adat*. However, in case of illegal state violence, a *teip* is usually either unable, or unwilling, to protect its member – even when the violence is committed by an agent of the state who also is of local ethnicity.

In Chechnya there are many instances of intra-*teip* blood feuds, mainly as a result of the recent wars. However, they cannot be enacted right now, as will be analysed in Chapter 10 below.

To conclude, blood feud and retaliation in case of humiliation is the strongest remaining mechanism (indeed, many say the only one) which can mobilize a descent group in Ingushetia and Chechnya today, but even this mechanism is being weakened. In Chechnya the lineage or segment of lineage, in Ingushetia the *teip* (if a small one) or lineage will offer moral and financial support, but retaliation itself is the responsibility of the closest kin. I return briefly to this phenomenon in the section on kinship and explain how it works within the extended family.

Rule of the Elders

Respect toward seniors is widely professed and displayed in both Chechen and Ingush societies. When an older person enters a room, everyone stands up and offers him or her the best place to sit. In fact, people do not sit down until invited to by the Elder (sometimes not even then). No one interrupts an Elder when he or she speaks. Elders are commonly invited to attend public events, religious rituals and political ceremonies. All politicians seek the symbolic support of 'the Elders'.

In the past, Chechens and Ingush were self-governed by councils of village elders selected by a *teip*. Adjudication was performed by Elders as well. *Mekhk-Khel*, or the Council of the Land, was composed of respected Elders from various *teips* or regions. Today, however, the Russian word *stareyshina*, or elder, is rarely used. More often, people use the term *starik*, or 'old man'. All my respondents noted the diminishing roles of *stariki* in Chechen and Ingush societies, but disagreed as to the reasons for the decline.

Some common explanations:

Very few Elders remain. All of our Elders died during these turbulent years.

This is a bad generation of Elders. They were ruined by the deportation. They are hungry or suffer from deportation syndrome.

All the best Elders are sitting at home because this is not the right moment to speak up. Those who are conspicuous in politics are trash.

There is a grain of truth in all of these explanations. A contributing factor in the decline of the influence of Elders is the toll that years of conflict and war have taken on their health. Many were killed or became ill. 'We have respect for the elderly, but we don't *have* the elderly', Mussa Aushev, 78, of the Aushev *teip*, told me. 'In our *teip* all the elderly are either very sick, or dead, and I have to perform all the seniors' functions. And very often, when I go to talk to other families, they don't even have one of my peers to represent them! I have to deal with the youngsters!'

Also, as noted in subsequent chapters, many politically active seniors discredited themselves during the early 1990s in Chechnya, and during the 1992 conflict between ethnic Ingush and Ossetians in Ingushetia. Recently these same seniors have been heard praising each new incoming president – prompting allegations that they are either being paid, or otherwise manipulated, by the administrations in question. At the same time, civic organizations using the Council of Elders idiom recurrently appeared in the post-Soviet Ingushetia and Chechnya. During the mass protests in Ingushetia in 2018–2019, such a council played a prominent role, which will be analysed in detail in Chapter 9.

In short, the value of Elders in Chechen and Ingush society has become merit-based (merit as defined by the members of the community). My years of field research show that the elderly are losing their functions in Chechen and Ingush societies – not because of deportation or high death toll, but primarily because the societies themselves are changing. No self-governing Councils of Elders currently exist in villages in Chechnya or Ingushetia, according to my interviewees. Sometimes village administrations may consult with respected seniors, but such actions are typically initiated by the authorities, on a case-by-case basis.

This is due largely to the fact that they have lost their religious authority, whereas the role of *imams*, or Islamic religious leaders, has grown significantly. The 'People's Islam of the forefathers' – traditional Islam deeply interwoven with ethnic tradition, rather than based on classical Islamic dogma, which the Elders promoted – is not popular among religious youth today. They turn instead to relatively young, learned clerics (village *imams* are often middle-aged) in matters of religion.

The influence of the market economy, and modern political processes, have further diminished the roles of seniors in Chechen and Ingush communities. Over the course of my five years of observation, with subsequent research, it became clear that, whereas the ritualistic lives of communities are regulated by seniors, the ins and outs of daily lives are managed by younger, energetic leaders with better education, greater financial resources and deeper political connections.

A resident of Ingushetia explained:

In the extended families, the decisions are taken by those who have economic power. Power is money based. In my family, the Elders really tried to impose their decisions, but they could only do so if they had my father's consent. My father made all his decisions himself, because he was the most financially successful in our lineage. In his household he was the boss, and, after the death of our grandfather, we consulted with our lineage Elders only formally.

Idris Abadiev, the successful Ingush businessman from the Evloev *teip*, told me that he had been elected to the Council of Elders when he was only 40 years old. The head of the council was an elderly man, a *mullah*, but younger members, such as Abadiev, performed most of the council's functions. In Chechnya, Akhmed, an energetic investigator for the Prosecutor's Office in his 50s, was the prime mover in the Bogur *gaar* of the Keloy.

Despite the diminished status of seniors in day-to-day functioning in both republics, respect for the aged among the populace remains high. The roles of Elders in religious rituals – such as funerals, weddings, and *mold* [*a ritual that involves reciting Koran in someone's home, usually for the deceased, or newborn or a new house*] – are central. If someone wants to get married, they ask their seniors to go to the family of the bride-to-be and deliver the proposal. The seniors of the bride-to-be receive them and give their response.

Moreover, elderly men in both Chechnya and Ingushetia continue to serve very prominent roles in the resolution of disputes that are decided in the people's courts – *Khels*. Abductions of brides, blood feuds or other disputes of honour can be resolved in *Khels* presided over by Elders who continue to engender a great deal of respect.

In such disputes a complainant may select his own judge. Typically, the judge is a senior who is respected in the community and known to have a pristine reputation as well as a thorough knowledge of *adat* (customary law), and *Sharia* (Islamic law). If a defendant opposes the designation of a particular senior as a judge, another will be chosen.

This *Khel*, or improvised court – which is held in a private home – will function for as long as it takes to resolve a particular dispute. Those I interviewed said that most complainants prefer to have disputes resolved in accordance with *Sharia*, and matters of procedure with *adat*. Still, such *Khels* are no substitutes for Councils of Elders.

According to Zalina, a resident of the Ingush capital of Magas,

> It's a very delicate balance. We seem to be listening to the Elders, but gradually there are more and more contradictions between seniors and the youth. And now young people just nod politely to the Elders but do things their own way. There's no open confrontation, there is always an attempt to convince Elders first, and sometimes it works. But when it doesn't work, in general I see that young people are independent, autonomous in their decisions, which of course causes huge dissatisfaction among the older generation. The problem is also that the Elders have discredited themselves. Too often they made wrong decisions. The young people don't say it outright, but it can be read between the lines.

During the 2020 COVID-19 pandemic, when government restrictions were not yet enforced or had already been relaxed, many families were split over how to bury their COVID-infected deceased. Many Elders felt that the proper rituals should be conducted, but younger people were generally more cautious and their voices were stronger. One resident of Ingushetia, whose father had died of COVID-19 in Moscow and had been brought to the family cemetery in Ingushetia for burial, said that it was her immediate family (sisters, brothers) that decided how do organize the funeral. 'We said no gathering of people, we are against it. And although some senior members of the family had insisted on following the usual procedure, they accepted our decision'. As a result, all the proper rituals were conducted several months later.

Another friend of mine from Chechnya became infected with COVID at the funeral of his cousin, who died of coronavirus.

> I had to attend and stand there for three days, to receive the people expressing their condolences, as I am the oldest in the family. The children [of the deceased] had decided to hold a regular funeral, and I had to follow their decision, although I thought it was a great risk. Several hundred people attended over those three days, and many became infected.

Thus, the nuclear family increasingly has a decisive voice in family-related decision-making, also concerning traditional rituals.

Religious rituals (funerals, weddings, *mold*)

Life-cycle ceremonies, especially weddings and funerals, are attended by very large numbers of people in Ingushetia and Chechnya. To express condolences at funerals is expected of all relatives, neighbours, friends, colleagues of the deceased and his/her family members, sometimes amounting to 500–600 people per day.

According to Muslim tradition, the deceased should be buried on the same or next day before sunset. Subsequently, for three days, mourning takes place in the house of the deceased, with people coming and going, expressing their condolences to the family. The ritual differs according to *vird*: some families offer food to their guests, others do not; some have groups of *murids* performing *zikr*, and others do not. Regardless, as Salavat Gaev of the Chechen village of Gekhi-Chu explained: 'when somebody dies in this village we leave all our work and are there for three days with the family, in support'.

The nearest kin and neighbours stay for three days; more distant relatives and people from other settlements usually visit once. Groups of close relatives often assemble, and in one convoy of cars arrive at the funeral together and leave together.

My respondent Mussa Aushev was among the oldest and most respected members of his *teip*, which is why he attended all the weddings and funerals. Mussa knew all the older people in his *teip*, who participated in ceremonies. As *teips* and lineages are quite large, funerals or weddings take place almost every week, becoming the main public space where seniors of a *teip* meet, as well as serving as a mechanism for maintaining *teip*/lineage cohesion in Ingushetia.

In Chechnya *teips* are much bigger, so people generally attend only the weddings and funerals of representatives of their own lineage or those with whom they maintain kinship relations. However, some highly respected elderly persons will be invited to ceremonies of other *teip* lineages and other *teips*.

Attendance and involvement in funerals/weddings are age- and gender-specific. Usually, all the seniors of the family are expected to express their respects on behalf of their kin. Middle-aged people are not expected to attend in all cases: one or two members of a family can come on behalf of all. Even less mandatory is the attendance of young people and their involvement in ceremonies of distant kin. In many families, women do not attend funerals; in others they do, but they sit separately from the men and express their condolences to the women of that family.

As a result, according to my respondents, the seniors know all (in Ingushetia) or many (in Chechnya) of the seniors in their *teip*/lineage; middle-aged people know each other much less, usually only those of their lineage; and young people often do not know each other.

However, within the segment of lineage, all adult members attend all weddings and funerals.

> Not a single Sunday passes without a wedding of one of Chapanovs in our village. We do not need to organize any congresses or councils; all political questions are resolved at funerals or weddings! If someone is going to get married, we get together there, the day or two before. And then there is the wedding itself … and then almost every day, we, the Achaluki Chapanovs, somehow bump into each other. I know all the elderly persons among the Chapanov, but I don't know all the people of my age, and as for the youngsters – they spring up like mushrooms you can't remember them all.
>
> – Vakha Chapanov, Achaluki village, Ingushetia

Weddings and funerals are not the only events which are attended by representatives of descent groups. Sometimes members of a lineage meet at religious rituals, like *mold* and *sakh*, which involve recitations from the Koran.

Based on the sections above, I conclude that in Chechnya the *teips* are not social organizations today. They have disintegrated and have not retained mechanisms for maintaining cohesion. Lineages, sub-lineages and territorial segments of lineages perform the function of descent groups, which is limited to mutual attendance at ritual ceremonies (weddings, funerals, *mold*) and support in cases of blood feud or humiliation. In Ingushetia, the *teip* has retained some degree of social cohesion, but it also is primarily limited to ceremonies and blood feud. However, some *familias* are still quite tightly knit units that can be said to serve as social organizations.

Other mechanisms which used to maintain *teip* unity in the past, such as common residence, common ownership of land/property and the rule of Elders, have ceased to exist. Blood feud has essentially moved to the domain of the extended family: the *teip* will express solidarity and provide financial support, but the actual killing is done or commissioned by the immediate kin. Moreover, there are many cases of intra-*teip* vendettas.

Kinship

Categories of kinship and relations between them

When speaking about *teips*, many of my respondents emphasized that although *teip* matters to some degree, everyday life centres on one's close kin. Chechens and Ingush are very kinship-rich societies. Close relatives are called *tsijna nakh* – ('ц1ийна нах' – Chechen, 'ц1е нах'/ 'ц1ентара нах' – Ingush) – lit. 'people of the same hearth or house'. '*Tsijna nakh*' includes patrilineal relatives: *shichoy* – (шичой) – cousins, *myakhchoy* (мяхчой) – second cousins, *vovtkhar (m)/yovkhatar (f)* (вовтхар/ йовхатар), third cousins. The term *yovkhatar* stems from the word for 'warmth', which indicates that this relationship entails some degree of closeness. For fourth cousins there is no special term, although they are sometimes included in *tsijna nakh*. After them, all other kinsmen are called *gergarlo* – 'relatives'. Chechens have another important kin-term – '*yukyokushverg*' (Юкъйоькъушверг) – 'dividing'. This is a relational term, the dividing line between kin and non-kin. Beyond *yukyokushverg*, people may marry.

There is a distinction between kinship terms on the mother's and father's line. Maternal relatives are called '*nenakhoy*' (ненахой); paternal relatives are '*dekhoy*' (дехой). Kinship is distinguished by prefixes: '*ne*' is added to maternal kinship terms (*nenavash* – maternal uncle, *netsi* – maternal aunt, *nenana, nenada* – maternal grandparents) and the prefix '*de*' to paternal kinship terms (*devash* – paternal uncle, *detsi* – paternal aunt, *deda* – paternal grandfather, and *denana* – paternal grandmother).

The *de* and *ne* prefixes are used usually only when one wants to specify the type of kinship. In directly addressing his grandfather, a man would seldom say *nenada*, but simply *dada*. Likewise, with grandmothers on both sides: they are normally addressed simply as *nana* or *baba*; similarly with uncles on both sides. Thus, kinship terms in Chechen and Ingush societies would seem to indicate that the closest relatives among one's kin are until the third cousins, that relatives on the mother's and the father's side are distinguished linguistically – however, in interacting with kin, the speaker does not differentiate between matrilineal and patrilineal relatives: kinship is perceived as cognatic.

Relatives by marriage (in-laws) are called *zakhalsh* (захалш). The wife's relatives are called *usttsa* (устца1а). The ethnic code presupposes special treatment of each of these categories of relatives. In Ingushetia these rules are still very strictly observed. Relatives on the female side are very important, and one must express more respect to them than to one's patrilineal kin.

Once married, a woman becomes a member of her husband's family – but she remains under the protection of *her* relatives. In Ingushetia, husbands rarely come into physical contact with their parents-in-law. In fact, they are obliged to avoid contact with their parents-in-law as much as possible – signifying feelings of shame for having sexual relations with their daughter. A husband will not park his car near the home of his in-laws, nor visit the home of his wife when her parents are present. However, Ingush husbands do maintain close relations with their wife's siblings and other kin.

As a result, the Ingush and Chechens are connected with many *teips* and lineages through various kinship ties – matrilineal, through marriage, marriage of siblings, one's own marriage. Especially in Ingushetia, relations with relatives on the female side are often very close, even more significant to a person than his own lineage relations.

In Chapter 1, I quoted Meyer Fortes, who held that kinship relations are between individuals, while 'clan relations' – between groups (Fortes 1953: 33). Fortes emphasized the importance of bilateral kinship relations for binding together the major groups by filiation through marriage. Fortes coined the term 'complementary filiation' to refer to the recognition of ties through whom descent is not traced. In daily life in Chechen and Ingush society, complimentary filiation though marriage is as prominent as are patrilineal relations.

Kinship relations and kin solidarity

The importance of kinship ties in Chechnya and Ingushetia can hardly be overstated. The sheer numbers of relatives mean that daily life in these societies unfolds within a tight network of kin; family lives are generally much more intense than the case in Russian families. In Chechen and Ingush societies, the average extended family is made up of three generations of relatives – both vertically and horizontally – extending to third cousins. With the high birth rates in the Caucasus, large numbers of kin mean especially large groups of relatives.

'We are a big family', said Alikhan, a respondent from the village of Gamurzievo, in Ingushetia. 'I have ten brothers and four sisters, all of whom are married and have children. I have 35 to 40 nephews and nieces whom I'm expected to see at least once a week. So I hardly have any [free] time, running around, celebrating all the birthdays and other important occasions.'

Alikhan's family is exceptionally large, but many of my local colleagues have between four and seven siblings – and keeping up with their lives makes my colleagues similarly busy. Family solidarity is strong: even when a young person is sent to study outside the republic, a close relative usually is sent along, and other close relatives are likely to follow.

In times of trouble, family solidarity can be as strong with the female side relatives as with patrilineal kin. I heard numerous stories of when, in deportation, families were helped by relatives on the female side, who got settled in big cities and assisted them in moving. During the recent wars in Chechnya many families found refuge with their *nenakhoy* (mother's relatives). In general, the most intense familial relations are with relatives up to second cousins.

'For me, my family first of all is my children, then my brothers and sisters', said Khazdimurat Kostoev of the village of Ekazhevo, in Ingushetia: 'If trouble comes, who will help? This is my immediate solidarity group … then come cousins and second cousins, they also are very close relatives. In our household four generations live under the same roof – cousins and their children. We all live as one family household.'

Close kin take the leading role in all rituals related to life-cycle events: they help to organize weddings and funerals, contribute money and food; and the women cook and clean up after such events. The end of the Ramadan fast is another occasion for maintaining kin connectivity. For three days all men are expected to visit their neighbours and relatives on all sides (starting with their in-laws), wish them a happy holiday and if time permits to have a meal with them. All the tables in each house are laid and people receive guests, who come in and out in small crowds.

Co-habitation: kinship enclaves

Many of my respondents said that in order to maintain close relations, it was important for relatives to live near each other. In Ingushetia, many settlements are patchworks of kinship enclaves, typically inhabited by segments of *familias* such as patrilineal kin. As shown in Table 4.1, every *familia* has one or several territorial centres, where descendants first settled before branching out.

Just as with *teips*, because Ingush families grow quickly, historical family centres cannot accommodate all successive families. Therefore, one of the sons will often buy land elsewhere and move out of his parents' village. Other relatives are likely to join him gradually. In this manner, new small kinship enclaves emerge. 'Our Merzhoevs live in the village of Barsuki, but there wasn't enough space for everyone, so we started buying land on Gvardeiskaya Street in Nazran. We already have ten houses here, in Nazran', explained one respondent.

Such micro-districts in more rural settlements, typically consisting of several streets, are known as *kuyans*. Residents of a *kuyan* usually know each other by name, and maintain especially close neighbourly relations – helping each other with household responsibilities, childcare, holiday and wedding/funeral cooking, home maintenance, and, given the often poor delivery of governmental services, ensuring steady access to water, gas and electricity.

Such kinship enclaves tend to be patrilineal, and usually are made up of *tsijna nakh* (extended family). This is explained by the widely shared belief that one should live close to one's *dekhoy* (patrilineal kin), because in case of conflicts or problems they will be the ones to help.

Magomed, a respondent living in Nazran, explained the dynamic this way:

I don't have brothers, but my cousins on my mother's side live in Dolakovo. They tell me, 'Why don't we buy you a plot of land here, with us?' but I won't go for it. Imagine, I settle in Dolakovo and one day I have a conflict with somebody. Right away, the people around me will say: 'It's that Merzhoev, who came here and settled with his mother's kin. And now he is making trouble.' They will already look down at me because I am not with my father's relatives.

My mother's cousins would, of course, intervene on my behalf – just to show people around them that they are not about to let a relative stand alone. But if a more serious problem occurs, they will say, 'Hey, you know you have your own kin, they should help you.' I will then have to turn to my father's relatives and ask for support. And they will tell me: 'Why on earth did you settle with your mother's relatives?! You should have come to live here, with us. Then, in case anything were to happen, we would always have been nearby.'

The invisible borders between kinship enclaves – in particular the distinctions along patrilineal lines – are observed and respected. It is very hard for an outsider to purchase land in such enclaves. Families living within these kinship enclaves, especially in the 'villages of origin', cannot sell land as they please. If they wish to sell land and a house, they first must offer it to their brothers or cousins. Such land ownership rules, however, do not apply in cities or newer settlements, where land purchases do not follow traditional property rights.

Kinship enclaves protect themselves. Anyone who came and tried to initiate a dispute or a fight would be quickly ousted. 'If he tried to sort things out on a neutral territory – this is another matter. But coming to us and making a hassle here, would be taken as disrespect of this family. Every guy down to the last idiot will jump out and protect the familial honour', said Albert, a respondent from Nazran.

In Chechnya, settlements are more mixed than are Ingush ones. In many bigger villages, representatives of 30–40 different *teips* might reside, not tightly together, but in constellations of kin groups often living in the same or adjacent streets. Even in Chechen villages of origin, close kinship is rarely maintained with relatives who do not live close to each other and are farther removed than third cousins:

> Nowadays we lose touch with each other very quickly. We maintain close kinship ties with our cousins, but our children will not know each other well. These days, time flies very fast, and everybody is scattered.
> – Fatima, from the village of Zumsoi

Indeed, the two wars in Chechnya have played a major role in the growing separation among nuclear and extended families.

Kinship and blood feud

Blood feud was examined in the section on *teip*, where I identified the role of the descent group in helping extended families to revenge their dear ones. In earlier times, blood feud was the function of the entire *teip*. Today, blood feud still falls strictly in the domain of patrilineal relatives, but, as noted, the *teip*/lineage 'supports' families in performing the blood feud as such, but the duty to kill lies with the immediate blood relatives.

> Brothers, cousins will take revenge. It hardly ever comes to second cousins. In exceptional cases, *vovtkhar* [third cousins – E.S.] can take revenge, because the prestige of the *teip* is always important.
> –Vakha Garsaev, Chechen ethnologist

If a blood feud cannot be carried out immediately responsibility for fulfilling the vendetta does not travel horizontally, from immediate to more distant members of the descent group, but vertically, to successive generations of direct descendant. This means that another mechanism of cohesion in descent groups is deteriorating, shifting to the extended family.

Thus, we have seen that kinship on the patrilineal and matrilineal sides and through marriage constitutes a vital structure of Chechen and Ingush societies: daily routines, support on important occasions like weddings and funerals, strong social solidarity and mutual responsibility, blood feud and social security – all fall in the domain of extended families. Where kin groups live in a compact fashion, they represent tight organic units. In the towns, however, the intensity of kinship relations is much weaker.

Regionalism

Historically most of the Chechen *teips* were united into nine *tukhums*, or military-territorial units. *Tukhums* are non-existent today, but their former contours coincide with cultural, regional, linguistic variations among Chechens. Thus, Akki is a *tukhum* of Chechens who reside primarily in Dagestan and are culturally closer to Dagestan. The Ortskhoy and Melkhi *tukhums* are geographically close to Ingushetia and speak a transitional dialect between Chechen and Ingush. In Soviet times, some of them were indicated in their passports as Chechens, others as Ingush. The Nokhchimakhoy *tukhum* is considered to be the nucleus of the Chechen nation. It comprises 30 *teips* residing beyond the Argun River. The Nadterechny, Naursky and Shelkovskoy regions' *teips* have traditionally leaned more towards Russia.

There is a widespread belief that certain regional identities influence political affiliations in Chechnya, and that Chechen towns and villages took independent positions in the turbulent political events of the 1990s. The town of Urus-Martan and the Nadterechny region were thought to be in opposition to the separatist regime of Dzhokhar Dudaev before the first war, while the same Urus-Martan was seen as the centre of fundamentalism in the Maskhadov era. Subsequent chapters examine these political processes in settlements and explain their special, or allegedly special, political standing; suffice it here to note that regionalism and territorial affiliation are certainly relevant in Chechnya.

In the past, the Ingush *teips* united into five or six 'societies', which, however, have no social or political relevance in Ingushetia today. For two decades after the collapse of the USSR, the Ingush have drawn culturally and politically relevant distinctions between those more urban and Russified Ingush who used to live in Grozny (*groznenskie ingushi*), those from the Prigorodny Region of North Ossetia (*prigorodnye ingushi*) and the indigenous Ingush, often called Nazran Ingush. For the last 20–30 years all three groups have been residing in Ingushetia and these distinctions have become very blurred.

Religious institutions

Since the mid-1990s, religion has occupied an increasingly prominent place in the life of Chechen and Ingush communities. Soviet anti-religion campaigns were not very successful: seniors continued to pray, fast and gather to perform *zikr* [*ritual religious dance*]. Today, Sufi believers in villages in both republics form so-called *murid* groups, followers of particular *sheikhs*. *Murids* are cells of larger religious structures known as *virds* (see Chapter 2), which, in turn, are part of still larger *tariqas*.

Two Sufi *tariqas* – the Qadyriya and the Naqshbandiya – are represented in the republics of Ingushetia and Chechnya. The Qadyri *tariqa* encompasses roughly 80 per cent of all Chechen and Ingush believers; the Naqshbandiya covers another 10 per cent, and other, very small *virds* cover the remaining 10 per cent.

Tariqas and *virds*

The largest Qadyriya *vird* is Kunta-Khadzhi, followers of a Sufi Sheikh Kunta-Khadzhi Kishiev, who introduced the Qadyri *tariqa* to Chechnya after the Caucasian War [1817–1864, see Chapter 2)]. Sub-*virds* have since sprung from the Kunta-Khadzhi *vird*, one of which, the *vird* of Vis-Khadzhi, was founded in Kazakhstan. Also, the Naqshbandi *tariqa* has several sub-*virds*, some of them very small. There are altogether 32 *virds* in Ingushetia and Chechnya, most of them Naqshbandi. The Qadyri *tariqa* is less fragmented.

The differences between the *tariqa* and *virds* are slight, and generally concern the performance of *zikr* – ritual dance and ceremonies during funerals. In one and the same family the wife could be of one *vird* and her husband of another. Fatima Bekova, a Qadyri Kunta-Khadzhi follower from Nazran, Ingushetia, explains differences between herself and her husband, a Naqshbandi:

> We [*Qadyri Kunta-Khadzhi followers – E.S.*] will spend our last kopeck to hold a dignified funeral. We spend a lot on rituals. When we buried our mother, we spent all our savings. For three days we serve lavish food and we give people little packages with food to eat for the soul of our deceased. For three days our men perform *zikr*.
>
> But my husband's *vird* [*Naqshbandi – E.S.*], they do not eat during funerals and do not do *zikr*. Their funerals are very quiet and inexpensive. On the seventh day they prepare a modest dinner and only the closest relatives come. Everyone brings what they can to contribute ... But I have no problem with us being different, my husband and I. I've told him that, when I die, I want them to bury me according to their [*Naqshbandi – E.S.*] *tariqa*, since I do not want my family to spend much on my funeral.

Despite the rather minor differences between the Qadyriya and the Naqshbandiya, *vird*-based integration and fragmentation remain relevant in Ingushetia and Chechnya. The most tightly integrated *vird* is Batal-Khadzhi, of the Qadyri *tariqa*, followers of Sheikh Batal-Khadzhi Belkharoev (1821–1914). This *vird* does not recognize *teip* divisions: members marry only within the *vird*, there is a monetary fund made up of its members' contributions, and until recently the *vird* used to control some important economic objects and government positions in Ingushetia.

In case of blood feud, they act as a *teip* and react quickly and efficiently. According to Makka Albogachieva, a scholar who has studied this *vird*, in Soviet times, members of this brotherhood refused to join Komsomol and were in opposition to the authorities. 'They always support each other in case of conflict, and people are afraid of them' (BBC, 5 November 2019).

Myths and prejudices about this group abound in the Ingush community, linked with their allegedly criminal nature and masterful skills in lobbying for their political interests. There is a consensus that the Batal-Khadzhi *vird* is the most politically organized and disciplined force in Ingushetia, one which every leader of the republic has to take into consideration. As will be analysed in Chapter 9, in 2019 and 2020 the federal authorities undertook very serious efforts to limit their influence and capacity to exert pressure after a national-scale scandal involving an attempt on the life, and subsequently the murder in Moscow, of Ibrahim Eldzharkiev, head of the Counter-extremism Department of the Interior Ministry in Ingushetia. The *vird* accused him of ordering the assassination of its leader, Ibragim Belkharoev, in 2018. All the accused of this murder were members of the Batal-Khadzhi *vird*, who apparently performed their blood feud (*Kommersant*, 30 July 2020).

The second most-integrated *vird* is of the Naqshbandi followers of Sheikh Deni Arsanov (1851–1917). It occupies a prominent place in Ingushetia as well as in Chechnya and is said to hold sway with the political heavyweights of both republics. The solidarity of this *vird*, too, is regarded as strong. The least-integrated *vird* is the most numerous: that of Kunta-Khadzhi Kishiev. Its followers are fairly evenly spread among most *teips* and, as noted, constitute some 80 per cent of the Chechen and Ingush populations.

Religious fragmentation is evident from the fact that in many settlements there are separate mosques for followers of different *virds*, and there are prejudices and stereotypes, with pejorative nicknames. All the same, the *virds* co-exist peacefully in both republics.

Murid groups and local religious authorities

In Chechen and Ingush villages, believers form *murid* groups, which meet for the performance of religious rituals and serve as cells of larger religious structures (*virds*), which, as noted, are part of the even larger *tariqas*. *Murids* are the followers of the spiritual leaders of their Sufi brotherhoods. Many respondents spoke of the strength and solidarity of these *murid* groups in their villages.

> My house was destroyed during the Second War. A tank shell fell on the roof. I was injured and spent about a month in the local hospital. At that time my whole family was in Ingushetia, in a refugee camp. So, the *murids* got together, bought construction materials, and built a new roof. That way the contents of the house were saved, and we were later able to rebuild.
> – Maskhud Musakhadziev, Samashki village, Chechnya

Several respondents said that *murid/vird* affiliation was as important to them as their *teip* – sometimes even more important.

Each village has a central mosque. Large villages may have several smaller mosques, usually one in each neighbourhood. In Ingushetia, a segment of a *familia* might even have its own mosque. For example, the Ingush village of Achaluki has a central mosque and seven smaller mosques, one for each of the six major *familias* living there: Chapanov, Bekov, Shadizov, Aushev and Gagiev (two). Achaluki also has one *imam* who is responsible for leading the prayers in the central mosque. Believers traditionally visit the central mosque on Fridays, and the neighbourhood mosques on other occasions.

Each village also elects a *tamada*, who is responsible for organizing religious rituals. In large villages, the *tamada* usually has assistants, called *turks*, for each neighbourhood.

Today, the *imam*, *tamada* and *turk* have largely assumed the responsibilities of the Councils of Elders.

> We don't have a Council of Elders, but if I need to discuss issues with the community, I can do it in the mosque on Friday, during Ruzban [Friday prayer – E.S.]. I gather people outside the mosque – in the mosque you are not allowed to deal with worldly

problems – and raise the issue. Usually almost everyone comes to Friday prayers. So I can discuss things with everybody. And later I can formalize it on paper as a 'meeting with residents'. The Councils of Elders have become transformed into this system.

Maskhud Musakhadziev, who was a *tamada* in Samashki for 22 years, said he was involved numerous times in negotiations with the military and local government during both wars. Moreover, the head of the village administration often asked him to talk with residents regarding sensitive issues.

It is quite natural that in the conditions of non-elective local governments, the religious authorities in the villages assume some of their function and act as representatives of the people in dealings with administrations.

Fundamentalists

Virds and *murid* groups are not the only patterns of religious integration in Chechen and Ingush societies. Fundamentalist movements – declaring open opposition to traditional *virds* – have been spreading across the North Caucasus since the mid-1990s. The fundamentalists call for a 'return to the origins of Islam' and speak out against what they see as elements of paganism in the Sufi *tariqas*.

The fundamentalists strongly oppose the adoration of saints and pilgrimages to their tombs, on grounds that such rituals contradict the main principle of Islam, or *tawhid*, the Oneness of God. (Here I might add that *virds* are indeed based on the adoration of spiritual leaders to whom are attributed supernatural abilities, such as flying to Mecca and back in a few minutes, emerging from a chimney as smoke, disappearing, and stopping an aeroplane in mid-flight to facilitate repairs.)

Moreover, fundamentalists see *zikr* as an innovation, and call for the simplification of expensive rituals (funerals, weddings) – in addition to the strict observance of all the duties stipulated by *Sharia* law. Fundamentalists, lastly, are opposed to all elements – including *teips* and *virds* – that they view as fragmenting the Muslim *umma* (community).

Many young people have been moving away from traditional *virds*, and toward fundamental Islam. 'Young people do not believe in these fairy tales anymore', one Ingush ethnologist told me. 'The *virds* got stronger after deportation, when people needed to believe in miracles. But now we have a 100 per cent literate population. Youth are moving away from *virds*.'

Fundamentalism is under pressure by the authorities in the North Caucasus, especially in Chechnya, where those who openly defy *tariqas* can become victims of arbitrary detention, murder and disappearance. Nonetheless, some young people risk persecution by gathering separately to follow their fundamentalist version of Islam. Such believers often form compartmentalized, closed communities.

In Ingushetia, where there has been greater freedom of religion starting from 2008 when the then-leader of the republic, Yunus-Bek Yevkurov, called for dialogue between fundamentalists and Sufi leaders, and ordered the republic-level Spiritual

Board of Muslims to include the seven republican Salafi mosques on their board. This caused a deep schism between the Spiritual Board and Yevkurov, and ended up in the latter disbanding the board. Such a move deepened the schism between the republican believers but overcame marginalization and compartmentalization among law-abiding Salafi youth.

Then there are the young people who do not join the fundamentalist networks but also do not participate in traditional *tariqa* rituals (*zikr*, *mold*), and prefer to perform prayers at home. Although they believe that local *tariqas* violate certain principles of Islam, they do not feel part of any fundamentalist community either.

Mechanisms of recruitment to office

In connection with my fieldwork, I sought to determine the main avenues for recruitment to political and professional office in Chechnya and Ingushetia. The consensus among the more than 40 respondents I interviewed – politicians or active professionals – was that relatives, neighbours and networks (personal friends, *vird* members, classmates, former co-workers, ideological comrades, acquaintances from mosques or prayer groups) play the biggest roles. Further, I found that the influence of any one of these categories varies, depending on personal values, level of education, occupation and place of residence (rural, urban).

Kinship and jobs

Among the primary channels of acquiring access to jobs/social goods are still relatives on either side or through marriage (more rarely, members of *familia* in Ingushetia). Most of my respondents had either found their jobs through relatives or thought this was the way to look for employment.

They viewed the intervention of relatives in finding work as not only morally acceptable, but pragmatic. 'Chechens have this understanding that if you have strengthened your position in life, you should help your relatives', explained one respondent, a person with a high political profile.

> If a *teip* member becomes the head of an enterprise, soon his relatives will appear there, down to the night watchman. A relative will not sell you or betray your interests. And if he steals, well, it's better if one of your own guys steals than a stranger.
> – Israil Murtazov, history teacher, agricultural college, Sernovodsk, Chechnya

However, respondents with successful careers and high levels of education downplayed the role of relatives in obtaining employment.

> In my personal network, relatives occupy less than 1 percent. I used to turn to my brothers and cousins in the past, now I don't – even if I need money. Instead, I turn

to friends. I have one friend from the same *familia* – but we're friends not because he is a relative, but because he is a writer and we feel close, spiritually. I have my own circle. I'll turn to relatives only when I need to perform wedding rituals for the marriages of my children.

– Nurdin Kodzoev, Ingush historian

That interview, along with a few others that I recorded, referred to the point made by anthropologist Marvin Harris: that, in more distant relationships, 'kinship ties can be chosen on the basis of personal liking – transforming them into relationships of a different kind' (Harris 1990: 62).

Some respondents said that, during the final years of the Soviet Union, when unemployment was high but less severe, family channels were less important in finding work. It was only after the Soviet collapse, when the economic crisis became more acute, that family solidarity increased – and so did kin-based nepotism.

Such nepotism deepened as the spheres of business and politics became highly militarized and criminalized, as many relatives felt more secure when they 'went into' jobs together. This was especially true for positions in government and law enforcement in Chechnya. 'To secure our family, we had to send one brother to work for the government. Soon we realized that it was hard for him to be there alone, so a second brother had to join him', Zura from Grozny told me.

In Chechnya in the conditions of sharp cleavages and warfare, securing employment in government or pro-government agencies has for many been a strategy aimed at ensuring the protection of their extended family. This shows that kinship is not only an effective tie, but also a resource used for risk reduction and securing employment.

Role of neighbours/*zemlyaks*, religious, professional and ideological networks

The roles of neighbours, community and location are recognized as no less important in finding work. Villager and regional connections constitute a prominent part of the individual's social capital. This was particularly evident with the incumbent administration of Ramzan Kadyrov, in Chechnya, who surrounded himself with villagers from his native Khosi-Yurt. Jokes abound about the nepotism of the current Chechen regime: in Khosi-Yurt every shepherd has become a government minister.

Village affiliation is strong, particularly in Chechnya. Urban centres are socially different from rural areas, but even the towns are often divided into smaller sectors, micro-districts – *kuyans* – comprising several streets or small residential areas. *Kuyan* residents usually know each other by name and maintain intense neighbourly relations. Neighbourly solidarity is very strong: mutual help in the household, maintaining infrastructure, water/gas/electricity supply, childcare, cooking for holidays or funerals are important, especially since some of these services are poorly provided by the state.

Among some respondents, particularly those in Ingushetia, religion also plays a role in social networking. The Qadyri Batal-Khadzhi and Naqshbandi *virds* are especially effective in using their solidarity to obtain employment and to lobby for their political interests. Fundamentalists, on the other hand, cannot find employment in government or pro-government institutions, but often find work for each other as labourers on construction sites.

Among professionally active individuals, none of these factors – close kin, neighbours, co-religionists – are deemed as important in finding work as are one's professional networks. Professional contacts, colleagues from one's previous or current workplace and other contacts are what count here. Many respondents have maintained close relations with friends from secondary school, from military service or the university. For those who studied outside the republic at institutions of higher education, such friendships could last the entire lifetime. Many have maintained close contacts with their ideological comrades *(nomenklatura,* members of national movements from the late 1980s); Chechen separatists (those who still cherish the idea) also maintain a loose, hardly visible network.

This chapter has analysed the main patterns of social integration in Ingushetia and Chechnya today, based on my many interviews and five years of continuous participant observation in the region.

Based on the detailed analyses of informal social structures presented here, I conclude that the *teip* (clan) has ceased to exist as a social structure in Chechen and Ingush societies today. Mechanisms for maintaining *teip* cohesion have been lost (except for small *teips* in Ingushetia); and the *teip* has become a loose identity, to which different people attach differing meanings, often stronger among ethnocentric men and traditionalists. Descent groups have disintegrated into lineages and territorial segments of *teips* and lineages, with very limited social roles, mainly involving the performance of rituals and 'showing solidarity' in rare cases of blood feud.

The daily routines of the people of Chechnya and Ingushetia are shaped largely by *close kin* (patrilineal, matrilineal, in-laws). Chechen and Ingush societies are very kinship-rich, the sheer numbers of close relatives due to high birth rates make kinship networks prominent in the life of each individual. Even blood feud, an institution which traditionally bound together the clans, has now shifted to the domain of immediate kinship. Chechen and Ingush kinship operates with strong biological connections. If a person has been integrated into a family (through adoption or otherwise), this will be always remembered and may be emphasized in certain circumstances. My fieldwork confirms Ernst Gellner's position in the earlier-mentioned dispute with Needham: while acknowledging a certain degree of fiction, kinship is closely linked to biology. This goes against the theoretical proposition of clan literature that kin, territorial and friendship ties are a variation on the theme that can be classified under the rubric of 'kinship'. Chechens and Ingush differentiate clearly between kin and non-kin, with each category involving a different set of rights and obligations.

Religious structures have become increasingly prominent in the life of Chechen and Ingush communities. *Murid* groups, *virds* and fundamentalist networks represent important patterns of social integration – many see them as more important than descent groups. In the conditions of non-elected local government, the religious authorities had become an important link between appointed administrators and the population. Regional and town/village/neighbourhood networks are also prominent. When kin groups settle in a compact manner, neighbourhoods become highly integrated organic communities.

My empirical research also involved uncovering the mechanisms of access to jobs and public office, for which interviews were conducted with professionals and politicians. Respondents identified various mechanisms as especially important, such as by kinship, religion, territory ideology and friendship/professional networks and descent as the weakest. Thus, this chapter has shown that descent and kinship structures are important, but in no way dominant, in shaping the social processes in Ingushetia and Chechnya today.

5

State-Building Project in Chechnya under Dzhokhar Dudaev (1991–1994)

Protest politics in Chechen-Ingushetia started – as was the case in many regions of the USSR – with ecological movements. Environmental protests against the construction of a biochemical factory in Gudermes were overtaken by political slogans and then the Peoples' Front of Chechen-Ingush Republic was formed, which was the avant-garde of the opposition until 1990. Between 1988 and 1990 several other 'informal' groupings emerged. They arranged public discussions on national history; some of them (like the organization *Bart* ['Unity']) went further, demanding that the status of the Chechen-Ingush Autonomous Republic within Russia be upgraded to full Union Republic of the USSR (Gakaev 1999).

The June 1989 appointment of Doku Zavgaev as the first Secretary of the Communist Party of the Republic was widely perceived as a victory for the democratic movement. This was the first time in the history of the Soviet regime in the Chechen-Ingush Autonomous Soviet Socialist Republic that a Russian communist functionary, proposed by the Central Committee of the Communist Party was outvoted, and an ethnic Chechen took the lead (Gakaev 1999; Tishkov 2001).

Zavgaev's rule brought a significant liberalization of the regime. As a moderate nationalist, he allowed sensitive issues of Chechen history to be discussed in the official press. This gave an unprecedented boost to the general awareness of past grievances, and a greater shared sense of historical injustice.

Protest sentiments were gaining force, gradually moving towards separatism. In February/March 1990, seven regional party bosses and several other party officials were replaced, after pressure from the People's Front. In May 1990 the Wainakh Democratic Party (WDP) was founded, with the creation of an independent democratic state as its main goal. In the summer of 1990, the WDP, together with several leading Chechen intellectuals, initiated the Chechen National Congress, where Dzhokhar Dudaev – a Soviet air force major general and an ethnic Chechen – made an impassioned speech, impressing the delegates with his strength of character and decisiveness (Dunlop 1998: 93). By the end of the year, Dudaev – then serving in Tartu, Estonia – would be elected chairman of the Executive Committee (*ispolkom*) of the Congress.

Dzhokhar Dudaev was born to a large family and lost his father at the age of 7. He was brought up on stories of deportation, and repeatedly experienced ethnic discrimination. However, he managed to overcome these obstacles and made a brilliant career as a Soviet military pilot. In late Soviet times, he found friends among nationalist politicians in the Baltic republics and Georgia, and wrote in his diary: 'I had been preparing to the decisive battle for the right to a dignified life as long as I remember' (quoted in Dudaeva 2005).

On 30 June 1990, three alternative drafts of the Chechen declaration of independence were published in the newspaper *Groznensky rabochij (The Grozny Worker)*, indicating three visions for Chechen independence: the first, proposed by the Supreme Soviet of the Republic, declared Chechen-Ingushetia an independent state within the Russian Federation and the Soviet Union; the second, proposed by the WDP, a sovereign Wainakh republic; the third, proposed by the Chechen National Congress, an independent Chechen Republic of Ichkeria (*Groznensky rabochij*, 30 June 1990).

The emergence of modern nationalism with formal political programmes transformed the Chechens from an ethnos, an ethnocentric community focused on the past, into a modern political nation projected into the future. As events developed towards separatism, national ideologues further politicized the 'memories of grievance' and cited security arguments to garner support for the idea of full independence from Russia. Protesters – most of whom were born in exile, unemployed and second-rate in their 'own' national republics – argued that Russia had historically inflicted massive suffering on Chechnya, and that in order to prevent repeated ethnocide, it was imperative for the Chechens to establish their own nation-state.

On 27 November 1990 the Supreme Soviet of the republic declared the independent state of the Chechen-Ingush Republic. In July 1991 the National Congress of the Chechen people declared that the independent Chechen Republic Nokhchi-cho was not part of USSR or Russia (Orlov and Cherkasov 1998)

The vision of the National Congress won, in the wake of the attempted *putsch* against Soviet President Mikhail Gorbachev on 19–22 August 1991. Zavgaev and the Supreme Soviet of the Republic had failed to take a firm stance against the *putsch* – whereas OKChN strongly condemned it, demanded that Zavgaev resign and that Chechnya be separated from Russia and the USSR. Thousands of people gathered in Grozny in support of this position. On 6 September, protesters stormed the building of the republican administration, forcing Zavgaev to resign. Temporary Supreme Council was set up for the transition period, with elections for president and Parliament scheduled for late October. This day entered history as 'Dudaev's revolution' or 'Dudaev's coup d'état'.

Khussain Akhmadov, deputy chair of the Executive Committee of the National Congress of the Chechen people (OKChN), and chair of the provisional government, the Temporary Supreme Council, told me of the events in 1991:

> When the attempted *putsch* took place, the authorities of the republic were disoriented. They supported those behind the *putsch*, and the people learned about it. By contrast, the National Congress knew what to do: they spoke out against the *putsch*, supported Gorbachev, and took the lead in the protest. The demonstration was massive – at least 100,000 people standing outside the palace of culture. And this human mass was ruled by Dudaev. They didn't recognize anyone but him.

On 15 September 1991 the Congress of people's deputies at all levels of Ingushetia declared the creation of the Ingush Republic as part of RSFSR, thus separating from

Chechnya. On 27 October 1991, elections were held for president and Parliament of the republic. The Electoral Committee declared that Dzhokhar Dudaev had received 90.1 per cent of the vote, with a turn-out of 72 per cent (Orlov and Cherkasov 1998). Dudaev's opponents did not recognize the results, however.

Thus, in 1991 the tide of social protest in Chechen-Ingushetia brought the slogan of political independence for the Chechens: a demand for congruence between the Chechen national and political units. In the definition of Ernst Gellner, famous scholar of nationalism, this was a classical slogan of political nationalism (Gellner 1983: 1). The amorphous pre-modern national feeling was 'abridged' and presented as a simplified platform for collective deeds. The past provided the future of the Chechen nation with a set of conditioned reflexes which were not deterministic yet crucial in shaping the range of potential trajectories and actions.

Following renoun scholar of nationalism Anthony Smith, one could argue that the Chechen modern political nation incorporated many features of its pre-modern ethnie and owes much to its general mode of ethnicity (see Smith 1986: 18). As analysed in Chapter 3, this mode of ethnicity was shaped by three types of memories, which alongside with memories of grievances, featured memories of success, development and positive co-existence of nations in the late USSR. These positive experiences can explain why the separatist ideology never established itself fully until war broke out in 1994.

A significant part of the national movement felt that Chechnya should have a national polity with extensive autonomy within the Russian federal state or be a national republic within the renovated Soviet Union. Many intellectuals, academics, members of the ex-*nomenklatura*, parts of the economic class and students held these views.

> My family was against full independence for Chechnya, and so were most of the intelligentsia. Many of us got our degrees in Russia. We maintained academic links. We were against radical nationalism and xenophobia of the kind that flourished under Dudaev.
> – Tamara, lecturer at the Chechen State Pedagogical Institute in Grozny

> I have never supported independence. In my view, you cannot build sovereignty on pure enthusiasm. I feel that we lack the economic, social, political preconditions for a functioning independent state.
> – Zura, journalist, Grozny

The supporters of Dudaev, however, saw these intellectuals as assimilated, alienated from Chechen society and not representative of its interests. A Chechnya independence supporter from Gikalo village told me:

> In 1976 my family returned to Chechnya from Kazakhstan. Our religion was under pressure. Our language was under pressure. There were no TV programmes in our native language. The first secretary [*of the Communist Party – E.S.*] was Russian, and the second secretary, Ingush. There was no work for the indigenous population. The Ingush occupied all the lucrative positions.

Russians held all the jobs for specialists. And Chechens had to sweat doing seasonal work outside the republic.

When Dzhokhar came, it all changed. It was a wonderful time. I can't remember him without tears. He was a star, an ideal, a meteor that visited the Earth and burned. Such people are born once in a thousand years. He was a romantic – a pure, conscientious soul. For romantic people he was everything ... I voted for Dzhokhar that day, and since then I've never cast my vote for anyone else.

Khozh, a former Chechen combatant, echoed some of this sentiment:

For me Dzhokhar was an ideal. The first time when I heard him at a rally, when I listened to Elders about the suffering they had to undergo, I understood that he was right. He wanted freedom. He did not want it repeated – the nineteenth century, the twentieth century, 1944 – all one massive pogrom of the Chechen people.

Notwithstanding the public support he enjoyed, Dzhokhar Dudaev was aware of ideological differences about the future of the Chechen national polity among his co-ethnics. He also understood that Chechnya was a multi-ethnic republic, and that his separatist project did not appeal to Russians, Ingush and other minorities. That is probably the main reason why no referendum on the status of the Chechen Republic had ever taken place.

State-building policies (1991–1994)

In his classic *States, War and Capitalism*, Michael Mann defined 'the state' as containing four major elements: (1) A differentiated set of institutions and personnel embodying (2) centrality in the sense that political relations radiate outwards from a centre to cover (3) a territorially demarcated area over which it exercises (4) a monopoly of authoritative binding rule-making, backed up by a monopoly of the means of violence (Mann 1992: 4).

Unlike Weber who equated the state with the military power (Weber 1995), Mann emphasized that the emergence of state and its maintenance are determined by two 'types' or two 'meanings' of state power: the *despotic* and the *infrastructural* powers of the state. In modern times, the despotic power of the state is still present (in the form of a wide range of actions that a state can undertake without routine, institutionalized negotiation with civil society), whereas infrastructural power is becoming increasingly more efficient (Mann 1992: 5). Such infrastructural power concerns 'the capacity of the state to penetrate civil society' (by subsistence: employment, welfare; means of communication, information maintenance), and 'implement logistically political decisions throughout the realm' (Mann 1992: 6, 7). The dependence of the state on its infrastructural power is enormous in modern times (1992: 6).

In 1991, all the ingredients of Michael Mann's 'state power' were lacking in Chechnya. This was a republic without experience of its own modern secular statehood, its own infrastructure, or even a historical experience of its own 'despotic' power (Imam Shamil had initiated his state from Dagestan). The republic had no precisely demarcated area over which it extended its power. There was no officially demarcated border with Ingushetia. There was no monopoly on physical violence or on binding rule-making.

What Chechnya did have in 1991 was the infrastructure inherited from the Soviet Union: many people were employed in the state sector, the welfare system was quite comprehensive, education and medical care were provided by the federal state, the state owned the railways, maintained sewage systems and lifts, paid subsidies for children. From 1992 onwards, Chechnya would have to maintain all these functions by itself.

Establishing institutions went smoothly enough: in 1991/92 all the relevant ministries, state departments and security services were set up. All state property owned by the Russian Federation and the Soviet Union was nationalized. The 1992 Constitution guaranteed all citizens of the Chechen Republic equal human, social, cultural and environmental rights. Islam was declared the state religion, but freedom of conscience to others was to be guaranteed. The languages of state institutions and judicial system were Chechen and Russian. Men and women were acknowledged as equal before the law and within the family (Constitution of the Chechen Republic 1992).

According to the 1992 Constitution, the Chechen Republic was a parliamentary state. The Chechen Parliament was granted extensive powers, including that of approving all Cabinet ministers, as well as the appointment of high-level officials, such as the Chair of the Constitutional and Supreme Courts, the Prosecutor General, the chairs of the Investigation Committee and the national defence service, etc.

The president of the Chechen Republic was the chief executive, the chief of Cabinet and the commander-in chief of the armed forces. Any citizen not older than 65 could be elected the chief executive by direct anonymous vote. The Soviet judiciary system at the republic, city and regional levels was to be preserved. An ethnic council was set up to represent the minorities in the republic.

> There was no mention of traditional institutions and very little emphasis on religion in that first constitution. All MPs had the Constitutions of the United States and of European countries on our desks. We produced many decent laws. We were oriented towards a European democratic model.
> – Khussain Akhmadov, Chair of the Chechen Parliament 1992–1993

The economy

Already in Soviet times the economic situation of the Chechen Republic had been very difficult: in 1990 it occupied the last, 73rd, place among the regions of Soviet Russia. From 1992 to 1994 Chechnya experienced a further sharp drop in industrial and agricultural production (Dunlop 1998: 126). Industrial and agricultural output fell in 1992 by an average of 18.8 per cent across all Russia, the drop was particularly acute (32 per cent) in the Chechen and Ingush Republics, according to the official Russian bureau of statistics, Goskomstat. In 1993, output improved throughout the Russian Federation, but continued to plummet – by 61.4 per cent – in Chechnya and Ingushetia. Food production fell by 46 per cent per capita (as against 18 per cent elsewhere in Russia), and output in the oil industry fell by nearly 60 per cent (Dunlop 1998: 126).

Unemployment increased: in 1992 the two republics experienced a 16 per cent increase, with the number of temporarily laid off workers exceeding 16,000 (Tishkov 1996:23). Chechen economists working in the government at that time do not trust the Russian statistics; however, they do not question the fact of a very significant economic decline.

The systemic problems were several. First, the economic sieges imposed by Russia had hit the Chechen economy hard. Second, after Chechnya declared its independence, all economic ties with Russia were cut. Chechnya tried to remedy this by creating cooperation contracts with individual Russian regions, bypassing Moscow. Initially there was some interest, but then the Kremlin put pressure on the regional authorities and the contracts were not implemented. The international cooperation projects created by the Ministry of Foreign Affairs and by Dudaev's own efforts failed to bring serious investment into the Chechen economy. Dudaev travelled to the Middle East, Turkey, Cyprus, the USA, Austria and several other countries, using Chechnya's own planes, often with himself as a pilot. However, most of the countries he tried to establish relations with were either reluctant to quarrel with Russia over Chechnya or were economically weak. As a result, the major state industrial enterprises in Chechnya lost their supply and sales markets.

Third, Chechnya was unable to develop a realistic economic strategy that could help it to survive under the prevailing conditions. Lack of such strategy was the result of what Dudaev's Minister of Economy, Taimaz Abubakarov, called 'an irrepressible striving for momentary political freedom', which, in his view, clashed with the economic basis of the republic, which had been created in Soviet times with different purpose in mind. 'The economy became a hostage of politics.' Although Dudaev was advised by economists in his government to seek new models of integration with the former USSR states, including Russia, he insisted on using Chechnya's own resources (Abubakarov 1998: 7, 8).

According to Abubakarov, Dudaev romanticized not only Chechnya but also its economic potential, viewing Chechnya as 'a depositary of enormous natural riches. Convincing him that this was otherwise was not easier than finding these very riches. His understanding of Chechnya as a self-sufficient country in all possible ways was usually based on insufficiently verified evidence, in abundance presented to Dudaev by his admirers' (Abubakarov 1998: 16).

The basis of the economy was the oil chemical industry, which constituted a 75 per cent share of the economy. In 1992 a unified tax was introduced for the strongest industries – oil chemicals, spirits and wineries, and cement producers (Abubakarov 1998: 154). Documents in the parliamentary archives show that Dudaev was trying to follow a flexible tax policy, to react to constrained economic conditions. For example, from 1 January 1992 he abolished the 5 per cent sales tax and the 25 per cent tax on 'goods in high demand'.[1] The agricultural sector was exempt from many taxes, as were state enterprises on the fringe of bankruptcy but deemed strategic by the government

---

[1] Decree of the President of the Chechen Republic 'On abolishing 5% sales tax on the territory of the Chechen Republic and 25% taxes from sale of goods in high demand', 16 December 1991.

Other tax collection proceeded efficiently in 1992, according to documents of the republic's State Tax Police.[2]

As Imran, a former tax collector from Grozny, explained to me:

People did pay taxes. Inspectors visited businesses, collected all dues. I don't know what happened with this tax money subsequently, but it was collected. You must bear in mind that, in those three years [of Dudaev rule], most industry stopped functioning and stopped paying taxes. Individual businesses paid. The tax service itself got funds from Russia, and we received salaries until 1994.

According to Abubakarov (1998), in 1992 the budget was fulfilled 77 per cent; in 1993 and the first ten months of 1994, 80 per cent. No hard data on tax evasion are available, however. Obviously, the large 'moonlighting' sector was outside the legal framework or reach of the tax authorities.

As a socialist, Dudaev strongly resisted privatization of state property in Chechnya and was keen to control prices. In January 1992, while Russia liberalized prices, Dudaev held down the costs of key consumer goods. He insisted that the price of bread remain a symbolic 1 rouble until July 1993 – by which time the policy had had catastrophic consequences for the Chechen economy: prices were so low in the Chechen rouble zone that small traders bought goods there and resold them outside the republic (Gall and de Waal 1997: 126). In addition, the government covered 50 per cent of the costs of local public transport from the budget, nearly 100 per cent of utility payments, including all expenditures for maintaining residential housing, gas and electricity. As a compensation for the irregularly paid salaries, the population also received gasoline and oil products, amounting to 150–200 thousand tons of fuel per year (Abubakarov 1998: 36, 100). Such social payments were a heavy burden on the already fragile budget; eventually the government was not able to keep these promises.

Despite Dudaev's resistance, de facto privatization happened. My respondents testified that they were able to privatize their flats in Grozny. Many buildings of state institutions or big state shops were sold. For example, the building of the Institute for Increasing the Qualifications of Education Workers was privatized, and its staff had to leave, according to its employee.

Gradually, small private companies took over the functions of the municipal services.

To begin with, the municipal services simply did not work in practice. For example, the central market was overflowing with garbage; after it rained, there were layers of paper and cardboard paper cluttering the floor, rubbish everywhere – the waste management services did not work. Eventually people started to make order themselves. Small private companies started to manage the waste, clean the streets. People paid for this, and they got high quality service in return.

– Khasan, businessman, Grozny

[2] Information letter by Head of Tax Police V. Alerkhanov to the Chair of Parliament of the Chechen Republic Yu Soslambekov, 5 May 1993.

Spontaneously there emerged an informal land market, a petroleum product market, a real estate market ... general creeping privatization took place outside the legal framework of the state (Abubakarov 1998: 41). The government did not intervene in business affairs:

> Dzhokhar gave people a chance to enrich themselves a bit. By 1993, anyone who wasn't lazy could earn money. People tried to survive on their own, and the authorities did not create any obstacles. Chechen planes flew to the Arab Emirates, other countries, brought lots of goods, the central market was bustling with life – full of goods, meat, even pork for the Russians ... Small businesses were flourishing.
>
> – Khusein Iskhanov, supporter of independence, member of Chechen Parliament 1997–1999

However, life was harder for those employed by the state. According to Taus Serganova, at that time associate professor and head of the Russian language department at Chechen State University:

> The situation started to deteriorate gradually. First, they started to delay salary payments for a month or two, then longer. By 1993 they had stopped paying altogether. Likewise with pensions and other social payments. At that time, I was working at a university and also in several newspapers, which paid small remunerations from their sales revenues. Later, the newspapers started to close down, people could not afford to buy them, and there was no state support for the media. This was a very difficult time for state-employed people.

Other respondents confirmed that by 1993 teachers and doctors were not paid for months on end; in some schools, the parents took up collections to pay the teachers.

A series of decrees issued by Dzhokhar Dudaev prevented the privatization of property belonging to educational, medical and cultural institutions.[3] However, hospitals experienced shortfalls in drugs and medical supplies as a result of the economic blockade. The social infrastructure of housing settlements was shattered.

Dissatisfaction with the regime was rising, and the government was unable to cope with the rapidly collapsing state. However, Dzhokhar Dudaev, declaring that freedom came at a price, called on his compatriots to tighten their belts and endure. From time to time he accused the pensioners who opposed him that they had been 'bought by the Russian pensions', and that in 'a normal society, the children should be the social welfare of their parents'. He advised others to 'knit socks or collect pinecones in the forest'. 'We gave you freedom', he would say, 'and now you must make your living by yourselves!'

---

[3] Decrees of the President of the Chechen Republic on state protection of institutions of culture and art (9.12.91), institutions of people's education (16.12.91) and healthcare system (23.12.91) These and documents below were accessed at a private archive in Grozny in January 2008.

Many of my respondents who knew Dzhokhar Dudaev personally insisted that he himself was not interested in material things and was prepared to live a harsh life for sake of his political dreams:

> I lived in the Tashkala area of Grozny, 500 metres away from where he was staying, I knew his older brother. He lived at his brother's place, in a simple Chechen cottage, two to four rooms. He didn't have any property, any Jeeps or Mercedes; he dressed modestly, either in a formal suit or in military uniform, depending on the situation. He was a very modest person in his daily life.
> – Khussein Iskhanov, supporter of independence, MP of Chechen Parliament 1997–1999

In the last years before the war, economic policy was focused on trying to keep the economy from complete collapse. Dudaev did not have a long-term development strategy for the republic; according to Abubakarov (1998: 82), he rejected all attempts to create one. He probably realized that war was approaching, and it was meaningless to create long-term economic plans.

According to his widow, Alla Dudaeva (2005), 'War was inevitable, and Dzhokhar understood that better than others. Speaking to the nation, he was very serious and concentrated. "Yes, war is approaching. Yes, it will be very hard in us, but let's finish it with our generation. For centuries, every 50 years Russia has been trying to eliminate our people. Let's pull ourselves together. Yes, they fought against us – but they have not won, let's us win now! Even if only 30 per cent of us are left."'

Law enforcement, justice and the military

Taming lawlessness and criminality was an issue of vital concern to the Chechen authorities. The illegal export of oil and petroleum products was one of them. Dudaev decreed that strategically important goods be dispatched by rail only after they had been inspected by customs officials and had received the necessary official approval.[4] Subsequently Dudaev ordered all oil-related transactions reported directly to him.[5] However, oil transactions remained in the dark, and the theft of such 'strategic goods' continued. In a resolution of 19 October 1992, the Cabinet characterized the safeguarding of oil and chemical products, and main oil pipelines as a matter of critical importance.[6] In May 1993, the Constitutional Court declared:

> The material losses of the state from unreasonable and, at times, questionable sales of oil and oil products amount to dozens of billions of roubles. By a decision of the government, despite the difficult material circumstances of the population,

---

[4] Decree of the President of the Chechen Republic 'On ordering the transfer of strategic goods beyond the Chechen Republic by railway', 4 January 1992.
[5] http://www.chechnya.ru/view_all.php?part=hist&offset=17
[6] Resolution of the Cabinet of Ministers of the Chechen Republic # 389, 'On appointing Atabaev M. as First Deputy Minister of Defense of the Chechen Republic', signed by Ya. Mamodaev,19 October 1992.

oil products were supplied according to questionable contracts, for which neither material value nor payments have been received to this day. Moreover, oil products were supplied for understated prices abroad, where bank accounts in foreign currencies have been opened, and which senior officials conceal from the public.[7]

Oil was not the only sector of the shadow economy in 1992. Criminal groups skilfully exploited the ambiguous status of the republic to make it a notorious centre of bank fraud. By forging the *avizo* (promissory notes) issued by the Russian banking system, these groups were able to procure spurious documents in one part of the former Soviet Union, and cash them for huge sums in other parts of the country. 'Some Chechen *avizovshchiki* brought home literally lorry-loads of roubles', claimed Carlotta Gall and Thomas de Waal (1997: 131). The Russian Central Bank did not manage to stop this practice until the summer of 1992.

Few obstacles stood in the way of these criminal transactions. In fact, 'certain corrupted Russian civil and army circles, and "mafia businessmen", zealously exploited the de facto free economic zone that had been formed in Chechnya', according to Sergei Arutounov, a leading Chechnya expert at the Institute of Ethnology in Moscow (cited in Dunlop 1998: 132).

In addition to organized crime, minor illegal economic activity, capture of previously state-owned property, industrial equipment, transport, taking over enterprises and using them for one's own good – all flourished. By a decree of 8 January 1992, Dudaev sought to get illegally captured administrative buildings and premises returned to the state, but the decree was not enforced properly.[8]

Overall, theft of state property increased by 234 per cent from 1991 to 1992, according to statistics gathered by the Constitutional Court of the Chechen Republic. Moreover, court records show that in 1992, crimes increased by 68 per cent over 1991 levels.[9]

The situation of lawlessness was exacerbated by the mismanagement of prisons, generous amnesties, and the escape of prisoners from the preliminary detainment facility (SIZO) in Grozny and from the Naursky penal colony.[10] President Dudaev and his supporters saw these escapes, some abductions and killings as provocations instigated by the Russian security services.

Imposing and enforcing discipline and order on Chechens by Chechens proved to be difficult – not least because, given the blood feud tradition, Chechens were reluctant

---

[7] Zakluchenie Konstitutsionnogo suda Chechenskoj Respubliki 'O sootvetstvii Konstitutsii Chechenskoj Respubliki dejstvij i reshenij visshih dolznostnih lits gosudarstva po ohrabe Konstitutsionnogo stroya, prav i svobod Respubliki' (Resolution of the Constitutional Court of the Chechen Republic 'On Compliance with the Constitution of the Chechen Republic concerning Actions and Decisions by High Officials of the State, Aimed at Protection of the Constitutional Order, Rights and Freedoms of the Republic') 18 May 1993.

[8] Decree of Dzhokhar Dudaev 'On the illegal capture of administrative buildings and premises', of 8 January 1992.

[9] Resolution of the Constitutional Court, 18 May 1993, p. 3.

[10] Prisoners escaped from SIZO of Grozny twice, in 1991 and in January 1993. In 1991 625 prisoners escaped from the Naursky penal colony.

to resort to violence against other Chechens. Realizing this, Dudaev issued decree #140 'On the use of weapons', which allowed security services and law enforcement officers to employ weapons against perpetrators, 'if it is otherwise impossible to stop their illegal actions'. Certainly, no decree could abolish blood feud. Implementing the law and ensuring law-abidance remained a major challenge. Many good initiatives came to nought.

Contributing to the rise in criminality was the drop in government funding and control that shattered the judicial system of the republic. In 1991, the functions of the Ministry of Justice were transferred to the National Committee for Legal Reform, whose work was subsequently hampered by a 1992 decree issued by Dudaev that ended state financing of courts, public notaries and civilian status (births, marriages, deaths) registration services. The committee was supposed to be financed by court fees and the notary public fees, collected by civilian registry offices and to be used for the maintenance of the institutions under its jurisdiction, and for the salaries of their employees. However, revenue collection was ineffective, and the courts became severely underfunded.

Consequently, the potential was high for local pressure to influence judicial decisions through bribes, connections or threats. In January 1992, Dudaev ordered strict punishment of those who 'prevented the courts ... from carrying out their duties'. His decree, however, was largely window-dressing: in 1992, only 327 persons were sentenced to prison in connection with 1,204 cases referred to the courts, mostly for minor offences which constituted a mere 12 per cent of all crimes registered that year, according to court records.[11]

Outside interference was usually limited to local courts. The Constitutional Court – until its dissolution in 1993 – sought to remain impartial – perhaps because it was highly visible, and subjected to checks and balances.

Although Dudaev had to struggle to enforce the laws of the new Chechen state, he succeeded in his efforts to create a military. From 1991 to 1992 the Chechen government appropriated or bought – mainly from Russian military officials – massive amounts of weapons, ranging from aeroplanes, helicopters, tanks, armoured troop carriers to automatic weapons and handguns. Twice a year the military drafted young men into mandatory service, for military training and drills. This unified system of defence was financed by revenues from oil-related transactions (Dunlop 1998; Gall and de Waal 1997; Tishkov 1996).

Political crisis: the Parliament vs. the President

According to the Chechen Constitution, Dudaev himself was the Chair of Government. The first government proved to be quite competent; apparently one-third of the government held PhDs (Abubakarov1998: 61). Of course, no Cabinet members had any prior experience of ruling a polity under such specific political and economic

---

[11] Resolution of the Constitutional Court, 18 May 1993, p. 4.

conditions. In fact, most members of the elite never had any experience of high-level governance: in Soviet times, it had been nearly impossible for a Chechen to rise to the highest positions of power.

Dudaev had three Cabinets in three years, fighting fiercely with the Parliament over the appointments. Despite his personal charisma, he did not manage to create an effective team. Mutual suspicion was widespread. Strong personalities in power clashed. Dudaev clashed repeatedly with his first vice-premier, Yaragi Mamodaev, and also with the chair of the Grozny City Hall, Bislan Gantamirov. Gradually, the Parliament became involved, which eventually led into a deep political crisis that paralysed state institutions.

Understanding the nature of this political crisis is crucial for grasping the essence of the state-building dynamics in Chechnya between 1991 and 1994, and of the role of informal political actors. The Parliament consisted of 41 deputies, with an average age of 35. All but one of the MPs had higher education, and all but one were non-Russian. The Russian Deputy, Gleb Bunin, supported Chechen independence; he chaired the Committee for Healthcare. Twelve MPs were advocates of independence, and committed supporters of Dzhokhar Dudaev, whereas nine were political moderates, and supporters of Khussain Akhmadov, the Chair of the Parliament. The remainder of the deputies occupied a political middle ground that was constantly fought over by supporters of Dudaev and Akhmadov.

According to Khussain Akhmadov, the main difference between the president and the legislators lay in the interpretation of the concept of sovereignty, saying in an interview:

> There were two concepts of state sovereignty. The first was Dudaev's: an independent state that could share a common economic, defence and monetary space with Russia. But in my understanding sovereignty was not absolute. It was always limited by something. We should have had less sovereignty because we have a historical connection with Russia, and we are located within Russia. We also had yet to gain compensation from Russia for the deportations and exile. The Chechens are a small people, and our sovereignty could be realized well enough on one-sixth of the world's territory.

These differences in the interpretation of sovereignty resulted in divergent positions on political and economic relations with Russia. Akhmadov and his supporters insisted that Chechnya should maintain a mutual budget with Russia, and remain in the rouble zone, whereas Dudaev and his supporters favoured separate budgets, and the introduction of a Chechen currency.

The major point of contention between Dudaev and the legislators concerned the process of negotiations with Russia. This peaked in November 1992 when Dudaev refused to receive the official Russian representatives, Ramazan Abdulatipov and Sergey Shakhraj, in Grozny. Dudaev saw Shakhraj as 'an enemy of the Wainakh people' because of anti-Chechen statements he had made, and the Russian intervention in the Ingush–Ossetian armed conflict – during which Russian troops sided with Ossetians, and participated in the ethnic cleansing of the Ingush. Instead of meeting Shakhraj personally, Dudaev sent four trucks of guardsmen to meet him, and stationed an APC [armoured personnel carrier] in front of the Parliament building – aiming a Shilka anti-aircraft gun at Akhmadov's office, Ilina Sadulaeva, a staffer in the Parliament's analytical department from 1991 to 1993, told me in an interview.

In fact, according to Sadulaeva, Dudaev demanded that Shakhraj be arrested and turned over to the Chechen government.

Akhmadov recalled in an interview:

I called Moscow and asked whether it was possible to do without Shakhraj, but Shakhraj was already on his way. We carried out negotiations, nonetheless. The head of the investigative committee organized lunch, we arranged for security guards – my relatives, relatives of MPs, some Moscow-based businessmen helped – because the Ministry of National Defence failed to provide any security.

That Moscow had appointed Shakhraj – a nationalist known for his public anti-Ingush and Chechen statements – as the lead negotiator was clearly a provocation. Still, most legislators in Chechnya felt that Dudaev was overreacting. Be that as it may, when negotiations resumed in late January [1994], Shakhraj was no longer on the Russian negotiating team.

Nevertheless, Dudaev still refused to sign the agreement negotiated by Bektimar Mezhidov, Deputy Speaker of the Parliament. As Mezhidov recalled in an interview:

We arrived at the airport in Moscow and were taken to the VIP hall. The tables were laid with cocktails, then, under escort, we went to the White House. Russia's representative, Mr Ryabov, chaired the meeting. We discussed the agreement between Russia and Chechnya on common and separate spheres of sovereignty. I emphasized that this was not about our political status, but about economic cooperation. In any case, it was decided that we would spend three days working on the agreement, and then come back. We were taken to the *dachas* [*country houses – E.S.*] of party bosses. I was placed in a separate palace. Beautiful girls attended us. Three days later we met again around the table. We had reached agreement on most points when – can you believe it? – Mr Ryabov pulls a telegram out of his pocket that states: 'I hereby delegitimize the credentials of the Chechen delegation.' (signed) President Dzhokhar Dudaev.' Can you imagine? Dudaev himself had hugged me before I left and said, 'May Allah help you, Bek!' And then after we had gone, he began declaring that the Parliament wanted to sign a unilateral agreement with Russia! But we knew that if we didn't sign some kind of an agreement with Russia, there would be no independence!

… So Ryabov said, 'What are we to negotiate? First, reach agreement among yourselves.' Our delegation included the Minister of Finance, the Minister of Education, the Minister of Oil and Chemical industries, legislators, senior bankers. It was a very representative delegation. We could have continued negotiations. The Russians could have signed a deal with us. But they were no longer interested. That was the last meeting we had at such a senior level.

The power struggle between Dudaev and the Parliament also concerned domestic policies. Dudaev wanted to create a strong presidential regime, whereas the Parliament – especially the politically ambitious Akhmadov – insisted on preserving the system of checks and balances.

The main battles between Dudaev and the Parliament were fought over control of institutions and key ministerial appointments. For example, in May 1992, Dudaev appointed – without first obtaining parliamentary approval – Yaragi Mamodaev as first vice-prime minister. As a result, the Parliament refused to accept his appointment. Nevertheless, Dudaev and Mamodaev set about trying to remove the power of Parliament to approve ministerial nominations to the Cabinet by creating state committees tasked with duplicating ministerial functions, only without the word 'ministry' in the title. In this way, Dudaev could appoint leaders of these committees without the approval of Parliament. Thus, the Committee for National Reform, the Committee for Management of National Economy (KoUNKh), and the Cabinet for Entrepreneurs, all headed by people loyal to Dudaev, were created as parallel agencies to the Ministry of the Economy.

Ironically, relations between Dudaev and Mamodaev were very competitive and tense. It is widely held that it was Mamodaev who helped Dudaev come to power; thus, Dudaev struggled but never got rid of his former closest ally.

Furthermore, Dudaev dismantled the Soviet system of regional and local government and appointed his representatives, 'prefects', to every region of the republic. Akhmadov responded by trying to place loyalists in local governments.

By late 1992 the conflict between the executive and the legislative branches had become so acute that Chechnya was moving toward a diarchy, or duumvirate. This cleavage obstructed the functioning of state institutions, with MPs and presidential loyalists sabotaging each other's manoeuvrings, playing legislative ping-pong: when Parliament passed a law, Dudaev would veto it; when Dudaev issued a decree, the Parliament would refuse to approve it.

Sometimes disputes led to open sabotage of efforts to combat criminality. In the archives of the Chechen Parliament, I found an appeal from S.M. Khasanov, the head of the republic's Investigative Committee, to the Chechen Parliament, dated 7 May 1993:

> From the moment the Investigative Committee was created, various power structures of the Chechen Republic, including law enforcement agencies, have erected obstacles to the committee's performance of its duties … The leadership of the Investigative Committee has credible evidence that several persons who had been arrested by investigative authorities and held in the preliminary detention facility of the Ministry of Internal Affairs, have been released. The lack of control by the prosecutor's office is critical to this situation … By doing so, they complicate the criminal situation and prevent the realization of the principle of inevitability of punishment.

In another document, S.A. Khasimikov, deputy head of the National Security Service (SNB), appealed to Khussain Akhmadov, then Head of Parliament:

Personnel of the SNB of the Chechen Republic detained 18 tankers of petroleum products at the railroad station in Gudermes ... We requested the necessary documents in order to determine the legality [...] of the contract in question. These documents were refused to us on grounds of an oral instruction by A.G. Albakov [*Minister of Internal Affairs – E.S.*] not to provide, or issue, any documents to the personnel of the SNB. Several obstacles have been thrown up to thwart our investigation into this matter.

The root cause of the problems was clear: the SNB and the Investigating Committee were pro-parliamentary institutions, whereas the Ministry of Internal Affairs and the Prosecutor's Office were pro-presidential. On 18 November 1992, Dudaev tried to abolish the Investigative Committee altogether on grounds of 'poor efficiency' – a move that was overridden by Parliament. The Parliament, in turn, fired Prosecutor General, El'za Sheripova – a firm supporter of independence, and of Dudaev.

This dynamic was brought into sharp relief following the collapse of Russo-Chechen talks. On 16 February 1993, the Parliament voted to stage a referendum on the governmental structure in Chechnya – whether it should be presidential or parliamentary. Dudaev vetoed the measure.

Two months later, in April, protesters rallied in Theatre Square in the centre of Grozny to demand the resignation of Dudaev, as well as a referendum on the governmental structure, and new elections (Tishkov 2001: 2). In response, Dudaev summoned his supporters to Freedom Square, also in downtown Grozny, seeking their endorsement of him, and of independence. Dudaev also sought new elections to the Parliament and the Grozny City Council.

Thousands of people flooded both squares, and protesters on both sides pledged to remain until their demands had been met. The centre of Grozny turned into a military encampment: field kitchens were set up and military troops were brought in, along with tanks and armoured personnel carriers.

By April 1993, not only Chechen institutions but also most of civil society and the media had taken sides in the crisis. On 17 April, Dudaev made an appearance at the Freedom Square rally, announcing the dissolution of the Parliament and establishing direct presidential rule. He also dissolved the Cabinet of Ministers, and appointed Zelimkhan Yandarbiev, a hard-line separatist, as vice-president. He returned El'za Sheripova to her post as Prosecutor General. Further, he imposed a curfew in Grozny and his armed supporters took control of the buildings of the Parliament, the Prosecutor's Office and state television.

Akhmadov recalled: 'The protesters started to flood into the Parliament. They tried to bully or hit people there, but each [deputy] had his crew, a crowd of relatives, standing in the lobby. So, they somehow prevented clashes.'

The Parliament considered Dudaev's decree illegal and remained in session. Twelve pro-Dudaev deputies walked out, which meant that the legislative body no longer had a quorum and could not legally adopt anti-Dudaev measures. However, parliamentary leaders then called in two other deputies, elected in the capacity of reserves, and a quorum was declared among the deputies present.

The Constitutional Court declared this move illegal. The Parliament then decided to hold a referendum on 5 June 1993 and formed a 'transitional government of people's trust'. The atmosphere on the streets was becoming increasingly tense and threatened to erupt in large-scale violence. The first fatalities were inflicted by opposition protesters when, on 25 May, four men – among them Dudaev's nephew, Shamil – were killed in Theatre Square. The following week, on 4 June, forces loyal to Dudaev stormed the city hall in Grozny, and dispersed the protest in Theatre Square. Dudaev then dissolved the Constitutional Court. As Deputy Speaker Mezhidov told me:

> After Dudaev ordered to shoot at Parliament and city hall, we all went home. People were telling me, 'Let's fight against Dzhokhar!' But I didn't want that. I didn't go there to fight for power, I went there to pass laws and build a state. This is the story of how the first and last independent parliament of the Chechen Republic ceased to exist.

Dudaev soon closed the opposition newspaper, *Golos Chechenskoi Respubliki*, and crushed strongholds of civic opposition. Moreover, criminal cases were initiated against opposition parliamentarians, some of which – including the one against Mezhidov – led to arrests.

As this account of the events indicates, the crisis was political-ideological in nature. It reflected the differences in approaches to the concept of Chechen sovereignty, to the future of the Chechen state, and to key domestic and international policies, like the state budget, privatization, local government and negotiations with Russia. Moreover, the crisis had a personal-power struggle dimension. 'All the energy of the main political actors was wasted, not for creative aims but on mutual combat with each other' (Abubakarov 1998: 75).

State-building and informal social institutions

> *In 1996, I was captured by the Russian military in Grozny. In the morning I was brought for interrogation. An investigator, an ethnic Russian, was writing something in his papers, didn't even look at me. Then he demanded to see my documents. 'Which* teip, tukhum, *who is your* veras [the Elder responsible for you in the clan], *he asked. I got really angry: 'Hey, look at me! Take a good look. Do I look like a tribal man? What kind of* teip *are you talking about! We are a Chechen nation fighting for its independence here!*
>
> – Khussein Iskhanov, supporter of independence,
> MP of the Chechen Parliament 1997–1999

Teips

The years starting from 1991 ushered in an intense revival of *teip* identity, which had been suppressed during the centuries of colonial rule. *Teips* were increasingly seen as a symbol of 'Chechen-ness'. The Chechen government encouraged the revival of the *teips* and other neo-traditional institutions; Dudaev gave considerable symbolic support to the Councils of Elders.

As noted by Lipkhan Bazaeva, then leader of the Chechen women's anti-war movement:

> With Dudaev, the fashion of *teips* started. It was something like a retro-fashion, a revival of our origins, our mentality. We began to remember past sufferings. The *teip* structure was romanticized.

On 22 November 1991, the first *teip* congress was held in Chechen-Ingushetia. It was followed by a wave of *teip* gatherings held either in villages of origin, or in large settlements in the plains. The main objectives were to meet and simply get to know each other – while promoting *teip* identity, solidarity and discipline. These congresses raised the issues of restoring *teip* borders and frontiers, boosting *teip* solidarity and morale, combating crime and helping representatives of *teips* to gain power.

Many *teips* attempted to establish *teip* banks, but after several instances of abuse – in which funds were misappropriated by *teip* members – the idea became unpopular. *Teip* congresses adopted resolutions that were published in the regional press, but, more often than not, they were distributed as leaflets.

> In the early 1990s the process of the revival of *teips* was initiated from above. There was a demand for new ideas, but nobody tried to predict how these ideas would behave in reality. We conducted our Congress, spoke about how we were so great and the best of all. We made an attempt to organize ourselves politically, but it proved impossible to agree on any political position. People were so different, everyone had different interests and views.
> – Ruslan Tsokuev, of the Biltoy *teip*, head of the administration of Zamaj-Yurt village, Nozhaj-Yurt region told me

My respondents have identified two reasons behind the upsurge in *teip* summits: politically ambitious people wanted to garner support of their *teips*, and *teip* members sought to build solidarity in an environment of increasing lawlessness, where the police could not protect the populace from burglaries and murders.

Nearly all elderly Chechens I interviewed maintained a reserved, if not directly negative, opinion of the *teip* congresses. Some tried to explain the rise of these congresses by conspiracy theories. As Yaragi Bagataev, an elder in the Pamyatoy *teip* from the village of Vyardi, in the Shatoy district, told me:

> The Pamyatoy *teip* wanted to hold a congress, here, in the school, which is located on our *teip* territory. I forbade them to hold it here. I told them that it was a special political trick aimed at dividing us. It was a method for [our] disintegration. The KGB did the same thing through teip agents all around Chechnya and Ingushetia in order to encourage disputes over teip borders – to divide, to clash. Dudaev was part of this KGB project.

Indeed, some *teips* deliberately chose not to hold congresses: 'We didn't have a Congress. At least I haven't been to any and haven't heard of any. They were unnecessary', explained Salavat Gaev, an elder in the Khajbakh *gaar* of the Nashkoy *teip* from the village of Gekhi-Chu, in Urus-Martan district. 'We needed to unite', he added, 'but instead they started to have their *teip* meetings. Our activists told me, "Let's call a Nashkhoy congress!" But I was against it. Older people didn't approve of it.'

Narkom Dadashev, an elder of the Biltoy *teip* in Khochi-Ara, in the Nozhaj-Yurt district told me about the Congress that his *teip* had held:

> There was one guy, Giriskhanov, a captain in the traffic police. He spoke up, said we shouldn't believe Dudaev, that he was an agent of Moscow. Then some people started to praise Dudaev, while others criticized him. Nothing good came out of it.

Many intellectuals and seniors were very aware of the danger of disintegration that such *teip* summits posed.

> It was a totally crazy idea. Our *teip* elders spoke out against it. But our activists nonetheless insisted that we go ahead and hold a congress. Everyone who came was told that, first and foremost, we were Chechens, and only then *teip* members. 'Those who do not understand this have nothing to do here' was the opening remark.
>
> – Said-Magomed Khasiev, Chechen ethnologist, member of the Alleroy *teip*

In 1993 there was an initiative to hold a congress of all *teips*. A steering committee was set up, but the Congress never convened. After Dudaev dissolved the Parliament, and opposition to his regime was growing he sought to instrumentalize traditional structures in order to maintain support for independence. According to the journalist Anatol Lieven, instead of working with political forces Dudaev started gathering hand-picked national councils, congresses mainly made up of village and *teip* elders 'to maintain the façade of democracy and consultation' (Lieven 1998: 343).

Dudaev even tried to revive the traditional *teip* function of discipline, then harness it to influence those opposed to independence. 'He said that everyone should know who these people were, which *teip* they came from, that their relatives should bring them to their senses', Khussein Betelgireev, a university professor, poet and bard-singer said in an interview.

This proved impossible, however, because the disciplinary functions of *teips* had already been lost.

> It seems easy to divide people by *teip* affiliation, but I witnessed how it worked during the protest rallies here. Some Benoy people were in the one square with Dudaev, while others were with me at Theatre Square. Benoy even fought each other in Urus-Martan. They decided to have an unarmed fight between themselves. The same thing happened with the Belgatoy people.
>
> – Magomed Muzaev, director of the Department for the National Archives

One sphere where *teip* (or rather, lineage) solidarity succeeded from 1991 to 1994 was in instances of security – or, more precisely, revenge. As Magomed Muzaev explained:

I know of several cases during Dudaev's time when *teip* solidarity morphed into action. At that time, armed bands appeared, 30 to 40 people each, who robbed civilians. Citizens were defenceless in the face of such groups. One such group was commissioned to kill Viktor Kan-Kalik, the rector of the Chechen State University. Kan-Kalik did a lot for our university, and for the republic. He introduced new technologies, new educational methods. He wasn't a revolutionary, but he was a creative person who did his professional work. The people's attitude toward him was very positive. However, some careerists and nationalists were jealous because he, a Jew, became rector of the university. Someone wanted his position. It also entailed money – access to bribes. So armed men in masks arrived. They surrounded him as he exited the university. A professor of physics, Abdul-Khalid Bisliev, quickly realized what was happening and tried to shield Kan-Kalik with his body. They shot Bisliev dead. Kan-Kalik was abducted and later found dead. After this happened the Bisliev *teip* got together, collected money, and swore to find these [abductors], and kill them. At that time blood feud was the only protection.

Dzhokhar Dudaev, however, considered the killing of Kan-Kalik to be a provocation instigated by the Russian secret services (Dudaev 1993).

Magomed Muzaev recalled another case involving attacks by armed groups:

One of the relatives of Said-Akhmed Isaev, a *doctor habitus* of science, was robbed. He was an elderly man. They caught him, humiliated and beat him, and kept him in a cellar. Miraculously, he survived. [Isaev] turned to Dudaev's Ministry of Internal Affairs, but they offered no help. Then he turned to his relatives. They summoned the members of the *teip*. The *teip* acted very quickly: they got together – in fact, some of them proved to be former police officers. They investigated, found these guys, surrounded the village, and identified the perpetrator who had humiliated the old man. He was crawling on the ground, apologizing, begging for forgiveness for the sake of his ill mother. So, they beat him up, took his pants off and threw him at the feet of that old man.

These instances of *teip* mobilization in cases of blood feud and humiliation are consistent with the findings of my fieldwork.

Teip congresses also succeeded in making people more aware of their roots. 'Until the 1990s I didn't even know which *teip* I belonged to. When they started discussing it all after the revolution, I went to my elders and asked them to tell me about our *teip*', said Khozh, a former combatant.

However, the political revival of *teip* identity failed for several reasons. First, during the Soviet period, *teip* identity had been heavily suppressed, and *teip* awareness was lost. Second, more and more educated persons, as well as seniors, had negative attitudes to *teip* identity, and felt that its revival could fragment the nation. Third, as discussed in Chapter 4, the *teip* as a social organization had disintegrated and divided into numerous large lineages, territorial segments, which were more relevant than the *teip* as a whole. The institution of Elders had lost its power, too. Remarkably, the Chechen Constitution had an age limitation: the president and MPs were not to be over 65, which clearly meant the rejection of any form of gerontocratic government. Fourth, the Chechen national project of 1991–1994 aimed at a European model of statehood, with modern democratic values. And finally, until 1993 a tough system of checks and balances existed, which prevented *teip*- or kin-based nepotism. The Chechen Parliament was popularly elected, freely deliberating and representing different *teips*, regions, sub-identities, and the MPs did their best to prevent Dudaev or Akhmadov from adopting personalistic approaches and making appointments on the basis of criteria other than merit.

Neo-traditionalism: the *Mekhk-Khel* and Elders in politics

Newly created neo-traditional institutions like the *Mekhk-Khel* (Council of Land) were strongly supportive of independence. Founded in Freedom Square during the revolution of 1991, it was chaired by a very active senior, Said-Magomed Adizov, who decided to set up an organization of Elders, and gave it a historical name – *Mekhk-Khel*. During rallies Adizov had asked people to nominate candidates for the new body. This meant that the *Mekhk-Khel* was constituted of separatist, rally-attending elders.

Unsurprisingly, then, the *Mekhk-Khel* was politically very active. It organized regional meetings and discussions in regions, and regularly held congresses in Grozny that were widely covered by the news media. Among the major political issues it took up were negotiations in 1993 on the territorial dispute with the Ingush. Dudaev attended meetings of the *Mekhk-Khel*, and paid respect to its members in a publicly ostentatious manner, but the council began to demand more authority.

> The *Mekhk-Khel* gained legitimacy at a public rally during the *putsch*. Its chair, Adizov, was a very resolute, brave, quick and talkative Elder. He took over the *Mekhk-Khel* and tried to dictate his conditions. For example, they wanted Baron Kindarov to be appointed Minister of Health. Baron was a doctor who had organized aid tents and medical support for protest rallies during the revolution. So Adizov proclaimed that only Kindarov should be Minister of Health. One day Adizov, along with a bunch of Elders, burst into Parliament and demanded that we approve Kindarov. Adizov threatened: 'the *Mekhk-khel* ousted Imam Shamil, it will also oust you!' my deputy, Bek Mezhidov, simply told him to get lost. Basically, we threw him out of the parliament.
> – Khussain Akhmadov, interview with author

As Mezhidov, Deputy Speaker of the Parliament, recalls this episode:

> There were several impostors in this *Mekhk-Khel*. I ousted them from the Parliament. I said, 'Please leave, the parliamentarians have to work.' And their leader said, 'What's with this bitchy talk?' then I told him to go to hell and ushered them out. And I suffered no political consequences because of that.

The famed Chechen respect for elders was seriously weakened when certain elders attempted to organize themselves into a real political force. In the end, they were treated like any other political rivals. According to Akhmadov:

> Adizov tried to revive the Chechen traditions in his own interests. It was very difficult to stop that old man. He crushed all authorities, except for Dudaev. Dudaev was the hero of the nation. He was a martyr who took off his general's epaulettes and placed his career on the altar of independence. Adizov organized congresses, demanded that the powers of the parliament be limited. He demanded my resignation. They even organized protests outside my windows. I did not like that man and behaved accordingly when they tried to interfere.

Popular respect for the *Mekhk-Khel* deteriorated further after it began to intervene more frequently in the routines of villages and grassroots organizations. Elders of the Council inspected warehouses and businesses, and intervened in professional disputes.

The pro-government newspaper *Ichkeria*, which had been independent until 1993, published several materials very critical of the *Mekhk-Khel*:

> The *Mekhk-Khel* is an organ sacred to every Chechen since ancient times. Its tasks are the issues of war and peace, support of national traditions, reconciliation of clans and blood-feud, but in no way the checking of warehouses and supplies bases, intervention in the work of the traffic police, resignation and appointment of people.
> – *Ichkeria* 24 May 1992.

In another instance, *Ichkeria* reported on the situation in Pervomajskaya village, where Elders intervened in the activity of a local *kolkhoz* director, and when he refused to comply, they started a smear campaign against him and threatened his father. Finally, they arranged a general meeting of the village, which ended up in a physical fight (*Ichkeria*, 28 July 1992).

An article in the 6 August 1992 edition of *Ichkeria* dropped all pretence at political correctness:

> Something strange has happened to a significant number of our Elders. They seem to have become obsessed with something. Day and night they sneak around the offices of those in authority. They look for ways to gain some kind of leverage, wherever they can. ... You see, 'during the revolution' they stood in rallies and caught a cold and sneezed and, now, for this, they need to be rewarded. If not, they organize self-styled '*Mekhk-Khels*' and '*Islamic centers*' and ... start preaching truth to the nation, using radio and television (for some reason without any restrictions).
> (Khizraev 1992)

By 1994 the *Mekhk-Khel* was discredited as an institution to such an extent that it had gained a pejorative nickname, 'Manure of the Land' (a pun: *Mekhk* in Chechen means both 'council' and 'manure'). Moreover, due to its aggressively nationalistic rhetoric, the organization had become associated with warfare.

And then, Said-Magomed Adizov was reportedly shot dead by a fellow *teip* member several months after the start of the First Chechen War. He had apparently been trying to flee to Turkey when he was confronted by a notorious criminal by the name of Alavdi, who had publicly accused Adizov of provoking the war. 'It was because of your ideology that we started fighting ... and now you want to escape!' Alavdi allegedly told the Elder. In response, Adizov hit Alavdi with a crutch, whereupon Alavdi shot both Adizov and Adizov's brother.

I heard another version of this story, according to which Alavdi had killed Adizov for disgraceful statements about independence and Dzhokhar Dudaev. The old man allegedly changed his political views as the Russian army approached.

The *Mekhk-Khel* as an institution, and largely the personality of Said-Magomed Adizov, discredited the idea of the elders' involvement in politics. Since 1994, no serious attempts or interest to revive the *Mekhk-Khel* in Chechnya have been noted.

Kinship

Dudaev had no close relatives – neither in his government nor in the broader political elite. My respondents recalled that one of his relatives had headed the Assay chamber, a commission for testing the purity of gold and diamonds. Otherwise, Dudaev had spent most of his adult life outside the republic; he had no support group of his own, he did not even have a house but lived in the home of his older half-brother (by his father's first wife), Bekmurza, whose wife was financial inspector of the Grozny market – a non-political, but lucrative position.

His family essentially did not benefit from his political standing, apart from small favours granted through official procedures. Once his brother, Baskhan, asked the Parliament for permission to use a car from the former garage of the Communist Party, now under parliamentary control. 'I signed a paper and Baskhan got a car', Akhmadov told me.

On the whole, Dudaev's immediate family did not approve of his political career. As Dudaev's older sister, Besira, told me:

> The family was unhappy when Dzhokhar headed the national movement. When he was accepted to the Higher Aviation school, we were happy. When he became a general, we were so proud. We thought that now life would be great: he had a good salary, a good job. But when he got involved in politics our mother and I were crying, and the brothers tried to talk him out of it. 'As if he would listen to us! He had no time for us anymore', she added.

However, 36 male members of Dudaev's extended family were killed during the two Chechen wars in the 1990s, Besira Dudaeva told me. This indicates that many of them had joined Dudaev in battle and continued to fight for independence even after his death.

Religion

The Islamic factor was not prominent in the 1991–1994 national state-building project in Chechnya, although voices were raised in favour of an Islamic state already at that time. Dzhokhar Dudaev's vision of Chechen statehood was secular and nationalist.

According to Minister of Economy, Taimaz Abubakarov, at one congress organized of the Council of Elders, Dudaev responded as follows when asked whether he was planning to introduce *Sharia*:

> The Koran and the Imamat are sacred matters, and we should not talk about them lightly. There's a right time for everything. If we today declare life according to *Sharia*, tomorrow you will demand that I start chopping off the heads and hands of sinners, without thinking that the day after tomorrow a rare participant of this Congress will preserve his head and hands. You are not ready for this, neither am I. That's why I say, let us make order in our souls by the Koran and in our life by the Constitution.
>
> (Abubakarov 1998: 36).

Some scholars claim that the separatist project was widely supported by the Qadyri *tariqa*, specifically the followers of the Kunta-Khadzhi *vird* – the *zikrists* (to whom Dudaev also belonged), but was opposed by Naqshbandiya *tariqa* (for details see Chapter 4). The *zikrists*, who constitute about 80 per cent of Chechen believers, are thought to have been more severely oppressed by the Soviet regime than the followers of the Naqshbandiya (Kulchik 1994; Muzaev, interview 2008). My respondents frequently expressed the opinion that the Soviet state had tried to provoke tensions between the two main movements in Islam by unevenly promoting the Naqshbandi *tariqa*. For that reason, *zikrists* are thought to be more supportive of independence.

Regarding the alleged support for Dudaev on the part of Kunta-Khadzhi *vird* followers, this seems to be more of a myth than a reality. The high representation of *zikrists* in the national movement simply follows from the fact that theirs was the most numerous *vird* (80 per cent of the population), and also the most conspicuous when performing their *zikr* prayers in the squares. However, there is also reason to believe that Dudaev was aware of the speculations regarding his association with *zikrists* and was careful to have representatives of the Naqshbandiya in his government. The main example here is Andarbek Yandarov, the first Chechen full professor of philosophy, who wrote a book on Sufism in Chechnya and was appointed Minister of Education, even though in Soviet times he had been the Second Secretary of the Chechen-Ingush Republican Communist Party. Dudaev avoided promoting former party *apparatchiks*, but Yandarov was the grandson of a prominent Naqshbandi sheikh, Solsa-Khadzhi from Urus-Martan, which probably weighed heavily in this choice.

Adam Dukhaev, editor of the regional newspaper *Terkjist* in the oppositional Nadterechny region of Chechnya, said that the *vird* factor did not play a role in the political orientation of the people in the regions. Khussain Akhmadov, Chair of the Chechen Parliament, also claimed that support for separatism cut across descent, kinship and *vird* ties.

Political elite formation: ideology, merit and loyalty

'Dudaev's people' usually shared the same ideology, had special achievements during the revolution, or were otherwise 'spiritually' close to him. Dudaev was also looking for qualified cadres who had no previous record of cooperation with the Russian government system – no easy task. Taimaz Abubakarov, Minister of Economy and Finance, recalled that Dudaev occasionally threatened to fire the members of the Cabinet and replace them with 20-year olds who, in his view, could compensate for lack of education and experience by their lack of complexes inflicted by the Soviet educational system. 'Dudaev was searching for cadres across the republic. Not a single well-known enterprise escaped his attention. Not infrequently he would return from business trips with names of candidates for cabinet posts' (Abubakarov 1998: 24, 25).

Dudaev did not allow kinship relations in the government, neither did the Parliament. During the first two years of independence, mainly active supporters of the revolution were promoted. Gradually, however, and especially as the post-revolution euphoria was ebbing and the regime was moving towards authoritarianism, kinship ties started to make their way into the political establishment. Members of Dudaev's government sought to bring people loyal to them into the administration. According to one member of the government, 'A person holding the insignificant position as unit manager, but who had access to economic resources and was linked through personal ties to a minister, could actually have a major influence on a political institution.'

Personal networks relatives, neighbours, friends and acquaintances were prominent at the medium and lower levels of decision-making. Disorder and lawlessness were largely the result of the generally shared opinion that reporting illegal activity to the authorities was not 'proper behaviour'. Unless they themselves were directly affected, people usually turned a blind eye to how their acquaintances and former colleagues misused public goods for private purposes.

Although the top political elite was not formed on the basis of particularistic ties, the regional and local-level governance was tolerant of informal and illegal practices, mutual cover-ups and non-reporting of illegal actions by neighbours, co-villagers, kinsmen, friends, members of personal networks and corporate groups of professionals. These practices had existed also in Soviet times, but after independence they proliferated. The new Chechen state was clearly unable to create anything approximating a Weberian rational bureaucracy which at the time was hardly possible in any of the post-Soviet polities.

The mountains vs. lowland divide?

Much of the literature on Chechnya 1991–1994 argues that support for the president or the opposition had geographical aspects. A widely shared opinion is that Dudaev was supported by the people from the mountain areas, whereas his opposition had the support of lowland Chechens (Gakaev 1999; Tishkov 2001). Experts explain this by claiming that more traditional, less educated and mostly unemployed mountain people supported more radical solutions. Many of my respondents noted that while their relatives on the plains were more critical of Dudaev, their mountain relatives were supportive of him. In fact, however, tens if not hundreds of thousands of Chechens living on the plains also supported Dudaev.

In the end, the cleavage between the opposition and the government boiled down to the issue of complete independence vs. some kind of agreement with Russia. People in the lowland settlements were far more dependent on the 'infrastructural power' of the state – for them a failed state meant not only lost income but also the lack of the basic state services on which urbanized populations are heavily dependent (Mann 1993: 6, 7). Chechen lowland settlements are usually very large, often with populations of ten thousand or more. These were small towns, strongly affected by the failed state, skyrocketing criminality and the food-supply shortages.

By contrast, mountain people were living in smaller, self-sufficient communities. Their daily lives were less affected by the failures of the state; they relied little on state infrastructure, and kept criminality at bay all by themselves. They were proud that the government was now Chechen, and that its leaders were respectful of religion, as well as the traditions of mountain people – even sometimes favouring rural traditions over the more urban lifestyle of the plains. They now felt at home in Grozny, and some bought flats there. Mountain people were more prepared to endure difficulties on the road to independence.

The explanation of their greater support for secession can be found not so much in a traditional vs. a more modern mentality, but in social realities and ideological cleavages rooted in specific historical experiences and memories. According to a Chechen ethnologist Said-Magomed Khasiev said it was not correct to say that the mountain people were more supportive of separatism: 'it all depended on a person's ideological orientation and economic position, not his mountain/ lowland origin' (Khasiev, interview, 2009).

Regionalism

Another common belief about this period is that certain regions supported the opposition. Clearly this was the case with the Nadterechny region, which had refused to recognize the Dudaev regime, and later with the Urus-Martanovsky region. My respondents among former Chechen combatants said that in the Urus-Martanovsky district many villages did not let fighters in during the First Chechen War and refused to help them with food and medical supplies.

In 1993, after the Chechen Parliament had been dissolved, Moscow began covertly supplying the opposition to the Chechen state with money and weapons. In fact, the first attempt of the armed opposition to take over Grozny took place as early as 31 March 1992, when 'the oppositionals' occupied the building of the state television and tried to take over the presidential palace. This attempt was quickly defeated, and it is not entirely clear whether this opposition was linked with specific regions. However, by 1993 several pro-Russia politicians had consolidated power in their regions, and took up arms against Dudaev, with the support of Russia. Among the most prominent of Dudaev's opponents were Umar Avturkhanov, from Nadterechny district; Bislan Gantamirov, former mayor and chair of City Hall of Grozny, who had quarrelled with Dudaev and moved back to his hometown of Urus-Martan; and Ruslan Labazanov, a hardened criminal who held a personal grudge against Dudaev, and whose criminal gang of 40 to 50 men was mainly based in the town of Argun, some 10 km east of Grozny.

On 16 December 1993, these three men, together with others, established the 'Temporary Council of the Chechen Republic' – declaring Chechnya to be part of the Russian Federation, and appointing Avturkhanov as their leader. Then, in June 1994, this council arranged a Congress of the People of Chechnya in the village of Znameskoye, the administrative centre of Nadterechny. Dudaev faced a no-confidence vote, and the Temporary Council was declared the 'highest organ of government'.

The rise of armed opposition to Dudaev is often cited as an example of clan-based politics in Chechnya. The fact that this opposition was regionally based, moreover, is usually attributed to the strength of Avturkhanov and Gantamirov: 'The money and backing that came from Moscow allowed pro-federal field commander Umar Avturkhanov to consolidate power in his native Naursky region [*Nadterechny – E.S.*] by paying wages and salaries to its inhabitants', Anatol Lieven wrote in 1998.

My fieldwork, however, reveals that regional opposition was of different nature in Chechnya in the early 1990s. The deep ideological divide that had split state institutions, civil society and the media also divided several regions which had varying historical experiences and memories of Russia.

I interviewed a host of residents who were politically active from 1991 to 1994 in the town of Urus-Martan, the second largest in Chechnya. According to these interviewees, Urus-Martan had opposed Dudaev long before the arrival of Gantamirov. The city's populace was well-educated, with its own active elite, or *intelligentsia*. This was also a city with a mobile labour force: many of the residents did seasonal work in other parts of Russia or had moved to Russia for a time – so they had a better idea than most Chechens of 'how people lived elsewhere, and how the state works', according to one respondent. Moreover, the layout of the city is urban, much more so than the republic's capital and largest city, Grozny, where some areas are like small villages where private homeowners raise livestock and grow vegetables on their plots. In Urus-Martan, by contrast, there was not enough land on which to raise animals or grow food, so people lived primarily on their salaries, which made them especially dependent on the state.

During the early years of *perestroika*, in the 1980s, several civic organizations were founded in support of democratic reforms in Urus-Martan – which was among the first cities in the Soviet empire to oust a communist mayor and replace him with a democrat. It follows that Urus-Martan was one of the first to support the Chechen independence after the 1991 revolution. However, people soon became disillusioned. According to a former local government staffer of the early 1990s:

> Changes did not bypass Urus-Martan. People enthusiastically elected the President. Many hopes and expectations were placed on Dudaev. The educated segment of Chechen society, a large percentage of whom lived in Urus-Martan, demanded some kind of democracy. But democracy proved to be merely a declaration. It was the louts who, from their positions of power, dictated their rules to the others.

A local lawyer added:

We expected that the Chechen authorities would implement some minimal policies: pay pensions, make welfare payments, create employment opportunities. Dudaev inherited an enormous economy, and an enormous amount of property. For example, in Urus-Martan, the Michurina state farm had assets valued at a million dollars. There were tens of thousands of livestock in the region, a good grain crop, functioning business enterprises and a very hard-working populace. Despite all this, Dudaev was incapable of organizing basic things. It was clear that he simply did not know how to govern. Everything we owned was gradually plundered, huge agricultural enterprises fell into decay, factories and plants were closed down. And when people begged Dudaev, 'Please, pay our pensions', he said on TV, 'Collect pinecones and knit socks.' People began to understand that nothing proper could be done with such leaders.

Not only had Urus-Martan a well-organized political elite, but, since the time of *perestroika*, it had a charismatic leader, Yusup Elmurzaev. He had previously worked as a history teacher, as well as an inspector for the regional department of education. He was also among those who created the Temporary Council and declared Urus-Martan free of Dudaev's rule.

As a journalist from a local newspaper recalled, 'Yusup Elmurzaev was a supporter of the historical co-existence of Chechnya and Russia. He said, "We will do our best so that neither Russian, nor Dudaev's, troops enter this city".

Urus-Martan created its own armed guard to protect the city. It was only in late 1993 that Gantamirov, the former Grozny mayor, arrived in the breakaway city with his own paramilitary fighters. Then, in August 1994, Dudaev's forces tried to take the city, but failed.

All those whom I interviewed from Urus-Martan asserted that Gantamirov had played a negligible role in the unique stance taken by the city.

I encountered a similar situation in the Nadterechny region of Chechnya, which is located on the right bank of the Terek River, and was the first region to reject Dudaev's government. Local activists elected a regional administration, and, with the support of religious leaders, persuaded the populace to ally themselves with Russia. Unlike the rest of the republic, the Nadterechny Chechens received their pensions, salaries and subsidies from Russia regularly – and on time.

Like Urus-Martan, the Nadterechny region was historically strongly oriented toward Russia. As Adam Dukhaev, editor of the Nadterechny regional newspaper *Terkjist*, explained in an interview, ever since the nineteenth century Nadterechny Chechens have been loyal to Russia. Doku Zavgaev, the first Chechen Secretary of the Communist Party, who was elected in 1990, came from Nadterechny. According to a member of the regional administration, Zavgaev did not recruit many of his Nadterechny people into the government, but his three brothers, who were all influential persons during the final years of the USSR, channelled Russian financial support to Nadterechny.

According to the above-mentioned editor, Adam Dukhaev:

The majority of our population was pro-Russian, but about 10 per cent were pro-Dudaev. One village in the region was fully pro-Dudaev. It was not linked with kin ties, but ideologically they wanted to be with their people. Dudaev's television was full of anti-Nadterechny propaganda. Nadterechny Chechens were called traitors who went against their own people.

The alliance of Nadterechny and Urus-Martan districts was a result of elite coalition. As a member of the Urus-Martan administration explained:

Bislan Gantamirov, the chair of the city hall of Grozny [city mayor], who was born in Urus-Martan region, quarrelled with Dudaev and moved to live in the Nadterechny region. He formed a coalition with Umar Avturkhanov and then established ties with regional oppositionals, and the two regional elites allied within the Temporary Council of the republic.

Slipping towards war

On 11 August 1994, Boris Yeltsin was interviewed on television. Regarding Chechnya, he stated that intervention by force was 'impermissible and must not take place', but then added, with a sly smile: 'However, the situation in Chechnya is now changing. The role of the opposition to Dudaev is increasing. So, I would not say that we do not have any influence at all' (cited in Dunlop 1998: 197). Dudaev reacted immediately, branding Yeltsin's remarks as an 'unprecedented provocation' which proved that he [Yeltsin] was personally directing the manoeuvres of the opposition. Dudaev declared a holy war, or *gazavat*, and ordered the mobilization of the military within the republic, against what he called 'Russian aggression' (Dunlop 1998: 197). Two weeks later, Russian Deputy Prime Minister Sergey Shakhraj announced that the possibilities for political dialogue with Dudaev had been exhausted.

On 26 November 1994, the forces of Umar Avturkhanov and Bislan Gantamirov, assisted by Russian security services, stormed Grozny. Tanks rolled into the capital without encountering resistance, and easily reached the city centre – where they were attacked, and destroyed, by Chechen forces wielding grenade launchers. Some 30 opposition fighters were killed and 30 were captured.

The next day, Russian TV channels showed footage of the captives, who confessed to being Russian forces under contract with the FSK [*federal service for counter-intelligence*]. Only one day later, however, on 28 November, Minister of Defence Pavel Grachev officially denied that the FSK had played a role in the ill-fated assault.

On 29 November, Dudaev declared that the captives would be executed unless Russia admitted its complicity in the attack, and admitted that the captives were Russian forces. That same day, the Russian Security Council approved a military operation (Orlov and Cherkasov 1998: 32)

On December 11, 1994, Russian troops entered Chechnya. The First Chechen War had begun.

The failed assault on Grozny had given Dudaev and his government, which had been in deep crisis, the lifeline he needed. When people learned that mercenaries had joined the Chechen opposition in storming the capital of the republic, popular support again rallied behind the president.

Mezhidov, Deputy Speaker of the Chechen Parliament, believes that war could have been averted, saying in an interview:

> Dudaev wanted to meet Yeltsin. For some reason, I believe that if he had met Yeltsin, he would have signed the agreement [on the status of Chechnya] that we had prepared. But he wanted parity. If this meeting had taken place, there would have been no war.

Thus, in 1991 Chechnya gave birth to a powerful political nationalist movement. According to the definition of Ernst Gellner (1983: 1), nationalism calls for congruence between the national and political units. Have Chechens become a *modern* political nation? Theorists of nationalism would probably give very different answers to this question. Foundational scholars, like Ernst Gellner or Anthony Smith, who saw political nationalism as a sociological condition and a likely result of modernization, would be cautious about classifying the Chechens as a 'modern nation'. In Gellner's view, a modern nation is characterized by an anonymous impersonal society, with mutually sustainable atomized individuals, held together above all by a shared standardized high culture which replaces the previous complex structure of local groups (Gellner 1983: 57). For Anthony Smith, a nation is 'a named population sharing a historic territory, common myths and historical memories, a mass public culture, a common economy and common legal rights and duties for its members' (Smith 1995: 57).

Although moderately industrialized, Chechnya's literate society had a high culture imposed through the educational system: this was not indigenous, but Russian or Soviet culture. Moreover, there was no common economy or a unified legal system. Subnational local identities still existed, albeit strongly diluted. Thus, the conditions outlined by the classics have not been fully met.

Other theorists of nation and nationalism have argued against standardized master variables or criteria for nations. For example, according to Craig Calhoun (1997: 99; 2007) a 'nation' must have social solidarity, a specific way of thinking about what it means to be one people. A nation must have some level of integration among its members: they share common ideas of boundaries, territory and population; have sovereignty or aspirations to sovereignty (usually through a self-sufficient state); share the idea that the government is just when supported by popular will; share a culture which involves some combination of language, common beliefs and values; share the idea that their nation extends from the past to the future; as well as sharing belief in common descent, and a special attachment to territory (Calhoun 1997: 4, 5). Clearly, Chechens do meet such criteria that define a political nation, based primarily on a common sense of solidarity.

No matter whether we classify the Chechens a nation or not, between 1991 and 1994 the Chechen political elites, who had come to power as a result of a national revolution, aimed to build a modern secular nation-state. The political process in that period was a secular one, and ideologically and economically driven. Up until 1993, the political actors tried to keep their commitment to stay within the framework of the law and a minimal definition of democratic procedure, with independent legislative and executive powers, a fairly impartial Constitutional Court, and a functioning system of checks and balances. But then the Chechen political system became paralysed by an acute political crisis, the outcome of the intense power struggle between political actors who sought to implement their differing visions of 'Chechen statehood' – separatist vs. sovereign in alliance with Russia.

Procedurally, the political process in Chechnya of 1992–1993 was in fact quite democratic and legalistic, despite many attempts to the contrary. The arguments of both sides were usually based on references to the Constitution; in cases of acute disagreement, each side resorted to the Constitutional Court, which tried to remain impartial. The absence of political actors embedded in traditional ties was a result of the significant autonomy of state institutions and political processes from society. Dudaev's state was a state-above-the-society, with elites playing a major role in the transition, as predicted by the democratization authors (Linz 1990; Huntington 1984). Dudaev himself was well aware that part of his political society maintained strong links and connections with Russia and had differing visions of the Chechen future. His problem was what Dankwart Rustow has called 'the birth defects of the political community'. The Chechens undoubtedly had a Rustowian 'strong prior sense of community' – but they did not agree on the political future of this community.

Another crucial challenge was the lack of knowledge and experience to build a modern state. Here we should note the low ability to govern and to deliver social services, to keep industries up and running and to preserve jobs, to maintain infrastructure, to keep the state coffers filled, to provide education and medical care, to combat crime, to enforce the law and to ensure a functioning judicial system. All these failings of Michael Mann's infrastructural power of the state were critical in shaping popular attitudes toward Dzhokhar Dudaev and proved far more important than *teip* affiliation (Mann 1992: 6, 7).

Despite Dudaev's support of neo-traditionalism in politics, of the revival of the *teips* and Councils of Elders, he did not attempt to incorporate them into the political system or let them play any significant role in the political process. The revival of the *teips* passed as an element of retro-fashion, whereas the political unification of the *teips* proved impossible. Except for a handful of cases, which were usually linked to a murder or the humiliation of its members, the *teips* (more precisely, lineages) were unable to mobilize for significant action. Neo-traditionalism in politics proved equally unsuccessful. Attempts by elders to intervene in important matters, politics in particular, encountered resistance from the Chechen people and the state. Moreover, the actions of certain elders apparently dampened enthusiasm for a meaningful revival of traditionalism in politics.

Relations between the state and the informal social structures in this period could be described as *accommodation*, or even cooperation, in the case of Dudaev's government and the *Mekhk-Khel* as well as other 'traditional' patterns of social integration. It was *competition/challenge*, in case of opposition forces; *compartmentalization*, in the situation of political crisis between the Parliament and the opposition, which resulted in duumvirate and division that cut across not only government institutions but also their supporting informal actors, the media and civil society groups.

My analysis in this chapter refutes the arguments of clan politics authors who have claimed that inter-clan tensions in Chechnya have led to group mobilization and violence (Collins 2006: 41) or that the 'subethnic *teips* became enshrined in Moscow's decision to launch a bloody invasion in 1994; some groups were most closely allied with Russia and others were more staunch supporters of independence' after the collapse of USSR (Schatz 2004: xvi). The clan politics literature lacks an understanding of what *teip*/clan really was at that time. It has misinterpreted the nature of the political process in Chechnya 1991–1994, and has underestimated the role of ideology, political/economic interests, and regional identities all of which were decisive to political outcomes.

Ascriptive ties, such as kinship, descent and religion had very low prominence, even negligible in the Chechen elite under Dzhokhar Dudaev, which is best explained by the nature of the political process, which was ideology-driven; and by internal constraints on the government, such as checks and balances (assertive Parliament, relatively independent judiciary) and organized opposition. As shown in this chapter, the special positions of the various regions were determined historically and sociologically – not by *teip* or any other primordial identities.

The low prominence of ascriptive ties in Dudaev's team is remarkable given the high-risk environment in which he operated. The risk of physical elimination of Dudaev was very high – but the source of that risk came mainly from Russia. Khussein Iskhanov, supporter of independence and later member of military headquarters in Grozny, who knew Dudaev quite well, has asserted in an interview:

> He understood that he would die on the way. He was hunted down, the regions where he travelled were subjected to aerial attacks. He realized that at any moment he could be killed. We all knew that in the next second we could be gone. But we didn't think about it. This was our duty in the face of the next generations, to create for them a secure and happy future.

With such a fatalistic attitude, Dzhokhar was not focused on ensuring security by surrounding himself with trusted relatives or other types of strong ties. He was still deeply loved and admired by a large portion of the population, which provided him with a degree of protection internally.

On 21 April 1996, Dzhokhar Dudaev was killed by two laser-guided missiles. His location had been detected by a Russian military plane while he was using a satellite phone.

As Said-Ali, a Chechen peasant born in 1911, told me:

> Dudaev declared freedom and independence, something people had been waiting for, for generations and generations. Our forefathers fought for it with arms. We were waiting for such a man, such a development, to start living in peace – to put an end to wars and extermination and subjugation. I am an old man, I don't understand many things. I don't know why it didn't work out for him. But I regret that it did not work out.

6

State-Building in Chechnya under Aslan Maskhadov (1997–1999)*

The victory of Chechen separatists in the first Russian–Chechen War of 1994–1996 was enshrined on 31 August 1996 with the Khasavyurt Accord, signed by Chechen Chief of Staff Aslan Maskhadov, on behalf of Zelimkhan Yandarbiev, President of the Chechen Republic of Ichkeria, and General Alexander Lebed, on behalf of Boris Yeltsin, president of Russia. The accord stipulated the end of the military conflict, which was to be followed by the withdrawal of Russian troops and a commitment not to use force, as well as a pledge to resolve any future disputes on the basis of international law (*Nezavisimaya Gazeta*, 3 September 1996). The question of the political status of Chechnya was to be determined by the close of 2001.

At the ceremony following the signing of the accord, Vladimir Lukin, then a member of the Russian delegation and MP of the Russian State Duma, and later Human Rights Ombudsman of Russia, made a remark that is remembered by many to this day: 'In five years Russia will be stronger, and we'll see what happens then.'

During the ensuing presidential electoral campaign in Chechnya, candidate Shamil Basaev, the republic's most notorious field commander, who had already resorted to active terrorism, repeatedly quoted Lukin's remark, while insisting that the political status of Chechnya should be resolved before 2001 (Tishkov 1998: 64). The unresolved status and the remaining threat from Russia were used by field commanders, including Basaev, as a pretext for not demobilizing their armed groups.

State-building resumed within Chechnya under difficult circumstances. An estimated 80 per cent of the republic's economy had been destroyed during the war, in addition to much of its infrastructure (Tishkov 1998: 73). The population was impoverished. Brushes with death had become routine. Many people suffered from grave psychological trauma. Although statistics on the death toll during the war are disputed, a reasonable estimate holds that up to 50,000 civilians died, and several hundred thousand were displaced (ICG, October 2012). Moreover, although the war had ended, the ready availability of weapons, and the desire for revenge – combined with the effects of paramilitarization of the male population – meant that the conflict was not yet over.

The Russian government recognized the scope of the damage and acceded to a package of economic agreements as part of the Khasavyurt Accord that would finance

---

* The anaysis of this chapter was first published in: Chechnya at War and Beyond (1st ed.), Le Huérou, A., Merlin, A., Regamey, A., & Sieca-Kozlowski, E. (Eds.) Copyright © 2014 by Imprint of Routledge. Reproduced by permission of Taylor & Francis Group.

reconstruction, and pay salaries and pensions within the republic. The Russian military campaign had not only greatly influenced the political situation within the republic but also brought about significant social change – in the form of profound Islamization, and the emergence of new patterns of social integration – paramilitary groups. Moreover, the war had drastically weakened the part of Chechen identity that held positive associations as to Russia. Indiscriminate violence at the hands of Russian troops had reduced the pre-war gains of the pro-Russian political opposition to almost nil – justifying old fears, intensifying memories of grievances and discrediting the idea of Russian statehood.

The war had also accelerated the re-Islamization of society. What had begun in 1994 as an anti-colonial conflict, with national liberation as the primary slogan of rank-and-file fighters, had by 1997 taken on a prominent Islamic character. All Chechen politicians invoked Muslim identity in their pronouncements. Much of the population, in the context of random violence and death, turned to faith. New fundamentalist trends in religion emerged: Salafism, Wahhabism. These beliefs proved very effective in promoting military organization and discipline. Foreign fighters who arrived in Chechnya in considerable numbers in 1995 were bearers of Islamic fundamentalist ideology, and invested much of their energy spreading this among former Soviet field commanders as well as the rank-and-file fighters.

Paramilitary groups had gradually grown in power. All former combatants I interviewed described the first two weeks of the war as chaos: the sheer numbers of men who had volunteered to fight were disruptive to military discipline. Moreover, there was no central command. Armed groups formed on their own – spontaneously and, often, randomly.

'It was difficult even to join in this nightmare', said one former combatant, Khozh. 'For two weeks I couldn't find a group. Most volunteers were forming groups on the basis of previous acquaintances, friendships, and I had no acquaintances. I had just arrived from Kazakhstan.'

Nonetheless, a unified command was quickly established, and the armed forces were divided into fronts and then, into sectors. The autonomy of military units was significant. Cohesion in the units was strong. Officers in the units were relatively free in their command, as many of the units were made up of volunteers who came and went, and operated in territory that was fragmented by areas under the control of federal troops.

Many armed groups were formed on the basis of village affiliation or previous acquaintance. Some emerged on the basis of mere happenstance. Often the social and regional composition of the units was heterogeneous. While commanders were usually men with prior military experience, they were not necessarily the oldest. As Khozh explained to me:

> In our group the commander was 49 years old. He was a schoolteacher who taught military education. We had other teachers with us, too. We called them the *intelligentsia*. I was 32. The oldest was 56, the youngest, 18. Two of us were from the Groznensky (Selsky) region, three guys were from Grozny, one guy was Adyg (Cherkessian), and the rest were from the Naursky and Nadterechny regions. We were 21–22 people altogether. All except for one had served in the army.

None of the former combatants I interviewed said that their group had been based on kin, or *vird*, affiliation. In fact, many said that their cousins and other relatives fought elsewhere, in other units. However, most fighters said that they preferred to be in a unit with people they knew, preferably co-villagers or neighbours.

'I wanted to be with my guys, those from my village, because I was 100 per cent sure that they wouldn't abandon me if I were injured, or killed', said Zelim, another former combatant.

The composition of the units fluctuated as the war progressed. Popular support for combatants was massive. Ruslan, another former combatant, explained:

The people's militia had to be fed, so women baked bread, sewed uniforms, and unloadings. The injured were treated. When a unit entered a village, the injured were immediately taken to homes – it was perceived as an honour to take care of them. The entire nation supported us. We were fighting for a pure idea, for independence. And you can't defeat a nation when it has an idea. When one side has patriotism, and the other side, vodka, it's clear who wins such a war (…) In the first war, truth was on our side, and we won with the support of the Almighty.

After the war, many of the units were dissolved, and most fighters returned to peaceful lives. Some units remained mobilized, however, and gradually evolved into paramilitary organizations with even stronger territorial components, and even greater personal loyalty to their leaders.

Former combatants were treated as national heroes. Quite a few felt entitled to their share of power. Achievements in the war effort became the main criteria for access to power, resources and social goods; paramilitaries were now seen as a social lift, which facilitated their institutionalization.

Elections and the early elite

Chechnya launched its second state-building project with presidential and parliamentary elections on 27 January 1997. The poll was carried out in keeping with the guidelines spelled out in the Constitution of 1992. More than 20 candidates ran for president; no pro-Russian or non-separatist candidates were permitted to run. There were three main candidates: Zelimkhan Yandarbiev, Aslan Maskhadov and Shamil Basaev. Yandarbiev, the acting president, had assumed the post after Dzhokhar Dudaev was killed by federal security forces on 21 April 1996. Yandarbiev had positioned himself as a supporter of Islamic values and was radically anti-Russian.

Maskhadov, a former Soviet army colonel who served in Hungary and Lithuania, had quit military service in late 1992 and joined Dzhokhar Dudaev. He was the chief of staff during the war, and now advocated a secular state and the normalization of relations with Russia. He also stressed the need to attract investment, and other support, from the West.

Basaev, a celebrated field commander – and most wanted terrorist – represented the radical Chechen separatists. He had gained fame in November 1991, when, in response to Yeltsin's imposition of a state of emergency in Chechnya, he had hijacked a Russian passenger plane to Turkey – an audacious act for which he was rebuked by the

Ichkerian government and placed on the list of Russia's most wanted criminals. Then, in June 1995, he commanded a unit that seized a hospital in the town of Budenovsk, in the Stavropol region of Russia, demanding that the Kremlin hold peace talks with Dudaev. After several unsuccessful attempts at storming the hospital, the Russian government announced a ceasefire in Chechnya, and Basaev released the hostages, returning home as a hero (Aliev and Zhadaev 2005).

Among the three leading candidates, Maskhadov was considered the most 'pro-Moscow' – and was therefore disliked by Chechen hardliners. 'The Kremlin obviously had a stake in Maskhadov. Because of that, I didn't trust him', said Shirvani, a former combatant from Grozny.

Most radical separatists and former combatants I interviewed shared this view. However, most of my respondents recalled the 27 January elections as an intensely meaningful civic experience. 'I cast my vote only once in my life. It was on that day. So many people were voting! There were queues at the polling stations. People were dancing. Everyone felt that, now that the war was over, we would start a new, better life', said Tamara from Grozny.

Maskhadov received an overwhelming 59 per cent of the vote, far outpacing his nearest competitor, Basaev, who netted 23.5 per cent. Yandarbiev received only 10 per cent of the vote. OSCE representatives observed the elections and recognized the results. Analysts of the Chechen newspaper, *Chechenskoye Obschestvo*, concluded: 'most people voted for Maskhadov because Basaev frightened them with his aggressive military biography, while Maskhadov was the symbol of reasonable and secular authority' (Aliev and Zhadaev 2005). Moreover, Maskhadov had personally signed the Khasavyurt Accord with Russia, and many voters looked to him to resolve outstanding disputes with Moscow. The overwhelming support for Maskhadov demonstrated that 'most Chechens wanted to avoid a new confrontation with Russian and favoured dialogue', according to Alexey Malashenko and Dmitry Trenin, two Russian scholars of North Caucasus. However, 30 per cent of the electorate had favoured radicals. 'These 30% of the electorate ... soon became the core fighting force of the anti-Maskhadov opposition' (Malashenko and Trenin 2004: 30).

If votes cast for president were many, votes cast for parliamentary seats were comparatively few. The two rounds of voting ending on 15 February garnered enough support to seat only 32 deputies from among a potential 63; the Central Electoral Commission reviewed the results, and seated another 11 deputies, creating a parliament of 43 representatives.

Maskhadov was sworn in as president on 12 February 1997. Under the Constitution, Maskhadov also was in charge of the Cabinet of Ministers, the Commander-in-Chief and the Chair of the Supreme Council with the president of the Chechen Republic. Maskhadov's selection of ministers – all of his chief political rivals were invited into the government – clearly reflected his firm desire to accommodate various interests, and avoid fragmentation within the separatist elite of former field commanders.

Shamil Basaev and Movladi Udugov became the first vice-prime ministers of the new government, responsible for industry and information, respectively. Two other prominent field commanders were appointed as vice-premiers: Ruslan Gelaev would be in charge of construction; Islam Khalimov would manage social issues. Maskhadov also appointed field commanders and former members of Dudaev's government to head various ministries and departments (Muzaev 1997). The defence and security ministries went to Maskhadov's top commanders and supporters in the electoral campaign: Magomed Khanbiev as Minister of Defence, Kazbek Makhashev as Minister of the Interior (Akhmadov and Lanskoy 2010: 81).

However, Maskhadov also realized the importance of experienced bureaucrats in government. He invited into government several former pro-Russian managers, a gesture viewed by his more radical colleagues as 'rehabilitation of communists' (Muzaev 1997).

Members of the government in Chechnya in 1997 were selected on the basis of their achievements – on the battlefield, and in furtherance of the idea of Chechen statehood. *Teip, vird* or kin affiliations did not play a role. In Parliament, the main faction was made up of more than 20 deputies aligned with the pro-Maskhadov Party of National Independence. The second-largest faction consisted of seven deputies from a union of political forces, Islamic Order. Both the Head of Parliament and his Deputy were former field commanders.

Maskhadov's decision to grant enough real power to his former comrades should have satisfied his potential rivals and bolstered his political clout. One can speculate whether this was the right choice – staffing institutions of government with former combatants, most of whom had no sufficient education, experience or knowledge of government. One can speculate, too, whether Maskhadov ever really had a choice: his approach was probably the only rational way to enlist the support of those who would otherwise have tried to challenge the political system from the outside.

Challengers to the Maskhadov regime

Despite Maskhadov's efforts, tensions among field commanders were increasingly evident. The first to openly challenge Maskhadov was a former presidential candidate, Salman Raduev, one-time prefect of Gudermes, the second-largest town in the republic. Raduev had headed the presidential guard from 1993 to 1996 and was married to Dudaev's niece.

Raduev was widely regarded a villain. However, he saw himself as the logical successor to Dudaev, and rejected the election results – refusing to accept the legitimacy of Maskhadov. Raduev renamed the Presidential Berets (the presidential guard) – which occupied well-armed bases in Gudermes and the Staropromyslovsky district of Grozny – 'the Army of General Dudaev'. And on 9 January 1996, he committed a terrorist act echoing the one carried out by Basaev earlier: his unit attacked a military base and airport in the Dagestani town of Kyzlyar, then, in retreat, seized a hospital, demanding safe passage to Chechnya.

However, the real challenger to Maskhadov was not Raduev, but Shamil Basaev. He took his electoral defeat very personally but was savvy enough not to oppose Maskhadov immediately after the elections. Former acting president Yandarbiev, too, remained on the horizon among opponents to Maskhadov, and after his electoral defeat travelled for several months among Muslim countries – probably to raise funds for his future political projects.

Other Chechen field commanders allied themselves with one political actor or another, but most maintained their armed groups despite Maskhadov's efforts to dissolve them after the war.

The forces led by Basaev and Raduev were major military units, well trained and experienced in daring military operations. Together, both groups could compete militarily with the official Chechen armed forces. Maskhadov did not maintain a loyal paramilitary group of his own: he relied on state security structures as well as a small number of faithful personal guards.

In addition to maintaining paramilitary groups, the aforementioned challengers to Maskhadov set up formal political organizations to represent their interests in the public sphere. Such 'public-political movements' essentially functioned as political parties with their own mouthpieces, usually newspapers.

One of these parties was founded in 1997 by Basaev. *Marshonan Toba* ('The Way To Freedom') pursued a radical separatist agenda that sponsored in June 1998 a congress of the Peoples of Chechnya and Dagestan, headed by Basaev (Malashenko and Trenin 2004: 34). In turn, Raduev founded the military-patriotic organization, Soldiers of Freedom, and, later, The Caucasian House; Yandarbiev, who had been elected emir of the Organization for Islamic Unity of the Caucasus, formed the popular movement Chechen Islamic State, which advocated for his return as head of state, only with more executive powers (Muzaev 1997).

Thus, a host of newspapers sprung up with editorial slants critical of Maskhadov, and favourable to specific political opponents. *Kavkazskaya Konfederatsiya* (Caucasian Confederation) backed Yandarbiev, while *MarshonanAz* supported Basaev and Raduev. *Put' Dzokhara* (Path of Dzhokhar] also backed Raduev, while *Put' Islama* (Path of Islam] and *Islamskaya Natsiya* (Islamic Nation] supported Udugov. *Veliky Dzikhad* (Great Jihad) backed another respected field commander, Ruslan (Hamzat) Gelaev.

The official state newspapers – like *Ichkeria* and *Zaschitnik Otechestva* (Defender of the Fatherland) – supported the new president. Independent newspapers, like *Groznensky rabochij* (Grozny Workers) and *Golos Chechenskoi Respubliki* (The Voice of the Chechen Republic), tended to support Maskhadov as well. All the same, while Maskhadov's rivals were engaged in formal political opposition, their real strength remained in their informal paramilitary abilities.

Ideological divisions fell along attitudes to Islam. All opposition leaders were pushing for the establishment of an Islamic state governed by Islamic law and were very sensitive to criticism of *Sharia*. Ideological divisions also emerged over internal and external policy. Whereas Maskhadov was pushing for privatization as a mechanism for the revival of the Chechen economy, his opponents were very cautious, and argued that privatization was likely to serve the interests of specific groups, and not the general populace. However, Maskhadov's opponents did all they could in the pursuit of an 'informal privatization' – direct seizure of state property by criminal groups. And whereas Maskhadov tried to combat organized crime within the republic, his opponents spoke primarily of the spies and 'collaborators of the occupation regime'.

Maskhadov's opponents also blamed him for inadequate response to what they called 'the cynical and insulting campaign against the Chechen state organized by Russia'. They demanded the swift settlement of outstanding issues with Russia, with full independence for Chechnya, the introduction of Chechen passports, as well as custom agents along the republic's borders within the Russian Federation – and even number plates for vehicles registered in Chechnya.

In matters of external policy, Maskhadov's challengers were displeased with what they saw as a lazy government reaction to changing geopolitical realities. They called for intervention on behalf of Islamist leaders vying for political influence in the neighbouring republic of Dagestan, and pushed for a more outspoken anti-Western stance in international affairs.

These were the 'indigenous' challengers to Maskhadov's state-building efforts.

By 1997, two groups of 'alien' challengers hosted by Chechen radicals were operating in the republic: Khattab, an Arab from Saudi Arabia who supported the spread of fundamentalist Islam financially, logistically and militarily, and Bagautdin of Kizilyurt (Magomed Kebedov), a Muslim scholar from Dagestan who provided ideological training and support to Chechen fundamentalists and inspired the transformation of Chechnya into an Islamic state. Both Khattab and Kebedov had their dedicated armed groups and had their hosts in the Chechen Republic from among field commanders.

Khattab, a Saudi citizen, had fought against the Soviet Union in Afghanistan before teaming up with Islamist rebels elsewhere in Central Asia, in Tajikistan and Uzbekistan. He said he first learned of the Chechen conflict from a CNN report in December 1994; within a month he had arrived in Grozny with an armed group of Arab fighters. Khattab also brought with him knowledge of the structure, skills and, most importantly, the financial support of international Jihadists. He organized stable inflows of funding to pay for weapons, ammunition, training and supplies. As a professional guerrilla fighter with a masterful command of weapons, landmines and mountain warfare, he also trained future combatants.

From 1995 to 1996 Khattab and his largely Chechen fighters carried out several successful military operations within the republic, the most infamous of which was an April 1996 attack on federal forces near the village of Yarysh-Mardy – during which, in the course of three hours, he destroyed a convoy of heavily armoured vehicles of the 245th Motor-Rifle Regiment, killing 95 troops and injuring 54. He attacked the head and tail of the convoy on a narrow pass with a steep mountain on one side, and an abyss on the other, killing the commander within minutes, then setting aflame the vehicles on each end, trapping those caught in-between.

The audacity of the operation impressed Chechen field commanders, but those I interviewed said that Dudaev, who was a consistent opponent of fundamentalist Islam, 'kept him quiet'. After the death of Dudaev in April 1996, however, that political isolation ended: Khattab was embraced by Yandarbiev, who in 1996 introduced *Sharia* courts, and granted more political power to proponents of fundamentalist Islam. Basaev, too, recognized the organizational benefits of fundamentalist structures, especially in generating support among youth. He became close to Khattab, who channelled money to his armed group. In fact, in 1996 Khattab married a Dargin woman from an Islamist enclave in Dagestan, and settled in Basaev's native village of Vedeno.

Also, that year Khattab, with the help of Basaev, founded the Kavkaz Centre, a training base on the territory of a former Soviet young pioneer camp near the village of Serzhen-Yurt, in the republic's Shali region. Over the ensuing three years, thousands of young males from the region were trained in this centre, where, according to my respondents, mostly foreign instructors taught the Koran, as well as how to use explosives and heavily artillery. They also taught tactics of guerrilla war, including attacks on the enemy's rear guard, according to interviews. Between 1,000 and 2,000 young people said to have been enrolled in each six-month training session, with Dagestanis interpreting for the Arabic-speaking instructors.

Youth from a broad spectrum attended, ranging from secular intellectuals who joined out of curiosity (or, perhaps, to learn something new about Islam), to radicals intent on becoming fighters. Each camp had a specialized programme offering ideological training (Koran study), training in explosives and military actions in the enemy's rear guard, training in heavy artillery weapons, and methods of guerrilla warfare. According to my interviewees, most were idle, bored young people seeking an all-expenses-paid adventure for whom the training was tantamount to *zarnitsa* – the sport game, imitating military exercises at Soviet schools. A great many of them had previously been disinterested in politics or religion, but successful completion of the six months of training was a sign of manliness and raised a young man's status among his peers. One of my Ingush colleagues, a secular intellectual, said that he had planned to attend, too, but had changed his mind after he was told he would first have to quit smoking. A Chechen attendee who took a full course in the camp told me that he had enrolled to learn more about Islam, but left very much looking forward to war.

Zelim, the former combatant who fought in both Chechen wars, told me that he received training at Kavkaz Centre together with about 1,000 other men:

There were Bashkirs, Uzbeks, Tatars, Tajiks, Ingush, Kabardins, Ossetians, Afghans, and even English there. There was also one black guy, a professional runner. He knew only English and Arabic. He had come to fight. And then there was one Bosnian, without legs. There were some real fighters there. They were wanted by security services all over the world. We were divided into Jamaats. There were Ingush, Kabardine Jamaats, both of which were closely united … After training the best among us were picked out and transferred to the military camp. Guys from Russia were taught mining, explosives and the like … This was real military training. These people knew there would be another war, and they were preparing … They showed us videos of Kashmir, Palestine. I was shocked. Although now I think it was brainwashing … And there was no authority in Chechnya that could approach this camp and reprimand them. All the taxi drivers knew the way to the camp. We would pass through military checkpoints, and the federal troops knew where we were going. It was impossible not to know about this camp. But it was too dangerous for them to touch us.

Another attendee, a former member of the Communist Party who later became a deputy editor of a regional newspaper, told me:

After the first war we went to Serzhen-Yurt. We thought it was a place where people worshipped God. The first week some Jordanian was lecturing. Gradually I started to feel tension. I saw people's eyes turning bloodshot. I thought this was some kind of hypnosis – they would often repeat words like *war, blood, murder*. Then I said to my friend, 'Something is wrong with this place', and we left.

Radical Islamist influences in Chechnya came not only from the Arab world but also from elsewhere in the North Caucasus. In the mid-1990s the Dagestani fundamentalist scholar Magomed Kebedov founded a *madrassah* [*religious school*], on the border between Chechnya and Dagestan. Some 700 students, both Dagestanis and Chechens, reportedly attended the school at any one time (Akaev 2006).

In 1997, after the authorities managed to crush many of the fundamentalist centres on Dagestani territory, Kebedov and families of supporters migrated to Chechnya, where they were invited to settle in the formerly pro-Russian town of Urus-Martan (Akaev 2006). There, Kebedov trained judges for the republic's newly introduced *Sharia* courts.

Both Khattab and Kebedov – careful not to infringe on the political ambitions of various Chechen field commanders – nevertheless manipulated Chechen politics from behind the scenes. Neither man ever expressed any personal interest in political office, but each consistently and forcefully pushed for an Islamic state. Each pushed, too, for more aggressive behaviour toward Russia and the West – for a Caucasus-wide effort in support of the international Jihadist movement. Each man regularly gave interviews to the Chechen media, most frequently to the pro-fundamentalist newspapers *Islamskii Poryadok* (Islamic Order) and *Al-Kaf* (sponsored by Khattab). In interviews, Khattab stressed that his credo was Jihad, and that Jihad was the obligation of every Muslim. He added that he did not believe that the war in the North Caucasus had ended, and called upon Chechens to prepare for another war (IGPI 1998–1999).

Both Khattab and Kebedov launched an outright assault on Sufism, to which most Chechens adhered. Salafism rejects elements of ethnic traditions in faith as well as the special role of Sufi saints or *sheikhs*, whose adoration they consider to be a grave violation of the Islamic principle of the Oneness of God. Both insisted there was no law other than *Sharia*, and that the Koran was the Constitution. Nationalism, in fact, was their foe. However, the majority of the population found their positions were hard to accept.

Maskhadov and his supporters tried to curb the anti-nationalist claims of Islamists. In early 1998, Maskhadov's close ally Lecha Khultygov, Director of the National Security Service, said that the propaganda of the 'Wahhabists' directly contradicted the national traditions of Chechens. Khultygov further condemned the imposition of what he called an 'Arab lifestyle', giving voice to fears that the replacement of national traditions by Islamic ones would erase the distinct identity of the Chechen nation (Muzaev 06/1998). 'Chechnya is for the Chechens', Maskhadov declared. 'We don't need [...] Arab advisors' (Muzaev 06/1998).

The military units that Islamic fundamentalists in Chechnya called *jamaats* were very well-trained, organized and combat-ready. Hostages seized for ransom had been discovered on their bases; Dagestani policemen released from captivity in Urus-Martan claimed that fundamentalists fighters had dug trenches, and were preparing for an attack by pro-Maskhadov fighters. My respondents, residents of Serzhen-Yurt, testified that they lived in constant fear of armed clashes between Khattab and Maskhadov at that time.

All the Chechen opponents of Maskhadov resorted to Islamist rhetoric: most of them were converts and allies of fundamentalists. Demanding a greater role for Islam served their political ends: amid the post-war chaos, calls for religious purity and strict adherence to Islam boosted one's own moral standing, and discredited one's rivals.

In a 1997 interview in the analytical magazine *Ogonek*, Raduev accused Maskhadov of fighting for power while claiming that he was fighting for Islam. 'I am a man of deep religious convictions', he said, 'I don't drink or smoke' (Belovetsky 1997). According to *Ogonek*, funds from the Global Islamic forum came through Raduev.

Maskhadov appealed to Muslim countries not to finance Raduev (Belovetsky 1997). Also Zelimkhan Yandarbiev openly acknowledged the instrumental value of financial support from the Islamic funds. In an interview to *Vremya Novostey* in December 2001, he said: 'Islamic fundamentalism is not dangerous. It is partnership, international relations. You don't consider it a problem if Western investors tour Russia, do you? One cannot divide help into help from Wahhabists and help from others' (Yandarbiev 2001).

Shamil Basaev insisted that he was continuing to fight a war for national liberation. For him, religious motifs, such as Wahhabism, were secondary, according to Andrei Babitsky, a reporter for Radio Free Europe/Radio Liberty, who was the last person to interview Basaev prior to his assassination in 2006 (Babitsky 2005).

Nonetheless, for the young followers of these opposition leaders – many of whom went through Khattab's training camp – radical Islam was already a part of their lives… lives that many of them sacrificed during the Second Chechen War, following the failure of the 1997–1999 state-building effort that they themselves had helped to derail.

State-building policies

The economy

At the core of the decline of the Chechen economy from 1997 to 1999 was the dramatic decay of the oil industry, and the lack of cash. In 1997 gross domestic product (GDP) amounted to 2 billion roubles ($340,000), less than half the expected 5 billion roubles. In 1998 GDP fell to 1.6 billion roubles, far below the projected 7 billion roubles. This had a deeply negative impact on financing for education, healthcare, infrastructure, law enforcement and the military (*Groznensky rabochij*, 10–16 June 1999).

Most economic activity was concentrated in small private businesses – food-stands, small cafes, shops, petrol stations, roadside sales of crude-oil products. Many field commanders turned their military units into military-economic groups that engaged in large-scale illegal economic activities, such as the clandestine extraction of oil, and hostage-taking for ransom. Although the radical Islamist opposition claimed to be opposed to the official privatization of state property advocated by Maskhadov, they were in fact already privatizing state property through their criminal enterprises – effectively squandering the property of the Chechen Republic.

The Maskhadov administration first looked to revenue from the oil industry to fill the republic's coffers, and afterwards to taxes (*Ichkeria*, № 13, June–July 1998). The government did not expect to collect much from individual taxpayers. By 1998, it had stopped collecting taxes from individuals altogether.

Many business enterprises were simply unable to pay taxes: they were on the verge of bankruptcy, and were further burdened by rising costs of production linked to the need of post-war reconstruction of buildings and equipment and for heightened security. Moreover, many of the tax exemptions generously adopted by the Chechen Parliament were applied not only to those who were eligible, which significantly decreased the state capacity to collect budget revenues.

The tax police could only pursue enterprises that were registered with the government, and most of the republic's economic activity was conducted in the shadows.

The cash shortage also meant that many transactions were performed via barter. Those transactions that were made in cash increasingly bypassed the banks. The government tried to coax businesses out of the shadows with a July 1997 'Resolution on Cash Collection', but the measure met with little success (*Ichkeria*, 18 January 1998).

Maskhadov also looked to Moscow to shoulder some of the economic burden, in keeping with its pledge under the terms of the Khasavyurt Accord. Nonetheless, shortly after the peace treaty had been signed, the Kremlin unofficially laid siege to the Chechen economy. Moscow fulfilled its obligations – but erratically. Payments were made partially and with delays. In 1998, Russia deducted from its obligations the costs of electricity debts of Chechnya.

In 1999, representatives of Grozny and Moscow negotiated a 2 billion roubles contribution by Russia to the Chechen budget. However, the Russian State Duma approved payment of only 240,000 roubles, while the Federation Council (the upper house) ruled out financial transfers to Chechnya altogether (*Ichkeria*, March–April 1999). According to the memoirs of Ilyas Akhmadov (initially an ally of Basaev, later Foreign Minister under Maskhadov), individual Russian ministries were open to agreements on subsidies for the Chechen counterparts, but parties stumbled on technical issues: how to sign official documents – as between the federal government and one of its regions? Or as an agreement between two equal entities? Neither side was prepared to compromise, and so Chechnya was unable to make use of these opportunities to revive industry and obtain economic assistance (Akhmadov and Lanskoy 2010: 84).

Industry

Some 80 per cent of the republic's economy had been destroyed during the war (Tishkov 1998). Most industrial enterprises lay in ruins. Several factories survived, but those that did had been compelled to change their scope. Among the survivors were furniture factories, which were using only 10 to 15 per cent of their production capacities (Tishkov 1998: 65). For example, Sintar, a radio-technical factory, began manufacturing plastic storage bins; workers were paid salaries in plastic bins (IGPI 06/1998).

Not all was doom and gloom, however. In June 1998, a Grozny manufacturer of iron and concrete goods was re-launched. A flour mill, sugar factories and battery farm were rebuilt in 1998. More than 3,000 new jobs were created with the re-launch of these factories (IGPI 06/1998). The reconstruction of the cement factory in Chiri-Yurt was financed by the Russian government. Seventeen of 44 major industrial enterprises were functioning by 1999, but their combined output reached only 5 to 8 per cent of pre-war levels (Tishkov 2001: 439).

Maskhadov had great hopes for the privatization of industry, which he saw as the only realistic means of reviving the Chechen economy. Negotiations over privatization began in the summer of 1997, and rapidly emerged as a major bone of contention between supporters of Maskhadov and the radical opposition. The first projects slated for privatization were announced in the summer of 1998, but the privatization process never really began in earnest.

Since the oil industry appeared to provide the most direct means of generating revenues, the Maskhadov administration regarded it as a top priority, and made great efforts to enforce order in the processing, realization and transport of oil. War had inflicted an estimated 340 billion roubles in damage to oil pipes in Chechnya. The largest processing factories in Grozny were bombed-out shells. Oil was now extracted mainly from fountain wells, because pumps were broken; thieves had stolen the electronics and cables during the war.

From mid-1998 oil revenues trickled into the budget of the republic in very small amounts. Since 1997, the industry had been gradually morphing from a profit-generating sector into a sector that inflicted damage on the Chechen economy (IGPI 10/1997). The government had to spend money not only on the maintenance and security of pipes and equipment but also on extinguishing fires caused by those who illegally extracted oil with disregard for safety measures. The profits from the oil industry were shrinking, month by month.

The primary challenge to the safe and reliable transport of oil through Chechnya were illegal taps in the pipelines. Between February and August 1997 more than 130 such taps were discovered, capable of siphoning off more than 30,000 tons of oil *(Groznensky rabochij,* 28 October 1997). Also, oil products were stolen directly from oil-processing factories. Firms responsible for security at the factories were often complicit in the thefts.

Ad hoc petrol stations and roadside stands hawking illegally extracted petroleum products mushroomed. The authorities banned such trade, but in vain: the illegal suppliers were selling fuel more cheaply than registered petrol stations. During the first six months of 1998, sales at state-owned petrol stations fell tenfold, as against the same period in 1997 (IGPI 06/1998).

In December 1998, the oil-processing enterprises had to stop functioning, due to the mass theft of oil. Five to six new taps were cut into oil pipelines daily. Moreover, the pipeline had essentially been divided up into sectors controlled by different armed groups. Only a small portion of oil reached the processors. In April 1999, representatives from the Chechen oil industry requested the government to deploy the military to protect the supply of oil (IGPI 03/1999). Maskhadov acceded. By July, consumers began to encounter fuel shortages at petrol stations. By then, however, most petrol stations were importing fuel from outside the republic because the Chechen government could no longer satisfy the demand for fuel (*Groznensky rabochij*, 28 July–3 August 1999). Around the same time, delivery of oil from Azerbaijan to Chechnya ceased as well. Chechnya's main source of revenue had nearly evaporated.

Agriculture

The most stable enterprises from 1997 to 1999 were *private* farms, as the agricultural output of Chechnya between the wars was growing steadily. Altogether 1,445 private farms were registered with the government, whereas state agricultural enterprises dwindled in number. Almost all the cattle at state-owned farms had been consumed during the war, and many buildings had been dismantled by local residents, for use in new construction. State-owned farms generally lacked fuel, machinery and qualified staff. The supply of fertilizers and pesticides fell by 35 to 40 per cent (*Ichkeria*, June–July 1998).

The government tried to correct these imbalances by creating coordinating centres aimed at boosting both state and private agriculture. Headquarters like Crop-98 and Crop-99 coordinated efforts aimed at providing farmers with seeds, fuels and spare parts, through a combination of money, barter and various forms of assistance.

Local administrations were worried that agricultural machinery was increasingly non-functional, so land had to be cultivated 'the forefather's way' – with oxen pulling a plough. The dearth of functioning machinery, combined with an insufficient labour force, meant that fields lay fallow. Moreover, cattle-breeding, a traditional industry in the highlands and mountains, also experienced difficult times: almost all veterinarians had left the villages, and many cattle were lost to disease *(Groznensky rabochij*, 27 May–2 June 1999).

Education and healthcare

The federal bombing campaign during the war decimated the republic's educational and medical infrastructure. Among government services, education was the most severely affected by the funding shortage following the war. As the government was unable to rebuild damaged schools, children in many villages studied in refugee wagons. The United Nations High Commissioner for Refugees (UNHCR) financed large-scale reconstruction of schools and medical facilities in villages across the republic, also in the mountains. In 1997 the UNHCR spent $2 million on reconstruction in Chechnya *(Groznensky rabochij*, 4–11 January 1998), but managed to complete projects in only 20 villages.

The republic's 13,665 teachers were not paid for months, depending on transfers from Moscow. However, the Chechen government sought various ways of compensating teachers. In October 1997 teachers reportedly received a portion of their salaries in refined sugar from a partially functioning sugar factory (IGPI 10/1997).

State educational policies sought to reduce not only the scope of school curricula, but the number of educational institutions. In January 1998 a several subjects were temporarily dropped as a result of budget cuts: music, painting, drawing and physical education, among others. New mandatory subjects were introduced: Chechen

Ethics, Arabic, Introduction to Islam and Introduction to *Sharia* and Civil Law. Islam would be taught starting from primary school, and instruction would be delivered in the Chechen language.

At around the same time, the government closed the Chechen Pedagogical Institute, on grounds that it duplicated offerings at Chechen State University, where it already had slashed 1,443 staff and shut down five departments, and 36 major subjects. About a third of all vocational-technical schools were shut down as well (IGPI 06/1998). Moreover, the educational system was suffering from brain drain as a result of the mass exodus of qualified personnel.

Villages in the mountains suffered most. Many teachers had moved to the plains in search of other kinds of paid work. Heating systems in schools had broken down, which made teaching, and studying, especially difficult during cold weather; families could not afford to buy warm clothing for their children. Classes of between 20 and 30 students often shared two or three textbooks. In the South-eastern Vedeno region all 32 schools were closed, due to insufficient funding.

Other schools across the republic reduced the frequency of classes to once or twice a week, and the length of lessons to between 20 and 30 minutes (*Groznensky rabochij*, 3–9 December 1998). Parents regularly took up collections to pay teachers. By May 1999, secondary education across the republic was no longer free of charge, yet the government mandated that no child could be denied an education if his parents were unable to pay (IGPI 06/1999).

Secular education was clearly in deep crisis. The same could not be said for religious education, however. The authorities took pains to support the creation of religious educational institutions, such as the Islamic Institute in Kurchaloy, in which 400 students were enrolled. Branches of the institute were opened in eight other communities. Further, the Grozny Islamic Centre taught children between the ages of 10 and 13 subjects such as Arabic, and how to read and translate the Koran. Most institutions of religious education were free of charge (*Golos Chechenskoi Respubliki*, 28 June 1998).

Also the healthcare system had been crippled by the war, particularly in the mountains. By mid-1998, most villages lacked ambulances, and local midwives had left (*Groznensky rabochij*, 28 October 1997). Some hospitals had been seized by paramilitary groups. Chechnya's tuberculosis hospital, for example, was occupied by a *Sharia* battalion, leaving the clinic to try to meet the needs of the population on its own – something it was not equipped to do. By 1998, the incidence of tuberculosis had doubled from 1994 levels, and deaths had tripled (IGPI 01/1998). The main maternity hospital in Grozny had been seriously damaged by bombing and required major reconstruction. It was ill-equipped to handle the post-war baby boom that swept the republic from 1997 to 1998. During that period, about 50 per cent of all newborns left maternity homes without the requisite vaccinations (IGPI 07/1998).

The depletion of state services, compounded by deteriorating sanitary conditions, resulted in a dramatic increase in acute intestinal infections, especially in cities. In 1997, reported incidences of such infections rose by 43 per cent over the previous year. Officials attributed this spike to the lack of modern infrastructure for the purification and chlorination of water, in addition to failing sewerage systems, unmonitored food sales, and water and soil pollution from illegal oil-processing activities (IGPI 06/1998).

The quality of treatment provided to former combatants was an exception: funding allocated to former fighters by the Health Ministry – for travel to Arab countries and Azerbaijan for prostheses and other medical care – was quite significant. A special foundation for participants in the war, Support, was established to address problems related to unemployment and the health of veterans; among the programmes was the creation of collective farms to be staffed by former fighters (IGPI 10/1997). In view of the high rates of unemployment, the government assisted field commanders in finding jobs for their fighters in order to ease their return to civilian life (IGPI 10/1997). Thus, the government delegated some of its functions to field commanders, who felt responsible for the financial well-being of their rank-and-file fighters during peacetime.

Former combatants also were permitted to enrol in Chechen State University without taking entrance exams. This resulted in serious disciplinary problems and disrupted the educational process, Tamara Elbuzdukaeva, former dean of the university's history department, told me in an interview.

The armed forces

Following the war, the official armed forces of the republic encompassed the special forces of the Defence Ministry, the National Guard and the Anti-Terrorist Centre. All three groups were nominally subordinate to President Maskhadov, who also was in charge of units of the Ministry of State Sharia Defence (the Sharia Guard, the Islamic Regiment), the National Security Service and the state frontier-customs troops (Tishkov 1998). Altogether, the armed forces in the republic had 53 generals – one for every 300 officers (IGPI 12/1998).

In the spring of 1997 Maskhadov set about re-organizing the command structure of the armed forces. On 13 March he founded the National Guard, which was designated as the only regular armed unit and was to consist of 2,000 troops (Muzaev 1997). In May that year he abolished the headquarters of the wartime fronts in favour of formal military bases and adopted the Statute of Armed Forces (Muzaev 1997). Then, in November, the Parliament adopted a law aimed at ensuring better control of the spread of weapons. Later government repeatedly introduced measures for buying confiscated weapons, none of which worked (Akhmadov and Lanskoy 2010: 97). There was a thriving weapons market in downtown Grozny.

On the whole, government efforts to demilitarize the republic proved ineffective. Field commanders brushed off Maskhadov's efforts at reorganization – most assuming various roles, such as police officers, private security firms and personal guards for field commanders (Muzaev 1997). 'Groups were splitting and multiplying. Authority was splintered among them into thousands of little pieces, so that in the end there was no real authority', former Foreign Minister Ilyas Akhmadov explained in his book (Akhmadov and Lanskoy 2010: 95).

Law enforcement and criminality

Criminality was the main domestic challenge for Chechen leaders from 1997 to 1999. The theft of oil, and the illegal seizure of oil-industry property, paralysed the industry to such an extent that farms were unable to keep the petrol tanks of their tractors filled, and the oil-rich republic began to *import* fuel. Hostage-taking and the murder of hostages severely undermined the Chechen cause.

Widespread housing fraud with residential property, and attacks on non-Chechens in order to take over their flats, led to another exodus of the non-Chechen population from the republic. Everyone in the government recognized that taming criminality was crucial to the very existence of the Chechen state. However, the sources of this social evil were differently perceived by supporters of President Maskhadov and by the radical opposition. Maskhadov's team saw crime as an internal problem, and considered paramilitary groups and criminal gangs to be the main disruptive forces. By contrast, his opponents blamed the soaring crime rates mainly on espionage and collaboration with Russia among some pro-Russian segments of the population. They agitated for a purge from the republic of spies and collaborators, and pushed for a strengthening of counter-intelligence, as well as the adoption of a law on lustration, which would allow a purge of Russia supporters from all levels of government.

Abu Movsaev, a close friend and ally of Basaev, and the first director of the National Security Service (SNB, or *Sluzhba Natsionalnoi Bezopasnosti*), was an adherent of the latter point of view. His agency was manned by ex-combatants, many of whom had dubious, even criminal, pasts; often these men provided cover for, and sometimes participated in, various illegal activities.

For this reason, Movsaev was forced to resign in July 1997. He was replaced by Khultygov, the wartime general and Maskhadov supporter, who took a tough line on crime. Khultygov basically declared war on crime, branding former combatants who engaged in illegal activities as enemies of the Chechen nation and state. He went on to purge the SNB of criminal elements, and even introduced public executions of criminals (IGPI 06/1998).

Maskhadov himself personally supervised law-enforcement agencies, which adopted three main priorities: to combat the theft of oil, hostage-taking and drug trafficking. Regular armed forces were deployed in support of combating oil theft, including local police and a special battalion of the Department for the Security of the State. Several times in 1998/1999 Maskhadov called up former combatant reservists in support of his efforts to stop oil theft and to tame criminal gangs.

The state policy on combat of crime involved routine measures along with special 'campaigns' – raids on criminal formations which usually mobilized almost all of the republican security services. The first round in a series of campaigns named the 'Shield of Legal Order' was launched in late May 1997. The next was carried out in June in response to the abduction of Russian journalists – three correspondents of NTV channel and two reporters of the TV Company 'VID'. Joint units of the security forces checked all vehicles in the main thoroughfares of Grozny, and searched all vacant buildings and basements, while special groups carried out checks in villages, including those high in the mountains. The journalists were not found, but the security services released six other hostages who had been taken for ransom, detained three persons wanted for murders, and arrested several individuals suspected of burglary and thefts (Zapodinskaya 1997).

The Maskhadov administration was well aware that the criminal groups were linked with the main regime challengers – radical opposition groups. Small gangs had patrons among major field commanders and their larger armed formations. Thus, each round of the 'Shield of Order' was accompanied with attempts to dissolve major political-military armed groups. The first of such raids against organized crime coincided with Maskhadov's June decree on dissolving the 'Army of Dzhokhar Dudaev' led by Raduev and another armed group regiment of special assignment troops – 'Borz' (Wolf). The Prosecutor's Office instigated several criminal cases against former combatants in connection with abductions and illegal violence.

In December 1998, Chechnya was shattered by a particularly shocking crime: the murder and beheading of four engineers of the British company Granger Telecom, which dealt a dramatic blow to the Chechen cause and the credibility of the incumbent government. A new round of the 'Shield of Legal Order' launched in December 1998 detained 596 persons, including 78 wanted criminals; and several hostages were released (*Groznensky rabochij*, 3–9 and 24–30 December 1998).

Despite large-scale efforts, taming organized crime was not easy. Russia and international organizations paid enormous ransoms for hostages, which led to further hostage-taking and brought resources into the hands of criminal gangs. Chechen law-enforcement agencies were confronted with large and well-armed groups. Thus, in June 1998 the Prosecutor General of the Chechen Republic Ichkeria instigated a criminal case into the capture of oil wells belonging to 'Grozneft' by an illegal armed group of around 200 people. Such criminal groups were prepared to defend their interests by arms, whereas Maskhadov was still cautious of spilling Chechen blood. As a result, his law-enforcement agencies were impotent when confronted with aggressive armed criminals. For example, in August 1998 the special battalion of the Department for the Security of the State, supported by police units, suffered a major defeat when it failed to gain control over two oil wells illegally captured by fundamentalist armed groups (*Golos Chechenskoi Respubliki*, 20 August 1998). The security services limited themselves to issuing warnings and trying to regain strategic objects by negotiating with criminals.

The law-enforcement agencies had some successes, but these remained inadequate. The security services were paralysed by the inability to resort to force, as was President Maskhadov in his political strategy. 'In the post-war society, taking on the opposition in an aggressive manner would have meant killing them. So to accuse Maskhadov of weakness is to blame him for not becoming a ruthless dictator and physically destroying his opponents', Ilyas Akhmadov wrote in his memoirs (Akhmadov and Lanskoy 2010: 100). However, building a state requires establishing a monopoly of violence – which Maskhadov spectacularly failed to do.

Judicial system

The judicial system in Chechnya from 1997 to 1999 was based on Islamic law: the transition from secular to *Sharia* law had taken place without the consent of the population. A major problem of the *Sharia* judicial system was the low qualification of judges. This was not surprising, as the republic was suddenly forced to staff all courts. Short-term courses for judges were taught by Kebedov, who typically trained young men with no background in law. *Sharia* courts in Chechnya initially based their rulings on the criminal codes of various Muslim countries, including Sudan (Akaev, interview 2008). On 1 June 1999, the Parliament passed the Criminal Code of Ichkeria (Muzaev 06/1999).

Political crises and government response

Although I rarely met a Chechen (apart from the current authorities) who held strongly negative opinions about Maskhadov, he is commonly characterized as a 'weak' or 'soft' politician by nearly everyone – average citizens, former combatants and outside observers.

Initially Maskhadov enjoyed a good reputation throughout the republic, and was respected by various paramilitary groups. But, unlike Dudaev – who had been accepted unquestioningly as the leader – Maskhadov was only one among many outstanding wartime field commanders, and many of his peers found it difficult to accept his authority.

'Maskhadov as a president, and as a person, was a far cry from Dudaev', said Salambek, a former fighter. 'You know how Dudaev talked to guys like Basaev and Gelaev? [*field commanders – E.S.*] He scolded them. "You're not doing your jobs! I don't see any progress – you're giving up positions!" Everyone respected him because he was clever, because he knew better. He taught them everything they knew [*about combat – E.S.*]. He was the authority for all of them.'

Khozh, the former combatant, also described Maskhadov as a good person, but very weak. 'His main mistake was to become president. When the war was over, they should have united and elected one candidate [*from among field commanders – E.S.*]. But Basaev decided to divide the people. He thought he was *the* national hero. Basaev resented not being elected president, I think.'

In evaluating the successes and failures of the Chechen state-building project 1997–1999, it is important to keep in mind both the legacy of the war, and the priorities of the ruling elite. The war was very destructive, but it was victorious. The achievements on the battlefield forged several national heroes, each of whom felt entitled to a chunk of state power. Moreover, the political status of the quasi-independent state had not been settled.

No country had recognized Chechen independence, so the lack of demobilization was tolerated by the society. The main priority of Maskhadov's government – repeatedly expressed by him and by members of his inner circle – was to avoid internal schism and civil war. His administration was challenged by heavily armed groups that used Islam to further their political ends and to raise money. They all got resources from somewhere: some from Islamists abroad, others from affluent Chechen businessmen who sought to buy influence, yet others from hostage-taking and illegal oil extraction (Akhmadov and Lanskoy 2010: 101–120).

The examples of Afghanistan and post-Soviet Tajikistan were fresh in Maskhadov's mind. He was well aware that while such groups, and not the entire society, were shaping the political future of his country, a civil war between them would tear apart the entire nation, and blood feud would come into play. He also understood that civil war would be used by Russia as a reason for another invasion.

Maskhadov's strategy was to keep field commanders at bay by means of concessions. For example, Raduev, the commander of the army of Dzhokhar Dudaev, began to challenge Maskhadov immediately after the elections. He criticized Maskhadov for compromising with Moscow, for including old communists in the government and for dragging his feet when it came to the Islamization of public life. Raduev organized numerous demonstrations, parades and rallies during which he threatened to 'take action'. In June 1997, only four months after the formation of the new Chechen government, other field commanders joined Raduev in accusing Maskhadov of facilitating the 'rehabilitation of collaborators' – those who secretly supported Russia. Basaev, Gelaev and Movsaev left his administration. The elite coalition was broken.

At this stage, the schism was only ideological – and limited to public criticism. Pressure on Maskhadov was mounting, and in late December 1997 he made his first serious concessions to the radical opposition. He appointed Shamil Basaev to the post of Executive Prime Minister, and transferred most executive powers (which according to the Constitution were to be in the hands of the president) to him. Basaev pledged to bring crime under control and solve social problems. He brought with him a team of people, including his brother Shirvani (Akhmadov and Lanskoy 2010: 135).

Khussein Iskhanov, Member of the Chechen Parliament 1997–1999, explained to me why Maskhadov made such a questionable choice to empower his main rival:

> Basaev was appointed as Executive Prime Minister to show how difficult it was, having no funding, to raise the country from the ruins. Shamil at that time was young and was hugely popular among parts of the population. His criticisms [of Maskhadov] were neither useful nor supported by facts. After being prime minister he understood and re-evaluated many things. Basaev had been a hero during the war, but he was totally unprepared for life in peacetime.

Basaev failed all social issues and used his new post primarily to advance Islamist values in Chechnya. By 1998 fundamentalist Muslims were aggressively codifying Islamic norms in the towns and villages. Crime did not concern them: but mores did. A Chechen friend described how every day her mother would accompany her from Argun to Grozny to attend university lectures, being afraid of aggressive bearded men who checked buses and harassed girls if their sleeves were too short. Another colleague described how when she travelled by car with her brothers they could any time be stopped, and bearded men would demand to know their relationship. *Sharia* courts issued lashes to drunkards.

As deputy editor at a local newspaper, told me:

> I had a café in which my wife and a female relative worked. One day, after the first war, [the women] ran to my office and shouted that bearded guy with guns had broken into the café. I rushed over. They didn't find any alcohol, but they screamed, 'Who is this woman? What kind of relationship do you have to her?'

I said, 'This is my wife, and this is my relative.' They said, 'Why are these women working here? Women are not supposed to work in places where men go. We'll give you two days. Unless you fix this problem, we'll burn down your café.'

By the spring of 1998 the number of kidnappings for ransom had soared. Some hostages were later discovered in fundamentalist strongholds. Moreover, fundamentalists active in the republic often quoted a section of the Koran which they said justified taking infidels hostage for ransom. Maskhadov's Anti-Terrorist Centre mounted an attack in March on the fundamentalist base in Urus-Martan, but failed to destroy the base, or achieve the release of hostages. Two months later, as Chechen radicals were increasingly calling for military intervention on behalf of their Islamist brothers in neighbouring Dagestan, radicals raided Alleroy, Maskhadov's village of origin. Several women were harassed, and a man from Maskhadov's *teip* was shot.

Government forces gave chase to the attackers and caught up with them in the town of Gudermes. There, nearly 2,000 men – among them Chechens, Avars and even Arabs – clashed after the leaders had agreed not to use guns, in order lessen the risk of blood feud. 'During several hours of the most brutal fighting, only one shot could be heard – injuring Maskhadov's guard, who knocked the Wahhabists off of him like sheaves of wheat' (*Vlast*, 30 June 1998).

This was the first violent clash between government and radical opposition groups since the end of the war. The protagonists were unarmed, but it was massive in scale because of the sheer number of participants. It also sent a signal to Maskhadov: armed clashes were on the horizon.

After the fighting in Gudermes, Basaev resigned in protest, citing government measures 'against comrades in the resistance'. His resignation came in the wake of severe criticisms in Parliament for his failures in office (Muzaev 2004).

Basaev's resignation was a political victory for Maskhadov: the main challenger to his authority, who had been given as much power as he wanted (short of becoming president), had failed. Basaev lost not only his political influence but also his credibility in criticizing Maskhadov – especially for the continued failure to alleviate social problems and crime, the issue over which Maskhadov was most vulnerable.

Following the Gudermes incident, Maskhadov's forces re-established control over government buildings and military posts in Grozny (Muzaev 2004). Peace was temporarily restored. However, Basaev was not prepared to give up. With his heroic image fading rapidly, he became increasingly involved in Salafism, and political projects aligned with it. In June 1998 he organized a permanent Congress of the Peoples of Chechnya and Dagestan, appointing himself its leader. Through the Congress Basaev hoped to revive the nineteenth-century imamate of Dagestan and Chechnya, which had been led by the legendary Imam Shamil (Malashenko and Trenin 2004: 34). Basaev's aim was to hijack the state from his rival, Maskhadov, by creating a new political entity – a union of Chechnya and Dagestan, with him as a new Imam Shamil.

The political power struggle in Chechnya came to a head the following month, when on 14 July the National Guard tried to disarm fundamentalist groups in Gudermes. Several dozen people were killed in the resulting clashes, and many more were injured. Later it was revealed that fighters in two government units – the Sharia Guard and the

Islamic Regiment– had switched sides during the operation, indicating that Islamists had seized control of a significant part of the republic's armed forces (IGPI 07/1998).

Two days later Maskhadov made his first tough public statements criticizing Wahhabists. He mobilized his supporters, among them former combatant reservists, and demanded that fundamentalist leaders leave the republic within 24 hours. He also dissolved the Sharia Guard and the Islamic Regiment. One week later, on 23 July, came a failed assassination attempt on Maskhadov. The government blamed the attack on radical Islamists, and prosecutors summoned leaders of the radical opposition for questioning. Fearing public disgrace, opposition leaders, including Basaev, declared their support for Maskhadov.

Later that year, Maskhadov made new concessions to opposition leaders, and agreed to adopt a law on lustration, which, through special courts, would regulate the participation of former communists in government and civil service. In doing so, Maskhadov sacrificed yet another principle of his administration for the sake of a sham consolidation. According to Akhmadov, government officials had to undergo a meaningless and humiliating procedure, in which they were asked professionally irrelevant questions, such as 'exactly how many times a day [they] prayed' (Akhmadov and Lanskoy 2010: 80).

On 3 February 1999, Maskhadov co-opted the slogans of the radical opposition and announced the introduction of 'full *Sharia* rule' throughout the republic. He created a special state commission for the drafting of a '*Sharia* Constitution of the Chechen Republic of Ichkeria'. In this new *Sharia* state, the Parliament would relinquish its legislative powers to the *Shura*, an Islamic council made up of prominent field commanders and Islamic scholars. (IGPI 2/1999)

The announcement caught the radical opposition flat-footed: Maskhadov had suddenly met all their demands. Basaev immediately declared his full support for the president. However, the Khattab-sponsored newspaper, *Al-Kaf*, wrote that the declaration of Islamic rule was a hypocritical political manoeuvre aimed at blunting the vigilance of all Muslims. Several days later, Basaev and his supporters said in a statement that they would not join the *Shura* created by Maskhadov, but would create their own *Shura*, with Basaev as emir (IGPI 2/1999). The Parliament – which had been previously extremely supportive of Maskhadov – now declared the introduction of *Sharia* rule unconstitutional and in violation of the basis of the Chechen state, and created a special commission to impeach him *(Groznensky rabochij*, 25 February –3 March 1999). The legislators refused to give up their posts.

As a result of this final concession to the opposition, Maskhadov both won, and lost. On one hand, he managed to show the Chechen populace the real face of his opponents: it was not Islam they were fighting for, but power. On the other hand, he destroyed the very foundation of Chechen statehood – the Chechen Constitution of 1992, and the institutions of direct popular vote and a secular executive – which also was the basis for his own legitimacy. Moreover, he further alienated his supporters – not least the Parliament, which had been loyal to him throughout the crises of 1997/1998. Nonetheless, Maskhadov continued to enjoy popular support, and on 15 March up to 50,000 people rallied in downtown Grozny in favour of his programmes (IGPI 03/1999).

In parallel, over the next two weeks two unsuccessful attempts would be made on his life.

In keeping with his methods of bold initiative followed by concession, Maskhadov had retrenched his position by the end of April. He returned legislative powers to Parliament – after the MPs agreed to cosmetic changes to the Constitution, by adding quotes from the Koran and hadiths ascribed to the Prophet Muhammad. He also pushed through a major reorganization of the security services.

In addition, Maskhadov began increasingly to whip up popular sentiment. His slogans calling for the eradication of crime – and blaming Arabs for unravelling Chechen unity – were resonating more and more deeply (IGPI 03/1999). In many villages, supporters of Maskhadov responded by forming militias and public councils aimed at keeping out those who did not live in accordance with Chechen traditions, who divided Muslims, who incited violence or who simply challenged the president (*Groznensky rabochij*, 1–7 April 1999).

By the end of the month the radical opposition had finally been neutralized. Even Yandarbiev, the most radical ideological challenger to Maskhadov, called for compromise (IGPI, April 1999). Thus, Maskhadov brought informal groups into power and had satisfied all their political demands – including the transformation of Chechnya into an Islamic state. At the same time, he launched several tough offensives on the radical opposition. And when his political opponents appeared weak, he quickly implemented reforms which they opposed, but which were instrumental to the state-building effort, such as the reorganization of the army, the purging of crooks from the security services, protecting Sufi *tariqas* or the introduction of educational standards for police and judges. In the words of Akhmadov and Lanskoy, 'he was walking a tightrope; every time he tried to do something constructive, all the splinter groups united against him' (Akhmadov and Lanskoy 2010: 100).

Maskhadov, as a state-builder, had lost. He was unable to dissolve the informal opposition presented by combat-ready groups or to revive the economy. He failed to resuscitate the oil industry, whose revenues would have provided him with resources to sustain the state sector, infrastructure and the courts.

As a politician, however, Maskhadov had won. By mid-1999, leaders of the radical opposition had realized that they had little to gain in Chechnya and accepted his moral authority. Moreover, Maskhadov had avoided bloodshed and civil war among Chechens, which was his key priority. However, he did not foresee that Basaev would set his sights elsewhere and, in the end, attack Dagestan.

In summer 1999 there were frequent armed clashes between federal and Chechen forces on the Chechnya/Dagestan administrative border. In August and September, Basaev and Khattab led a military incursion in support of their 'Muslim brothers' for 'freeing [...] Dagestani Muslims from occupation by the infidels' (ICG, October 2012). Shortly thereafter, Russia launched the Second Chechen War.

All former combatants whom I interviewed strongly disapproved of Basaev's excursion into Dagestan. Ruslan said: 'This was such a terrible mistake, to go into Dagestan! To give such a trump card to Russia!' Later Shamil tried to explain himself, saying that [Russia] had already planned it, and would have invaded, anyway. But he was given $16 million to $17 million to prepare for new war with Moscow. So, in order not to lose this money, he invaded', Ruslan told me with strong resentment. 'But I always thought, "Shamil, you had to understand, it's one thing if they attack first, and another thing if we attack first!" How could we expect any support for our cause after that?! But he could have cared less. Honestly, I have never wished death to any Chechen, but when I learned that he had been killed, I felt malicious joy, and revenge. This man pushed our nation to the abyss. And I had voted for him in 1997.'

Salambek described the period from 1997 to 1999 in this way: 'We were not able to preserve our patriotism, our victory. We defeated the Russian soldiers and went home. But instead of creating and multiplying, we started to destroy. That's why the second war was Allah's punishment.'

State-building: informal institutions and practices

The lack of success in post-war state-building projects in Chechnya may be attributed to the incapacity of the Maskhadov government to subdue the radical opposition and paramilitary groups that openly challenged the regime, undermining the political process in a perpetual struggle for power. Criminal groups, usually linked directly or indirectly with paramilitaries, squandered state property and paralysed the oil industry – the main source of revenue – in the republic. Without the oil revenues, the government did not have enough money to restore the shattered education and healthcare systems, let alone rebuild infrastructure and the transportation system. And then the second war broke out.

Unlike the state-building project under Dudaev, when mountain people suffered less than those living on the plains, during the second bout of state-building, the mountain areas were particularly hard hit: schools and medical clinics were destroyed, and people reverted to 'the ways of their forefathers' to cultivate land. *Sharia* was perhaps the only thing that the state was able to deliver.

Paramilitary groups

The rise of paramilitary groups directly engaged in crime was new to Chechnya. Most of the paramilitaries positioned themselves as formal political forces (political parties) with their own mouthpieces, or newspapers – but they remained armed groups, first and foremost. The social make-up of the paramilitaries was heterogeneous. Their differences with the government were over power but were framed as an ideological divide.

Initially, former combatants constitute the core membership of these groups. Gradually, others were drawn in – friends, relatives and co-villagers – with whom members had personal connections. After the war their main activities were political-economic; they provided resources to their members and supporters. Concerning the distribution of resources, the social composition of the groups leaned toward more ascriptive ties.

Religion and ideology

The emergence and vigorous dissemination of a new religious trend – Islamic fundamentalism, primarily in the forms of Salafism – created a deep schism between Sufi and new fundamentalist leaders. The schism has persisted to this day.

The Islamists who dominated the public sphere under Maskhadov opposed the traditional Chechen *virds*. As a result, the political role of *tariqas* was next to nil until the near-breakout of the Second Chechen War. Only in late 1998 – when popular resistance to Islamic fundamentalists had become stronger – did Sufi leaders, wary of being attacked for their own religious practices, join in efforts to reduce the influence of fundamentalists.

The then-*mufti* of Chechnya, Akhmad-Khadzhi-Kadyrov, a Sufi, emerged in 1998 as the republic's most outspoken opponent of Wahhabism. He described Muslim fundamentalists as 'enemies of Islam', and demanded that they be deported from Chechnya. Several attempts were made on his life, but that did not stop him from defending his religious convictions. Maskhadov had worked with Kadyrov, but they were not close allies. In an interview, a close relative of Maskhadov told me that Maskhadov ultimately did not trust Kadyrov.

The Islamists sought to erase not only *vird* divisions in Chechnya, but nationalism as well. Political nationalism – the driving force behind Dudaev's revolution, and early state-building, and the First Chechen War – was hijacked by Islamist slogans. Maskhadov was a nationalist. But he also was an Islamist. With the spread of rigid Islam throughout government and among youth, secular nationalists did not dare to expose themselves in public.

Regional opposition

The town of Urus-Martan again occupied a special place during the second attempt at state-building, but this time it underwent a remarkable change from being pro-Russian to being pro-Islamist. According to my interviewees, several factors contributed to this development: 1) 'The betrayal of Urus-Martan by Russia', as it was popularly believed; 2) Maskhadov sought to control anti-separatist Urus-Martan by allowing Islamist leaders and military bases there; 3) repressions against pro-Russian elites after the withdrawal of Russian troops

As a former official in the local administration explained to me:

> During the war, Urus-Martan maintained neutrality. Neither federal forces nor Dudaev's troops entered the city because we had our own guards and defended the city. At the same time, both sides in the war saw Urus-Martan as a haven. Injured fighters and federal troops were brought here and given medical assistance in the hospital. After the withdrawal of Russian troops, Urus-Martan was taken over by Maskhadov's fighters. In 1996, our leader, Yusup Elmurzaev, was killed. After Urus-Martan lost its leader, the people were disoriented. They were tired of combat, and felt they were alone against this armed barrage. A law on lustration was passed. Everyone who worked in pro-Russian institutions was fired, including

the cleaning ladies. Former opposition leaders were arrested, thrown in cellars, beaten and subjected to torture. In order to protect themselves, many joined the Islamists.

Interviewees recalled how Islamist groups established themselves in Urus-Martan gradually, almost imperceptibly. By 1997, they were firmly in control. According to a journalist at the local newspaper, it had become impossible to resist their influence:

> There was a local family, the Akhmadovs. There were nine brothers, one of whom fought in Afghanistan, and then in Abkhazia with Basaev. They joined the Islamists and helped them settle into the town. The Islamists set up headquarters in administrative buildings, at a boarding school. Maskhadov supported their resettlement in order to keep Urus-Martan from rising up against his regime. Islamists from all over the region moved here. They had money, they bought houses. They were from Dagestan, from Arab countries. They married local girls. Then the veils, black dresses for women, started appearing ... At some point there were checkpoints at the entrances to schools, for enforcement of dress codes.
>
> Conflicts sprung up within families over schisms between Wahhabists and supporters of traditional Sufi Islam. Families were falling apart. People stopped talking to each other – brothers and cousins, for example. There were so many fights over this, even incidents of murder. A son killed his father for rejecting Wahhabism.

My respondents noted that the Islamists tended to stay within the confines of their headquarters while the population of the town moved about, living as they always had – but taking additional basic precautions. As a local journalist told me:

> We had a wedding for my nephew, a regular wedding with alcohol and all that. One of our neighbours came in and noticed that some people were drinking. As he was leaving he said, 'I'm going to report this to the Sharia police!' I said, 'Just go ahead and try it! We'll see how you'll come back here and live among us.' He left – but he never reported us.

Chechen communities like Urus-Martan had become accustomed to living under politically repressive regimes: on the surface they complied, but underneath they tried to live their normal lives.

Teips and Elders

In February 1999, a well-known Chechen businessman, Khoz-Akhmed Nukhaev, issued a declaration 'On the basis of organizing state institutions in Chechnya'. In it he proposed re-organizing the state according to the traditional *teip* hierarchy. The highest authority would be the *Mekhk-Khel* (Council of Land), and the head of state would be the popularly elected *Mekhk-Da* (Father of Land). Instead of a parliament there would be a Supreme Legislative Council (*Lor Is*) made up of representatives of the nine *tukhums* (*teip* unions).

Nukhaev believed that a government based on national institutions would guarantee state sovereignty, and unity, for the Chechen people (*Groznensky rabochij*, 23 January – 3 February 1999). His proposal resonated with some nationalists, particularly supporters of the marginal nationalist party, *Nokhchi* (Chechens) (IGPI 04/1999). No other political institutions or groups embraced the cause, however.

According to historian Timur Muzaev, this proposal of a *teip*-based system of government was largely an attempt to find alternatives to *Sharia* rule and the 'Arabization' of Chechnya (IGPI 04/1999). The main drawback with this proposal was its very foundations: its proponents assumed that the *teips* were still accountable to their members, and that each member was still accountable to his *teip*. However, if that had been the case, the rampant criminality in Chechnya in the 1990s would never have been allowed to emerge in the first place.

Another instance when *teip* representatives tried to play a role in Maskhadov's period was when a delegation visited Maskhadov and offered him their support – on one condition. The Chechen ethnologist, Said-Magomed Khasiev, recalled the meeting:

> After he had been elected, a delegation of representatives of *teip*s – people concerned about the fate of the state, both old and young – came to Maskhadov and said, 'All these generals, their headquarters should be liquidated. Everyone should take up spades and axes and get to work. If you cannot stop them, we will.'
>
> 'These are my comrades in arms, my friends. We fought together. I can't do that', was his response. That was the end of the conversation.

The role of the Elders gained no more traction than did the *teips* in state-building under Maskhadov. Elders were not visible in the public sphere, nor were they paid any special respect. Even at the local level, their roles were dramatically diminished.

'When young people have weapons in their hands, they don't ask Elders for advice. Leaders from among the youth began to distinguish themselves, and they took control of villages', said Ilyas, from the village of Shatoy.

*Teip*s and their most respected members played negligible roles in the political process from 1997 to 1999 – but one longstanding element of traditional Chechen life – blood feud – played a very prominent role. Indeed, Maskhadov's notorious 'weakness' stemmed from his caution over inciting a series of blood feuds across the republic.

Descent, kinship and personal networks in Maskhadov's elite

Maskhadov's hiring practices, much like those of Dudaev, were not oriented toward *teips* or other kinship affiliations: more important were ideology and shared values, as well as the political necessity of appeasing the radical opposition. The only member of Maskhadov's inner circle who was a relative was his nephew, Turpal-Ali Atgeriev, Minister of Defence.

The Minister of Agriculture was from the Alleroy *teip*, as was Maskhadov, but this had little to do with nepotism: Alleroy is one of the two largest *teips* in Chechnya. If anything, they were not overrepresented in Maskhadov's administration. As noted by the ethnologist, Said-Magomed Khasiev, also a member of the Alleroy *teip*:

> [Maskhadov] had the support of the Alleroy people, but if he had listened to the most respected members of his *teip*, there would not have been such anarchy. He dismissed all their suggestions, didn't follow even one bit of reasonable advice he was given. For Maskhadov, *teip* had no relevance whatsoever. He was outside the *teip* framework.

Maskhadov came from the Alleroy people in the village of Zebel-Yurt, in the pro-Russian Nadterechny region. His wife was also a Nadterechny Chechen. When Russia retreated after the first war, Nadterechny Chechens recognized the Maskhadov government – and many in the region supported Maskhadov, not only as the most moderate among the major field commanders, but as their *zemlyak* ('countryman', a person from the same geographical area).

Adam Dukhaev, editor of the regional newspaper, *Terkjist* in Nadterechny, said that, although Maskhadov clearly had the support Nadterechny Chechens, he deliberately chose not to bring them into the government. 'He was afraid of being accused of favouritism, of being called a traitor for inviting Nadterechny Chechens, who were known for their pro-Russian stance. That's why Basaev, in fact, overthrew and betrayed him in the end, because [Maskhadov] was not surrounded by people close to him.'

In practice, the constant challenges to Maskhadov's legitimacy by his opponents served as a peculiar system of checks and balances that deterred nepotism. Relatives could be found among his personal guard responsible for his security, but mostly his guards were his former comrades in arms during the war. Khussein, Maskhadov's close associate and a member of personal guard, told me:

> Maskhadov's security problems started long before war. I worked in the general staff and in his personal security team. Already at that time there was real risk for him, I was staying next to him 24 hours a day. After the elections of 1997 when he was elected President, the risks really increased. The first attempt to blow up his car came one month after the elections: it was unsuccessful, his car was slightly damaged, that's all. The second attempt was made on the Staropromyslovsky highway of Grozny. He was on his way from home to work when a remote-controlled explosive went off. He was in an armoured jeep, the security guard in front lost one eye and the driver was killed on the spot. No one else in the vehicle was injured. The jeep was in flames, Maskhadov got caught inside, something happened with the locks, the guys hardly managed to open the doors and get Maskhadov out. After this, we took routine security measures – changed his routes, as much as that was possible in a small place like Grozny. Our special services also worked to prevent new attempts on his life. But he did not focus too much on his own security, he never had strong fears. Even during the war I saw

how in the some of the worst bombings and shootings even his eyes would not blink. He was a real military man, he was not afraid of death, he never had any kind of paranoia about security.

When I asked Khussein how Maskhadov protected himself from the traitors in his inner circle, he explained that there was no such a risk at that time. 'After such a horrendous bloody war, in which we lost our comrades in arms, there was no place for betrayal. Possibly there were attempts to infiltrate, to emplace agents closer to him, but such infiltration was impossible because we all knew each other too well.'

Thus, it seems Maskhadov, just like Dudaev was fatalistic about his future, and probably understood that he was likely to die on the path that he had chosen. His risk management was based on surrounding himself with a tight group of trusted people, most of whom were not relatives but brothers-in-arms, united by the common wartime experience which had made them very close.

This chapter has demonstrated that under Maskhadov, the Mannian infrastructural power deteriorated much further than it had been under Dzhokhar Dudaev (Mann 1993 6, 7). Chechnya lay in ruins, and from 1997 to 1999 the government's ability to deliver social services was extremely limited. The systems of education and healthcare remained standing thanks to the enthusiasm of employees and to financial contributions (sometimes in the form of barter goods) from students and patients.

State-building in Chechnya after the first war came to be defined by the emergence of field commanders backed by sizeable paramilitary groups who agitated for the Islamization of the fledgling state and unflagging defiance in negotiations with Russia. Under the cover of slogans calling for the incorporation of a stricter interpretation of Islam not only in government, but in public life, these radical rivals of President Aslan Maskhadov – effectively warlords – kept trying to undercut his ability to govern, while at the same time gaining more power for themselves and refusing to demobilize their groups.

Maskhadov responded to threats to his power and life primarily through concessions – interspersed with rare offensives. Despite the highly flammable situation, Maskhadov managed to avoid civil war, and to purge the state security services of criminal elements. He begun to finally register modest successes in combating organized crime when Basaev and Khattab invaded neighbouring Dagestan, marking the beginning of the end of his government, and the second attempt at building an independent Chechen state in the North Caucasus.

Similar to the 1991–1994 state-building effort, the main challengers to the stability of the government from 1997 to 1999 were not pre-existing but newly emerging patterns of integration – in this case, paramilitary groups and ideological and regional oppositions. *Teips* and *virds* – marginalized by an ascendant Islamist ideology deeply opposed to ethnic and subnational divisions, played no role in government appointments or in state-building, in general. Their attitude to the government was accommodating. *Vird* affiliation grew slightly in importance as anti-fundamentalist sentiment became stronger in 1999, but never served as a source for popular mobilization.

Relations between the state apparatus and its informal challengers between 1997 and 1999 can be described as *compartmentalization* and *competition*, but also to a certain degree *capture* of the state by informal challengers, which occurred with the consent of Maskhadov and at his invitation. The internal constraints on the government were strong, mainly due to very strong opposition which prevented nepotism based on ascriptive ties. At the same time the formal system of checks and balances was weak.

The risk of physical elimination by Russia and by the domestic armed opposition was very high. While the risk of prosecution for illegal economic activity was negligible. The very high risks of physical elimination in Maskhadov's case were mitigated by basic precautions, like entrusting his personal security to close brothers-in-arms and his ability to look openly on the face of death. Maskhadov did not aim to build a clan for protection.

Chechnya under Maskhadov most closely approximates Migdal's concept of 'state-in-society', where control maybe concentrated among various groups rather than in the state; and where states not only mould societies, but can be continuously shaped by them (Migdal, Kohli and Shue 1994: 2; Migdal 1988: 28). According to this model, Maskhadov's state was not a fixed ideological entity. It changed under pressure from informal actors, which grew in strength proportionally to their capacity to deliver protection and generate income for supporters, providing them with what Migdal called 'individual strategies of survival' (1988: 27). In this mélange of social organizations, Maskhadov's state was one organization among many, just as Maskhadov was one of the many prominent field commanders of the First Chechen War, who claimed a share of power.

The Second Chechen War proved to be bloodier and more brutal than the first one. Aslan Maskhadov led the Chechen separatist armed forces until 8 March 2004, when he was killed in an operation by the Russian Federal Services in the village of Tolstoy-Yurt. A few hours after this, my colleagues from Memorial and I arrived at the site to document the arrests of his host and comrades, who had been captured alive. We saw what remained of the bunker where Maskhadov had spent the last two months of his life: a closed underground space, roughly $2 \times 2 \times 2$ metres. From there he had tried to reach out to Moscow with an initiative to conclude some kind of peace. There has been no peace accord after the Second Chechen War, which is officially termed a 'counter-terrorism operation' that was declared to be completed in 2009.

7

State-Building in Ingushetia under Ruslan Aushev (1992–2001)

National movements, founding of the Republic

The Ingush national movement emerged during the early years of *perestroika*. The driving force behind the movement were Ingush intellectuals who agitated for the return of the Prigorodny Region, which formerly belonged to Ingushetia but had been declared part of North Ossetia in 1944 following the Stalinist deportation of Ingush and Chechens to Central Asia.

That autumn 1988, a congress of ethnic Ingush was held in Grozny, then the capital of the Chechen-Ingush Republic. The main issue was the return of former Ingush lands, and the restoration of Ingush autonomy. The Congress elected Issa Kodzoev, a schoolteacher, poet and dissident, to head the Organizing Committee for the Restoration of the State Autonomy of Ingushetia. Two months later, Kodzoev was replaced by the law professor, Beksultan Seynaroev, which generated the first major schism in the Ingush national movement: Kodzoev, who had the support of rural Ingush, went on to lead the public movement Nijskho, while Seynaroev, backed by urban intellectuals and Communist Party members in Grozny and the city of Vladikavkaz, went on to lead the People's Council of Ingushetia.

In terms of ideology, the two rivals were not opposed. Both advocated for Ingush autonomy within the Russian Federation, including the return of Prigorodny and parts of Vladikavkaz. The Nijskho movement, however, was more radical in its ideology and more proactively engaged in protests featuring anti-communist slogans and rallied to oust the corrupt *nomenklatura*. In the first months of 1990 Nijskho, supported by deputies from Ingush rural councils, staged demonstrations that drew many thousands of protesters, and succeeded in replacing regional party bosses with the democratically oriented ones.

According to many of those I interviewed, the rivalry between Nijskho and the People's Council came to radicalize the national movement, contributing to armed confrontation in 1992 with Ossetians.

As noted by Yakub Patiev, an Ingush ethnologist and former Minister for Nationalities Policy in Ingushetia, 'There were situations when one would rally in Nazran, and the other would rally in Ekazhevo [*two Ingush towns – E.S.*]. One rally would claim that the others were KGB, and the other would do the same.'

On 23 March 1991, Boris Yeltsin, who was running for the Russian presidency, visited Ingushetia. He was the first top-level Russian politician to visit the republic, let alone to publicly recognize the injustices committed against the Ingush, and to pledge his support. He began his speech with the traditional Muslim greeting, *Salaam-aleikum, Ingushis!–* which won the hearts of the Ingush nation.

In the following month, the Supreme Soviet of the Russian Federation adopted a law, On the Rehabilitation of the Repressed Peoples. Its Articles 3 and 6 stipulated the rights of repressed peoples to 'territorial rehabilitation' – the return of lands that had been illegally taken from them as a result of Stalinist repressions. Human rights groups warned against such territorial rehabilitation, which they saw as a potential flashpoint for ethnic conflict. However, their voices were drowned out by the rhetoric of historical justice. In the national elections held on 12 June 1991, the Ingush cast 94.7 per cent of their ballots for Yeltsin – the highest level of support for him registered anywhere in the Soviet Union.

At that time, the leadership of the People's Council of Ingushetia appeared to be downplaying the difficulties of regaining control of the region. 'The council's leaders would say: "No Russian soldier will shoot at you. Yeltsin is sitting in Moscow and waiting for us to take the region." They incited people to action', Patiev later recalled in an interview.

Following the attempted *putsch* in August against Soviet leader Mikhail Gorbachev, and the national revolution in Chechnya, deputies of Ingush regional councils adopted a declaration on the Establishment of the Ingush Republic, claiming the territory that was part of Chechen-Ingushetia with Prigorodny region of North Ossetia and the right bank of Terek in the city of Vladikavkaz *(Ingushskaya gosudarstvennost. Normativno-pravovie akty* 1997: 46).

On 30 November 1991, 97.4 per cent of the voters came out in favour of creating the Ingush Republic as part of the Russian Federation (Khamchiev 2002). On 4 June 1992, the Supreme Soviet of the Russian Federation adopted the law 'On Establishing of the Ingush Republic, Part of the Russian Federation'. This day is now celebrated as the birthday of Ingushetia. The restoration of national statehood is seen by most Ingush as the main achievement of the post-Soviet transition.

'I can't describe how happy I was when the republic was created. Overwhelmed with joy ... I couldn't sit down for even a minute', Osman Khadziev, an elderly peasant in the town of Malgobek, told me. 'Even if we are brothers with the Chechens, each brother wants to live in his own house.'

After the Ingush republic was created, Moscow dispatched representatives to help regional leaders in setting up a government. It was decided to postpone elections to the Supreme Soviet of the republic until negotiations over the border with Ossetia had been concluded. Thus, Ingushetia functioned without a government for more than a year, by which time clashes between Ingush and Ossetians in the Prigorodny Region had already begun to get out of control.

Ever since spring 1991, clashes between Ingush and Ossetians in the Prigorodny region had been occurring with threatening regularity. People's militias had already emerged on both sides. Then, on the night of 30 October 1993, full-scale armed conflict broke out between the militias in two villages. As news of the clashes reached

Ingushetia, followed by news of Ingush casualties, hundreds of Ingush males raced to Prigorodny to help to defend the ethnic Ingush. At about the same time, a few hundred men from South Ossetia (breakaway republic of Georgia) arrived in Prigorodny to defend ethnic Ossetians.

By 9.30 pm on 30 October, ten large villages were embroiled in battle. Both sides were equipped with machine guns, grenade launchers, anti-aircraft guns and sniper rifles. In the afternoon of 31 October, a federal delegation flew from Moscow to Vladikavkaz. The next day, the official position of federal government was announced by General-Colonel Filatov on Ossetian TV:

> Today at 12:45 p.m. the first plane carrying paratroopers, equipment and ammunition arrived, to be emplaced on the territory of Ossetia. Russia has not forgotten its faithful sons, the Ossetians, who served it with full faith and honesty for many years. Already today [...] the paratroopers, together with the interior forces of the Russian Federation and the interior forces of North Ossetia, will undertake military action against the aggressors, and every hour this resistance and pressure upon the aggressors will grow.
>
> I want to warn all those who find themselves in the zone of military action. I think it won't take us long to cleanse the area of all those who disrupt the peaceful workings of Ossetia, or want to ... I want to warn them that they should leave this territory and not disturb the people who live here, on this territory, and who have lived here in peace and harmony for many years.
>
> (quoted in Zdravomyslov 1998: 65)

On the next day, regiments of Russian troops arrived in the region, first separating the warring parties, then joining with interior forces of North Ossetia, and paramilitary fighters from South Ossetia, forcing between 40,000 and 60,000 Ingush civilians out of Prigorodny and Vladikavkaz. Some 3,000 Ingush homes were deliberately destroyed (Zdravomyslov 1998: 65). The Ingush forced from Prigorodny and Vladikavkaz found refuge in neighbouring Ingushetia, as well as in the Chechen capital, Grozny.

The conflict between Ingush and Ossetians – in which the Kremlin took the Ossetian side, holding that the Ingush attacked Ossetia – has remained unresolved. It dramatically intensified Ingush memories of grievances and is still perceived by the Ingush as a genocide of the Ingush people at the hands of Ossetians and Russian troops. However, some Ingush intellectuals and officials now acknowledge that ethnic Ingush bear some of the responsibility for the tragedy. Mukhtar Buzurtanov, former Deputy Minister of Internal Affairs in Ingushetia, and a Deputy in the People's Assembly of the Republic of Ingushetia from 2003 to 2008 told me in an interview:

> Many people say that it was a provocation on the Ossetian side, aimed at ethnic cleansing. I think that the conditions were such that they naturally hurtled toward conflict. The Ingush lobbied for the law [*on rehabilitation of repressed peoples – E.S.*]. They just wanted to have this law and didn't care about the means by which it would be implemented. Only a few people understood that it would not be easy to reclaim the region. The Ingush leaders thought that, once the law

was adopted, we would redraw the border, and that would be that. They did not realize that human beings are not a mechanical aggregate, that there are different characters, forces at work.

Not surprisingly, the Ingush–Ossetian conflict prompted ethnic Ingush to close ranks, strengthening the sense of ethnic belonging normally conducive to building a unified polity. Since Yeltsin sent in tanks to drive the Ingush from Prigorodny and parts of Vladikavkaz, his pre-electoral greeting – *Salaam-aleikum, Ingushi!* – is usually remembered with bitter irony, and has come to embody the Ingush 'betrayed nation' identity.

Creation and consolidation of institutions

Two days after the outbreak of violence between ethnic Ingush and Ossetians in 1992, Yeltsin declared a state of emergency on the territory of North Ossetia and Ingushetia, and created a temporary body, the Provisional Administration in Ingushetia and North Ossetia, to govern the territories. Ruslan Aushev, a 38-year-old ethnic Ingush born in Grozny – and a former Soviet army major general who was awarded the medal, Hero of the USSR for combat in Afghanistan – was appointed to lead the body.

On 28 February 1993, Aushev was elected president of Ingushetia with 99.94 per cent of the vote. Voter turn-out was reported to have been 92.66 per cent; however, Aushev was the only candidate running (*Ingushskaya Gosudarstvennost* 1997). Because the state of emergency continued into 1993, members of the People's Assembly, the Parliament of Ingushetia, were not elected until 27 February 1994. By special decree, Aushev allocated three of the seats to representatives of the Chechen minority, and three to ethnic Russians. The vote also resulted in the adoption of the Constitution of the republic.

The Constitution established Ingushetia as a presidential republic. Any citizen between the ages of 35 and 65 who could speak both of the official state languages, Ingush and Russian, was eligible to run for a five-year term as president. Ingush legislators had fewer powers than their Chechen counterparts, and could approve only the heads of the administration, and of the supreme and arbitration courts. The Ingush Constitution made no special mention of Islam. Further, according to Article 11, 'return by political means of lands illegally annexed from the Ingush territory and the preservation of the territorial integrity of the Republic of Ingushetia is a state goal of the utmost importance.'

However, Aushev did not invite any participants in the Ingush national movement to government posts. The nationalists were powerless to object, as they had been discredited by the devastating armed conflict with the Ossetians.

Ingush nationalists 'brought us to the tragedy of 1992', said Magomed-Sali Aushev, a member of Ingush Parliament from 2003 to 2008. 'They gave the pretext for Ossetia to get ready for war. They screamed that several thousand horsemen were prepared to take Vladikavkaz. Which horsemen?!'

Ruslan Aushev 'categorically refused to allow leaders of nationalist movements anywhere close to the government. He got irritated just hearing about them. He felt that they had inflicted tremendous damage on the Ingush people. He never talked to them, or made any concessions to them', Akhmed Malsagov, former Minister of Finance, later Chair of Cabinet 1997–2001 told me.

Aushev, therefore, did not seek to consolidate the political forces in his elite, but marginalized rivals and nationalist leaders. Unlike Dzhokhar Dudaev, his counterpart in Chechnya, who repeatedly heated up memories of grievance, Aushev used every opportunity to tamp down emotions of past injustices among ethnic Ingush. Instead, he emphasized finding ways to remedy evils and overcome hardships, irrespective of the difficult recent past. 'Enough of complaining, "Oh, we are such a long-suffering nation!" We need to work, not forever keep looking back', Aushev said in a speech (Aushev 1994).

Even though he marginalized potential opponents and prevented informal groups from being heard in the government, Aushev won over the Ingush electorate through his resolute, yet moderate, style of leadership – which also was defined by an independent, yet cooperative position with Moscow, and a genuine capacity to find solutions to numerous seemingly unsolvable problems. On 1 March 1998, Aushev was re-elected to a second term, with 66.5 per cent of the vote.

State-building, 1992–2001

The economy

Ingushetia is a rural, agrarian republic. After the breakup of Chechen-Ingushetia in 1991, Ingushetia inherited less than 10 per cent of the former republic's production capacity (Gutseriev 1997: 195). It had little industry, and an underdeveloped social infrastructure and public transport. There were no institutions of higher education, no airport, no hotels, stadium or railway stations – not even a cinema. Few villages in Ingushetia had running water, natural gas or telephone lines. In 1994, some 90 per cent of the republic's budget was funded by Moscow. Ingushetia was at the bottom in per capita income in the entire Russian Federation (Gutseriev 1997: 195).

Moreover, Ingushetia had the highest birth rates in Russia. That meant that the republic was densely populated for its size – and its population increased further in 1992 with the arrival of at least 45,000 internally displaced persons (IDPs) from North Ossetia, and in 1994 with more than 100,000 IDPs from Chechnya. Then, in 1999, the population grew again, as another 300,000 IDPs fled to Ingushetia during the second military campaign in Chechnya.

Of course, the decline in industrial production affected post-Soviet Russia in general. However, the severe economic depression in Ingushetia was made more acute by its proximity to conflict zones, and the proportionately large role of the military-industrial sector (massively underfunded after the Soviet collapse) in the economy, according to the Ingush economist Ruslan Malsagov. Moreover, the scant industrial capacity that remained in Ingushetia needed urgent modernization, or outright replacement. (Gutseriev 1997: 195).

Nowhere was this more evident than in the oil sector. In the Soviet times, the oil industry in Ingushetia constituted 70 per cent of all its production. However, by 1992, only three major wells remained; 274 smaller wells had ceased to function. Between $14 million and $16 million were required for the reconstruction and modernization of the smaller wells – funds that the republic did not have (Toriev 2004: 4).

In 1995 the Aushev administration developed a programme of socio-economic development for the coming decade. The priorities were promotion of economic self-sufficiency, the development of social infrastructure and improvement in the standard of living. Aushev proposed to accomplish this by boosting the profits of local businesses, modernizing the petro-chemical industry, improving fiscal discipline, re-organizing the agricultural sector, and attracting outside investment (*Serdalo*, 16 April 1998, 8 December 1999). Implementing the programme would cost $1.65 million, some $700,000 of which would be required from 1996 to 1998 (Gutseriev 1997: 195).

Although Moscow was supposed to fund the development programme, it was not able to provide for even the most urgent needs of Ingushetia. Consequently, the Ingush government, with the support of regional economists, proposed that the federal government should create, within the republic, an experimental offshore economic zone, as well as an offshore international business centre. Both projects were to be named 'Ingushetia'. And both Yeltsin and his prime minister, Viktor Chernomyrdin, agreed.

The free economic zone provided legal and tax incentives for businesses, in a bid to stimulate economic activity. It worked in the following way: the Ingush Republic's Cabinet of Ministers was granted a loan by the Russian Federal Finance Ministry equal to the taxes and fees required by the federal government from the business enterprises newly created in the zone. The loan could be used for the social-economic development of the republic *(Ingushetia,* 30 July 1994). The zone, approved initially for one year, was extended several times through 1997, in the course of which 3,069 companies, including 140 foreign firms, were registered in the republic (Gutseriev 1997: 208).

Altogether 88 projects were constructed with the profits generated by the free economic zone between 1995 and 1997. These included a hotel, a sweets factory, a boarding school, a publishing house, half dozen outdoor cafes, five dozen modern single-family houses and nine children's parks. In subsequent years the government built a modern airport, a railway station, a TV station, a hydroelectric power station, a brick-making factory, a military school and various sports stadiums. It provided gas and communications infrastructure to mountain villages, and extended water pipes to the Malgobek district, which for decades had suffered from shortages of drinking water (Aushev 1997; Gutseriev 1998: 213).

After the loss of what had been Ingush urban centres, Grozny remained in separatist Chechnya and Vladikavkaz in now-hostile North Ossetia, President Aushev decided to construct a new capital, Magas, also financed by profits from the free economic zone.

Like Aslan Maskhadov, who succeeded Dudaev in Chechnya, Aushev prioritized the revival the republic's petro-chemical and gas industries. By 1994 some 20 oil wells had been restored, and a new well with a daily yield of 50 tons of oil was in operation, according to Mustafa Akhriev, deputy director of the oil and gas company

Ingushneftegazkhimprom. By 1995, oil extraction had risen by 4.2 per cent, and production had increased by 9.7 per cent.

In addition, the Ingush government purchased an oil-processing refinery station that would make possible the collection and delivery of oil to other regions in Russia. This, in turn, generated revenues that were used to modernize and purchase equipment, as well as pay salaries and – importantly – taxes. In 1997, Aushev even netted a big foreign fish: the US oil company Pacific Petroleum signed a contract to boost the extraction of oil in the republic (*Serdalo*, 18 October 1997).

Aushev was still not satisfied: 'The level of oil extraction in recent years has stabilized at a level that enables the industry to barely survive. The new wells have not been re-activated, oil-processing enterprises have not been built, and cases of major theft have been revealed by the Department for Control and Inspection', Aushev was quoted as saying in a 1999 report by the Congress of the Ingush People (Aushev 1999). On the other hand, and in contrast to Chechnya, Ingushetia managed to stave off the total collapse of industry in the republic, and even spurred a very modest revitalization.

The Aushev administration made considerable efforts to enforce budgetary discipline and increase the rates of tax collection. Unlike Maskhadov, who virtually gave up on collecting taxes from individuals, Aushev tightened the controls on tax evasion. He ordered commercial banks to follow Russian tax laws strictly, and to file monthly reports to the tax police on all taxpayers (*Ingushetia*, 27 October 1993). In 1995 Aushev abolished all tax waivers for businesses except for those registered in the free economic zone (*Ingushetia*, 24 January 1995). The ban on illegal sales of petroleum products was strictly enforced. Moreover, the government introduced inter-ministerial joint action plans for increasing budget discipline, which the president oversaw personally.

Agriculture

In 1992 the agricultural sector of Ingushetia faced problems similar to those in Chechnya. Not only were state-owned farms in need of reform, but most of their equipment was also outdated, or missing essential parts. Unlike Chechnya, however, Ingushetia was part of the Russian Federation, and could benefit from federal programmes that subsidized the purchase of fuel, seeds and livestock. However, that is where the benefits ended: employees at state-owned farms in Ingushetia were sometimes not paid for as much as eight months (*Serdalo*, 29 April 1995).

The government's plan was to reorganize the state farms into joint stock enterprises, privately owned farms and state-owned farms. Aushev was opposed to the privatization of land, however, so most agricultural enterprises were transformed into joint stock enterprises. These changes were not enough to prevent the considerable decline in agricultural production from 1995 to 1996; however, by 1998, the agricultural sector had begun a slow recovery.

The Ingush government tried to appoint entrepreneurial, successful people to head the state farms, who in turn looked for ways to motivate workers who, in the cash-strapped economy, were often not paid for months.

Batarbek Akiev, head of the Dolakovo collective farm, told me in an interview:

In Grozny I was the director of a passenger transport enterprise with more than 1,500 employees. In 1994, we moved to Ingushetia. They asked me to work as the director of the *sovkhoz* in my native village of Dolakovo. I had a degree in agriculture, but had never worked in agriculture, never lived in a rural area. However, they said, 'No problem. You just need to have the right style of management.'

The squalor was terrible here. The farms had no windows, or doors. The fields were overgrown with weeds. I brought in cattle from Krasnodar. We fixed the farm buildings, planted the fields. Later we set up a butter workshop, a breeding nursery and vegetable teams. Our fields looked beautiful! I paid additional benefit to the workers in natural products – barley, corn.

Still, despite gains in some aspects of Ingush agriculture (grain production increased fourfold from 1998 to 1999), the sector remained mired in crisis through 2001 – fulfilling less than half of the republic's needs. Moreover, less than half of the agricultural enterprises that received state loans ever paid them back, further straining the budget.

Many locals praise Aushev's efforts to revive the Ingush economy, especially the free economic zone, which Gagiev, the former Justice Minister, calls 'the core around which everything else revolved'. 'Ingushetia had no economy in 1992. A blank page. This zone gave shape to the entire economy', he said in an interview.

Others, among them opposition activist Idris Abadiev, consider the economic zone a failure. He told me:

This offshore zone wasn't profitable. The structures that they built didn't bring anything to the citizen, or to the budget. For example, take the railway station. What does it give to the Ingush people? [Aushev] spent $10 million on it. I could have built 50 enterprises for $10 million that would be still replenishing the budget. I would have built a cheap railway station for one train, with two cars. The costs of construction were inflated at least ten times. Aushev was not corrupt himself, but his close associates took bribes behind his back.

Critics of Aushev stressed in interviews that Moscow was anyway obliged to finance the infrastructural projects constructed with the help of the profits from the zone. Moreover, the Kremlin was to use the zone as a bargaining chip in Ingush–Ossetian negotiations over the status of Prigorodny.

In an interview, Akhmed Malsagov, Minister of Finance and Chair of the Cabinet under Aushev, acknowledged that the economic zone was used by Moscow to cool Ingush territorial claims. However, he added, the zone went a long way toward affirming Ingush statehood:

The zone was a distraction so the Ingush wouldn't demand Prigorodny back. But Aushev thought Ingushetia wouldn't survive without the zone. He was always saying, 'Unless we strengthen ourselves economically, we'll never get Prigorodny back.' He was right, in a way. The zone helped us not so much economically, but psychologically. The people became more optimistic. There was hope that the republic would develop.

Magomed Tatriev, First Vice-Premier Deputy Chair of Government, explained to me that Aushev was determined to develop economic resources on his own, because 'waiting for the favours of the federal centre in the prevailing very complex economic situation – which will prevail in Russia for a long time – is an almost hopeless endeavour' (*Serdalo*, 12 March 1996).

Law enforcement

Following the collapse of the Soviet Union, criminality surged in Ingushetia as it had in neighbouring Chechnya. Ingushetia ranked 63rd in crime-fighting effectiveness among republics in the Russian Federation.

'Everything had to be created from scratch', recalled Mukhtar Buzurtanov, the former Deputy Minister of the Interior. 'State institutions had been virtually destroyed, including the Ministry of Internal Affairs. But we had professional cadres. Without good cadres, the president would not have been able to do anything.'

Between 1992 and 1993 – in only one year – the republic rose to third place in crime-fighting in a Russia-wide rating. Two years later, in 1995, it occupied first place, with a case resolution rate of 77.6 per cent (*Serdalo*, 14 June 1995).

Aushev employed a wide array of measures to strengthen law enforcement. He regularly held meetings of the heads of various law-enforcement agencies, personally coordinating and controlling their activities. Villages with the worst criminal environments were placed under special government control. Curfews were regularly introduced in areas notorious for crime.

Central to this approach was an emphasis on training law-enforcement personnel. In 1996 some 200 police officers were fired because they failed to meet professional standards, according to Daud Korigov, then Minister of Internal Affairs. In 1997, on Aushev's orders, police departments purged their ranks of 300 officers by 'getting rid of dirty [*corrupted – E.S.*] people and those who failed to meet the requirements of the job' (*Serdalo*, 14 April 1997). In the course of his first term in office, Aushev replaced three ministers of internal affairs and four prosecutors.

These efforts were not limited to violent and run-of-the-mill crimes. In 1993 Aushev issued a decree invoking a series of measures aimed at preventing the illegal privatization of state property; he intended to use all income from privatization to build the new capital, Magas. He also prohibited the registration of commercial enterprises in conjunction with state institutions, so as to 'prevent the emergence of conditions conducive to abuse and theft of state funds'.

In the course of the first six months of 1995, the law-enforcement authorities conducted 61 inspections of enterprises and businesses and found more than a hundred violations. The results of these investigations were publicized in the press, along with the names of the accused and the damage they had inflicted on the regional economy. Kin or *teip* relations did not count.

For instance, on 25 July 1995, the newspaper *Ingushetia* reported on a case against Kiloev, former head of the milk factory Nazranovskoye, and a senior mechanic, Aushev. The two were accused of falsifying documents and appropriating monies intended for paying salaries and benefits to workers and children. The men were accused of misappropriating more than 317 million roubles in total.

It was quite unexpected to read in a newspaper about the misdeeds of a person with the same surname as the president. Open criticism of officials and publicizing crimes – naming names and publishing photos of some of the republic's most brazen criminals – was new to Ingush society, where tradition instructs people to avoid direct confrontation and be diplomatic, so as to preserve the honour of the family. Aushev simply ignored these traditions. His efforts to combat corruption, and economic crimes, ensured that significant funds were channelled into the republic's coffers.

After 1996, however, security in the republic again began to deteriorate as kidnappings for ransom by criminal groups in Chechnya spread into neighbouring regions. These criminal networks singled out wealthy victims in Ingushetia, abducted and transported them to Chechnya, then demanded ransom. During the first ten months of 1997, 44 people were abducted, 35 of whom were rescued by Ingush security services (*Serdalo*, 15 November 1997). During the first six months of 1998, 26 people were abducted for ransom. Korigov attributed this rise in crime to poor cooperation between security services in Ingushetia and Chechnya, where the government was turning a blind eye to criminal gangs acting under the umbrella of leading field commanders (*Serdalo*, 30 July1998).

Aushev personally saw to investigations of abductions. In an effort to stem the tide of growing criminality, Aushev in 1998 called a referendum on broadening the powers of the state over judicial and law-enforcement institutions, seeking to reduce some of the federal powers over appointment of judges and top security officials. However, the Supreme Court of the Russian Federation struck down the referendum on 17 November.

Undeterred, in the following year, Aushev organized a congress of the Ingush People to discuss the deterioration of security throughout the republic. He urged the populace to protect themselves against criminals and proposed that the Parliament hold a special hearing on 'activities of law-enforcement agencies aimed at ensuring the security of the citizens and combating abductions' (*Serdalo*, 15 June 1999). As a result, the Ingush government under Aushev succeeded impressively in managing to contain crime – particularly challenging in such a turbulent region.

Education and healthcare

In 1992, Ingushetia ranked last among all republics in the Russian Federation in number of hospital beds per capita (*Serdalo*, 14 June 1995). There was not even a hospital emergency ward, or any specialized medical clinics. Ambulance crews in many villages lacked not only basic drugs, but staff with higher medical training. Ingushetia's maternity clinic required a major reconstruction (Toriev 2004: 7). Even the Ministry of Health, established in 1992, was housed in two refugee trailers parked in the courtyard of the district hospital in Nazran, now renamed the Clinical Hospital of the Republic.

As Khadizhat Musieva, director of the children's polyclinic at the hospital, explained in an interview:

> The situation was very difficult. There were no qualified doctors, only nurses. Then, in 1992, after the Ingush–Ossetian conflict, all the qualified Ingush doctors

who had worked in Ossetia fled to Ingushetia and took up jobs. By 1994 our [healthcare] capacities were strengthened even further, after the inflow of refugees from Chechnya. Among them also were qualified doctors. Specialized health clinics began to open because, now, we had specialists.

Initially the Ingush government sought to combat the dearth of qualified staff by requesting additional places for Ingush students in medical schools throughout Russia. In 1993 the government opened a medical college for nurses in Nazran, and in 1997 inaugurated a medical department at Ingush State University. Dr Musieva continued:

At first the quality of instruction [at Ingush State] was not very high. But the dean invited guest faculty from Grozny and, later, our local specialists got degrees, defended dissertations. Now we have qualified academics in the department.

The Ingush health system came under tremendous stress during both Chechen wars. Magomed Gadaborshev, urologist at the republican hospital in Nazran, told me:

The inflow of IDPs was enormous. We didn't know what to do. The first winter was very difficult. The refugee camps were the responsibility of the republican hospital. Sometimes each doctor received 50, 60 patients a day. International organizations helped a lot, but the doctors were from local institutions, and for several years worked under emergency conditions.

The Ingush education system also was strained by the inflow of IDPs from conflict zones in Chechnya and Prigorodny (and the steady departure of the Russian-speaking population from the republic). Schools operated in three shifts to try to compensate for the lack of space – estimated at 20,000, or the equivalent of 63 additional schools – to account for the surge in population (Toriev 2004: 8, Bednov 1995).

International aid organizations helped to establish schools in Ingush refugee camps, but many IDPs lived in private housing and sent their children to regular schools. The quality of elementary and secondary school education in Ingushetia was extremely low as a result of the overcrowding, as well as the lack of textbooks and equipment (Toriev 2004: 8). The Aushev administration had a new, modern lyceum building constructed from the revenues generated by the offshore economic zone, as well as Mountaineers Cadet School, which the president envisaged as a boarding school for the future Ingush elite (*Serdalo*, 22 November 1997). Overall, however, Ingushetia had nearly four times fewer specialists with higher education, and four times fewer specialists with secondary education, than the average Russian republic (*Ingushetia*, 22 December 1993).

In 1994, Ingush State University was founded, by 2001, the university was offering 17 major subjects, and housed a centre for research into Ingush language and literature. The university was especially important to efforts at boosting education in the republic: most families could not afford to educate their children outside the republic; in particular, the existence of a local university helped to ensure that more female students gained access to higher education.

As Magomed Mutsolgov, a local human rights activist, explained to me: 'Because of our mentality, many people didn't let girls go away to study. Now the Ingush are sending girls to school. This is a very important change.'

In addition to secular institutions of higher education, the Imam Ash-Shafi Islamic Institute was founded in the town of Malgobek – the first Islamic institution of higher learning in Russia. This institute was privately funded and employed both local and foreign instructors. Its vice-rector and later rector, Issa Tsetchoev, had been educated in Algeria and was (and remains) a Salafi *imam*.

Many students were initially drawn to the institute by its non-competitive admissions policy, and the potential of obtaining the lucrative profession of *mullah*. However, many eventually became activists for fundamentalist Islam. Some were arrested and killed by the security services after allegedly joining the Islamist insurgency.

As one graduate of this Institute, 39-year-old Moldi, told me:

After serving in the Army, I went to Saratov and tried to get into the law school there, but failed the essay-writing exam. I studied to retake the exam the following year, but I only got a 4 [*equivalent to a B grade – E.S.*] and, again, was not accepted. The next year I was again studying for the exams when everything was decided by fate. My uncle stopped by and said that an Islamic Institute had opened in Malgobek, and that it had been decided that I should study there. Before that I hadn't performed *namaz* [*the mandatory five times daily prayer*] and had drunk alcohol with my mates during military service ... There [*at the Islamic Institute – E.S.*] I learned that Allah is our president, tsar and protector. Who are the other presidents? Once you have recited *La ilahha il Allah* ['*There is no God but Allah*'], then there are no Russian laws anymore. The Koran is our law. The *Sharia* is the Koran. Everyone must live according to the laws of the Almighty.

The Islamic Institute was shut down in 1997 by the Ingush government. Aushev, who had fought against the Taliban in Afghanistan, did not want to nurture Islamic fundamentalism on Ingush soil.

Political discord, and the Chechen Wars

The primary sources of political disagreement in Ingushetia from 1992 to 2001 were the policy toward Chechnya, and negotiations with Ossetians in the wake of the deadly conflict. Regarding the latter, Aushev focused on ensuring that Ingush IDPs could return to their villages in Prigorodny.

As early as January 1993 the presidents of Ingushetia and North Ossetia signed a protocol that served as a symbolic peace treaty in which both sides agreed to abide by the Constitution and laws of the Russian Federation, and to resolve the outstanding issues concerning IDPs. As a result of pressure from the Aushev administration the first IDPs began to return to villages on the Ingush–Ossetian border in 1993, less than a year after the war. Efforts to disarm Ossetian groups still active in Prigorodny, however, were unsuccessful. Convoys carrying IDPs hoping to return to Prigorodny were systematically attacked to prevent their resettlement. Some returnees were killed; others were wounded and forced to return to Ingushetia. Often the attacks occurred in the presence of federal military units. Despite the dangers, hundreds of Ingush IDPs managed to return to their homes in 1993.

On 24 June 1994, the presidents of North Ossetia and Ingushetia signed the Beslan Accord, which many Ingush came to regard as a betrayal of their cause. The agreement spelled out the guidelines for the return of Ingush IDPs and stated that both parties agreed to 'recognize the territorial integrity of the Republic of North Ossetia'.

Ingush nationalists were outraged and viewed the Beslan Accord as tantamount to the effective surrender by Aushev of Ingush claims to territory within North Ossetia. His refusal to insist on the return of land, and emphasis on IDP returns to their villages, was widely seen as an unacceptable compromise. Moreover, the accord came as Aushev was building the new capital of Magas, already seen as a major retreat from Ingush claims to the right bank of Vladikavkaz.

'The greatest crime was the establishment of Magas', Bamatgirej Mankiev, a member of Ingush Parliament from 2003 to 2008, and a former Deputy of the Supreme Soviet of Checheno-Ingush Republic said in an interview. 'The Ingush already had their capital – Vladikavkaz. Aushev was sent by Moscow to ensure the territorial claims of Ossetia.'

Criticism of Aushev's policy on conflict with North Ossetia, combined with the extremely difficult economic and political situation, resulted in a 33 per cent drop in support for Aushev in 1997 elections.

A further contributing factor was the political controversy over policies on Chechnya. Deeply critical of the federal government for launching the wars in Chechnya, Aushev had facilitated negotiations between Moscow and Chechen leaders. He also had opened the Ingush borders to Chechen IDPs and invested considerable energy and resources in helping them – drawing the ire of Ingush nationalists, who accused him of protecting Chechen interests over those of the ethnic Ingush.

Ingushetia was affected by the Chechen War not only as a host to refugees but also directly. In 1995 the Ingush mountain villages of Dattykh and Arshty were repeatedly bombed by Russian forces, resulting in human casualties. Moreover, the civilian airport of Ingushetia was attacked in October 1995 by seven helicopters flown by Russian federal forces (*Serdalo*, 3 October 1995).

Aushev demanded that military prosecutors launch investigations. He travelled to the mountain villages that had been bombed, urging the population 'not to react to provocations and not to let Ingushetia be dragged into the war' (*Serdalo*, 27 February 1996; 6 March). Aushev continued to hold press conferences strongly condemning the wars in Chechnya. He hosted Russian and international organizations in Ingushetia, which documented war crimes by the federal forces.

Yeltsin did not like Aushev, but he tolerated him. Then, shortly after Yeltsin handed power to Vladimir Putin, who launched efforts to 'strengthen Russian statehood', Aushev resigned on 28 December 2001, before the end of his term. He never publicly explained the reasons, but most observers agree that he must have realized it would be impossible to work with the new Kremlin leadership.

Until his voluntary resignation in late 2001, Aushev kept the security services in Ingushetia on a tight leash, and succeeded in preventing the spillover of federal 'counter-terrorist' operations from Chechnya. After his resignation, 'clean up' operations similar to those underway in Chechnya – and involving grave abuses of human rights – began in Ingushetia. Moreover, armed groups hostile to Russia became more active within the republic, attacking the security services and federal troops.

By 2007, Ingushetia had become a fully fledged hot spot. Critics of Aushev hold him responsible for these developments: by opening up borders to Chechen IDPs, they say, he created breeding grounds for Islamist radicals and fundamentalists in largely peaceful Ingushetia. His supporters, however, say that Aushev protected Ingushetia from security services as long as he could.

All the same, even Aushev's critics were largely toothless in standing up his administration.

> After his first term there were people who wanted to overthrow him. They came to me and said, 'Let's organize actions of civil disobedience.' I said, 'I'm not going against him. The Ingush republic is a feeble child. It could die if we start fighting. I respected him for not allowing military forces to cross over into Ingushetia.
> – Issa Kodzoev, the leader of Ingush nationalist movement Nijskho (author's interview)

State-building and informal social institutions

Teips and *familias*

The national revival in Ingushetia, as in Chechnya, went hand-in-hand with a revival of the *teips*. Ingush *teips* held congresses in the mountains of their origin, and in their hereditary towers, in an effort to promote solidarity, and discuss social and political issues.

'Three years ago, our Elders organized a trip to the mountains for all our men. We spent three days in the mountains, cleaning up our tower, recounting stories and legends about our *teip*. It was great fun', Roustam Yandiev, a 24-year-old from the village of Vezhery-Yurt, told me in an interview. 'I now know so many things about my *teip*', he added. 'We have a rich history. There are so many of us. I was surprised!'

Idris Abadiev, former MP and a nationalist activist, told me why he sponsored gatherings of his Evloev *teip*:

> In the late 1990s my brother and I organized several congresses, invited people to the mountains. We slaughtered cows and boiled the meat. We also invited Chechens who belong to our *teip*. Their elders had tears in their eyes when they learned about their family roots. In Soviet times only those who were close maintained kin-based relationships. The rest had already forgotten that they were Evloevs, had begun to intermarry. We wanted to unite them.

Visitors to the mountainous areas of Ingushetia will notice that many *familias* have taken steps to restore their family relics, the hereditary towers. Some have provided the buildings with electricity and planted orchards on the surrounding land. Moreover, sometimes *teip* representatives (usually one elder per *teip*) have moved into the towers to live.

A member of the Ozdoev *teip*, Alikhan Dozariev, told me that, during their *teip*'s first congress in 1995, the *teip* leadership decided to pave a 5-kilometre stretch of road leading to their most famous historic construction, Vovnushki Tower. The *teip* raised money, and paved the road, but is still awaiting the restoration of the tower because this must be overseen by professional architects working under the auspices of the Ministry of Culture. 'We decided to have one representative of each *familia* in the Ozdoev *teip* actually live in the towers, to help maintain them', Dozariev added.

Ingush *teips* also have raised money to beautify up their cemeteries and build small premises for prayer. The Aushev *teip*, for example, built a prayer house and posted an engraved model of the family tree at the entrance to their cemetery, literally showing members their roots. Three members of the Uzhakhov *familia* donated money to build a prayer house at their *teip* cemetery in the village of Barsuki. At the same cemetery a young businessman, Ruslan Uzhakhov, funded the construction of a building in memory of Teshal Uzhakhov, an associate of nineteenth-century Sheikh Kunta-Khadzhi Kishiev, founder of Qadiri *tariqa* – in which to read the Koran. Six other *teip* members have arranged a 99-year lease on six hectares of land surrounding the cemetery, in order to prevent others from buying the property and settling on what was formerly recognized as their *familia* land.

Other measures taken by many Ingush *teips* have involved assembling telephone lists of all known members and creating WhatsApp groups, following serious efforts to reconstruct *teip* histories, lineages and family trees. Some Ingush have recreated *teips* heraldic symbols, coats of arms from petroglyphs (*tamgi*) carved into their towers and castles in the mountains. The symbol of the Evloev *teip*, for example, is registered with the Russian Heraldic Society. A group of *teips*, comprising the *Tsori* society, has created a website dedicated to its history, culture and current affairs.

Most *teip* activity has centred on issues of culture and ritual. For instance, the minutes of the 12 January 2002 meeting of the Council of Elders of the Uzhakhov *familia* show that 22 representatives from seven settlements were present. Magomed Uzhakhov, a middle-aged history buff and former opera singer, delivered a report summarizing the results of various joint projects, and proposed new issues for discussion:

1. Alcohol consumption by adults and some youth had been creating 'anxiety in families, and in society', with 'damaging effect on their health.' Measures to be discussed: how to make them undergo treatment, whether to excommunicate them from the *familia*.
2. Drug addiction and distribution were also deemed problematic. Measures to be discussed: forcing abusers to undergo treatment, excommunicating them, resettling them in other parts of Russia or putting them in jail.

3. Resolving land disputes and issues of inheritance. Question for discussion – which law to use [*secular, adat, Sharia* – E.S.].
4. The resolution of ongoing financial disputes.
5. The creation of a commission to address the 'urgent issue of timely marriage for youth of both sexes, and of the divorced'.
6. Assistance to sick members who were in their homes, in hospitals or outside the republic.
7. Regulating issues of blood feud and reconciliation.
8. The moderation of cases of abduction of brides or other family members.
9. Better coordination of weddings and funerals. (How, when and who should inform others? Who should organize the events? How much time, or how many days, should various *teip* members remain to assist with the event? How should seniors be dressed, especially at funerals? Why is the same food cooked at both types of events? Why is there no longer dancing at weddings? How can dancing be encouraged, and when should it be prohibited?)
10. Maintenance of cemeteries. Should all members be obliged to supply a *vosket* (a will, composed in accordance with Muslim tradition)?
11. Restoration of the tower of the Uzhakhov *teip*.
12. The organized support of members 'who would be useful to the entire Ingush and Russian populations, as well as our *teip* of Uzhakhovs', especially in matters of positive state-building processes.

Persons whom I interviewed from other *teips* and *familias* reported similar agendas, and similar discussions, at their gatherings, so this is a typical case.

This grand agenda laid out by Magomed Uzhakhov proposed tackling serious issues. However, discussion at the meeting was dominated by other matters, such as the pros and cons of the creation of a religious council to resolve matters of ritual. The meeting also considered mores, uses of *teip* land that had been rented for 99 years, and the creation of a monetary fund for mutual assistance.

None of the issues considered by the Council of Elders of the Uzhakhov *familia* involved enforcement or even serious commitment to issues such as the expulsion of drug addicts, or the resolution of financial disputes. Elders limited their guidance to the importance of leading moral lives and resolving conflicts according to law.

Magomed Uzhakhov, the most active member of his *familia*, was disappointed at the low level of participation by his fellow members. Most of the initiatives that were proposed were never implemented, he told me. Moreover, he said, it was difficult to raise money for almost every project, as members began to lose interest after the first few meetings. He lamented:

We elected the Council of Elders and the *tamada* [*responsible for religious ritual*]. But the train never went much further than that. Even the council fell apart! I made a list of people who were worthy of commemoration [*mainly heroes of various wars* – E.S.], but we couldn't raise enough money for it. The book about the Uzhakhovs has still not been published, because we lack the funds. I even created special Uzhakhov postcards, to be used as invitations to weddings. But they haven't caught on.

In fact, the Uzhakhovs – who refer to themselves as a *teip* in all their documents – are technically a lineage (*nek'an*) of a larger *teip*, the Gazdiev. The Ingush word, *nek'an*, – which reminds members that they are included in the larger *teip* – is found only on the Uzhakhov coat of arms.

One of my acquaintances, a member of a *familia* generally identified as belonging to the Gazdiev *teip*, argued with me at length about the accuracy of this classification. He said the historical records were incorrect and insisted that his *familia* was a separate *teip*. He even requested me not to identify him, or his *familia*, as he did not want any written mention of a possible link between his *familia* and the Gazdievs.

I offer this example to underscore the degree of confusion still existing between Ingush *teips* and lineages – as specified in Chapter 4. Moreover, the example demonstrates the dynamics in most *teips* – where several middle-aged activists take the lead in retrenching ideology within the *teip*, often romanticizing its history and sometimes trying to manipulate it toward political ends, whereas most other *teip* members, including elders, are uninterested in enforcing *teip* discipline over individuals or extended families.

According to Daud Uzhakhov, from the village of Altievo, the Uzhakhovs, a medium-sized *familia*, have never tried to achieve political consensus. 'We could never agree over political matters. Moreover, it would have been dangerous for our [internal] security', he told me.

Larger Ingush *teips*, however, did attempt to mobilize politically (or at least they discussed the possibility) during the presidential election campaigns of 1998 and 2002. None of the Ingush *teips*, however, managed to vote in an organized manner, and some were strongly divided over it.

Some *teips* refrained from discussing politics altogether, for various reasons. The Barkinkhoev *teip*, for example, decided that promoting one candidate over another be divisive, automatically positioning all members of the *teip* against all those who favoured other candidates. Since election outcomes at that time still were far from predetermined, such a position would be risky.

As Magomed-Sali Kotiev explained:

Prior to Aushev's 1998 election victory, the elders of the Barkinkhoev *teip* got together. I was elected to represent the Kotiev *familia*, which is part of this *teip*. Our Barkinkhoev scholars, professors and other academics spoke, expressed their opinions. Afterwards, we deliberated and concluded that everyone should vote the way he wanted, even though everyone had the right to express his opinion and share it with others. One of our elders spoke up and said, 'All the candidates are dignified, educated people, with their own *familias*, their own convictions, and we can't say anything against any of them. We should not divide people by *familias* or categories. We have suffered enough. We shouldn't split people. That's why everyone should vote for him or herself.' You see, if we had decided to vote in an organized manner, we would have had to declare so publicly, in front of the nation. And such a thing would never be forgotten, or forgiven. This would be remembered for generations. It could have had an impact on our offspring. So, our elders said that they forbade even raising the issue of organized voting in the future.

The two largest Ingush *teips*, Ozdoy and Yovloy, put up their own candidates for the presidency, and tried to organize disciplined voting among their members. The efforts of both *teips* failed. In both instances, moreover, the initiative was spurred by politically active members who were seeking to use *teip* unity as a tool to boost their own political success.

According to Alikhan Dozariev, a member of the Ozdoy *teip*:

The second time, during the election of Aushev in 1998, there was an attempt to get all the Ozdoevs together. Boris Ozdoev, a judge, was also running for president. There was an attempt to organize support for him. I remember how our elders argued: 'Boris is an educated, decent person. He is our relative. But what can Boris give to the entire people?' So, they issued a statement that said that electing a president is a responsibility that every person must decide for himself, because tomorrow everyone will have to bear responsibility for this decision. They said that electing a president should not centre around the *teip*. And in fact, everyone supported Aushev, not Boris. It shouldn't be this way, that we elect a relative to become the president. The presidency is a national post.

Perhaps the most dramatic example of political division occurred within the Evloev *teip*, which split completely while trying to reach consensus regarding the 2002 presidential election. Aushev had already resigned, and eight candidates were vying for his post. Among the frontrunners were Mikhail Gutseriev, an Aushev proponent and the administrative head of the offshore economic zone, and Murat Zyazikov, an FSB general backed by the Kremlin.

Idris Abadiev, of the Evloev *teip*, recalls the campaign in this way:

In 2002 my brother and I were running for the presidency. We had the following tactic: initially we would both, because he was better-known in Moscow, and I had more influence in Ingushetia. Then, at the last moment, one of us would drop out and focus the attention of voters on the other. Evloev is a huge *teip*. If all the Evloevs unite, that's it – no president can be elected without their support. We had a tremendous chance to win. So what did Gutseriev do? He had the head of his guard – also a Evloev, a good guy. Then he was in close contact with Vakha Evloev, a European champion in wrestling. And then there was a third Evloev, Zakri, who had run for parliament several times. And the fourth [Evloev] was Maskurov, the vice premier in the Aushev government. Gutseriev encouraged all of them to run! Combined with me and my brother, that made six Evloevs! In this way Gutseriev fragmented us. Zakri Evloev immediately acknowledged that he was Gutseriev's man. Vakha Evloev later announced it on TV and withdrew in favour of Gutseriev. Maskurov turned out to be stronger, but even he proved to be a Gutseriev man. That was how we were fragmented. As a result, neither Gutseriev, nor an Evloev, but this Zyazikov came to power.

(author's interview)

Some observers say the inability of *teips* to mobilize should have been expected. Mukhtar Buzurtanov, a former Deputy Minister of the Interior, noted how an earlier election, the presidential campaign won by Aushev in 1998, provided some faint hopes for *teip* political unity:

> When Ruslan Aushev was running for the second time, there were eight other candidates. Among them were representatives of big *teips* – Issa Kostoev, Albogachiev (Leimoev), Evloevs. These candidates calculated that, if the members of their own *teips* voted for them, Ruslan wouldn't get more than 50 per cent of the vote. I understood this situation, and told them, 'Don't expect your *teips* to give you many votes. Ruslan is well-respected. People are interested not in which position you attain, but how the republic is governed. All the candidates from big *teips* jointly got 33 per cent in the first round. Ozdoev, who has the largest *teip*, got about 1,000 votes. Albogachiev got 600! They had tried to mobilize the *teip* factor, but they failed. Now the times have changed. Now it is the individual family that is the centre of everything, not the *teip*. The *teip* can only give moral support, especially in the cases of blood feud. For political positions, however, we now choose respected individuals.

Thus, I have shown how *teip* identity flourished in Ingushetia from 1992 to 2001. Many *teips* and their lineages made significant strides by consolidating, as well as researching and popularizing their histories. *Teips* improved coordination of their popular rituals, and came together more often – in the mountains or through Councils of Elders – to address social issues, such as immorality, alcohol abuse and substandard state care for the sick and needy.

However, despite these efforts, *teips* effectively had no real impact on the resolution of social problems. They had even less success in uniting politically behind the same candidate, or cause. The *teips* strengthened their profiles during this period, but they remained loose identities that meant different things to different people. Consequently, *teips* were unable to maintain much in the way of commitment.

My fieldwork showed that, in Ingushetia, much as in neighbouring Chechnya, the influence of lineage superseded that of the greater *teip*. Some lineages in Ingushetia have forgotten their ties to the larger *teip* altogether; they feel no attachment. The most *teip*-conscious and politically active members are usually middle-aged men, not elders, whose roles – like those of the *teips* in general – also are reduced, confined primarily to ritual.

A new movement toward Islamic fundamentalism emerged in Ingushetia, as in Chechnya, over the decade that followed the Soviet collapse. These previously unfamiliar fundamentalist forces sowed tension throughout the Muslim community in the Ingush Republic.

As Moldi, a student at the fundamentalist institute in the Malgobek town, recalled:

> I was brought up in the Sufi tradition. I appealed to my Sheikh when I prepared to take university entrance exams. My father carried a strand of hair from Deni-Sheikh in his wallet. After I was accepted into the Islamic institute, I would come back home and tell my father and mother what we had been told at school, and how we were doing things wrong.

They were so indignant. 'What are you saying about our Sheikh!' And so we, the students at this institute, were labelled Wahhabists ... The religious conflict was superimposed on the Wainakh hierarchy. The older generation has this attitude, 'Who do you think you are, milksop?!' It was hard for them to accept us.

The Islamic Institute in Malgobek had been given textbooks from Saudi Arabia, tomes that were personally delivered by the country's ambassador to the Russian Federation. However, Aushev shut down the fundamentalist institution, and instead introduced traditional Ingush Sufi teachings of Islam as a school subject. Although Aushev himself was not religious, according to those I interviewed, he felt it was important to revive Islam, which he believed could play an influential role in the upbringing of youth in the republic. However, he favoured a more customary low-key, ostensibly calmer form of Islam.

Akhmed Malsagov, the former prime minister, recalled that once Aushev even sent away an official delegation that had arrived from Saudi Arabia at the behest of Moscow.

By the late 1990s, issues related to the spread of Islamic fundamentalism had emerged as a serious concern of the Ingush government, which was aware of developments in Chechnya, and viewed radical Islam as a threat. In his 1997 annual speech to the nation, Aushev called Wahhabism 'a harmful movement'. In 1998, he issued a decree regulating the activities of religious educational institutions, and supervised the development of a joint plan of action between his government and republic's Spiritual Board of Muslims (*Muftiyat*). Under this plan, all *imams* in Ingushetia would receive salaries paid by the state, and missionaries from other countries would be advised to leave the republic (*Serdalo*, 5 August 1998).

It was not until the start of the Second Chechen War that Islamic fundamentalism really began to take hold in Ingushetia. Until then, Aushev had managed to control and marginalize fundamentalist groups – while, at the same time, giving them little cause for complaint. The state preserved freedom of religious conscience, and mosques mushroomed around the republic. The two major Muslim holidays of *Uraza-Bayram (Eid al-Fitr)* and *Kurban Bajram (Eid al-Adha)* were declared state holidays. The sale of alcohol was prohibited during Ramadan. Islam was introduced as a subject in schools. Aushev even de facto legalized polygamy. Moreover, the people recognized that the Ingush government was doing its best to deliver social services under very difficult circumstances. There were no major violations of human rights in the republic, which denied Islamic fundamentalists of a rallying point they commonly used to elicit support. And Aushev's openly critical position of Russian policy in Chechnya garnered the respect of Chechen field commanders, who refrained from challenging his authority.

Kinship, personal networks, ideology in the Ingush elite

Opinions on the role of kinship during the period of Aushev government differed greatly among those living in Ingushetia at the time. His opponents tell of how Ingushetia was effectively turned into the state of 'Aushetia', where all prominent posts were held by relatives of the forceful leader.

'In Karabulak, all the city mayors were Aushevs. This happens when a person becomes president, his *teip*, which has otherwise been dormant, wakes up and rallies around him', noted the Ingush historian, Nurdin Kozdoev in an interview.

Magomed-Sali Kotiev, who was part of the national movement, also pointed to widespread nepotism under Aushev:

[Aushev] said, 'What can I do if the Aushevs are educated? They were studying while others made money performing seasonal labour.' But Aushev has a big *familia*. He often trusted them not as relatives, but as specialists. Take Gutseriev [*a close supporter of Aushev, and a successful businessman – E.S.*]. He belonged to the Beshtoev *teip*. The Gutserievs are a very small lineage, 10 to 15 households. What has [Gutseriev] done for them? He is one of the 30 richest men in this country! He could have given a million roubles to every household, bought plots of land for everyone in the same area, and ensured that they lived comfortable lives. But he didn't do that.

Idris Abadiev, who possesses a very strong '*teip* consciousness', invested a great deal of time, and money, in galvanizing the Evloev *teip*. He told me, with unconcealed bitterness, that even though he had helped Evloevs to attain positions in government, they supported Aushev far more than other members of their *teip*, or the *teip* itself:

There were Evloevs in Aushev's government, The Minister of Labour, Deputy Minister for Social Development. But any Evloev who was appointed by [Aushev] stopped listening to the Evloevs. *Teip* affiliation doesn't matter. There is the president, and everybody does what he says. This has destroyed Ingush democracy. We have never had presidents, or tsars.

Still, even the greatest critics of Aushev's rule – and of the disproportionate role they say kin played in his government – concede that, in the end, the main criterion for appointment to positions in government and state enterprises under Aushev was adherence to his approach to government. One had to do his job well, and resist opportunities for corruption.

Mukhtar Buzurtanov – who has held posts in every Ingush government, from Aushev to Yevkurov, said that the term 'Aushetia', was merely invented by 'malicious gossipers', mainly members of national movements whom he did not invite to power. 'There were only four or five Aushevs in prominent positions in the republic, and he fired them just as often when they underperformed'. Notably, among the main political challengers during Ruslan Aushev's second term were two other Aushevs.

Indeed, there was a high turnover rate among Aushev's ministers, and heads of various state departments and agencies; from 1993 to 1994 ministers were often replaced after only several months in office. Frequently, after the president had fired a minister or mid-level official, the main newspapers published government documents stating that the person had been dismissed 'for inadequate performance' (see e.g. *Serdalo*, 25 March 2000).

Unsurprisingly, by the end of his second term, Aushev had made quite a few enemies in the republic. Some explain the frequent dismissals of state employees as a two-pronged effort by Aushev to break the old networks of nepotism and corruption dating back to Soviet times, and to simply rid the government of unprofessional and ineffective public servants. Others attribute the frequent layoffs to the president's quick temper.

In order to gauge the truth of the claims of kin-based preferential treatment under Ruslan Aushev, I scoured decrees and articles published in the editions of the newspapers *Serdalo* and *Ingushetia*, from 1992 to 2001. I then compiled a list of top- and mid-level government officials hired or dismissed by Aushev. Because some editions of both newspapers are missing from libraries in St Petersburg, Moscow and Nazran, the list might be incomplete.[1] Still, it contains most of the names of those fired, along with their job titles. Some of the officials held their posts only briefly, but, for the purposes of this examination, it is important to include them because they were recruited, at least for a time, into the Ingush elite.

As noted, Ingush *familias* may represent either lineages, or *teips*. Therefore, by examining the surnames (and sometimes the villages of origin) of public servants one can determine kinship links with a fairly high degree of certainty. Analysis of hirings and firings over the nine-year period shows that seven senior government officials were of the Aushev *familia*, while another two hailed from the Aushev *teip* (Toldiev *familia*). The next highest level of representation under the Aushev administration were found among representatives of Evloev *teip*, eight of whom held office, followed by the Barkinkhoev *teip* (seven), the Gorokoy *teip* (five) and the Ozdoev *teip* (three). All other Ingush *familias* and *teips* had three representatives or less.

The results of my analysis show that critics are correct in saying that Aushevs (members of both the *familia*, and the *teip*) were represented more than any other kinship group in state institutions in Ingushetia over the course of the period studied (see Table 7.1).

When presented with these figures, Akhmed Malsagov – who earlier acknowledged that Aushev was not without '*teip* consciousness' added:

Table 7.1 *Teip* representation in Ingush political elite 1992–2001 (four representatives or more)

Teip	Number of officials
Aushev	9
Yovloy	8
Barkinkhoy	7
Gorokoy	5
Malsag	4
Barakhoy	4
Khulakhoy	4

[1] A copy of the list can be found on the webpage of this book.

There was no clanship, but there was an element of kinship. There were Aushevs on the team. But, importantly, if an Aushev performed badly or behaved in an inadequate manner, Ruslan would punish him very strictly. There were many cases like that. For example, Bashir Aushev was the first Minister of Internal Affairs, but he was caught taking a bribe and was fired and punished.

Aushev's team also included a considerable number of officials who were not of ethnic Ingush origin (Russians, other non-Caucasian ethnic groups). For many years the prime minister was an ethnic Russian from the city of Voronezh, Boris Agapov, with whom Aushev had fought in Afghanistan. Several other veterans of the Afghan war among them, Ruslan Pliev, Emergencies Minister – also served on Aushev's team (Kovalskaya 1996).

Interestingly, even ethnic Russian officials adopted the rhetoric and approach of their Ingush colleagues. Agapov, for example, referred to the Ingush as 'our people', and Ingushetia as 'our republic'. He condemned the First Chechen War and the tactics of Russian generals. And he, more than Aushev, often spoke of the 'imperial ambitions' and 'Russian chauvinism' of the Kremlin (Kovalskaya 1996). Thus, Russians who served under Aushev were of the same mind as the president himself.

This chapter has shown that the defeat of ethnic Ingush at the hands of Ossetians and Russian troops in 1992 intensified feelings of insecurity among Ingush, stirred up their memories of grievances and alienation from the Russian state. At the same time, the ethnic conflict promoted feelings of solidarity that provided what Dankwart Rustow, a prominent scholar of democratization, called 'a strong sense of prior community' that 'was taken for granted' (1970: 346). Rustow considers such feelings to be important prerequisites for successful nation-building.

Unlike Chechnya, the Ingush subnational state was not born with 'birth defects'. Its first president, Ruslan Aushev, managed to consolidate post-conflict Ingush society through his resolute, but non-confrontational, style of leadership and his ability to defend the interests of the Ingush people vis-à-vis the federal centre, as well as to play an important role in regional affairs.

His creative approach to governance, compounded with his ability to find solutions to seemingly intractable problems, prevented the economy of the republic from total collapse, protected society from criminalization, and gave an impetus to the development of the educational system, healthcare and infrastructure of Ingushetia.

Ingush *familias* and *teips*, like their counterparts in Chechnya, experienced a revival. However, Ingush descent groups were unable to find a significant niche in the modern life of the republic. The role of religion grew during the first decade of Ingush statehood yet religion was not a factor in Aushev's choices of government officials and other public servants.

According to the Constitution of the Ingush Republic, the Parliament had very limited leverage over cadre policy, and the opposition was not organized. This lack of an effective system of checks and balances contributed to nepotism in the Aushev administration. A much greater share of descent and kin groups were represented in the Aushev government than in the administrations of Presidents Dzhokhar Dudaev and Aslan Maskhadov in Chechnya. However, all of those I interviewed agree that, at least among top-level government officials, Ingush appointments were meritocratic. The first president of Ingushetia did not give his relatives preferential treatment: they got jobs if they were qualified, and were dressed down or fired if they failed.

Using Migdal's classification of the relationship between the state and social groups (1988: 25), Aushev's government could be said to follow the 'accommodation' pattern toward traditionalist informal actors, such as Ingush *familias* and Sufi brotherhoods. The Aushev administration, like that of Dudaev in Chechnya, did not actively seek the participation or legitimization of informal actors, but allowed them to co-exist as long as they were peaceful. In turn, pre-existing informal patterns of social integration had internalized the idea of 'autonomy of the state', and did not press for greater participation in politics.

Aushev *marginalized* nationalists and Islamists but stopped short of persecution or repression.

Thus, 'the clan politics' argument does not apply to Ingushetia during the Aushev presidency, 1992–2001. The main criteria for elite recruitment were shared values and efficiency. In the conditions of low risk of physical elimination for Aushev or his prosecution of illegal economic activity, the president could afford not to have a tight-knit political team, based on strong ties.

Quite high degrees of secular national consolidation achieved by the Aushev government are acknowledged even by his critics. However, Ingush state-building 1991–2002 did not result in the institutionalization of the system: it produced a highly personalized, presidential political regime heavily dependent on the consolidating capacities of President Ruslan Aushev.

8

In the Authoritarian State: Ingushetia under Murat Zyazikov (2002–2008)

The weakness of Russian federalism of the 1990s is often explained by the weakness of the federal centre. When Vladimir Putin came to power in 1999, he aimed to strengthen the federal centre, which provided a window of opportunity for Russia to build balanced federal relations on the principles of 'strong centre – strong regions' (Busygina 2018). However, instead of developing and strengthening the federation, the Kremlin started to build what it called 'the vertical of power', gradually depriving the regions of their former sovereignty.

These processes included changes in the order of formation of the Federation Council, the Russian Senate, whereby the elected governors and republican presidents were replaced by republican representatives, significantly weakening this once-powerful body; the abolition of direct regional elections (in most entities, election by the regional legislative assemblies after the nominees had been approved by the president of the Russian Federation); reduced status of national languages; consolidation, leading to a reduction in the number of federation entities; redistribution of power in favour of the centre; and a growing imbalance of federal, regional and local budget incomes, with more and more of the revenues concentrated in the federal centre, depriving other governments levels of economic self-sufficiency (Isakova and Jalilova 2018; Busygina 2018; Zulkarnay 2018). In addition, all regional leaders except for Chechnya's Ramzan Kadyrov lost their leverage on security services.

The abolition of popular-vote elections deprived regional leaders of legitimacy, minimized the level of political competition and dramatically reduced the accountability of the leaders to their constituencies. In turn, this significantly lowered the status of the highest officials of the republics, gradually turning them into executors of the will of the federal authorities – not of the voters. With Dmitry Medvedev's 'thaw' (2008–2012), elections in some regions returned, but a 'municipal filter' was introduced, which prevented independent candidates from running. The increased control of the federal centre over the economic, social and political activities of the regions deprived the regional leaders of their political independence. The concept of free and fair elections at all levels of governance gradually became obsolete, as large-scale electoral fraud turned elections into a political ritual rather than a meaningful mechanism for selecting representatives of the people.

In 2010, Chechnya's President Ramzan Kadyrov proposed changing the title of regional leaders from 'President' to 'Head' of a republic, arguing that only one person should be entitled to be called 'president' in the country. This proposal was eagerly 'accepted' by the Kremlin (which probably used Ramzan to imitate a bottom-up initiative).

'A highly centralized government system was formed in Russia in the 2000s', according to Natalia Zubarevich (2018), a leading expert on Russian regions. As Irina Busygina has rightly pointed out, 'given the huge area of the territory, diversity and multinational population composition, some degree of decentralization will be present, but this decentralization will not make the country a federation' (Busygina 2018).

Given these developments, it is not possible to speak of autonomous subnational state-building in this period. The regional leaders did not have to struggle to earn their own money, devise special measures to combat crime, or find creative solutions for managing underfunded education and healthcare. The federal centre significantly increased its contribution to regional budgets; it provided for the state-employed sector; the situation when salaries and pension payments were delayed for months would not be repeated.

Further, there was greater funding for regional schools and hospitals; the federal centre set up specially targeted programmes to improve social infrastructure and roads, support cultural activities and resettle people from shabby housing or landslide zones. However, at the same time, the federal centre deprived the local population of leverage over the performance of the authorities and security services. These were granted full impunity for economic crimes and sometimes grave human rights violations, in return for loyalty, ability to keep public protests under control and for ensuring the 'proper' electoral results for the ruling party.

Murat Zyazikov, a lieutenant-general in the Federal Security Service (FSB), and a protégé of then-president Vladimir Putin, is a classic example of a new regional governor. In May 2002, he became president of Ingushetia in an election widely regarded as neither free nor fair. This was probably the least remarkable period in recent Ingush history as Zyazikov never had any serious ambition of changing the republic: he simply followed his own, highly self-centred, agenda. Zyazikov lacked any notable economic, social, law-enforcement policies – thus this chapter on to his time in offices is the shortest in this book.

Conflict spillover

The ascent of Zyazikov dramatically changed the profile of Ingushetia. Whereas Ruslan Aushev had managed, as president, to protect Ingushetia from the spillover of the bloody conflict in Chechnya, Zyazikov had been installed primarily to ensure the freedom of operations of the federal security services in the republic. Mop-up operations similar to those carried out by Russian forces in Chechnya were now carried out in Ingushetia as well. As I moved to the North Caucasus from St Petersburg in early 2003 and spent most of the next five years in Ingushetia, so I was able to follow these processes closely.

In my new job at Memorial human rights group in Ingushetia, one of the first cases was that of Visadi Shokarov, a Chechen IDP, a resident of the refugee camp Satsita in Ingushetia. My colleagues and I were in the camp when his dead body was brought;

waves of shock, terror and indignation shattered the camp. A big crowd gathered; women were crying and shouting. Shokarov's body was brought into the mosque, where we later examined it. It was a shocking sight: burnt and mutilated with numerous cut injuries, split skull and one arm missing. Shokarov was among the first persons to be abducted by unidentified masked armed military servicemen from this IDP camp early in the morning on 6 January 2003. A few days later, relatives were notified that Visadi Shokarov had been officially arrested on the suspicion of participating in an armed attack. A month later the investigator contacted Shokarov's wife and told her to pick up the body of her husband in the morgue. He was said to have died as a result of a car accident when being driven in custody from one place to another. Clearly (I saw it with my own eyes), the nature of his injuries was incompatible with the official explanation offered to the family. This man had been very brutally tortured and mutilated before his death. Shokarov's story is typical of many other summary executions; indeed, his family was relatively lucky to have got Visadi's body back. Nearly 5,000 Chechen men who had detained in a similar way disappeared without any traces.

Initially, the abductions and summary executions in Ingushetia mostly affected Chechen IDPs. From 2003, however, security operations, often accompanied by enforced disappearances, targeted ethnic Ingush, and insurgency forces were increasingly carrying out attacks on Ingush soil.

The situation escalated rapidly after 21/22 June 2004, when a group of up to 600 men attacked Ingushetia and took control of several towns including the largest, Nazran and Karabulak. The attack started in the evening when many people were still outdoors. I myself was at home in Nazran alone, working on a text, when I heard heavy gunfire in the neighbourhood. 'Strange, such a loud wedding on a Monday', I mused, and continued my work. Apparently, many people were thinking along the same lines, as curious mothers with their children rushed towards the nearby police station where the sounds were coming from, to see what was going on. Ingush residents simply did not expect a street fight in the middle of their peaceful city. After some time, I saw red tracer bullets flying close to my window, then grenade launchers went off and the pane of one of my windows cracked. In the yard downstairs armed men in masks, some with very long beards, started to push women and children into the houses. My neighbour Madina knocked on my door and took me into her home. Her husband was downtown at the time and could not come back home as the whole city was now controlled by the attackers. I spent the night together with Madina and her five little children; we had no idea how long the clashes would continue.

The only forces who resisted the attack were the local Ingush police, many of whom were killed or summarily executed that night. Neither the federal army nor the internal troops stationed in the republic provided support to the Ingush police. In total, the attackers killed at least 79 people, including 43 policemen, and injured another 88, before retreating in the morning.

During the first 48 hours there were no security operations carried out in Ingushetia; then, after the attackers had retreated, major mop-up operations were launched in the Chechen IDP camps. Furious Ingush police blocked the camps, dragged Chechen men out of tents, forced them on the ground, beat and humiliated them, and dozens of men were arrested. Women were told to return to Chechnya.

My colleagues and I happened to be in a camp during one such mop-up that was conducted by heavily armed and masked police, shouting, shooting into the air, dragging men into buses in what was a truly intimidating episode. Ethnic hatred was in the air; many of us were very concerned that outright clashes might ensue. As more information about the attack became available, it became clear that there had been many ethnic Ingush among the insurgents – probably as many as Chechens, perhaps more. The Ingush insurgency, closely linked with the Chechen, was beginning.

After the events of 21/22 June, Ingushetia was quickly sliding into a raging conflict zone: security services carried out operations that severely violated human rights: suspects were seized, subjected to beatings and torture, and sometimes summarily executed; criminal charges were falsified against them. The insurgents attacked the Ingush police, federal servicemen, officials and sometimes civilians.

Zyazikov turned a blind eye to the mass abuses of human rights, not even trying to pretend that he was concerned. He let the security services do as they wished. In return, the Kremlin granted him full freedom over the republic's economic affairs. In June 2005, by which time regional elections had been abolished across Russia, Murat Zyazikov was appointed to a second five-year term.

Corruption and 'clanship'

Zyazikov's government became famous for its unprecedented corruption, violence and general incompetence. His team was unable to solve any of the problems of the republic: ensure security to the population, support socio-economic development, or defend Ingush interests in the Ingush–Ossetian conflict. While most residents of Ingushetia were struggling to make ends meet, the political elite were building luxurious mansions. The Kremlin granted impunity to the loyal local elites, and closed its eyes to the clearly fake reports of 'success'.

In 2007, Zyazikov told reporters that his administration had nearly doubled the amount of public housing in the republic: 'In the last three years we built 3,233,000 square metres of residential housing. For a small republic, this is a huge figure.' That figure was indeed difficult to fathom, considering that total public housing under Aushev had accounted for less than 3 million square metres, and residents across the republic were hard-pressed to find any new construction apart from the private homes of their better-off neighbours (Velikovsky, 24 September 2009).

In a report to President Putin, broadcast on the central TV channels, Zyazikov claimed to have launched 80 industrial enterprises in the republic. That produced furious reactions in Ingushetia, which was too small for members of the public not to notice such enterprises (Velikovsky 2009) – especially since the gross regional product fell by 25 per cent during his first two years in office, and unemployment and poverty soared to 55 per cent and 80 per cent, respectively. Corruption was also reported to have risen significantly (*Wild West*, 30 January 2009).

The prominence of kinship in Zyazikov's team was minor, but the role it played was significant. His most trusted aide was a matrilineal cousin, Rustambek Zyazikov, who held the relatively minor post of manager of Zyazikov's personal guard. He also relied on another cousin, Rashid Zyazikov, who was the head of his administration.

Despite his modest post, Rustambek became the most powerful man in the republic. It was common knowledge that, in order to gain a post in the Zyazikov government, one had to pay a bribe – and these bribes were allegedly arranged for by Rustambek Zyazikov. In fact, all financial agreements with the state were thought to be negotiated by Rustambek.

'Who stood behind Zyazikov? Only his relatives, friends, confidants', explained Azamat Nalgiev, a Member of the Ingush Parliament. 'What Zyazikov presented as his team was, in fact, his clan, his associates – an association of human exploiters who stole from their people in a climate of complete lawlessness and impunity. It was an interest group united by the interests of thieves.'

For example, Rashid Zyazikov was implicated to be involved in a scheme whereby he represented the interests of certain businesses – helping them, for a fee, to gain no-interest loans and credit, as well as permissions for various construction projects. The credit and loans were signed by Finance Minister Aset Ustilgova. The opposition website Ingushetia.org investigated various illegal schemes which they claimed were used to channel public funds to private pockets. In 2006, the Prosecutor's Office opened a case against Ustilgova on suspicion of large-scale embezzlement of public funds (Caucasus Knot, 19 August 2006); however, it was inconclusive and Ustilgova was never made accountable. Zyazikov used his lobbying capacities to make sure the Prosecutor (who was surprisingly his brother-in-law, married to the sister of his wife) left Ingushetia, and the case was closed.

One of the biggest scams is alleged to have involved Musa Medov, the Minister of Internal Affairs. Medov reportedly orchestrated the large-scale corruption surrounding the disbursement of benefits awarded to policemen after an attack by armed insurgents on the night of 21 June 2004. Following the attack Ingush police officers – sensing that the situation in the republic was hurtling toward armed conflict – began to leave their jobs, *en masse*. The Kremlin responded to the defections by paying police officers 'emergency money', (чрезвычайка) supplementary funds – retroactive to 1992, the period of the Ingush–Ossetian conflict – for working in a zone designated officially as being an 'emergency situation'.

Under this plan, even police officers who had been employed for only a few years would receive sums sufficient for the cash purchase of a house. However, throughout the republic, police spoke of having to keep between 40 to 50 per cent of the 'emergency money' as a bribe before they received anything. Moreover, officers said they were compelled to pay judges to confirm that they had been legally employed as police officers during the relevant periods. (Moreover, lawyers prepared the necessary court documents, then served as 'postmen' who delivered the documents, along with bribes, to judges.) In the course of my fieldwork, I met several people who had not worked a single day on the police force, yet – after paying the requisite bribes – received emergency pay-outs.

My acquaintance, Musa, a defence lawyer, put it very succinctly: 'This might be the only opportunity in my life to make such money, and I can't pass it up.' He bought a luxurious apartment in downtown Magas, the new Ingush capital, after only several months of work representing police officers in such 'emergency' cases.

Thus, members of Zyazikov's team were 'doing business' by virtue of their office – all the while engaging in a cover-up of their machinations that was emblematic of what a respected scholar of the Russian informal economy, Alena Ledeneva, has called the 'exchange of favours' (Ledeneva 1998). All this was possible due to the tightly integrated trust network, whose members were complicit in *krugovaya poruka*, with each covering up for one another. Zyazikov's closest allies in government were neither relatives, nor members of his *teip* or *familia*. All five were united by common economic interests, and the mutual trust and dependence deriving from detailed knowledge of the others' conduct. Zyazikov's only relatives with significant posts in government were his matrilineal cousins; several other relatives occupied less prominent positions, not playing any significant role.

Following Zyazikov's resignation, the news portal Ingushetia.org, published a list of alleged members of 'Zyazikov's team', which it claimed were responsible for the plundering of the republic. According to the news portal's list of 46 of the closest associates of Zyazikov, only two were members of his *teip*.[1] Moreover, the republic's largest *teip*, Evloev, was represented in government by only five members, and the second largest, Ozdoev, had only two persons in the government. Otherwise, representation was spread quite evenly among the republic's other *teips* and *familias*. There were also two ethnic Russians on the list – one of them, Yuri Turygin, Prosecutor of the Ingush Republic, was once among the most loyal supporters of Zyazikov, and eagerly tried to suppress reports of financial and other misdeeds committed by the president and his inner circle. Once Zyazikov was replaced, however, Turygin joined his successor, Yunus-Bek Yevkurov, in efforts to unmask frauds committed under Zyazikov by his former comrades. Subsequent investigation of the republic's coffers by the Federal Audit Chamber uncovered violations amounting to 1.74 billion roubles, or 13.4 per cent of the republic's annual budget.

This chapter has demonstrated that the government of Murat Zyazikov, probably the most corrupt and inefficient in the history of Ingushetia, was a trust group, linked by common economic interests and the high risks.

The physical risks to the lives of Zyazikov and his near family were indeed high due to insurgency and criminality. There was an attempt on his life committed by a suicide bomber in April 2004. In 2006 his 70-year-old father-in-law, a Member of the Ingush Parliament, was abducted; two months later, he was released after lengthy negotiations with the perpetrators. Then in 2007, his 72-year-old uncle was abducted from a mosque, the perpetrators demanding millions of dollars of ransom for his release.

His risks of prosecution could be related to economic and other even more serious crimes if he fell out of favour with the Kremlin. After all, Zyazikov's resignation came two months after the most brazen assassination of his time, of his most outspoken critic, Magomed Yevloev, committed on 31 August 2008.[2]

---

[1] Zyazikov grew up in the family of his mother and bears the name of his matrilineal kin. His actual *teip* members (Borovs) were not represented in the ruling elite.

[2] On that day, Zyazikov was travelling on a flight from Moscow to Ingushetia. He noticed among the passengers one of his main critics, Magomed Yevloev, who ran the oppositionist website, Ingushetia. ru. Zyazikov made a phone call. When the plane landed, he disembarked and was met on the tarmac by Musa Medov, Minister of Internal Affairs of Ingushetia. Medov hustled Zyazikov away – but not before gesturing to security agents of the ministry to board the plane. The agents seized Yevloev. Some 30 minutes later his body – a bullet in the temple – was dumped outside the republic's main hospital in Nazran.

To mitigate his multiple risks Zyazikov relied on his tight support group. His elite had only a minor kinship element, his 'clan' consisted mostly of non-relatives. Yet, compared to the Aushev presidency, when the percentage of *teip* members was much larger, the strength of ties was much higher in Zyazikov's period. He hardly ever dismissed any of his close allies for underperformance and the cadre rotation was very low. In Ingushetia 2002–2008, the absence of elections, the lack of any system of checks and balances, virtually no political autonomy from the federal centre, dependent courts and ineffective prosecution – all this combined to create a predatory system, where persons with access to channels of public goods redistribution extracted resources for their own benefit.

The Ingush opposition disclosed numerous cases of corruption, and detailed the corruption schemes – but their allegations never resulted in *bona fide* official investigations and sentences. Federal journalists who tried to investigate corruption were harassed, also after Zyazikov's resignation. For example, REN-TV journalist Leonid Kanfer and cameraman Victor Muzalevsky were threatened by Rustambek Zyazikov, and their driver was beaten in Ingushetia in 2009. The crew had been working on an investigative reportage into corruption under Zyazikov and were filming from the outside the property allegedly belonging to the Zyazikov family (Committee to Protect Journalists, 15 October 2009).

Ingush opposition leader, Maksharip Aushev, who also made public the corruption schemes in this period and was involved in a personal conflict with Rustambek Zyazikov on this score, was killed by unidentified perpetrators in October 2009. Prior to his assassination, Aushev had received multiple death threats (Memorial, 8 December 2009). After completing his term, Murat Zyazikov was transferred to Moscow to become advisor to the then Russian President Medvedev. He has never worked in Ingushetia since then.

9

Ingushetia under Yunus-Bek Yevkurov (2008–2019)

On 30 October 2008, General Yunus-Bek Yevkurov was appointed president of Ingushetia by the then-president of Russia, Dmitry Medvedev (Caucasian Knot, 31 October 2008). The Ingush Parliament – the People's Assembly of Ingushetia – approved the appointment on the next day.

Yevkurov, an Ingush from a large rural family, was born in the disputed Prigorodny district of North Ossetia, but left the republic in 1980s, when he was drafted into the Soviet army. There he went on to make a successful military career: a paratrooper and a reconnaissance specialist, he was involved in numerous combat operations, including in Kosovo and Chechnya, for which he was proclaimed a Hero of Russia. The replacement of the FSB general Murat Zyazikov by a GRU (Military Intelligence) general Yunus-Bek Yevkurov was received with enthusiasm in Ingushetia: crowds thronged the streets, dancing *lezginka*, to celebrate the departure of the detested leader (*Echo Moskvi*, 31 October 2008). Also, the local opposition expressed readiness to support and cooperate with Yevkurov (*Lenta*, 31 October 2008), who declared his intention to engage in dialogue with various forces in society to resolve the numerous problems of the region.

> His first moves were encouraging. He communicated easily with the common people. Zyazikov would never talk to people without tight security measures and bodyguards. Yevkurov started to turn up alone at some religious gatherings, in the streets. He was open and without fear. This is what our people like, such unreasonably brave people. Gradually he showed himself as a more active politician who had assumed responsibility for the nation, especially compared to Zyazikov whom many considered a leader with no will of his own.
> – Akhmed Buzurtanov, businessman and public activist

Many of my respondents mentioned this openness that won the hearts of the Ingush people.

> We had high hopes. He chose the right policy line. He would put on his *tubitejka* [*traditional skullcap*] and go into the mosques, to talk to people. And people appreciated this possibility of dialogue.
> – Fatima, housewife, resident of Sunzha

Many expectations were related to the fact that Yevkurov came from Prigorodny district; there were hopes that he would try to get the disputed lands returned to Ingushetia.

– Isa, driver, resident of Nazran

Yevkurov was appointed at a time when Ingushetia was a full-fledged conflict zone, indeed the most unstable region of the North Caucasus. There were insurgency attacks, armed clashes or counter-terrorism operations nearly every day.

Yevkurov announced a new policy of countering the insurgency based on a combination of soft and hard measures. The security services continued to carry out law-enforcement operations, killing and arresting suspected insurgents. Yevkurov insisted on the integration of law-abiding Salafis and intra-confessional dialogue; furthermore, he defended the continued functioning of Ingushetia's 13 Salafi mosques, declaring that they should be properly registered and represented on the Spiritual Board of Muslims (Borodikhin, 29 May 2018).

In May 2009 he met with representatives of the various religious groups in the republic and called for dialogue among them, also on some points of dogmatic disagreement. Extra-judicial persecution and harassment of law-abiding Salafi were stopped. The number of registered cases of abductions, enforced disappearances and torture in Ingushetia also dropped, although security operations aimed at the capture or killing of active insurgents continued (Human Rights Centre Memorial, 26 June 2015).

Yevkurov has been credited for stopping abductions of people by security service personnel in Ingushetia, the investigative authorities also tried to react to the most extreme cases of abuse and falsification of criminal files. Most notably, in December 2016, the director of the Centre for Countering Extremism, Timur Khamkhoev, his deputy and two other officers were accused of 'overstepping their legal authority and for the violent treatment of detainees that resulted in substantial violations of the rights of citizens' – in other words, torture that led to one death. Khamkhoev and his team received prison sentences of three to ten years – unprecedented in the North Caucasus, where the security services had enjoyed almost total impunity.

This was a radical change compared to the time of Zyazikov, whom many Ingush blame for 'letting the security services rule the republic', when there had been systematic abductions and killings, and non-violent Salafi communities were persecuted, treated by security services as supporters or accomplices of the insurgency (HRC Memorial, 26 June 2015).

Human rights defenders appreciated the new approach and started to cooperate with Yevkurov:

We turned to him because he turned to face the problems we raised [grave violations of human rights]. He started to speak publicly about them, raise them with the federal authorities. This won him support. This was the time when Medvedev was in power in the Kremlin, he was a kind of liberal. And Yevkurov was the continuation of Medvedev's liberal line in our region.

– Timur Akiev, director of the Memorial Human Rights Centre in Ingushetia

Then, on 22 June 2009, Yunus-Bek Yevkurov survived a serious attempt on his life, when his cortege was attacked by an insurgent car filled with explosives. His bodyguard was killed, Yevkurov himself was severely injured and remained in a coma until successfully treated by some of Russia's top physicians.

Fatima, a resident of Sunzha, explained: 'He changed after he hardly survived [the attack], they assembled him back from pieces. And he started to distance himself from the people.'

Many of my respondents, especially women, emphasized how much they had wanted Yevkurov to survive and return to office.

> When he was blown up I remember how *every time in my prayer I was asking /God/* that he would recover and come back to the republic. I know that many people were really praying for his recovery. But he came back very different. He stopped trusting people, he was no longer close to people, he had decided to be wary. There were even some conspiracy theories circulating that he had been targeted [by the security services] because they didn't want Ingushetia to have a people's leader.
> – Laura, resident of Malgobek

Yet, after returning to office, Yunus-Bek Yevkurov deepened his soft-measure approaches to counter-insurgency. In 2011 he established a commission for the rehabilitation of former fighters which aimed to help insurgents surrender to the authorities and return to peaceful life (Yevkurov, 28 July 2012). A similar commission, set up in Dagestan in 2010, had been criticized for being largely a PR exercise aimed more at promoting its chairperson and not working for the surrender of real fighters. The Ingush Commission, having learnt from its Dagestani counterpart, adopted a different, non-public *modus operandi*.

The Commission's first chair, Akhmet Kotiev, at the time Secretary of Ingushetia's Security Council, explained to me in 2012 that the Commission worked mainly through kinship relations, informally negotiating individual surrenders through relatives. In the prevailing conditions of widespread application of torture to individuals suspected of participation in armed groups, Kotiev and the Commission provided informal guarantees to the families that physical mistreatment of their surrendering family member would not be practised. Such informal guarantees served as an additional, perhaps even primary, mechanism that supported the formal procedure.

Once I spent four hours in Kotiev's office after business hours, discussing the root causes of radicalization with him and his deputy. He was very keen to hear about the 'social portrait' of violent extremists and the typical trajectories of radicalization. However, he seemed disappointed to learn that I thought that there was no one social portrait or stable trajectory, but rather push and pull factors. This made things look too unstructured and difficult to address, in his view. He also had difficulty admitting that the peaceful protests that he had crushed when he headed the city police in Nazran, or assassinated opposition leaders (in one case, he was allegedly involved indirectly), were among most powerful push factors.

Starting from 2012, after the return of Vladimir Putin, most of the soft measures of counter-insurgency were rolled back; Ingushetia, however, managed to defend its approaches. 'The winds have changed, but thanks to the head of our republic [Yevkurov] we defended our Commission, even though it was against the general political trend at that time', Kotiev explained to me. It is hard to determine whether it was due to Yevkurov or to Akhmet Kotiev himself that the Commission kept working, because after Kotiev was killed by the insurgents in August 2013, the activity of the Commission fell dramatically, and in the following year it nearly stopped operations.

Intra-confessional schism

Ingushetia maintained its soft-power religious policy, but Yevkurov's attempt to liberalize government attitudes towards Salafi mosques resulted in a sharp public clash with the Sufi Mufti of the Republic (the Chair of the Spiritual Board of Muslims), Isa Khamkhoev, who mobilized the support of Sufi believers against Yevkurov and the Salafis. The Spiritual Boards of Muslims, or Muftiyats, in Russia are self-governed organizations of Muslims in a given territory that coordinate the daily activities of religious institutions (mosques and religious schools). After the collapse of the USSR, these boards represented the official, government-loyal Muslim organizations; in turn, the government supported the boards (politically and by paying salaries to *imams*), which in many places turned into semi-government institutions. The *mufti* usually holds a very important position in any Muslim-dominated region of Russia.

Isa Khamkhoev, who had been elected as a *mufti* in 2004, was an influential, affluent person backed by a large support group of local *imams* – members of the Spiritual Board. These *imams* were often elected by the local communities with the endorsement of Khamkhoev and received small salaries from the state through the Ministry for Nationalities. Khamkhoev was strongly opposed to dialogue with Salafis, in particular the inclusion of Salafi mosques in the Spiritual Board. On 5 June 2015, he and his supporters tried to take over, by force, one of the Salafi mosques in Nasyr-Kort run by a charismatic and very popular *imam*, Khamzat Chumakov (INKavkaz, 5 June 2015). Fist fights erupted in and near the mosque, but the believers and the security services prevented Khamkhoev's men from taking control of the mosque. This episode had deep repercussions in Ingush society and beyond, as Chumakov was an outspoken figure, popular far beyond Ingushetia, a celebrity *imam* among youth (Khamzat Chumakov, 5 June 2017). To mediate in the conflict, representatives of Yevkurov first visited the mosque, and spoke with the Salafi clerics and the congregation (Khamzat Chumakov, 5 June 2017). In the following week, Yevkurov attended Friday prayers in the Nasyr-Kort mosque; he blamed both sides for the incident and called on them to restore the peace (Yevkurov Ingushetia, 13 June 2015).

The *mufti* recorded a series of video appeals in which he claimed that Chumakov was an illegitimate *imam* and should be replaced. He also stated that no new trends in Islam were needed in Ingushetia (Imams, Alims of Ingushetia, 8 June 2015). Subsequently Yevkurov blamed the mufti for polarizing local society and called for his resignation. The Ministry of Justice then initiated procedures of dissolution of the Spiritual Board of Muslims (the Muftiyat), which was registered as a public association – an unprecedented move in post-Soviet Russia (Official website of the Republic of Ingushetia, 5 February 2016).

This markedly deepened the intra-confessional schism among believers. Khamkhoev and his supporters were not prepared to give in, and they mobilized support, also at high levels. Yevkurov tried to call for the Congress of Imams of Ingushetia to elect another *mufti*, but he eventually gave up on this idea: a spiralling of the confrontation seemed very likely. The Council of Alims (Islamic scholars) that did get together refused to dismiss Isa Khamkhoev, even though Yevkurov threatened to withdraw their (state-paid) salaries – which he eventually did. Quite unprecedentedly, the usually dependent court went against Yevkurov, and found no grounds for dissolving the Spiritual Centre of Muslims (Muradov and Chernykh, 12 April 2020). In 2017 the Ministry of Justice of Ingushetia rescinded its decision on dissolving the Muftiyat, and Yevkurov stepped down before his upcoming re-appointment for the next term as head of the republic (Department of the Ministry of Justice, 14 September 2017).

However, the conflict remained simmering. After a new episode of confrontation over property rights to a large plot of land intended for the new mosque in Magas, the Muftiyat even excommunicated Yevkurov from the Muslim community of the republic – another development unparalleled in post-Soviet Russia (Borodikhin 2018).

How did it come about that the usually dependent court and the religious authorities, who otherwise tended to be reluctant to oppose the secular authorities, resisted Yevkurov's attempts to dissolve Muftiyat or get rid of Khamkhoev?

According to one local analyst:

No one wants to become an enemy of the Qadiri *tariqa* [which Khamkhoev and the Spiritual Board largely represented], because that is the largest and the best organized community in Ingushetia. If the judge is Ingush, he is socially dependent on society, he can't become enemy of the individuals whom Yevkurov is prosecuting. Yevkurov is in Ingushetia today, and he will not be in Ingushetia tomorrow – but the Qadiri Sufis will remain. If there are legal grounds to prosecute them, the judges will do so, but if there are none, why should they run such risks?

Another question is why the federal centre did not intervene in Yevkurov's clash with the Sufis, whom it usually supported across the North Caucasus. Some local observers hold that Moscow had not even noticed the conflict until mass protests broke out in Ingushetia in 2018; other analysts claim that the dialogue with Salafis was the initiative of the federal centre, which explains why it tolerated Yevkurov's clash with the Muftiyat.

The aim of the federal centre was to weaken some of the Sufi groups which had become significantly strengthened recently. For years they had been supported by the state in their clash against Salafis, so they accumulated resources and power. The federal centre did not want such strong players, especially if they had political ambitions. That's why Yevkurov started to create divisions inside these groups, aiming to weaken them. He supported and promoted alternative leaders among the Khadzhi-murid *vird* and he really weakened the Batal-Khadzhi *vird*, while the Naqshbandi *vird* was naturally weakened because many of its young people moved closer to Salafis.

– Akhmed Buzurtanov, local businessman and activist

Isa Khamkhoev clearly had political ambitions, according to many of my respondents. An affluent businessman, not particularly learned in Islam but with strong support of the Sufi *alims*, he had a popular radio station at his disposal and good connections outside the republic. 'He was always part of the political establishment, I've never thought of him in any other capacity than as a politician', explained Hava, a resident of Nazran.

'The Sufi *alims* who supported the *mufti* went into opposition to Yevkurov and they were the ones who had deep influence in the local communities. There has never been such a deep schism among the Ingush believers since the Ingush adopted Islam', a Sufi activist told me. Isa Khamkhoev began travelling to Grozny, where he participated in the anti-extremism events (ChGTRK 'Grozny', 28 December 2015), including with Ramzan Kadyrov, who offered the Ingush *mufti* support against Yevkurov, with whom he had very tense relations.

On the surface, the conflict between Kadyrov and Yevkurov was mainly about approaches to combating insurgency and violent extremism. Kadyrov implemented very heavy-handed measures against Salafism and the insurgency, and was highly irritated by Yevkurov's soft-power approaches. He repeatedly accused Yevkurov of being too lenient, or reluctant to fight extremists: in Chechnya itself all Salafis were treated as accomplices of terrorists (Grishina, 6 August 2012). Yevkurov, on the contrary, tried to maintain the image of a liberal, open politician, who preferred dialogue to repression. According to some of my respondents, he even intentionally played on the contrast with Ramzan Kadyrov in order to reap political dividends inside and outside the republic. In my view, there was also a personal dimension to this clash: Ramzan wanted to be the regional boss and get leaders of other republics to recognize his special status, whereas Yevkurov, himself a man of strong character and impressive military achievement, treated Kadyrov as a (younger) equal, which greatly irritated the latter.

The soft measures, liberalization of attitudes towards Salafis, visible improvements in the sphere of human rights, combined with vigorous law-enforcement measures aimed at capturing or eliminating the remaining fighters – all this significantly reduced violence in the republic. By 2016 the activity of the Islamist insurgency was sharply reduced, and Ingushetia became one of the most tranquil regions of the North Caucasus (Gadzhiev, 8 June 2016). The general level of crime under Yunus-Bek Yevkurov also reduced by 21 per cent (Russian Federation, General Prosecutors Office 2021; Republic of Ingushetia, Ministry of Internal Affairs 2018).

This of course cannot be credited to Yevkurov alone. Since 2010/2011, the Imarat Kavkaz insurgency had been in deep crisis, as was its Ingush section, *vilayat Galgaiche*. Most of the high-ranking leaders of Ingush insurgency had been killed by the security services, including the notorious Amir Abdullah (Artur Getagazhev) who had reportedly organized the assassination of the Chair of the Commission for the Rehabilitation of Fighters, Secretary of Security Council Akhmet Kotiev and several other high-target attacks. From 2014, many Ingush radicals had begun to leave for Syria and Iraq, which also contributed to reducing the level of violence in the republic.

Economy and governance

Yevkurov's appointment as president of Ingushetia came with significant federal funding. The targeted federal programme for 'Socio-economic development of Ingushetia 2010–2016' made possible the construction of 70 new industrial, agricultural and social objects for 16.5 billion roubles (*RIA Novosti*, 12 May 2016). A new programme, 'Socio-economic development of Ingushetia 2016–2025' followed. However, despite this significant funding, there was little improvement in the quality of life. Moreover, by the end of Yevkurov's time in office it had become clear that most of the newly constructed industrial enterprises were unfeasible (*Tass*, 9 September 2019). In 2019 the Ingush government acknowledged that most of the industrial enterprises funded through the federal programme, and 16 agricultural enterprises, were running at a loss, due to lack of contracts (Kostoeva, 13 November 2019). Some of the agricultural enterprises were put up for sale at prices far lower than the construction costs, which had been paid by the state (Russian Federation, Ministry of Property and Land Relations of the Republic of Ingushetia 2019).

> In the North Caucasus, the economy is shaped by the way corruption is organized. During Yevkurov's time, the circle of people who could benefit from corruption was significantly narrowed compared to Zyazikov's time, consequently, the income of the population went down visibly, business and services were suffering because purchasing power had fallen so steeply. I felt that my business reached its ceiling by 2014, people just had no money to buy my services. The money which was accumulated by the elites was not invested in the republic – they had no plans to live in this republic, they invested in real estate and businesses in Moscow or other regions of Russia.
>
> – local businessman

The average salary of employees in the health care and education system in 2018 was USD 384 and 300 USD respectively; actual salaries of schoolteachers seemed to be getting lower. 'My son and daughter are both schoolteachers. She gets 17,000 (240 USD) and he gets 16,000 roubles (230 USD), working fulltime with extra hours', a resident of Nazran told me.

Initially, Yevkurov's declared (and highly publicized) economic policy gave new hopes to the people. Ingushetia participated in prestigious economic forums, and signed fat investment contracts – however, according to local experts, most of these either remained on paper or proved dysfunctional. The enterprises, schools and hospitals constructed during the programme were of very low quality; their budget prices were inflated while actual costs were reduced to a minimum.

For example, in November 2021 the court temporarily closed one of the schools (704 places) constructed within the framework of the federal targeted programme 2016–2025 in the town of Malgobek (*Tass*, 15 November 2019). The building was full of cracks, several rooms had high humidity, and there had been numerous security violations in its construction. This school had been completed in 2018, and 290 million roubles had been allocated to it. Moreover, in the same region, the new (2013) water purification system was not functional – a serious matter, given Ingushetia's chronic problems with clean water supply. Further, a kindergarten constructed in 2012 was eroded by cracks and no longer fit to be used; a new multi-flat building constructed as social housing was also covered with cracks and declared not usable (Press Service of Ingushetia, 27 April 2021). Another three kindergartens had been planned for construction in the same region by 2018, but as of 2021 they were not even close to completion, and the funding had been used up. The same thing happened with another school, for which 400 million roubles had been allocated, but only 50 per cent of the building constructed. Enterprises were in a similarly pathetic condition: for example, a factory producing energy-saving lamps was constructed, but closed in 2019, due to lack of demand for its products.

The Ingush opposition leaders Akhmet Pogorov and Barakh Chemurziev investigated these grave facts of corruption and recorded a series of videos showing sites of several enterprises that were to have been constructed under the federal targeted programmes but were either non-existent or not functioning. For example, they showed a residential neighbourhood in Malgobek which had been constructed for the resettlement of the residents of landslide areas. According to Pogorov, Yunus-Bek Yevkurov had reported to President Putin that the micro-district was completed; however, the video showed that most of the houses were empty: 'We see that this is a dead zone. No one has been resettled here', Pogorov concluded (Fortanga Org 7 March 2019a, 8 March 2019b, 11 March 2019c, Fortanga.org, 3 March 2021).

Akhmed Buzurtanov, a businessman and activist, explained:

The targeted federal programme in Ingushetia was implemented fully, with all the planned social objects (like schools, kindergartens, hospitals) constructed, but most of the enterprises that were supposed to create employment were totally ineffective. They were planned without due market research, needs and resource analysis. The sewing factory, factory for baby food production, glass factory, factory for production of lamps were constructed but could not be properly launched.

Naturally, 'by the end of his term people, were very angry at Yevkurov. They blamed him for corruption, and that despite the very significant federal investment, the region was not developing', said Laura, a resident of Malgobek.

The federal centre simply ignored the large-scale embezzlement of funds. Recently, the Investigative Committee of Ingushetia has instigated criminal cases of fraud by commercial companies – subcontractors implementing the construction projects or local-level officials accused of fraud and embezzlement of state funds. However, high-level officials have not been affected. The Ingush opposition leaders claim that if investigators dig more deeply, the trail will lead to Yevkurov and his 'clan', but that there is no political will in the Kremlin to make him accountable.

The Yevkurov 'clan'

Having no previous experience as a civilian government official, Yunus-Bek Yevkurov came to the region without any support group or specific clan behind him. As such he managed to alleviate some of the severe tensions in the republic between various power groups and strong individuals.

> At first, he was not a politician, he was a security official and agent of the security services, but he was definitely not corrupt, he had nothing to do with illegal economic schemes, he did not even understand what corruption and big money meant. This changed in a few years.
> – Magomed Mutsolgov, director at Mashr NGO, an opposition leader, interview with author

Yevkurov failed to create a stable team that he could rely on. In the course of 12 years in office, he dismissed the government six times, beginning with his return from hospital after surviving the assassination attempt in 2009. His last government was formed in September 2018, less than one year before his resignation (Press Service of Ingushetia, 21 August 2018). Yevkurov explained these actions by the low efficiency of the Cabinet of Ministers and their incapacity to solve social problems in the republic.

He often stressed that corruption was one the most severe evils in the republic. In 2017 Ingushetia ranked first in the Russia-wide rating of the 'most corrupt' regions (the authors of the rating had apparently not dared to accord this place to Chechnya) (*Regnum*, 5 March 2018). Several criminal cases were instigated against officials at various levels. For example, the last chair of the government Ruslan Gagiev (in office 2016–2018) was accused of illegally renting to a commercial enterprise a government-owned meat and milk factory built under the targeted federal programme (*Kommersant*, 19 June 2020). A minister of construction and residential housing was accused of fraud during the construction of a secondary school in a mountain region (*Kommersant*, 3 February 2017). Another minister concluded a state contract with his own private company, for the amount of 700 million roubles (*Caucasian Knot*, 20 August 2014).

Both during Yevkurov's time and after his resignation, dozens of criminal cases were instigated against former officials, ranging from heads of municipalities to ministers and MPs. However, most of these persons were not sentenced to real prison terms. They were temporarily deprived of freedom during their preliminary detention; in some cases, the decisions on their cases have never been made public (*Fortanga*, 16 August 2020).

Despite Yevkurov's declared combat against corruption, the opposition has repeatedly accused him of being very corrupt personally. His brothers, nephews and other trusted people are said to have engaged in mass embezzlement of federal funds channelled through targeted federal programmes as well as other programmes aimed at improving the social infrastructure and social services in the republic and reducing the unemployment. He put his relatives everywhere, they controlled the financial flows, a local expert explained to me.

Yevkurov brought relatives into power. He has a very big family – six brothers and five sisters. But he was a very cunning and smart politician, he tried to conceal his nepotist networks. He tried to maintain his image as a democratic politician.

– Izabella Evloeva, founder and chief editor of the opposition news-site *Fortanga*

According to various sources, state contracts were concluded with construction companies owned by Yevkurov's circle of trusted people, such as nephew Akhment Shovkhalov and his cousin Abuezid Yevkurov (In // Line, 8 November 2018). Sources have also accused his brother Uveis of being involved in illegal schemes for appropriating oil from the Ingush oil companies (Bezformata, 11 January 2019). Some have claimed that the illegal schemes of the Yevkurov family were coordinated by his brother Magomed, who lives in Moscow, but most agree that Uveis ruled the show (In // Line, 8 November 2018).

His brother Uveis controlled all the financial flows very tightly. If the distribution of profits was violated, if people from outside the circle benefited, this had to be confirmed personally by Uveis or Yunus-Bek.

– interview with Akhmed Buzurtanov, businessman and activist

It seems that Yevkurov, as a federal-level bureaucrat, involved relatives and acquaintances discreetly, not to attract attention and criticisms: 'He placed relatives in second or third-level roles. Even now, many heads of departments in the government come from among his relatives. He preferred not to put his own people in conspicuous positions but would always have such persons as deputies', another opposition leader explained to me.

How was the loyalty of the inner circle maintained? Mainly through carrot-and-stick mechanisms, a local expert explained in an interview:

If he hired you, you got the chance to earn good money – but you were also tied, being part of their 'themes' [shadow business]. And then you were caught. Once you were involved deeply enough, he would send security services to you, so that you knew that you were on the hook, then he would also hire your son or daughter. By hiring several relatives, he tied you even more to the group, everyone had some share in the profit, several family members became dependent and this kept them together.

My sources report that Yevkurov's management style was based on a maximum of personal control. As one resident of Nazran explained, 'Yevkurov tried to be everywhere and to replace all ministers and public figures himself. He either tried to be personally involved in as much detail as he could, or he placed trusted people to oversee any relevant project.'

One businessman told me how a big investor from another region was allegedly told to employ a local subcontractor from a company affiliated with the local elite. The investor refused and left the republic. Large-scale corruption and embezzlement of state funds were among the main reasons for the mass protests that shook Ingushetia in 2018–2019.

Opposition and protests

The first serious political clashes started in 2013 when the Ingush Parliament cancelled direct presidential elections, based on the amendments to the federal electoral law that empowered it to support or reject direct elections. Yevkurov strongly endorsed this decision, which significantly curbed regional authority, depriving the Ingush of the right to elect their top leader. The opposition was incensed and threatened to organize protest rallies in Moscow and in the capital of the republic, Magas. The security services responded with repression. One opposition leader, Magomed Khazbiev, fled to Chechnya. There he remained in hiding for two years, featuring on the federal and international wanted lists for having insulted the representative of authority (the head of Ingushetia) and for illegal possession of firearms (Caucasian Knot, 25 July 2019).

Many others were somehow accommodated or maintained dialogue with the authorities as Yevkurov continued his open policy line to activists. Civil society leaders and opposition members also told me that the administration of the republican head tried to 'buy' opposition leaders, including themselves, by offering prestigious employment, money, cars and other opportunities. One example is the case of Bamatgirej Mankiev, an outspoken opposition figure, whom Yevkurov made Minister of Agriculture, but soon afterwards fired him for corruption. 'He tested critics with power, tried to find out whether this particular activist could be bought', a local activist told me.

In 2010, the *Mekhk-Khel* (lit. the Council of Land: the Council of *Teip* Representatives) was revived, and declared itself an alternative parliament whose main goal was to stop abductions and disappearances. The activities of this movement had been suspended in 2008 after Yevkurov stated that he was ready to work with various civil society institutions. Earlier, *Mekhk-Khel* had been in deep opposition to Zyazikov and had demanded his resignation. The movement was founded by a highly controversial leader, the hard-core nationalist Idris Abadiev, self-styled leader of the largest Yevloev *teip*.

However, it was impossible for the *Mekhk-Khel* to be 'representative', because of the deep disagreement on political and social issues among the various *teips*; moreover, there was no single goal that could unite them all. In essence, *Mekhk-Khel* was an association of oppositionals from various *teips* who agreed with Abadiev (Caucasian Knot, 16 December 2011). The organization issued video statements, including an appeal to the republic's self-styled *Sharia* court to have Yevkurov made accountable for falsifications during the elections to the Russian State Duma in 2011 (Caucasian Knot, 15 December 2011). That move is a clear example of the legal pluralism in Ingush society: a traditional descent-based institution appeals to an informal religious court to have a political leader held to account for corrupting a secular election.

In 2012 the *Mekhk-Khel* issued its 12 demands to Yevkurov, which included new parliamentary elections, new municipal elections and taking a strong position on the Ingush territorial dispute with North Ossetia (Caucasian Knot, 23 February 2012). Yevkurov met with representatives of this movement and declared that he would continue dialogue with the representative of opposition and civil society – but also noted that the *Mekhk-Khel* had taken a very high-profile name,[1] whereas in fact it was simply a non-government organization (Caucasian Knot, 13 June 2012).

At the same time it seems that Yevkurov liked the idea of mobilizing traditional structures for political purposes, In 2009 he created a Council of Teips under his own auspices, made up of representatives of the most numerous and famous Ingush *familias*. At that time, he justified the creation of the new institution by his intention to engage the Elders in re-introducing order in the republic. Not unlike Kadyrov, who introduced moral spiritual passports, Yevkurov stated that he was hoping that the Elders would be able to prevent youth in their families from joining the insurgency; he promised to allocate to each *teip* a proportional number of quotas for students to enter universities outside the republic, to prevent corruption and nepotism in the educational sphere (Muradov, 15 October 2009). These initiatives were never realized, however, and the council did not last long.

Disagreements started quite early on. Local activists say that Yevkurov tried to distribute favours to council members, for example presenting some of them with plots of land or finding good jobs for their sons or daughters. Nonetheless, eventually this council faded away; its members stopped attending meetings, apart from a handful of Elders whom Yevkurov continued to invite to events for various purposes. For example, during the border demarcation crisis, he invited his loyal Elders, who then expressed support for his position (Ingushetia tv, 1 October 2018a).

Yevkurov had ordered the creation of the Council of Teips so as to overcome blood feuds and prevent crime. In many *teips* elections were held under great time pressure, and the council started to work. However, it soon emerged that certain developments were against beliefs of the council members, who, after all, had gained their authority because of their clean reputations. Contradictions appeared, and many members left. Subsequently those who left actively participated in the creation of an alternative, the People's Council of Teips. In Yevkurov's council, there remained only collaborators, who finally discredited themselves when they tried to justify the transfer of Ingush land to the neighbouring region, a member of the alternative Council of Teips, Dhzambulat Dzaurov, explained to me.

This independent Council of Teips was inspired by Yevkurov's idea but was conceived as an authentic, representative alternative to the failed official council in 2016. In fact, this organization came to play an important role in the protests of 2018/2019.

---

[1] As described in Chapter 2, historically *Mekhk-Khel* was the Land Council: it consisted of representatives of all *teips* and had real power in Ingush and Chechen societies.

The border agreement and massive protests of 2018

A real political crisis broke out in Ingushetia quite unexpectedly in September 2018. Information was leaked that the leaders of Ingushetia and Chechnya, Yunus-Bek Yevkurov and Ramzan Kadyrov, were to sign an agreement demarcating the administrative border between Ingushetia and Chechnya. The two republics had not had a formal administrative border since they split in 1992 (Caucasian Knot, 28 September 2018). Two agreements had been signed in 1993 and 2003, but the issue was not considered formally resolved by the federal centre; Ramzan Kadyrov used this opportunity to claim large territories for Chechnya – which would endanger the very existence of Ingushetia as a republic, already the smallest region of the Russian Federation (HRC Memorial, 2019).

Historians and activists on both sides clashed, citing various maps compiled at different points in colonial history when borders were drawn and redrawn arbitrarily. Ramzan Kadyrov promoted Chechen interests and Yevkurov resisted – but many in Ingushetia believe that signing this document was a precondition for his re-appointment for the third term as head of Ingushetia (Kara-Murza, 27 September 2018).

Be that as it may, on 26 September 2018 the document was signed behind closed doors, with no prior information or public discussion. Rumours had circulated the night before, and in the morning of 26 September the first small group of protesters gathered spontaneously in Magas. Once the agreement became public, Ingushetia rose up. Opposition leaders and national activists started to mobilize youth, declaring that the authorities had, under conditions of secrecy, signed an anti-national agreement which transferred one-third of Ingush territory to Chechnya.

Initially Yevkurov insisted that not a single metre of Ingush territory had been given to the Chechens, whereas the Minister of Agriculture of Ingushetia stated that the republics had exchanged plots of 1,290 hectares each. However, the Ingush activists claimed that thousands of hectares of land had now been detached from Ingushetia and given to Chechnya. Geographers hired by the independent media outlet Caucasus Knot confirmed that Chechnya was to receive plots of land 25 times bigger than the plots transferred to Ingushetia (Caucasian Knot, 8 October 2018).

I myself was in Ingushetia on the day when the agreement was signed, and clearly remember how the secrecy aspect was the key initial trigger of protests. 'As if we didn't even exist', 'behind our backs', 'as if the Ingush people meant nothing', could be heard again and again. One young leader of the protest who was subsequently arrested in Belorussia and is currently behind bars explained how it started:

> In the end of August, a member of the municipal parliament in Sunzha district discovered a six-kilometre road that Chechen workers were constructing under protection of Chechen security servicemen. The public organization 'Opora Ingushetii' (Support to Ingushetia) issued a statement, demanding that the authorities explain what was going on. We, the young people, activists, also demanded explanations. I personally sent a letter to the authorities, we tried to

approach the members of the elite. One of them told us, 'It's none of your business, the seniors are aware of what's happening, they will sort it out'.

– Ismail Nalgiev, chair of the NGO 'Choice of Ingushetia' youth leader of protest, currently recognized as a political prisoner

However, the young people were not content with the explanation that 'the seniors are aware, and they will sort it out'. They did not trust the seniors in power to resolve the problem properly: they wanted accountability and were ready to take action themselves. On the same day as the agreement was signed, several dozen young men moved on foot towards the gates of the capital of the republic. As one activist told me: 'I was ashamed to stay at home. A piece of your motherland is given away, the authorities have sold out their nation, they are silent. We just wanted an answer from the authorities, what exactly they were signing there?!'

Initially there were no Elders in the streets. I remember how, on the first days of protests, young people said to me: 'Where are the Elders? Why are they sitting at home? We need them today'. Their presence would make the protest appear more legitimate – and indeed, the Elders did appear in the city square several days later.

According to the leaders of the protest whom I interviewed, mobilizing support was not easy. In the first days they travelled around in the republic, spoke with influential people, explained to them what had happened and convinced them to come down to Alania Square, in front of the Parliament. One of them explained:

I went to Khamzat Chumakov [*the celebrity Salafi imam*] to explain him what was happening. We had a map with us to show how much exactly was taken, and I told him that tomorrow the agreement would be signed, this was roughly the map. He didn't listen to me, he said he was busy and left. At that time there were many people who did not believe us. They trusted Yevkurov, they thought he was against Kadyrov and he would not give our land to him. At first few people realized how serious the situation was – not until after the agreement had been signed and made public.

Eventually none of the senior Salafi *imams* openly supported the protest, although privately they sympathized with and supported the cause of 'resisting the injustice'. However, younger Salafi activists and *imams* actively joined the protest. As one protest leader explained: 'Later, we came to understand this [the decision of senior *imams* not to support the protest]. If they'd come out and joined the young people, that would have been used in official propaganda to discredit the protest.'

In fact, the position taken by the senior Salafi *imams* reduced their support among young people. Many stopped attending the Nasyr-Kort mosque run by Khamzat Chumakov, who had otherwise been the only channel consistently critical of the authorities.

The activists emphasized that convincing the Sufi Elders took time: 'You have to explain every detail patiently, make them believe you. Even Akhmet Barakhoev, who would later become the symbol of protest, a man of Isa Khamkhoev's [the Mufti's] inner circle, who was initially against Yevkurov, was hard to convince', a member of the protest organizational committee told me.

The Sufis played a key role in the mobilization. According to one of the leaders of the protest, a resident of Magas, 'the Imams would choose topics for their Friday prayer service in such a way that the message was not pronounced directly, but metaphorically it was clear: "*go to the square*". Only Chumakov said clearly "*don't go*" – and he lost his support among the young people'.

'The mobilization took place quickly because everyone was doing what they could. Just as with our weddings or funerals: when they happen, no one is in command, people just start doing what they should. Of course, that doesn't mean that there wasn't any coordination among us', explained Izabella Yevloeva, Fortanga media founder and editor-in-chief.

On 4 October, the local parliament was to ratify the border agreement made between Yunus-Bek Yevkurov and Ramzan Kadyrov. Thousands of protesters gathered in Alania Square. Yevkurov came out to speak to the crowd, but he was whistled at, insulted and bottles of water started to fly in his direction, so the guards had to ensure his retreat by firing shots into the air (Caucasian Knot, 26 July 2021). That evening, the Parliament ratified the agreement and Yevkurov signed it. However, some MPs declared that the votes were faked, so it was decided that the Parliament would vote again on ratification of the agreement (Caucasian Knot, 4 October 2018a).

The protesters remained in the square for the night, and the authorities issued official permission for the rally (Caucasian Knot, 4 October 2018b). Kadyrov's made a statement that fuelled mobilization even further. Many interpreted his words that he 'would also not mind fighting' [for these lands] as a threat of war.

The protest rally was not solely about land as such. It was a question of the defence of the statehood of the republic itself, mobilized and reinforced by collective memories of 1992, when the Ingush had lost their lands in Prigorodny district of North Ossetia and experienced a bloody ethnic conflict and ethnic cleansing. Now the protesters greatly feared entirely losing their republic and again being forcefully merged with Chechnya, which would mean losing their Ingush identity. 'I felt it was about saving the republic, as if it were a great Patriotic War', a female activist told me. In addition to statehood and land, the rally was also about lack of accountability, and egregious corruption and the lack of legitimacy of the regional authorities.

In the first days the demonstrators brought tents, tables, benches and started an open-ended permanent demonstration. The space was organized in accordance with Ingush etiquette: Elderly men seated in front in their traditional woollen hats (*papakhas*), young people standing behind them, the women with a separate area. Special tents were organized for Elders and women to rest; hot meals were supplied by volunteers; cauldrons of meat and broth were boiling on the site; meat broth was distributed to warm the participants in the cold weather; rubbish was managed, order and cleanliness maintained; and mandatory prayers were conducted jointly on the pavements. The weather was cold and rainy; and starting from day two, internet services were shut off in and around the square. The protesters managed to coordinate regardless of these inconveniences.

> Of course, we discussed the seating set-up, according to the etiquette, according to *sharia* rules, so that everyone could be able to participate comfortably. We

organized water supply, toilets, benches. We set up volunteer security guards to ensure order. I remember how a volunteer guard came to me and said that an operative investigator from the town of Karabulak was among people guarding the protest. He asked what to do with him. I said: 'If he is not harming or spying on anyone, let him stay, he is also part of our society'. The Muftiyat people came, Salafis came, no one was excluded.

– Magomed Mutsolgov, Director at Mashr NGO, one of the leaders of the protest

The protest had an organizing committee – the Ingush Committee of National Unity (ICNU). As a member of the organizing committee explained to me:

There was not one leader, but a group of leaders. Akhmed Barakhoev, an Elder, became the symbol, Musa Malsagov, the chairman of Russian Red Cross in Ingushetia, a person of very clean reputation, was his co-chair. There were other people who wanted to stand forth, but no one wanted to take full responsibility alone, so we had a group leadership.

The ICNU had three groups of members: representatives of leading organizations in the republic (such as the Muftiyat, the Council of Teips, the Council of Elders, representatives of political parties, civil society leaders and activists and technical support coordinators. All members had an equal voice, but members of participating organizations had to coordinate their decisions with their associations first. According to one ICNU member, the Council of Teips, represented by its chair Malsag Uzhakhov, usually took longest time to make decisions. 'We always had to wait for them, they had many members, many opinions and it took them time to reach consensus. But at the end of the day, their decisions were wise.'

All my respondents in some way involved with the Council of Teips noted that their decision-making procedure was pluralistic and democratic, with due respect accorded to each opinion. Each member of the council represented a long patrilineal lineage and thus felt responsibility and accountability for his relatives; and his position was not to be ignored by the others.

Thus, the Council of Teips was among the members of the ICNU, and one of the many who contributed to these protests. However, it had a special role and enjoyed special legitimacy. This legitimacy convinced many, especially of the older generation, to join the rally.

Although the picture of the protest looked very traditional – with picturesque Elders in the forefront and Council of Teips as a leading force, with Ingush etiquette fully implemented in detail, with frequent references to *Sharia*, *adat* and the traditions of forefathers – the Ingush protest was in fact a modern national movement:

According to Akhmed Buzurtanov, member of ICNU:

This was a hybrid protest made up of various social groups, led by politicians of the new generation, a new generation of civic activists who turned into politicians. The average age of the leaders was 30–50, and youth were the driving force of this movement. They were the ones who convinced the Elders, convinced the religious leaders, the traditional leaders. Young people needed these traditional actors because otherwise this would be only a protest of youth. They protested because their rights were violated, Elders protested because of the land. But the seniors many times said very directly: 'You are young, you know better what needs to be done, you explain to us what's needed, and we will support you.'

Further, Izabella Yevloeva, founder and editor-in-chief of Fortanga media, and an ICNU member, explained: 'This is our life: everything is organized by the strongest, which means the young, but then they give the floor to the seniors, while the young people step back and stand at a distance. This is our usual and normal way of behaving.'

The overwhelming majority of the protesters followed and agreed with the ICNU, but there were also more radical youth: they wanted more decisive steps, they were not content with standing peacefully in the square.

> There were 2,000 to 3,000 of them and they were self-organized. At one point several of them came up to me and said: "We don't know your plans, we don't want to harm them. We can break up into groups of 1,000 each, we will get into the government buildings and bring these beasts here [Yevkurov, chair of parliament and chair of government]. Ahmet [Barakhoev] was standing next to me, he turned pale. I told them 'No. Under no circumstances can we do that.' After we told them this, some 1,000–1,200 young people left the square.
>
> We wanted to prove to these young people that we could achieve our goals by peaceful methods. We told them we don't need war. Wars and conflicts have dragged us many years backward; some nations were sending manned rockets into space, and here we are still struggling with the sewage system. Every summer the republic must struggle to get clean running water. But young people get angry when there are no results.
> – Magomed Mutsolgov, director of Mashr NGO, member of ICNU

It was probably these young people who later clashed with the police on 27 November 2019. However, in autumn 2018, very a-typically for the North Caucasus and for a leader with a military background, Yevkurov did not order the protests to be crushed. The protests continued for two weeks, until 17 October, when the organizers decided to suspend the rally as the matter was to be scrutinized by the Constitutional Court of the republic.

On 20 October, the collective Friday prayers held in the Ingush capital, Magas, united the supporters of the Spiritual Board of Muslims (Sufis) as well as the communities not represented on the Spiritual Board (Salafis). This was the first-ever united prayer of that kind (as reported in Caucasian Knot, 26 July 2021). Subsequently, the co-chair of ICNU, Elder Akhmed Barakhoev, apologized publicly for his antagonism to the Salafis, adding that for him one of the main achievements of the protest was that representatives of different strands in Islam had achieved unity:

> I couldn't have imagined even in my dreams what has happened to me during this rally. For example, Bagaudin [Khautiev, Salafi, close supporter of the *imam*

Khamzat Chumakov, one of young leaders of protest, currently a political prisoner] and me. We have become brothers here, at this rally. A week earlier we wouldn't have thought this would be possible. We have forgiven each other and have united. If Bagaudin does not want he will not follow the *tariqa*, but I will honour my *ustaz* [*spiritual leader*]. My beliefs don't disturb Bagaudin, and his beliefs don't disturb me. This is due to this rally that our unity has been restored.

Some of my respondents noted that, ironically, it was Yevkurov's policy of dialogue between different strands in Islam that had prepared society for overcoming the intra-confessional schism against Yevkurov's own policies.

'The main thing that these protests have shown is that when it comes to the Ingush statehood, all the differences evaporate, they no longer exist', said Laura from Malgobek.

Indeed, informal patterns of social integration were all united and contradictions put aside in defence of the threatened Ingush statehood and nationhood.

When the rally dispersed, the opposition leaders continued to work for the cause through institutions. Despite the mass public outcry, it was not possible to assemble the quorum necessary to submit the agreement to a re-vote. Heavy pressure on the MPs was exerted from both sides: 'The rally appealed to the *teips* of each of the MPs requesting to put pressure on their representatives who were in their turn under huge pressure of the Yevkurov's administration' (Caucasian Knot, 26 July 2021). According to members of ICNU, the Council of Teips played the key role in the process of mobilizing *teips* against their members' MPs who voted for the agreement.

They put direct pressure on *teip* leaders to take action against the agreement. As a result, 'one MP, Nalgiev, was excluded from the *teip*. Another MP, Sultygova, was also excluded', one activist explained. Heavy pressure was put on other MPs and 'even though these exclusions were not of much practical consequence, they did cause huge discomfort' to those concerned.

On 15 October the self-styled Sharia court working under the auspices of the Muftiyat planned to investigate the situation with falsification of the parliamentary voting on the land issue, based on the testimonies provided by the MPs (Caucasian Knot, 26 July 2021).

As one local expert explained it:

The chair of the Council of Teips, Malsag Uzhakhov, suggested inviting the MPs to the Sharia court and asking them how they voted on the land issue. The logic was that they wouldn't be able to ignore this invitation because they are Muslims. Of course, this wasn't a real court; it was a meeting chaired by a *kady* [*Sharia judge*], and normally a *Sharia* judge can't investigate secular issues. This was just a ploy to learn who voted and how. As a result, the only MPs who came were ones who had voted against the border agreement. The others didn't show up.

This was a clear case of interference, pressure and lobbying of government officials – but the result was all-important for the *teip* activists at that time.

The Ingush crisis was unprecedented in Putin's Russia – not only because several traditional and informal mechanisms were mobilized for a political cause, not only because in Putin's Russia it is very rare for an action that draws 20–30,000 protesters to stay in the streets for two weeks, but also because it led to a schism in the elites. On 30 October, the Constitutional Court of Ingushetia ruled that the border agreement with Chechnya was illegal, as, according to the Ingush Constitution, issues related to the administrative borders of the republic could only be resolved through popular referendum:

'The position of the Ingush people is absolutely legal and justified on this issue. Whoever can speak out and say [whatever] in return for material goods or positions – history will decide and condemn everyone', said the Chair of the Constitutional Court, Ayub Gagiev (Caucasian Knot, 26 July 2021).

Eventually most part of the Parliament, the Cabinet, and some of the local police took the side of the protesters. Police and protesters prayed together on the pavement, sharing food and a clear commitment to the cause.

Yevkurov tried to negotiate with the protesters and convince the population that Ingushetia had not lost any of its land. I was present at one of the meetings that he organized with opinion leaders – Elders, civil society representatives (the few who agreed to come), loyal Elders, academics, federal representatives in Ingushetia. Pointing to the map, he repeated that there was an equal exchange of several plots of land, that Ingushetia had not lost any of its territory. 'Metre for metre' was the phrase he repeated several times that day. However, later on, when confronted with the reality of the matter, he had to retreat and acknowledge that some territories that had been de facto part of Ingushetia since 1992 had been now transferred to the jurisdiction of Chechnya.

Finally, on 6 December 2018, the Constitutional Court of Russia upheld the agreement on the Ingush–Chechen administrative border. Obviously, the Kremlin had decided to close the issue in favour of the Chechen position.

2019 protests and clashes: Russia's biggest politically motivated criminal case

A new wave of protests came in late March 2019, when the Ingush Parliament was to discuss amendments to law on referendum (Caucasian Knot, 26 March 2019). The opposition noted that in the clauses listing possible reasons for a referendum, the paragraph on the issue of administrative borders had 'disappeared'. The Yevkurov administration admitted that this was a technical mistake, but it was too late. New protests flared up in Magas on 26 March.

The main slogans denounced the border agreement, demanding the resignation of Yevkurov, and that direct popular elections be held for the head of the republic. In essence, the Ingush people were calling for true federalism, as stipulated in the Russian Constitution. The authorities issued permission for a protest only for one day, but the protesters stayed for the night. The authorities brought in the Russian Guard units from other regions of Russia and stationed them around the demonstration.

Early in the morning of 27 March, the security services tried three times to expel the protesters from the square but were met with resistance. The organizers then asked the protesters to leave. Most of them did leave, but some remained. When they started their morning prayer the security services went into action, using clubs to beat the demonstrators, including the Elders. A group of Ingush policemen tried to form a live shield to protect the demonstrators, but they could not prevent the clash: in response the protesters threw bottles and sections of metal fence at personnel of the Russian Guard.

Magomed Mutsolgov, a protest leader, reported:

The protesters took off their shoes and started the morning prayer ... The security servicemen attacked people then. We did everything to prevent clashes, we told the people 'these guys (the security servicemen) also have parents waiting for them at home, we don't want any bloodshed.

Kaloy Akhilgov, the lawyer of one of the participants later accused of using force against the Russian Guard servicemen, quoted from the interrogation of his client:

– Why did you use force against the Russian Guardsman?
– He was hitting an old man in the face with a stick – am I not a man? In the Caucasus we can't treat Elders this way. Any man in my place would have acted as I did.

– Akhilgov, 21 July 2021

Beating peacefully protesting Elders was a sure way of eliciting a violent reaction in the North Caucasus. However, the leaders of the protest managed to remove the youth from the square in return for the authorities' pledge to grant permission for another rally in ten days' time.

Despite their successful attempts to prevent large-scale violence and put an end to the protest, six leaders were arrested and accused of organizing an extremist community and violence dangerous to the health of representatives of authority. Several key activists of the ICNU fled the country.

Altogether 300 people were prosecuted and either fined, arrested or sentenced to mandatory labour. Forty people were charged with criminal offences. All of the accused were kept in preliminary detention centres in neighbouring regions outside Ingushetia; moreover, the Supreme Court of Russia acceded to the request of the Prosecution General to move the court hearings to the predominantly Russian populated Stavropol Krai. That request was based on information provided by the FSB of the Russian Federation that the accused persons had strong kinship and *teip* ties within the judicial system of Ingushetia and could put pressure to bear on the judges; moreover, that mass protest rallies were planned to be held during the court hearings, aimed at destabilizing the situation in the region (HRC Memorial 2019a).

Nearly all the arrested organizers, except for one female academic, were leaders of various local NGOs, including the director of the Russian Red Cross in Ingushetia, Musa Malsagov, whom I have known since 2003 as an intelligent and peaceful person. The 13 Ingush policemen who had refused to disband the demonstration by force were also on trial (HRC Memorial, 8 April 2021). All six leaders of the Ingush protests were declared political prisoners by human rights NGOs. These organizations were confident that the accused had not committed the crimes of which they were accused: they had organized a peaceful rally and had tried to prevent clashes with police, as shown on numerous videos. Indeed, Elder Akhmed Barakhoev became the recipient of the Moscow Helsinki Committee award 'for courage in protecting human rights'.

> The overwhelming majority of the people, even those in power, somewhere deep in their hearts, strongly care and sympathize with the political prisoners. There were of course some people who didn't support the rallies: those in power, those whose interests were in line with those in power, there were those who said: why did you all demonstrate for a piece of uninhabited land, but when security services were killing young Ingush chaps you sat at home? But the overwhelming majority were supportive. What makes us a nation? Our territory and language! If you take our land and our language, the Ingush as a nation will cease to exist.
> – Timur Akiev, director, Memorial Human Rights Center, Ingushetia

After the protests, the Council of Teips came under intense pressure: searches, administrative arrests, fines, the security services pressured those who had rented premises for meeting rooms to the Elders, and they were evicted. The council started to meet in private homes. At one point, entry to an entire village was blocked by APC and military cars when the Council of Teips wanted to hold a meeting there (Yevloi 2019).

On 24 June 2019, Yevkurov announced his resignation which he said was voluntary, and caused by the 'disunity of the nation'. Despite his initial efforts to reach consensus with the opposition, Yevkurov had failed to build bridges with the protesters or avoid violence. With no strong and influential team that could help him through this turbulence, he lost all support in the population and was transferred to Moscow, where he became Deputy Minister of Defence of the Russian Federation.

Ingush society remained deeply traumatized and alienated from, even hostile to, the authorities. Several of my respondents told me that they would not have any relations, particularly kinship relations (intermarriage), with the Yevkurov's family or their supporters. Some mentioned that Yevkurov's supporters were not welcomed at funerals and weddings. Isa, a driver from Nazran told me:

> When his brother Uveis or other supporters come to a funeral, some people say to the family of the deceased: if you don't oust them from here, we will leave ourselves. Sometimes they are asked to leave … So they try to come at odd times, when there are few people around, quickly come and go.

Isa, who is an active *Khadzhi-murid* of the Qadiri *tariqa*, also told me that inside the *vird*, the *mullahs* who supported Yevkurov have lost all support. 'People don't want to hear them. They used to pray with them and listen to them, but now they reject them as traitors.'

Teips in Ingushetia under Yevkurov

In late March 2020, the Ministry of Justice of the Ingush Republic agreed to the request of the Supreme Court of Ingushetia to liquidate the regional public movement 'Council of Teips of the Ingush People'. The reason given for de-registering the organization was that it intervened in the work of government agencies, published information held to be state secrets, and had contradictory clauses in its statutes. The chair of the council, Malsag Uzhakhov, was arrested in April 2019 and sentenced to nine years in prison in the end of 2021 for 'organizing an extremist organization and violence against representatives of authority'.

Thereby the life of a *teip*-based organization, one which had played a key role in one of the largest protests in Putin's Russia, was officially finished.

However, it proved to be difficult to crush an Ingush institution based on familial structures, short of banning them altogether. As activists told me, the state does not know how to combat such institutions: infiltration is impossible, because people know each other well in the *familias*, and would identify any possible agents immediately.

> The Council of Teips is deliberately supported [by the opposition] because today this is the only institution that the authorities can't influence. After the protests they managed to de-register and liquidate several other civil society organizations, but not this one. They banned them and closed them, but the Council still meets, and no one can do anything about it. They can't ban *teips*, after all. Traditional Ingush institutions cannot be liquidated, at least not now.
> – Izabella Yevloeva, founder and editor-in-chief, Fortanga media

How representative is the Council of Teips? That remains a question. As mentioned, the council was created in response to Yevkurov setting up an official 'council of teips' working under his auspices in 2009. The new institution was created as an independent parallel structure and was intended to consist of delegates from the people.

One activist explained to me: 'We are seven *familias* of Yevloevs in Nasyr-Kort. I was elected from my *familia*. In Nasyr-Kort there were also other Yevloevs, they made a selection from among themselves and delegated one person in the Council.'

Many *teips* have in such a way selected representatives and sent them to the council. Other *teips* are represented by activists who were in touch with the council at the time when it was created, and joined as members.

> I joined the Council of Teips after the two-week protests in 2018. There I met many good people, including Malsag Uzhakhov, Chair of the Council. He was a very open, honest and intelligent person. His attitude to life, to developments in the republic, was close to mine. After the protests I started to attend the Council meetings. I liked their goals and how open and democratic their process was. They took up very difficult issues, they listened to different opinions and then voted when making decisions. Pretty quickly, I decided to join – and not just me: soon the Council represented 120 *familias* and *teips*, most of our society.
> – Dzhambulat Dzaurov, member of Council of Teips

In some *teips*, according to members, it is impossible to choose one delegate, as the *teip* is so large and there is more than one competing leader. The structure of the council has accommodated this issue: every *teip* and every *familia* may send representatives to the council. Big *teips* with many *familias* could choose whether to send one person from the *teip*, or many from the various *familias*. In this way, the council made the status of the lineage de facto equal to that of the original *teip*. Moreover, if a senior person in the *familia* found it difficult to attend meetings because of his age, a deputy could be appointed to represent him.

At the village level, *teip* representatives are not always elderly people: they are often successful, middle-aged individuals. However, at the higher levels, Elders generally predominate.

A representative of a *familia* part of the Yevloev *teip* told me:

> I was elected from my *familia*, but I didn't want to join. I was busy, and also it's not my kind of thing. But they kept asking me, and I agreed ... I attended two or three meetings at the grassroot level. But I didn't like it. I don't like these tribal relations, for example that you must always give preference to a member of your own *teip*. They want our Evloev people to be in the government. In my view, government selection should be based on merit, not *teip*. Like most of the young people, I felt uncomfortable there. Young people can't express themselves freely when Elders are present. We have our traditional etiquette: younger people must give precedence to the seniors, and this is still respected. As a result, the opinions of young people become peripheral. People in these Councils have traditional ways of perceiving social reality. So, I left. I didn't even know who was finally delegated to the Council from our *teip*.

My respondents agreed that this respect for the Elders as prescribed by traditional etiquette constrains the young members of such descent-based institutions. If they want to do something or to speak out, they don't feel entitled to do so.

> In our society you have to reach a certain age in order to feel that you have some weight in society and can speak up. But these days young people more and more feel their own agency, that they should take on responsibility. They don't treat the seniors as authorities, many of them are just older people, the young people don't have trust in them. All the events of the previous years have taught them distrust.
> – Izabella Yevloeva

Thus, the Council of Teips does not represent all the *teips*. It does not represent unified positions in these *teips*, not does it reflect generation or gender differences in perceptions of realities. It is a public association with a broad social base that enjoys real legitimacy because employs an authentic indigenous idiom, a symbol of Ingush distinctness.

On the other hand, in the situation of total lack of democratic procedures, when Ingush society could not elect any of its institutions for over 20 years, the Council of Teips proved to be the only institution with some degree of representativity.

> In essence, the Council of Teips has replaced our impotent parliament. They were the ones who reacted to Kadyrov's advances, other key issues, and challenges. They made statements, investigations, what had to be done on behalf of the nation, what the parliament did not do ... The Council became a kind of informal parliament, because it consisted of representatives of the people.
> – Akhmed Buzurtanov, businessman, member of ICNU

Clearly, the council functions as a civil society organization. The traditional idiom of *teip*ism remains attractive and still enjoys legitimacy, whereas the *teip* as such, especially the big ones, no longer has a significant political role.

Isa, a driver from Nazran, confirmed this observation:

> Now everything modern is trendy; some children don't even listen to their fathers. Who will follow the *teip*? No-one is afraid of anything anymore. In the past, the *teip* had power, but no longer. I don't know even one third of my *teip*, it's a very large one, there's no unity anymore. [During the protests] it wasn't the Council of Teips that raised the people, the people rose up by themselves, because land is something sacred for us.

Religious groups (*virds*, Salafi communities)

My respondents reported that during ten years in the office Yunus-Bek Yevkurov followed the divide-and-rule policy towards the Sufi *imams* which resulted in fragmentation and disagreements in the major *vird* – Kunta-Khadzhi-*murids*. Yevkurov brought some *imams* close to himself, supporting and promoting them, which, against the background of conflict with Isa Khamkhoev, created strong internal tensions. *Khadzhi-murids*, like the rest of Ingush society, were further polarized and divided over the issue of territorial dispute with Chechnya. Some *imams* continued to support Yevkurov, and are now quietly ostracized by society, whereas the majority supported the protests.

In parallel to fragmenting the unity of *Khadzhi-murids*, the authorities created and supported a new Spiritual Centre of Muslims which took the place of the abolished Spiritual Board of Muslims and was headed by a cleric loyal to the government. In the last two years this centre has been invited to represent Ingushetia in official or high-level meetings of the Russian Muslim clergy, instead of the Muftiyat. Thus, in addition to fragmenting and marginalizing the established pattern of integration, the authorities have tried to replace it with a loyal clone.

The Batal-Khadzhi *vird*, also known as the *batlaki*, was a Sufi brotherhood that suffered a powerful blow in Yevkurov's time: not only were they squeezed from the economic niches that they used to control, their top leadership was killed or jailed. A local expert explained:

> First, Yevkurov tried to attract them. He let them get into Parliament, gave them various government positions, including that of the city mayor of Magas. However,

gradually a conflict emerged between Yevkurov and the Belkharoev family [*the descendants of Batal-Khadzhi, the spiritual leader of this vird*]. Yevkurov started to push them out of various economic spheres. They lost their influence in the Interior Ministry, in the Ministry of Construction [from which most funding is allegedly embezzled]. Yevkurov started to push them out of the big bazaar, pushed their construction companies from subcontracts to the government-funded objects – the relatives of Yevkurov took them. Yevkurov gradually took over all the positions where he could earn money and placed his own people there – not necessarily relatives, but members of his inner circle.

The turning point in relations between the Batal-Khadzhi *vird* and the state was the assassination of the leader of the *vird*, Ibragim Belkharoev, in December 2018. Unidentified gunmen opened fire on his car, killing him on the spot. The *vird* leadership declared a blood feud with the head of the Anti-extremism Department, Ibrahim Eldzharkiev. The first attempt on his life was carried out already in January 2019. The second attempt was successful: Eldzharkiev was killed in Moscow in a car, together with his brother in November 2019. Subsequently, official investigators announced that Eldzharkiev had been killed by 'the militant wing of the Batal-Khadzhi *vird*' for investigating crimes committed by the wing's members, including killings of *vird* members who had been excommunicated from the community for serious misdemeanours. By 2021 twelve members of the *vird* had been arrested, another five put on the wanted list, all accused of terrorism and other crimes. Another leader of the Batal-Khadzhi *vird*, Ibragim Belkharoev, former Member of the Ingush Parliament, was also arrested and accused of large-scale embezzlement of state funds (*Tass*, 23 March 2021; RBK, 29 July 2021). According to my sources, after these events the Belkharoev leadership has split into two conflicting groups who accuse each other of the events described here.

Despite government pressure, the role of Sufi brotherhoods remains quite strong, especially among the older generation and in rural areas. However, the dispute with Salafis made it clear that Muftiyat is a rigid organization, unable to respond to the challenges of modern life. One main point of disagreement was Salafi criticism of the Sufi traditions of arranging very lavish funerals and weddings, which, according to Salafi *imams* were too burdensome for the population. They called for the local Muslims to follow the Sunnah of Prophet Mohamed in their life-cycle rituals. According to a local expert:

> The old laws are part of national traditions in our religious practices. They complicate the already difficult life of our society. If someone dies, we of the Qadiri *tariqa* do *zikr* for three days and three nights, we must feed people. Nowadays more and more people want to be buried according to Sunnah [without such expense]. Now there are groups of young men who offer the burial services by Sunnah. You can reach them by WhatsApp and they come, perform the ritual quickly, and take the body to the cemetery. And they do it free of charge, in the name of Allah. So, you don't need to depend on these official *mullahs* and prepare the whole ceremony for them. My uncle is 80, he is a *khadzhi murid* [*quadiri tariqa*], but the

last time we were together at a Sunnah funeral he told me: 'Please bury me in the same way.' There are such tendencies in our society, but Muftiyat does not catch them, doesn't notice them. If they want Khadzhi-murids to remain the leading force, they should recognize the needs of society, reduce the burdens. But they don't. So, society quietly ignores them. They ban shooting [in the air] at weddings, but people still shoot. The decisions of their *Sharia* court are often ignored. But regardless of such internal dissent, we are still a conservative society, we are slow at changing. So, the nucleus of the Khadzhi-murids remains strong, even though young people are looking for other solutions, for other kinds of mosques, other values. They adopt these new ways, and slowly they start to influence their fathers.

Some experts think that the generation of the 1990s, even the Sufi youth, are now ready to change their ways and move away from Sufism, but they are under the pressure and influence of their seniors. 'But after some time, they will understand that their peers are living differently. Now their fathers maintain strong control over them, but once their seniors die, the situation will change', one activist predicted.

Yevkurov's policy enabled the law-abiding Salafis to gain more weight in the republic, as they were officially recognized as part of the religious landscape. However, the refusal of the senior Salafi *imams* to support the protests dealt a strong blow to their popularity among youth. As Russian expert on North Caucasus, Irina Starodubrovskaya has rightly noted (author's interview), the Ingush Salafis are well-integrated in the Ingush community, and follow the same, mainly rural, Ingush lifestyle. Salafi youth is very proud of their Ingush identity and eager to defend it that is why they actively joined in the protests.

It is not clear whether it was Yevkurov's own idea to suppress, divide, marginalize or replace the informal patterns of social integration, or if it was the decision of the federal centre – or perhaps their joint policy. In any case, Yevkurov played a major role, and his 'clan' of relatives and non-relatives benefited financially pushing strong actors among Sufi brotherhoods out of certain spheres of the economy.

Yevkurov tried to capitalize on the public legitimacy of the *teips*, but failed: being selected from the people, *teip* representatives proved unwilling to support his policy lines. Eventually the alternative Council of Teips, became the only quasi-representative organization in the republic. It tried to take on some of the political functions of the Parliament that this thoroughly controlled institution was unable to perform.

Under conditions of lack of accountability on the part of the authorities or proper democratic mechanisms for channelling discontent, a society tries to revive the mechanisms it has at its disposal to self-organize and defend its interests. As one activist told me: 'In critical situations, people turn to traditions or to institutions that helped them to survive before. This works at the subconscious level.' However, the alternative Council of Teips was shut down and marginalized by the authorities and proved unable to have any impact on the situation after the crackdown on the protest. It effectively functioned and was suppressed as any other civil society organization.

10

Chechnya under the Kadyrovs (2000–)

In August 1999, the Second Chechen War broke out. By 2002, the Russian military had gained control over almost the entire territory of the republic. In the process, several formerly separatist political-military groups had switched sides and supported the Russian invasion. The Kremlin put a stake on the group led by the former Ichkeria Mufti, Akhmad-khadzi Kadyrov, who was a consistent ideological opponent of the Islamists, and ensured peaceful transfer of the Gudermes region under Russian jurisdiction. Kadyrov had real power on the ground and still enjoyed some respect among separatists; moreover, he was deeply embedded in the local social context, which probably tipped the scales in his favour as regards the Kremlin's choice, not in favour of those Chechen politicians who initially supported Russia.

On 12 June 2000, Akhmad Kadyrov was appointed Head of the Administration of Chechnya. In 2003 the Kremlin launched its 'Chechenization policy', which stipulated a 'political process' as well as the transfer of law-enforcement functions to pro-Kremlin paramilitary groups made up of ethnic Chechens who set about targeting the remaining pockets of separatist resistance. The political process involved a series of staged elections: a referendum on the Constitution of the republic (March 2003), presidential elections (March 2003), and elections to the Parliament of the Chechen Republic (November 2005). I myself monitored all these elections in Grozny and elsewhere in Chechnya. They were conducted under conditions of acute insecurity, fear, abductions by armed camouflaged men followed by the subsequent disappearances of people, continued armed clashes, recurrent shelling of settlements and roadside booby trapping.

Voter turn-out figures were hugely inflated, and numerous violations were reported. Officially, on 23 March 2003, a full 95.97 per cent of the electorate had voted – 95.37 per cent in support of the Constitution (*RBC*, 27 March 2007) placing Chechnya under the dominion of the Russian Federation. I remember that on the day of the referendum, the streets of Grozny were remarkably empty, as were the polling stations. That morning, together with colleagues I was counting voters leaving a polling station in Staropromyslovsky district of Grozny. The Electoral Commission of the station reported that more than one thousand voters had arrived by 11 am – but we were able to track only seven elderly men. Later we moved on to other polling stations where the commissions never checked on the domicile registration of those voting, so my journalist friends, some of them French citizens, managed to vote several times in different locations, as a test.

The results of the subsequent 'election' of the president and Parliament were also a foregone conclusion: Akhmad Kadyrov was declared the 'First President of the Chechen Republic', with a new Parliament fully loyal to him. Neither PACE nor OSCE recognized the elections as legitimate, but this lack of recognition was not the greatest challenge facing the new government: establishing control over breakaway Chechnya proved to be a much harder task.

The birth of 'kadyrovtsy'

By 2003 the separatist insurgency had largely gone underground. Akhmad Kadyrov emerged as one of the strongest actors in the republic, which was informally divided into sectors controlled by pro-federal paramilitary groups, serving as the proxies of various Russian security agencies. The largest of these was the Security Service (*Sluzhba Bezopasnosti, SB*) of Akhmad Kadyrov – widely known as '*kadyrovtsy*'.

A resident of one of the eastern regions of Chechnya explained to me:

> He started to form the SB back in 2000, few people knew about it then. In our district he had three people, two from our village and three from the neighbouring village. When he was appointed the Head of Administration, he started to pay them small salaries. They were not his relatives, but activists who were opposed to the Ichkerian authorities. Gradually he built up his SB.

SB was initially responsible only for the security of Kadyrov; however, it gradually grew into a powerful force that was tantamount to Akhmad Kadyrov's private paramilitary group. The nucleus of the group consisted almost exclusively of relatives, neighbours and friends of Akhmad Kadyrov whom he could trust, under the command of his young son, Ramzan, then 28 years old. After Akhmad became Head of Administration, the SB began recruiting young men who had not been involved in the conflict previously. The prevailing conditions of mass unemployment throughout the republic meant that the SB was the only stable source of income for many (International Helsinki Federation for Human Rights, November 2005). Once employed by the pro-Kremlin security services, men who had been on the sidelines automatically became involved in armed conflict – and, therefore, personally dependent on the good graces of the Kadyrovs.

In addition, Akhmad offered an informal amnesty to former combatants, essentially freeing them from prosecution by the federal authorities. He negotiated with various groups and tried to convince key figures in the resistance to lay down their arms under his guarantees.

A former supporter of independence told me:

> Some left [the insurgency] because they realized that the conflict had turned into intra-Chechen war, they understood that it was time to get out of the forest [the insurgency]. Some saw that it was impossible to win the war. Still others were caught [by the kadyrovtsy] and forced to surrender. But at the time of Akhmad most people left voluntarily.

Increasingly, however, as Ramzan Kadyrov gained more power, forced surrenders prevailed. At the time I was working for the human rights group Memorial; among the issues we documented was hostage-taking of the relatives of fighters. A short paper 'Chechnya 2004: new methods of Counter-Terror', issued by Memorial in spring 2005, listed 28 cases of hostage-taking or burning of the homes of family members of combatants, mostly in order to make them surrender. A highly publicized case was the surrender of Magomed Khanbiev, defence minister of the self-proclaimed Chechen Republic of Ichkeria on 29 February 2004. Kadyrov forces seized over 40 relatives of Khanbiev – men and women, elderly and children from several villages. One teenage boy was severely injured during detention, and another relative – a medical student – was brutally beaten and then thrown, semi-conscious, out of a car in his home village of Benoy (Cherkasov, 11 March 2004). After this massive detention operation, a message was sent to the Ichkerian Defence Minister: he should surrender – otherwise his relatives would be in big trouble. On 4 March, Magomed Khanbiev 'voluntarily surrendered' (Caucasian Knot, 10 March 2004) to the authorities.

Dozens of lower-rank field commanders also surrendered at different times. In an interview with the *Kommersant* correspondent Olga Allenova, who spoke to several recently surrendered 'brigade generals' in 2004, they emphasized that it was not surrender, but that they had 'put down arms' (Allenova, 19 March 2004).

At that time Kadyrov treated the surrendered commanders with respect and dignity, even offering them posts in his security forces and money – which they appreciated.

For example, Khanbiev became an MP of the Chechen Parliament. His official biography on the parliament's website modestly states: 'Between 1994 and 2005 he worked in various capacities' (Parliament of the Chechen Republic, 2013).

Initially, to save face and preserve their dignity, former Ichkerian leaders informally continued to claim their commitment to independence – which deeply angered those Chechens who had always been ideologically opposed to independence and supportive of Chechnya as being part of Russia. They called them '*perebezhchiki*' – defectors. Ramzan provided these *perebezhchiki* with resources and power, and gradually they reconciled with their position:

As one person formerly part of resistance told me:

When XXX*** [currently a high-level Chechen politician] surrendered to the FSB he and a few of his comrades swore to kill Kadyrov at the first opportunity. With such an *amanat* [*here – commitment*] they had surrendered. But switching sides proved profitable and XXX is now loyal.

Not all the Ichkerian commanders received equally dignified treatment. For instance, eight relatives of Aslan Maskhadov, including his brothers and his elderly sister Buchu, were taken hostage on 3 December 2004. They were released two months after Maskhadov had been killed in a security operation on 8 March 2005. At Memorial we followed the case closely and I interviewed the relatives when they were released. They said they had been kept at a Kadyrov base in Tsentoroy, in a small concrete cellar without beds or other furnishings. They were not interrogated, and were taken out only to the toilet and were not allowed to shower. They were released only after one of the elder brothers became so ill that he was close to death. It remains unknown whether the disclosure and killing of Maskhadov was facilitated by this hostage-taking – but he had not surrendered, and it was clearly beyond Ramzan's authority to guarantee him any kind of informal amnesty.

With the rank-and-file fighters, however, the process of surrender often involved capture by *kadyrovtsy*, torture and then the choice between joining the Kadyrov forces or being killed. Umar Israilov, a former fighter captured by Kadyrov forces, escaped to Europe and filed a complaint with the European Court of Human Rights, accusing Ramzan Kadyrov of personally torturing him in 2003. Umar's case became highly publicized, as his father was later taken hostage and spent 11 months in a secret prison, trying to force Umar come back to Chechnya. Umar himself was killed by a group of Chechen assassins in the centre of Vienna in January 2009 (BBC, 1 June 2011).

Some months before his death, Umar told me in an interview in Vienna that, after his capture by *kadyrovtsy*, he had been kept incommunicado for three months at the main SB base in Kadyrov's native village of Tsentoroy, where he had been systematically tortured, beaten and hideously mistreated, and then offered the choice between life or death. 'The threat was very real, several people who were kept together with me were either tortured to death or shot dead', he explained. Umar chose life and was transferred to Tsentoroy base as a Kadyrov guard but effectively remained a prisoner. He was not allowed to leave the base, even to visit his family, and had no weapons for nearly one year, after which he was transferred to his native village of Mesker-Yurt, where he had initially fought against the federal forces. He was now tasked with capturing or killing the remaining rebels – his former comrades and friends.

This was a typical strategy of Kadyrov forces: to secure people's loyalty through blood. Often, as in the case of Umar Israilov, after Kadyrov's men captured fighters who had opposed his rule, these were transported to secret prisons where they were tortured, and killed, in front of other captives. In this manner they intimidated other captives and convinced them to change allegiance. The new recruits – now as ranking members of Kadyrov's forces – would then be sent to the villages where they had fought, now tasked with eliminating their former comrades. In this way, new recruits were forever 'linked with blood' to Kadyrov's group.

This proved very effective in eliminating the remaining groups of organized resistance. However, the issue of loyalty remained acute. Akhmad trusted his own forces more than the federals, especially in matters of personal security.

As Said-Selim Peshkhoev, deputy director of the FSB in Chechnya 1999–2001, explained in an interview to *Kommersant*:

> ... The President believed unconditionally in his inner circle – he didn't even let FSB participate in his own protection, he trusted them less than his own fighters. However, as subsequent events showed, the presidential guards were not up to standard. Walking around with formidable expressions and guns, next to the President, is not enough to ensure reliable protection. Most of these presidential guards were incapable of professional implementation of security functions.
> (Muradov, 25 May 2004)

Akhmad Kadyrov was killed in a bomb blast during the Victory Day parade on 9 May 2004, at the Dynamo Stadium in Grozny. The bomb had been planted under his seat in the VIP section; seven people were killed and another 50 injured. It is generally believed that the bomb had been sealed in the concrete of the stadium during reconstruction. Shamil Basaev claimed responsibility for the attack, although it was widely rumoured that it was the FSB that had commissioned the murder of Akhmad.

In 2008 Ramzan Kadyrov declared that all those who had been behind the death of his father had been killed. 'Eliminated is the one who claimed the responsibility, eliminated are those who were indirectly involved. Whatever the Prosecutor's Office is doing is a secondary issue. As a Chechen, as a Muslim, as the son of my father, I have done everything to ensure that these people are no longer alive', he said in an interview to Echo Moskvi (*Izvestiya*, 29 January 2008).

Earlier, Ramzan had admitted that there was a traitor in his father's inner circle (Borisov, 22 March 2006). Clearly someone had leaked the detailed plans for the ceremony. This assassination shaped not only Ramzan's future life but also his 'state-building strategies', which became a perpetual politics of survival.

Establishing control (2004–2008)

After the assassination of Akhmad Kadyrov, Ramzan Kadyrov was still too young (28) to inherit the presidency. Alu Alkhanov temporarily replaced Akhmad in an election-by-appointment manner. In 2004 Ramzan Kadyrov was awarded the title of a Hero of Russia. He had a few years to prepare for the formal takeover. Strengthening his own army was a prerequisite for control.

After Akhmad's death, the SB was formally abolished, but Ramzan Kadyrov was appointed Vice-Prime Minister for Security Affairs. SB which, according to various estimates, numbered between 4,000 and 12,000 well-armed and well-trained people – was fully legalized as part of the Ministry of Internal Affairs of the Russian Federation. Four months after Ramzan turned 30 and became eligible for the presidency, he was appointed by Vladimir Putin, first as executive president and as president of Chechnya.

Crushing or submerging competitors and insurgency

After the death of Akhmad, Ramzan Kadyrov set about crushing or dissolving competing pro-federal armed groups, to establish full control over the territory which meant eliminating other strongmen. First, relations became strained between Kadyrov and the leader of a small paramilitary group, Movladi Baysarov, a close associate of the late Akhmad. In 2006 Baysarov led *Gorets* [Mountaineer], an armed group of between 200 and 400 men from the township of Pobedinskoye, adjacent to Grozny. Although *Gorets* participated in 'anti-terrorist' operations alongside federal forces and was subordinated to the operational-coordination department of the Federal Security Service in the North Caucasus, it lacked official legal status.

After the assassination of Akhmad Kadyrov, Movladi Baysarov refused to subjugate his group to Ramzan, relying on support from the FSB and hoping for legalization within the Ministry of the Interior. Subsequently, the *Gorets* fighters were besieged by Kadyrov forces (*Echo Moskvi*, 21 September 2006) in Pobedinskoye. While Baysarov was in Moscow, his guards, who had been provided by the FSB, were called off; and on 18 November 2006, he was gunned down by Chechen special forces in downtown Moscow – officially while resisting arrest. Kadyrov's right-hand man, Adam Delimkhanov, was implicated in having organized and personally participated in this operation (Mashkin and Sergeev, 23 November 2006).

Next on Ramzan's list was *Gruppa Vostok (East Group)*, a division of the Ministry of Defence led by Sulim Yamadaev. It had controlled the mountain areas of Chechnya and served as the special company of the military commandant's office of the Chechen Republic. The nucleus of the group were the former fighters of the National Guard of Ichkeria, who had switched sides and joined the federal troops. The group enjoyed high political standing: it participated in the Georgian–Ossetian conflict on the Russian side; and Sulim and his brother Dzabrail were posthumously awarded the Hero of Russia medal for fighting the separatists, and another brother, Ruslan, became an MP of the Russian State Duma.

Tensions between the Yamadaev brothers and Ramzan erupted in open conflict in spring 2008. It started as a traffic quarrel over whose cortege should give precedence. Ramzan Kadyrov initiated a major smear campaign against the Yamadaev brothers, calling them war criminals and demanding a criminal investigation of their activities. Eventually, in autumn 2008 – despite the political clout of the Yamadaev brothers, and Vostok Group's decisive role during the Georgian–South Ossetian conflict – the Defence Ministry dissolved the group without explanation. Two days later, on 24 September, Ruslan Yamadaev was shot dead in downtown Moscow. Some members of Vostok Group fled; others joined Kadyrov's forces. The following year, on 29 March, Sulim Yamadaev was gunned down by an assassin in Dubai in the UAE. The law-enforcement authorities of Dubai demanded the extradition of Adam Delimkhanov but Russia refused to hand him over.

After what happened with *Gorets* and Vostok groups, the remaining small paramilitary group led by Magomed Kakiev – the *Gruppa Zapad*, which nominally fell under the jurisdiction of the Chief Investigating Department (GRU) of the Defence Ministry, became fully loyal to Ramzan.

Thus, in the course of a few years after his father's death, Ramzan used the military and political resources available to him to eliminate his rivals and ensure that his armed forces were not only the largest and most powerful, but indeed the only ones existing in Chechnya. Unlike Maskhadov there was no talk of accommodation: the sole options were to submit or be eliminated. As of today, Ramzan Kadyrov is the only Russian regional leader who controls all the security services on his territory through the chain of command though relatives and loyal people.

Kadyrov has systematically invested in training and equipping his forces. The special task forces trainings are supervised by Kadyrov's personal assistant for security services, Daniel Martynov, one of Russia's most prominent special task experts and former 'Alpha' group fighter. Ramzan invites some of the best Russian instructors to teach specific skills. YouTube features numerous videos of such trainings and competitions (MsOnlysee, 13 December 2013; EnemyOpsBelNews+, 25 April 2015; EnemyOpsBelNews+, 13 December 2013). Since 2015, considerable attention has been paid to the construction of the International Training Centre for Special Task Forces, for training anti-terrorism groups for combat in the forests, mountains and under water (Yevgenii Argunov Live, 14 February 2017). The centre has the most modern equipment, including one of the best aerodynamic tubes in the world. Another training centre is located in Kadyrov's native village of Tsentoroy (*Groznyinform*, 21 October 2017).

In the eyes of the Kremlin, Ramzan's real success, which allowed him to accumulate power and build up muscle, was his victory in the war against the parts of armed insurgency that refused to surrender. This task involved massive violence, and extremely high risks – particularly in view of the Chechen tradition of blood feud. The secret of Ramzan's efficiency in suppressing insurgency lies in his excellent local knowledge of family structures, access to local intelligence, the use of high levels of violence, and the principle of collective responsibility, according to which family members of fighters, including distant relatives, could be detained, beaten, tortured or threatened, kept hostage, expelled from the village, their homes burnt, in order to get members of separatist movement to surrender or be captured.

This method has also been used very effectively to deter future recruitment. There is no insurgency left in Chechnya today.

Silencing the critics

In parallel to training his own forces and eliminating political rivals, Ramzan established control of all criticism and dissent: incorporating, submerging, threatening or destroying all alternative centres of thought through money, influence, violence or threat of violence and public humiliation. Some NGOs and activists have voluntarily switched sides and joined the Kadyrov establishment. Courts, judges, defence lawyers and even juries have been threatened, streamlined or abused and intimidated (*Meduza*, 16 May 2016; Milashina, 11 October 2016). All human rights organizations (apart from a handful of a-political women's rights groups) have been forced to halt open operations after their offices were burnt or attacked, their staff killed or abducted or threatened. Journalists have been attacked repeatedly. Critics of the regime have been beaten, killed, abducted; individuals who simply complained about social problems and corruption have been humiliated, beaten and forced to publicly repent and apologize to Kadyrov (BBC News, 12 October 2018). Collective responsibility and threats against relatives are also widely used. Such abuses against civil society leaders are well documented (Freedom House, 6 February 2020; Human Rights Watch, 28 August 2018; HRW, 7 June 2021; HRW, 15 July 2019; HRW, 31 May 2019; *The Guardian*, 11 August 2009).

Not only direct criticism but also jokes and ironic remarks have been brutally punished. For example, Khizir Ezhiev, an associate professor of economics at Chechen State Technical University, was abducted by armed men in December 2016 after making ironic remarks about the Chechen leadership in a closed Vkontakte social media group. His body was discovered 11 days later; he had been beaten and tortured to death for his remarks and reportedly for refusing to publicly repent his sins (Umarova, 7 Junuary 2016).

Alternative religious trends in Islam, such Salafism, Sufi khabashism, are banned; Shiism is considered to be a sect (HRC Memorial Winter 2014). Official *imams* tirelessly praise Ramzan Kadyrov and his policies; local *vird* leadership lacks political organization or influence and remains silent.

Today's Chechnya is a full dictatorship, where all independent thought is deeply concealed underground, and most independent opinion leaders fled, given the unprecedented climate of fear. It is based on the personality cult of Ramzan, whose inner circle promotes him as royalty, calling him *padishah* ('master king'). Others are treated as vassals, including the elderly, who can be reprimanded, humiliated and even beaten by representatives of Chechen elite – regardless of the tradition that prescribes subordination to and respect of the elders. The climate of fear explains why in this chapter of the book all of my respondents provided testimonies on the conditions of anonymity.

The only open challengers to the regime among Chechens are Europe-based bloggers from the diaspora. The regime tries to silence them with threats and targeted killings in Europe, by putting pressure on their relatives or helpers inside Chechnya, and by deterring society from listening to them. My sources among schoolteachers say that teenagers' cell-phones are routinely checked; if they are found to be following critical channels or YouTuber sources, their parents are called in, reprimanded and threatened.

Pseudo-legitimacy

Lacking real electoral legitimacy, Ramzan Kadyrov tries to maintain control by populism and charity. He is the centre of media attention, with a massive state propaganda machine using television and social media to promote the image of Ramzan as a strong, tough but fair leader, the supporter of Chechen traditions, but also a modernizer and innovator who brings technology, fashion and celebrities to Chechnya.

His populism is based on Chechen nationalism, the promotion of Chechen 'moral-spiritual values', and traditional Sufi Islam, Chechen culture, sport and youth initiatives. Ramzan has built mosques, and restored *ziyarats*, the sacred places of Chechen *virds*. Unlike the case in most other Russian national minority regions, where minority languages are dramatically declining in power and use, Chechnya under Ramzan Kadyrov has become Chechenophone. The elites often come from rural areas; they feel more comfortable speaking Chechen than Russian, and thus prefer to speak Chechen in the public space. Over the past 15 years, this has significantly elevated the role and status of the Chechen language in daily use.

One very popular move undertaken by Ramzan Kadyrov was the delineation of the administrative borders with Ingushetia. It caused deep conflict with the neighbouring Ingush, but ensured him support of all Chechen nationalists, including the Chechen separatists in Europe (for detailed of the situation around the border, see Chapter 9). Also, the delineation of administrative borders with Dagestan caused tensions, on a much smaller scale. Ramzan managed to ensure support for the Chechen position at the federal level, and thus succeeded in getting the Chechen borders fixed even more favourably than in the times of Ichkeria.

Another mechanism of popular legitimation is Ramzan's famous charity and capacity to help people solve their problems. He and his circle are exceptionally rich. Their wealth comes from informal levies on Chechen business inside and outside Chechnya, routine exactions from state-employed workers, whereby they must transfer certain financial contributions to the foundation named after Akhmad-khadzi Kadyrov or simply 'above'. The totally non-transparent reconstruction and appropriation of federal funds are also a big source of income. The 'dead souls' – hugely inflated staff number at government institutions where only some people are employed and actually work, while others do no work but receive their salaries, which they transfer 'above' – also contributes to large-scale enrichment of the incumbents. Having accumulated such wealth, Ramzan then distributes part of it as charity to the needy, also to families formerly in opposition to him.

When government-funded projects distribute social welfare, it is always linked to Ramzan. When new social housing is built, he personally hands the keys to the new flats and houses, while media promotes this as being a present from Ramzan or his mother, Aymani Kadyrova, the president of Kadyrov Foundation. Some of the houses have probably been constructed by the foundation, but clearly not all of them. A Chechen activist told me

> For people who are waiting for years, sometimes decades, to get housing, it is not important who financed the construction. For them the benefactor is the one who handed over the keys. Popular belief in the fact that only Ramzan can solve problems is only growing.

The same principle applies to any other positive developments in the republic. A new factory opening, new mosque, museum or school being constructed, children returning from Syria and Iraq – the media explain to the public that this would have never been possible without the leader of the republic.

According to a local expert

> The rhetoric of the authorities and of the government media is such that the postwar republic was reconstructed by Kadyrov and his father, as if with their own money. The role of the state budget, federal finance, contributions by Chechen businessmen is never mentioned. Ramzan comes to the opening of every big construction and delivers a speech, in which he speaks of Akhmad Kadyrov and his team.

This way in recent years Kadyrov has promoted himself as an effective manager. Demonstrating an impressive ability to function within the existing Russian political system, Kadyrov has become a highly influential politician at the Russian federal level. Thanks not least to his close personal relations with Vladimir Putin, he has some of the best lobbying capacities among regional leaders, and has managed to deal with the various federal ministries and get financial preferences and lucrative projects for Chechnya.

His pronounced loyalty to Vladimir Putin is central to this success. Such expressions of loyalty have ranged from ensuring over 99 per cent election support to Putin and the United Russia Party, to bringing 100,000 people onto the streets during Putin's birthday celebrations, aggressively supporting Putin's foreign policy, including by actively involving Chechen security forces in Russian war efforts abroad. As to ideology, Kadyrov copies and intensifies the key pillars of Putin's policy lines, with a discourse more aggressively great-power Russian and anti-Western than that of the Kremlin. In parallel Kadyrov capitalizes on his Muslim identity, and wants to be the leader of the 20 million Russian Muslims. He is famed for making strong statements on issues that resonate throughout the entire Islamic community, on matters like the Charlie Hebdo cartoons, Rohingya Muslims and others. Further, Kadyrov has strengthened his international position: although most of his international communications are arranged through the Russian Foreign Affairs Ministry, he has gradually developed close personal ties with several Middle Eastern leaders, particularly King Abdullah II of Jordan, the Saudi royal family, the leadership of Libya and of Bahrain. Kadyrov has spearheaded several important Russian initiatives in the Middle East – including the return of women and children in ISIS, which he personally initiated and convinced the Russian president to support.

Ramzan skilfully capitalizes on his political influence; moreover, the flow of revenues into the republic over the past ten years is unprecedented in recent Chechen history. State-funded projects, however, are non-transparent and corruption remains egregious.

Given the absence of elections at any level, the lack of checks and balances of any kind, and full impunity combined with high levels of violence against political opponents, a regime could hardly be more personalized and more dependent upon strong, organic ties than that of Ramzan Kadyrov. That is not to say that the issue of trust has been resolved, however.

Trust and betrayal

In February 2008, two of my senior colleagues from the human rights group Memorial and I met with Kadyrov at his private residence in Gudermes. Closer to midnight Kadyrov sent a car to bring us in order to discuss the activities of Memorial within the republic. A lavish table was laid with all kinds of Chechen delicacies, but during all the 3.5 hours of the meeting no one – not us, nor Ramzan and his team – touched the food. The conversation was very tense and far-ranging. This was the first and last meeting like this with Memorial. Initially, Kadyrov clearly tried to charm my Moscow colleagues – renown human rights defenders. Sometimes he was surprisingly sincere. He repeatedly spoke about the risks to his life, from his fighters and from the Russian security services. He recalled an episode from when his father was still alive, when he seriously considered walking away from the struggle for power in Chechnya:

One day I told my father, 'Why are we doing this? The Russians hate us. The Chechens think we're traitors. Can't we get out of this?' Then my father said, 'Have you chickened out? Pick any university, I will buy you a ticket and send you there.' I said, 'No, I'm staying with you.'

After that he regarded me not only as his son, but as his associate.

Ramzan Kadyrov also recounted how, following the assassination of his father, he felt that could no longer trust anyone, and always tried to display a tough exterior when in the company of his men. His only confidant, he told us, was his dog:

I had to be strong. I could never show my hesitation, or feelings, to anyone. I had a dog there at the stables, and in the evenings, I would go to him and tell him about all my troubles. He was a young, healthy dog and, in a few months, he became sick. I sent him to Moscow, to Rostov-on-Don, to all the best vets in the country. They couldn't do anything. There was nothing to diagnose. He died because I had poured too much of my grief into him.

Naturally enough, given this environment of distrust and extreme risk, Ramzan Kadyrov surrounded himself with a network of the people he trusted most: kin, classmates, co-villagers he grew up with. A local expert explained to me

When a person comes to power, he has to rely on someone, he is looking for faithful people. You rely on relatives because you know that they can't escape you. Others can betray you or run away with money, but relatives are tied to you, they have nowhere to run. So, he relies on those with whom he was raised.

Ramzan's inner circle includes several trusted people who are not kin or co-villager but who have proven their loyalty or are otherwise strongly linked to the Chechen leader. He generally values those who have proven their loyalty by disclosing and/or eliminating enemies, whether insurgents or critics.

One of Kadyrov's closest allies is the Chair of the Chechen Parliament, Magomed Daudov, better known by his nickname 'Lord'. In one of his speeches Ramzan explained how Daudov personally killed the assassin of Akhmad Kadyrov

… All my remaining life I am indebted to Daudov because he stretched his brotherly hand to me and did what first and foremost the Kadyrov clan had to do. He proved, not with his words, but in reality that he is 100 per cent, in all different aspects, on the path of Akhmad-khadzi Kadyrov.

– Kadyrov, 23 April 2020

Kadyrov also highly values those who were injured during security operations or relatives of those who were killed during attempts on his life or that of his father. One such example is a friend and co-villager of Ramzan, Zelimkhan Matsuev. Matsuev was killed during a security operation in Kadyrov's native village in 2010 (Grozny.tv, 17 July 2020). Later, his son Viskhan married Ramzan's older daughter and became the director of the federal migration service in Chechnya at the age of 22 (Caucasian Knot, 1 December 2019).

Another ticket to elite membership is direct kinship, where the chances of betrayal are much lower than with unrelated people. In addition, every family member in power strengthens the influence of the Kadyrov family. One of the first relatives in the government was Odes Bisultanov, Ramzan's cousin, who subsequently made a career at the federal level and since 2016 has held positions at the Deputy Minister level. Gradually the number of relatives in the key positions has increased. Kadyrov is very generous to his inner circle, supplying them with money, real estate, power, guns and impunity. He has enough resources to do this; unlike previous leaders, he cares about cementing his elite.

Apart from the good life that members of the Kadyrov inner circle can enjoy, they also share his risks, like getting involved in activities that can result in criminal prosecution by the federals and blood feuds with other Chechens, where many kill and can be killed. Ramzan also controls his trusted people through fear. In addition to security control checks and tapping their phone calls, routine physical punishments can be applied for misdemeanours, which keep the elite in fear. The leadership style of the Chechen top officials is said to be unpredictable and often humiliating to subordinates. Thus, sources claim, there is considerable hatred in the inner circle.

This breech in loyalty was proven by the failed plot on Ramzan's life, reportedly organized in the spring of 2016. According to *Novaya Gazeta*'s investigation, the plot involved close relatives, co-villagers, nearly all members of the Benoy *teip* members (to which Kadyrov belongs), people from famous Chechen families, hundreds of whom were subsequently detained, subjected to severe torture and all their property expropriated. The assassination had been commissioned by the two remaining Yamadaev brothers, who declared blood feud on Kadyrov family for their killed brothers Sulim and Ruslan; the key person who transferred information to Yamadaev was the cousin of Kadyrov's nephew, Islam Kadyrov, then the Deputy Chair of the Chechen Parliament (Milashina, 29 January 2017).

Novaya Gazeta reported that the assassination was planned to take place in Benoy, the village of origin of Kadyrov's Benoy *teip*, where Ramzan has a large house. A powerful explosive was planted there. Simultaneous attacks on several of his other residences were planned (including in Grozny). Searches revealed large quantities of modern weapons, grenade launchers and explosives. This, claims *Novaya Gazeta*, was the biggest plot against Kadyrov's life organized by the members of his elite. It was only by chance that it was disclosed that numerous people had been involved in the preparations (Milashina, 29 January 2017).

After this failed plot, the number of relatives in the inner circle only increased. If previously the state propaganda tried to convince the society that the appointment of a relative was meritocratic, recently Kadyrov promotes his family members simply because they are kin, and does not find this practice shameful or unacceptable. 'Yes, indeed, this appointment was facilitated by the fact that they are grandchildren of Akhmad-khadzi Kadyrov', he commented on the appointment of two of his nephews (aged 30 and 23) to ministerial positions (*Znak*, 13 February 2020).

Kadyrov also emphasizes that relatives are treated more strictly than non-relatives. We know situations when relatives were punished, for example the third nephew of the Chechen leader, Islam Kadyrov, who was indirectly involved in an attempt on his life (Milashina, 29 January 2017). He reportedly lost his titles and was beaten, his both arms broken, forced to work as a street cleaner in Kadyrov's native village of Tsentoroy, and then was made the guard at the entrance to the same village. All property had been expropriated, but Islam remained alive.

Another example: Kadyrov's cousin Turpal-Ali Ibragimov, who was guilty of a fatal car accident, remained unpunished (Caucasian Knot, 21 December 2018). The accountability of relatives will depend on the type of mistake they committed and their personal value in Kadyrov's hierarchy. The value of Turpal-Ali Ibragimov in the team was investigated recently by *Novaya Gazeta (NG)*, which claims that Ibragimov tortured and summarily executed the detained individuals (Milashina, 15 March 2021).

The appointment of relatives has produced resentment in the elite, especially when old and experienced cadres are replaced by Kadyrov relatives in their 20s. Another round of a major cleansing of the Chechen elite started in August 2019, three days after Ibraghim Temirbaev – the mayor of Argun, the second-largest town in Chechnya – was replaced by Ramzan's 28-year-old nephew, who had no professional experience. Temirbaev, who had served as mayor of Argun for 15 years, was one of the few remaining officials with independent backing and connections. Moreover, he was not an Ichkerian defector, but an initial opponent of independence. After his resignation Temirbaev called many people in the elite and spoke unfavourably about Ramzan. According to *NG*, recordings of these conversations were brought to Kadyrov, who was shocked to realize that so many of his close associates, who praised and glorified him in public, were saying ugly things about him behind his back. Further, according to *NG*, dozens of high-level officials, their family members and their guards were thrown into cellars, tortured and all their property taken. This applied to two ministers, one vice-premier, Deputy Minister of Interior, among others. At least one of the detainees was a co-villager and friend of Kadyrov senior; one was quite a close relative – the husband of the sister of Ramzan's wife. Temirbaev himself was severely tortured and kept in illegal detention for a year and a half. He died in a car accident under suspicious circumstances in 2021.

Predictably, after such cleansings, the vacant places were replaced by young relatives of Kadyrov and his close friends.

The Chechen elite today

As mentioned, the Chechen elite today is a trust group consisting of people related to Ramzan Kadyrov through ascriptive ties – kinship (both female and male lineages), co-villagers, classmates and friends. The non-kin members of the team are those who have been with the family since the early years of SB and have proven their loyalty by risking their lives for Ramzan on numerous occasions, they also do some very sensitive work for the Chechen leader; some are under international sanctions.

The number of relatives on the team is growing day by day. In the past, Kadyrov-close people were mostly employed in high positions in security services; now, more and more are represented in the executive and legislative power. Many of those who get positions in the republican government or city-level authorities are transferred into civilian positions from the security services, especially as regards non-kin members of the team. It seems they first need to prove their loyalty in the security sector, to win the trust as regards civilian affairs. They often continue to wear the camouflage, as with the Minister for Youth affairs, for example (*Chechnya Sevodnya*, 27 June 2018). Here it should be noted that the official titles of the closest members of the inner circle are a secondary issue: their main tasks are unrelated to their official roles.

Examples include three of the closest people in Kadyrov's team, all of whom are not his relatives. I have already mentioned Magomed Daudov (nickname 'Lord'), a former fighter who surrendered to the FSB and started his career as a commander of a platoon in SB. He went on to hold various positions in security, including the head of Shali police station. Daudov participated in numerous operations against the insurgency, including eliminating Hayrulla, a Dagestani Islamist thought to be responsible for the terrorist act that killed Akhmad Kadyrov. Since 2015 he has been the Chair of the Chechen Parliament; but he is de facto responsible for security, dealing with critics, and many other sensitive issues.

Adam Delimkhanov was an Ichkerian fighter in the group under the notorious commander Salman Raduev, the organizer of the 1996 Kyzlyar raid on the hospital where some 3,000 patients and medical personnel were taken hostage. Delimkhanov switched sides in the face of the second Russian invasion and eventually joined the SB. Later he became the commander of the Oil Regiment (the regiment of extra-departmental security with the Interior Ministry of the Chechen Republic for security of the oil and gas industry), which carried out numerous anti-insurgency security operations. He was in charge of the 2006 operation for eliminating Movladi Baysarov, the commander of *Gorets* paramilitary group, in Moscow. After the assassination of Ruslan Yamadaev in Dubai, Delimkhanov was put on the international wanted list, but after numerous diplomatic efforts and a staged 'reconciliation of blood feud with Yamadaev' his name was removed from the list in 2012. Since 2007 he has served as MP in the Russian State Duma from Chechnya, with parliamentary immunity. Kadyrov has repeatedly called him his closest friend and successor. According to some sources Delimkhanov is a distant relative, but others claim they are not biological kin.

Abuzaid Vismuradov (nickname 'Patriot') is a Kadyrov childhood friend from schooldays. He officially started his career in Gudermes police station in 2002 and became the commander of Special Task Force regiment 'Terek'. Since 2020 he has been Vice-premier of Chechnya for Security; he is also the president of the UFC club 'Akhmad' – but, most importantly, he is the personal security guard of Ramzan Kadyrov and his family.

This trio of Kadyrov's closest associates is also embedded in the system through family ties. The closest members of the inner circle have relatives in key positions in the government. This ensures additional trusted people to Ramzan, but also makes the associates even more dependent on him.

For example, one of Vismuradov's brothers is an MP of the Chechen Republic; another one was, for many years, the head of the Grozny police department, until he was replaced by a nephew of Kadyrov. Vismuradov's father Dzhandar served as personal assistant to Ramzan until his death in 2017.

Adam Delimkhanov's brothers play a key role in controlling the security agencies in Chechnya. Adam's brother Alibek is the deputy commander of National Guard troops of the Russian Federation in the North Caucasus, Sharip heads the department of the Russian Guard in Chechnya, and Amkhad is a senior police officer (BBC News, 25 June, 2018). In total, five of his relatives hold important positions in the security sector.

The career pattern from a security serviceman to state official frequently applies to senior members of the Kadyrov team. Young relatives, especially the recent newcomers, are directly appointed to government positions. For example, three Kadyrov nephews received appointments in various ministries and government agencies immediately after their university studies, one at the age of 23, another at the age of 21. Ramzan's daughter Ayshat became Deputy Minister of Culture at the age of 21.

Research undertaken in 2018 by BBC Russia found that the state system of Chechen government mostly consists of persons close to Ramzan Kadyrov. According to BBC, of the 158 high-level officials in Chechnya, 30 per cent are Kadyrov's relatives, 23 per cent are co-villagers and another 12 per cent are friends of the Chechen leader or their relatives. Nearly all close relatives of Kadyrov who have reached the age of 20 have already been given government positions, as illustrated by this list:

1. Aymani Kadyrova (mother): President of Akhmad-khadzi Foundation, the main informal resource accumulator of the family
2. Medni Kadyrova (wife): Vice-President of the Akhmad-khadzi Foundation
3. Ayshat Kadyrova (daughter): First Deputy Minister of Culture
4. Viskhan Matsuev (Ayshat's husband): Director of Federal Migration Service in Chechnya
5. Khadizhat Kadyrova (daughter): Director, Department of Pre-school Education in Grozny
6. Zulay Kadyrova (sister): Deputy Director, Department of the Head of the Republic and Parliamentary Affairs
7. Salman Zakriev (Zulay's husband): Deputy Chair of Parliament, reportedly placed there to follow up the activities of the non-family Chair of Parliament, Magomed Daudov (Lord) (*Kavkaz Reali*, 18 December 2019)
8. Sahab Zakriev (brother of Zulay's husband): Head of Administration of Gudermes district, strategic region where the Kadyrovs have property and real estate
9. Yakub Zakriev (nephew): Vice-Premier of Government, Minister of Agriculture of Chechnya
10. Zargan Kadyrova (sister): Assistant to the Chechen Head for Pre-school Education
11. Ramzan Cherkhigov (Zargan's husband): Minister of Transportation and Communications of Chechnya
12. Idris Cherkhigov (nephew): Director of Traffic Police of the Interior Minister of Chechnya

13. Adam Cherkhigov (nephew): Chair of Sheikh Zaed Foundation for Entrepreneurship and Innovation
14. Khamzat Kadyrov (nephew): Minister of Sport of Chechnya
15. Idris Bisultanov (maternal cousin): Minister of Health
16. Khas-Magomed Kadyrov (nephew): City Mayor of Grozny

These are only the closest relatives of Kadyrov. Also, more distant relatives hold lucrative positions. For example, among the seven assistants of Ramzan, two are Kadyrovs (BBC News, 25 June 2018).

In post-conflict Chechnya, the security bloc is central. According to the BBC, among the leading positions in the Interior Ministry, the Russian Guard and other federal security agencies are four close friends of Ramzan, two nephews, two close associates of his father, three more distant relatives, nine co-villagers, as well as five relatives of Adam Delimkhanov (BBC News, 25 June 2018). Such penetration ensures effective control over the federal agencies in Chechnya, essentially their capture by the Kadyrov network.

Social reactions

Chechen society has responded to the tendencies of the past 15 years by closing up, trying to survive, and adapting to realities. According to some of my respondents, little has changed in Chechen social relations in the last ten to 15 years: interactions inside nuclear families remain the same, unless the family faces some extraordinary challenge that requires the intervention of other relatives.

Some of my other interlocutors hold that, in the conditions of authoritarianism, earlier tendencies have been developing faster: family and religious structures have been suppressed and continue to lose any remaining elements of power. Respect for the elders has been nominally preserved, but the elders themselves are often fearful and reluctant to take responsibility for major family decisions.

Much probably still depends on the family. According to one senior, the key function of the elders now is surveillance.

> The elders are afraid to take responsibility, to interpret traditions, religion, teach norms to the youth. They are afraid to be dragged on television and made to apologize. Some elders I know regularly call on their family members, checking, warning, begging them to comply with all the rules. In particular the elders don't want young people to create any problems for them. Young people use this, deliberately or not, and increasingly consult them only nominally, or inform them about their affairs. And if there are no problems, the elders are happy.

In the villages the coordinators of *murid* groups (so-called Turkhs) are no longer elected but appointed by the authorities; this institution has also largely lost its meaning as an informal solidarity group based in religious brotherhood and trust. As one resident of Grozny explained:

We now only have one big *vird* in the republic to which our leader belongs. In the past, the *vird* was stronger than the *teip*, but now it has only symbolic significance. For example, in our *vird*, the *murids* are supposed to meet twice a week, to pray and discuss various current matters, but this is not done. I know in some mountain villages they still do, but that is the exception. Moreover, young people are not supportive of *murid* groups.

It seems that yet another social institution is losing its traditional functions.

Dictatorship and fear make people atomized. Moreover, and independently from the regime, modern technology is conducive to less intense communication in the neighbourhood and family communities. A resident of Grozny explained:

Mobile phones have really influenced human relations. People don't visit each other to drink tea and chat, they don't know how their family members live. Instead of a polite visit, now they call you or send a voice message. For example, take the *Uraza-Bayram* [Eid al-Fitr] celebrations. This used to be a very warm, happy holiday. Relatives you might not have seen for a whole year would come to celebrate the feast. I would be waiting for these days just to see them. Now, this has all diminished. Third cousins don't come, they send you a card on WhatsApp, or at best make a phone call. Relations have weakened between relatives, and between neighbours as well.

This probably applies more to the urban centres, whereas villages life remains more conservative.

According to a local activist:

In the mountain villages there are still patriarchs whom people listen to. There the communities remain relatively stable. On the plains there's a lot of change and movement, migration, people coming and going, everything is different there …

The descent group, *teip* or lineage has weakened even further: it has completely lost its final remaining function – that of security protection and revenge. According to the elder of one lineage:

In effect, the *teip* is dead. It doesn't play any role in the life of an individual family or person. It remains a kind of ritual services club. *Teip* members get together for funerals or weddings. Some romantics still try to revive it. They build guest houses in the mountains, so that people can travel to their village of origin, to the birthplace of their forefathers. But it's just a hobby. In the past, the main function of the *teip* was protection of life, honour and the property of its members. Even in the Soviet times, if it was known that a person had a *teip* behind him, no one would create too many problems to him, even his boss. Nowadays, the *teip* cannot offer protection, from the boss nor from the security servicemen. All that is now beyond the *teip*'s sphere of influence. That's why the *teip* is dead.

Ramzan often speaks very emotionally of Chechen traditions, and the need to protect them. However, the Chechen leadership has long distorted and adapted traditions and the customary legal system of *adat* for their needs. The most striking example is instrumentalization of the blood feud, which greatly contributed to *teips*' (rather lineages) incapacity to protect its members. Many new feuds were created during two wars, and especially since the policy of Chechenization was launched. As has been noted earlier, blood feud is strictly regulated, and can only be declared by male relatives of the killed person against either the killer or his direct male relatives. One life can be taken for one life, and if the murderer has already been killed, no one else in the family should be affected. However, Kadyrov security servicemen declared blood feuds for their killed comrades and colleagues against relatives of insurgents, also when the guilty insurgent had already been killed. Moreover, officials convinced relatives of the deceased to expel extended families of insurgents from their villages. *Adat* does not permit colleagues 'to take blood', and especially so if relatives of the victim have not declared a feud, but this however is practised.

In parallel to announcing feuds, in 2010 Ramzan created a reconciliation commission, which in the course of one year settled 451 cases; thereafter, it was then declared that there was no longer 'any blood feud conflict in the republic'. Many of my sources report that, although many old cases were indeed authentically reconciled, in other situations of premeditated murder these were forced reconciliations. People staged a reconciliation performance on camera, but later some of them let their enemies know that this had been imposed, and the act of vengeance was simply postponed.

Moreover, the families of victims of violence, summary executions and enforced disappearances cannot currently enact blood feud against anyone in the ruling clan.

As one Chechen journalist told me:

> There is complete chaos with regard to the blood feud. It remains to be seen whether the reconciliations that were facilitated by the government will hold when Kadyrov is not in power anymore. It is unclear if the rejection of blood feud against authorities will work in the long run. However, no one is taking blood-feud revenge now.

Thus, for the present, Ramzan Kadyrov seems to have established a monopoly over violence in Chechnya, depriving descent groups from their last remaining function.

'If we can talk about clanship at all, then the most vivid example of clanship is being displayed today. Today you can put your relatives and co-villagers in different positions and call them a "team"', former prominent politician and historian told me.

A Chechen ethnologist further explained:

> Maskhadov didn't use kinship connections, or his co-villagers. Ramzan Kadyrov learned from [Maskhadov's] mistakes and adopted a style of government that was the opposite of Maskhadov's. He had to suppress [armed] groups. Also, he bought people, aware of their lust for money, for power. He bought clerics and civil servants. He bought his relatives, too.

However, even organic ties, wealth, power, impunity and protection cannot ensure full loyalty to the Chechen leader. Several plots against Ramzan Kadyrov's life have proven that the elite has repeatedly displayed poorly concealed discontent, even direct hatred of its leader. Elite purges have been harsh, and fear rules not only Chechen society – it also rules the elite.

Chechnya today could be called a clan society – but this political 'clan' has nothing to do with the Chechen traditional structure or descent. It is what Charles Tilly has called a trust network (Tilly 2005: 5, 7), which places significant value on common enterprise, *inter alia* protection in high-risk politics. As we have seen, the key resource for recruitment to office in Chechnya has been the multi-vector kinship, patrilineal, matrilineal, recruited from families related through marriage of sisters, daughters as well as close friends who have proven loyalty through blood. Chechnya can probably be called a 'patronalistic society', as its regime encompasses various mechanisms and concepts connected with patrimonialism, corruption, clientelism and fully informal politics, when the positions of top officials rarely correspond to their actual roles (Hale 2014: 20).

Disgraceful as it is, today's regime in Chechnya has been most successful state-building project in post-Soviet Chechnya. Today the republic closely resembles a sultanistic, dictatorial but independent state – with its borders, parallel taxation system, well-trained, well-equipped combat-ready security services under the control of one leader, bureaucracy, the national language used at all levels, an established monopoly over violence, all alternative power centres submerged (including competing social institutions), a national ideology and traditions developed and applied as per the wishes of the elite.

Kadyrov's Chechnya meets all the criteria of Michael Mann's definition the modern state, outlined in Chapter 1 of this book. The only thing this state lacks is an economy capable of feeding the population and satisfying the appetites of its elite and gaining international recognition.

The main problem of this regime and why its state-building achievements are unlikely to transform into real independence (if Chechens again get a taste for it) is the utter lack of legitimacy or institutionalization. If and when the Kremlin support should be withdrawn, the regime is likely to collapse in no time, destroyed by its own members, opponents and by numerous blood enemies who – in line with *adat* – may wait for decades to 'take their blood'.

Conclusions

This book has examined recent subnational state-building and political integration in the two most volatile Russian regions: Ingushetia and Chechnya. After the collapse of the Soviet Union, both entities have experienced devastating armed conflicts as well as periods of acute instability. The analysis of the Ingush and Chechen state-building projects presented here has offered a window into polity-building processes in unevenly modernized societies – where traditional identities and patterns of integration still matter, and informal networks play a prominent role in politics. These chapters also offer some insights into how changes in post-Soviet Russian federative relations have influenced local dynamics in the national republics.

One aim of this study has been to provide the analysis of informal patterns of social integration usually deemed 'traditional', and to assess their role in subnational state-building and political leadership.

My argument was constructed primarily in response to the literature on clan politics, as well as noting important points of disagreement. Scholars of clan politics writers have claimed that regime transition and state-building in such contexts are shaped by and organized around clans – understood as pre-existing informal identity organizations based on kinship (Collins 2006: 24; Schatz 2004; Sultan 2003).

I started from the same position but arrived at different conclusions. The ten chapters of this book have refuted the clan politics arguments, both bottom-up (starting from the *teips* and working towards the political systems) and top-down (analysing state-building projects 1991–2021, and the role of *teips* and other informal actors in the underlying political processes).

The historical chapters have analysed the colonial wars, the repeated forced and voluntary resettlements, as well as the deportations, expropriation of *teip* ('clan') lands, destruction of traditional economic systems, and integration into the capitalist and the Soviet economies. All these have transformed the *teips* and traditional political structures in Ingushetia and Chechnya, far beyond the weakening trends identified by historians as early as in the eighteenth century.

Further, the ethnographic findings, collected between 2003 and 2021, have enabled me to offer a detailed analysis of the current state of *teips* and other informal social structures, providing a link between the macro- and micro-levels of social and political integration. I find that the *teip* is no longer a functional social organization, as the mechanisms for maintaining *teip* cohesion have been lost – except, perhaps, for small *teips* in Ingushetia.

The next layer of dilution came with the demographic growth of the *teips*. They have mushroomed, dispersed over large territories – losing their unity in the process. Descent groups have disintegrated into lineages and territorial segments of *teips* and lineages, with very limited social roles, mainly involving the performance of rituals and 'showing solidarity' in rare cases of blood feud. Today the *teip* has become a loose identity to which different individuals attach various degrees of significance.

Through participant observation and interviews I found that the daily routines of Chechen and Ingush individuals today are largely shaped by *close kin*, religious groups and regional/village identities. Coupled with personal networks of acquaintances, colleagues, ideological comrades and friends, these often constitute a person's 'inner circle' – useful for getting employment, solving problems or acquiring social goods. The informal patterns of social integration and the state interact in five main ways: *accommodation, compartmentalization, competition, marginalization* and *capture*.

The case studies in Chapters 5–10 analysed the socio-political processes underlying specific subnational state-building projects pursued from 1991 to 2021 in Ingushetia and in Chechnya.

All my case studies serve to refute the 'clan politics' claim. The case of Chechnya 1991–1994 shows that, despite attempts to revive and politicize the *teips* and traditional political structures, clans failed to play any significant role in the political process: they served more as elements of retro-fashion. Dzhokhar Dudaev was challenged by moderate national intellectuals and state-employed workers who wanted an agreement with Russia – and a functioning state. The fragmentation lines in 1991–1994 were highly ideological.

This state-building project failed – partly because of the government's inability to maintain Mannian infrastructural power and deliver public services, but mostly as a result of the subsequent invasion of the Russian troops. State separatist ideology appealed to many Chechens, but state capacity to deliver the public services on which many people relied, was also very important. Which of these mattered more proved more crucial than *teip* affiliation in determining individual attitudes to the regime. A strong Parliament and opposition were crucial to preventing nepotism and the dominance of affective ties in the government.

The failure of the 1997–1999 state-building project in Chechnya can also be attributed to the incapacity of the government under Aslan Maskhadov to maintain infrastructural power, but also to subdue the paramilitary and criminal groups that challenged his authority, squandered state property and paralysed the republic's oil industry – the main income-generating sector of the economy. The situation was characterized by acute competition and compartmentalization of formal and informal subsystems within the polity (the state, foreign Islamists, local and regional Islamists, and criminal groups), controlling patches of territory or certain institutions and resources, and each following its own specific logic of behaviour. Maskhadov tried to consolidate the situation by empowering and accommodating the leaders of these competing groups. Although this strategy brought temporary peace, it eventually failed due to the fatal provocation of his challengers, who attacked Dagestan and invited the second Russian invasion of Chechnya. Strong ties played a negligible role in Maskhadov's government, which was formed primarily on the basis of ideological and religious convictions and programmatic beliefs, loyalty, merit and his strategy of accommodating ideological opponents. The main cleavages had nothing to do with kinship or *teips*.

In Ingushetia, the relative success of the 1992–2001 state-building project was due largely to the ability of the government of Ruslan Aushev to marginalize the radical nationalist challengers in 1992, and subsequently keep the Islamists under control and prevent informal groupings from stabilizing as political actors, without resorting to violence. Creativity and consistent efforts to deal with a tremendously difficult socio-economic situation helped the Ingush government to maintain the infrastructural power of the state. Aushev prevented the republican economy from a collapse and society from criminalization. Moreover, the government managed to give a modest impetus to the development of the Ingush educational system, healthcare and economy. Although Aushev's government included significant representation of relatives and members of descent groups, 'the clan politics' argument does not apply to his regime either. The system was meritocratic, with main criteria for elite recruitment being efficiency and programmatic agreement. Kinsmen in positions of power were treated like anybody else, and were dismissed if they performed poorly.

The situation changed dramatically in the new decade of the 2000s, with the restoration of the unitary state under Vladimir Putin. *Ingushetia* under Murat Zyazikov (2002–2008) and Yunus-Bek Yevkurov (2008–2018) as well as *Chechnya* under Ramzan Kadyrov (from 2003) were not engaged in proper subnational state-building. Their budgets have been over 80 per cent funded by the federal centre, which has also provided the leaders with administrative and security resources and guaranteed impunity. The Ingush leaders have had very little real political autonomy, but have enjoyed the freedom to form their elites and, to a certain degree, choose the style of governance. Ramzan Kadyrov has freedom to rule Chechnya as he pleases, provided he keeps his republic quiet and loyal to the Kremlin.

Since 2002, all three regimes have produced highly personalistic elites based on strong ties, characterized by massive corruption, and, in case of Zyazikov and Kadyrov, also violence. The government of Ramzan Kadyrov is strongly embedded in ascriptive ties of kinship, descent, village affiliation; in recent years, government positions have been given to direct family members. By contrast, the political elite under Zyazikov and Yevkurov had a very insignificant number of relatives, co-villagers and *familia* members in official posts. Both these governments were classical Charles Tilly's 'trust groups' of unrelated people, linked by common economic interests, and awareness of each other's economic misdemeanours (Tilly 2005: 9). Analysis of these governments indicates that even very predatory, personalistic regimes in traditional settings do not need to be based on ascriptive ties of blood or descent. Trust may develop as a function of interdependence and shared involvement in risky political projects. The widely employed mechanisms of *nepotism*, *krugovaya poruka* (mutual covering) and *corporatism*, similar to those described by Alena Ledeneva (1998) in her influential study of Russia's economy of favours, as well as more context-specific methods – to sustain these trust networks – such as 'tying with blood feud to the group' (which could involve making a newcomer kill, in turn making him dependent on protection from the new group); hiring several relatives to create greater dependency of the whole family on the authorities.

My case studies confirm Charles Tilly's claim that trust networks do not have to be linked by kinship in order to maintain strong solidarity (Tilly 2005: 9). Today's Chechnya, ruled as a fiefdom by Ramzan Kadyrov, most closely approximates what Charles Hale terms a 'patronalistic society' (Hale 2014: 20): political power represents hierarchical networks 'through which resources are distributed and coercion applied' (Hale 2014: 10), and the economy is mainly shaped by corruption, controlled directly by a regional leader and his network of trust. Because of the immensely high risks to physical security from within the community (Ramzan Kadyrov has numerous blood enemies) and large-scale economic crimes, Kadyrov created an inner circle that is most tightly knit trust network. The organic bonds of kinship (patrilineal, matrilineal, through marriage filiations) are prominent in this network; however, it also includes brothers-in-arms who have proven their loyalty over the years, co-villages, some friends of Ramzan's father, and his own classmates.

However, the situation of Ramzan Kadyrov is unique: he knows that his biological survival is dependent on one person – Vladimir Putin – and that if left one-on-one with his constituency, his life will hardly be long. Unlike Dudaev or Maskhadov, he is not prepared to die for his cause, but wishes to live a long, peaceful life enjoying power and luxury. He has set about controlling the risks by surrounding himself with relatives, and marrying members of his inner circle with the state. In practice, his personal network and private paramilitary have *captured* the state institutions in Chechnya.

The findings presented in this book suggest the following generalizations:

- In the 1990s, the popularly elected governments in Ingushetia and Chechnya did not produce authoritarian clannish regimes based on strong ties. The polities had fairly free elections, with organized opposition and systems of checks and balances. Chechen President Dzhokhar Dudaev was the only leader to attack democratic institutions, after his conflict with Parliament and Grozny city hall had reached a deeply embedded stalemate, compartmentalizing and paralysing the government institutions and spilling over into street violence. This indicates that the 'authoritarian turn' in these subnational polities was not predetermined, nor is it necessarily permanent. In line with the argument put forward by Vladimir Gelman (2016: 458), the Chechen and Ingush cases show that, although 'legacies' are important, future paths are not necessarily shaped by them. To a significant degree, the post-Soviet authoritarianism and dictatorship in Ingushetia and Chechnya were the result of the deliberate actions of political actors, lost wars or Kremlin-imposed rules of the game – and not of indigenous social dynamics and political culture.
- Collective memories and traumas related to the history of colonialism, Stalinist deportations and the recent armed conflicts are among the key 'legacies' that play a prominent role in the collective identity of Chechens and Ingush, with a considerable impact on subnational state-building and political processes. Manipulation of these memories and traumas (Dudaev) or their constructive

management (Aushev) largely determine the capacity of regional leaders to consolidate their constituencies for conflict or peace.
- Generally, as predicted by 'democratic transition' scholars, the role of leaders in the post-Soviet transition period was crucial for the future of democracy (Huntington 1984; Linz 1990). Under conditions of weak institutions, leaders' choices largely determine the outcome of state-building. However, in fragmented societies, social consolidation is a particularly challenging task, as informal actors may differ in their visions of statehood (as in Chechnya); they may be eager to challenge the authorities or even try to capture the state (as with Islamists in both republics). The Chechen case demonstrates the high importance of what Dankwart Rustow called the pre-existing sense of community ... 'preferably ... quietly taken for granted that is above mere opinion and mere agreement' for not only democracy but the survival of subnational statehood per se. Indeed, one of the hardest struggles the leaders of the de facto independent Chechnya had to fight were against 'the birth defects of the political community' (Rustow 1970: 363). Even though Chechens share a common sense of community, they do not agree on what kind of state they would like to have.
- Pre-existing patterns of social integration (*teips, tariqas, virds*) no longer play a role in the state-building and political process in Chechen and Ingush societies. The political process is shaped by agency, integrated based on ideology, programme, religion, economic and security interest, personal loyalty or patronage. Chechens and Ingush politics are not clan-based.
- The past three decades in both republics saw several attempts to revive *teip*-based political organizations – Councils of Teips, Councils of Elders or *Mekhk-Khels* – and mobilize them for an active role in politics. Such attempts were either unsuccessful and/or unpopular in society (as with Adizov's *Mekhk-Khel* in Chechnya) – or they managed to play important public roles, but in the capacity of civil society organizations, as with the Council of Teips during the Ingush 2018–2019 protests). Regardless of the public symbolism of such councils and the public respect for the Elders, the actual driving forces behind these organizations were younger activists, aged 35–50. Remarkably, in Chechnya nationally oriented activists were negative to attempts at reviving the *teips*, viewing them as a challenge to national unity. By contrast, in Ingushetia, nationally oriented activists viewed them quite positively as indigenous, traditionally legitimate grassroots mechanisms for self-organization.
- The cases analysed in this book indicate that, contrary to popular perceptions, the strength of ties in the government does not directly covary with the prominence of kinship; and that the prominence of kinship/descent does not directly correlate with strong personalistic government.
- The model of elite composition and nature of ties within the government in Ingushetia and Chechnya is as follows:

Subnational state-building has an impact on factors which shape the composition of the elite by dictating certain criteria for their recruitment. Thus, the 1991–1994 nationalist project in Chechnya required marginalization of strongly pro-Russian actors; and the Islamist regime would not allow atheists in the government. There is also an impact on the system of checks and balances (via constitutional design and law) and on opposition (dictatorial and authoritarian regimes do not leave room for opposition). The factors shaping the nature of ties within government include the five patterns of integration analysed in this book (descent, kinship, regionalism, religion, ideology) together with other integrative patterns (such as acquaintances, colleagues, friends and professionals). The prominence of each factor will depend on elite choices and the demands of the state-building project. The nature of ties will depend on systemic constraints (such as checks and balances and the existence of an opposition) as well as on the political risk environment. High risk of physical elimination or prosecution for economic crimes will tend to strengthen the ties within the government – unless the leaders are prepared to die for the cause. In turn, elites may alter the systemic constraints and reduce or increase risks through their policies.

From the cases analysed here, it would seem that successful state-building and effective governance for Ingushetia and Chechnya will require, first and foremost, free and fair elections, to enable constituencies to place their elites under control and make them accountable. It will also require a very strong system of checks and balances, with an opposition, civil society watchdogs, reduced risks for elites and meritocratic legal-procedural bureaucracies. In fragmented kinship-rich societies,

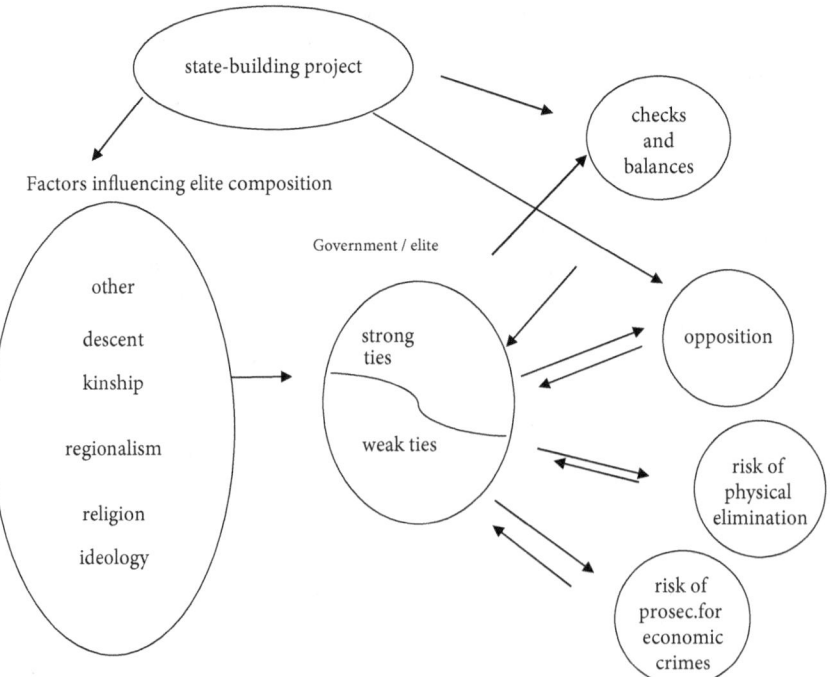

Figure 11.1 The model of elite composition and nature of ties within government in Chechen and Ingush societies.

strong parliaments entitled to control government appointments and plural political process are conducive to reducing nepotism among the elite. Modern-day clanship is not a problem of traditionalism in society, but of bad governance and the lack of democratic procedures.

Therefore, in parallel to the returned democratic procedures, Ingushetia and Chechnya urgently need to set the goal of creating a Weberian bureaucracy. For the past 30 years, the leaders of these republics have all been high-level security officers with little experience of routine political governance. Training new, efficient political managers, as well as boosting governance capacity in the elite and promoting Weberian meritocratic bureaucratic culture will be important for combating criminal trust networks in the power apparatus.

This book has shown that, in the cases of kinship-rich societies with strong informal patterns of social integration, even very imperfect democratic procedures have prevented kinship or clan-dominance, and strong ties in the government. The desire to turn to traditional social mechanisms increases when there are no other channels of voicing discontent or making the elites accountable, like in the case of the Ingush protest movement in 2018–2019, when the informal Council of Teips sought to take over the functions of the powerless Parliament and tried to articulate the problems of the people in this time of acute political crisis and deadlock. Under current conditions, such an institution cannot be effective in achieving political goals: essentially, it acts as a civil society organization. However, because it is so deeply embedded in local identities, the authorities have a hard time of crushing it completely, and can only marginalize it. Completely suppressing Sufis, their *virds*, *imams*, or organizations like the Ingush Muftiyat is also difficult for the authorities.

In the future, we may well observe new attempts at reviving the traditional institutions of *teips*, Councils of Elders or *Khel*s. However, such attempts are extremely unlikely to succeed: the *teips* as relevant political organizations in Chechnya and Ingushetia ceased to exist a long time ago.

Bibliography

Abrams, P. 1988. Notes on the difficulty of studying the state, *Journal of Historical Sociology*, 1(1): 58–89.
Abubakarov, T. 1998. *Dzhokhar Dudaev's Regime: Truth and Fiction*. Moscow: INSAN.
Ajtberov, T. and Akhmadov, Y. 1982. Izvestiya araboyazychnih dokumentov XVI–XVII vv ob obshestvennih otnosheniyah u vajnakhov, *Obshestvennie otnosheniya u Chechenstsev i Ingushei v dorevolutsionnom proshlom*. [Information in the Arabic-language documents VI–XVII centuries about the social relations of the Wainakhs]. Grozny: Chechen-Ingush Publishing House.
Akaev, V. 1994. *Shejkh Kunta-Khadzhi, Zizn' i uchenie* [Sheikh Kunta-Khadzhi, Life and Teaching]. Grozny: Scientific-Research Institute for Humanitarian Studies of the Chechen Republic.
Akaev, V. 2004. *Islam i sotsiokulturnaya realnost na Severnom Kavkaze* [Islam and sociocultural reality in the North Caucasus]. Rostov-on-Don: Izdatelstvo SKNTs VSH.
Akaev, V. 2006. *Kto, zachem i kak eksportiroval vahhabizm v Chechnu* [Who, why and how exported Wahhabism to Chechnya]. http://www.annews.ru/news/detail.php?ID=60968&print=Y. Accessed 4 May 2009.
Akhmadov, Ya. 1991. *Syn Kishi* [The Son of Kishi], *Respublika*, 11 June.
Akhmadov, Ya. 2001. *Istoriya Chechni s drevnejshih vremen do kontsa 18 veka* [History of Chechnya from ancient times till the end of the 18th century]. Moscow: Mir domu tvoemu.
Akhmadov, I. and Lanskoy, M. 2010. *The Chechen Struggle: Independence Won and Lost*. New York: Palgrave Macmillan.
Akhmadov, Ya and Khasmagomadov, E. 2005. *Istoriya Chechni v 19–20 vv* [History of Chechnya in the 19–20th centuries]. Puls. http://www.Chechnyafree.ru/article.php?IBLOCK_ID=359&SECTION_ID=0&ELEMENT_ID=66729. Accessed 27 December 2008.
Akhriev, M. 1995. Kontsern Ingushneftegazkhimprom, Nastoyashee i budushee [Ingushneftegazkhimprom, present and future], *Serdalo*, 28, 1 August, p. 1.
Aliev, T. and Zhadayev, R. 2005. Maskhadov i Basaev, dva lidera odnoj voini [Maskhadov and Basaev, two leaders of one war], *Chechenskoje obshestvo* 2 (40), 1 February.
Aliroev, I. 1990. *Yazyk, istoriya i kultura vajnakhov* [Language, history and culture of Wainakhs]. Grozny: Checheno-Ingushskoje izdatelskoje ob'edinenie 'Kniga'.
Allenova, O. 2004. Я из лесу вышел, был сильный Ахмат [I left the forest, there was a strong Akhmat], *Kommersant*, 19 March.
Almond, G. and Verba, S. 1963. *The Civic Culture*. Princeton, NJ: Princeton University Press.
Aushev, R. 1994. Bit chelovekom na zemle ... Dialog na fone portreta [To be a human on Earth ... Dialogue against the background of a portrait'], *Ingushetia*, 11 January.
Aushev, R. 1997. Rech na prazdnovanii pyatiletiya obrazovaniya Ingushskoj Respubliki. [Speech at the celebration of the 5th anniversary of the creation of the Ingush Republic]. http://www.youtube.com/watch?v=qVvo-a9p73A&feature=related. Accessed 1 August 2008.

Aushev, R. 1999. Doklad Presidenta Respubliki Ausheva na S'ezde naroda Ingushetii [Report of the President of the Republic Aushev at the Congress of the Ingush People], *Serdalo*, 8 December.

Avtorkhanov, A. 1991. *Ubijstvo Checheno-Ingushskogo naroda, Narodoubijstvo v SSSR* [Killing of the Chechen-Ingush people. Nation-killing in USSR]. Moscow: Ves mir.

Avtorkhanov, A. 2005. *Gorskaya sovetskaya respublika* [Mountain Soviet Republic], *Dosh* 7, p. 2.

Babich, I. 2000. Pravovaya kultura Adygov (Istoriya i sovremennost) [The legal culture of Adygs (history and modernity]. Dissertation. Russian State Library.

Babitsky, A. 2005. Yarost' iz-za samoj vstrechi s Basaevim [Fury at the very fact of the meeting with Basaev], *Russian Newsweek*, 14 August.

Baddeley, J. (1908) 2005. *The Russian Conquest of the Caucasus*. London: Adamant Media Collection.

BBC News – Русская служба. 2018. Кто и за что извинялся перед Рамзаном Кадыровым? [Who and for what did people apologize to Ramzan Kadyrov] [online]. YouTube. https://www.youtube.com/watch?v=1SqDcbm87cY

BBC News 1 June 2011. 'Austrian court convicts Chechens over dissident's death'.

BBC News – Русская служба. 25 June 2018. [Chechnya of Thrones: Who and how do they govern the Republic. Detailed map].

BBC News – Русская служба. 5 November 2019. Кто и почему мог убить ингушского силовика Эльджаркиева? [Who and why could kill an Ingush security serviceman Eldzharkiev?].

Bednov, S. 1995. Malen'kij mir riadom s vojnoj [Small peace next to war], *Serdalo*, 17 October, № 39.

Belovetsky, D. 1997. Salman Raduev: S pervomajskim privetom [Salman Raduev: May-day greetings], *Ogonek*, 8 May.

Bennigsen, A. and Wimbush, E. 1979. *Muslim national communism in the Soviet Union: A Revolutionary Strategy for the Colonial World*. Chicago, IL: Center for Middle Eastern Studies.

Berge, A. 1859. *Chechnya i Chechentsy* [Chechnya and Chechens]. Tiflis: Publishing House of the Caucasus Viceroy.

Bezformata. 11 January 2019. Загадочная Асет [No. 421 Mysterious Aset]. https://penza.bezformata.com/listnews/421-zagadochnaya-aset/2380987/.

Bilalov, M. 2019. Родственника Кадырова утвердили на работу [Kadyrov's relative approved for work], *Kavkaz Realii*, 18 December.

Black, C. 1996. The politics of modernization, in *The Dynamics of Modernization*. London: Harper & Row.

Bliev, M. and Degoev, V. 1994. *Kavkazakaia Voina* [The Caucasus War]. Moscow: Roset.

Boas, F. (1897) 1970. *The Social Organization and the Secret Societies of the Kwakiutl Indians*. New York: Johnson Reprint Corporation.

Boissevain, J. and Mitchell, C. (eds). 1973. *Network Analysis: Studies in Human Interaction*. The Hague: Mouton.

Borisov, T. 2006. Бить или не быть [To beat or not to beat], *Rossiskaya Gazeta*, 22 March.

Borodikhin, A. 2018. Отлучить от республики. Как давний конфликт привел к отрешению Юнус-Бека Евкурова от мусульманской общины [Excommunicated from the republic. How an old conflict led to the removal of Yunus-Bek Yevkurov from the Muslim community], *MediaZone*, 29 May.

Bronevsky, S. 1823. *Novejshie geograficheckie i istoricheskie izvestiya o Kavkaze, sobrannie i popolnennie S. Bronevskim* [New geographic and historical news of the Caucasus, collected and complemented by Semen Bronevsky], part 1. Moscow: Selivanovsky publishing house.

Busygina, I. 2018. Зачем и как реформируют российский федерализм? [Why and how the Russian federalism is being reformed?] Контрапункт апрель 2018. https://www.ponarseurasia.org/wp-content/uploads/attachments/busygina_countepoint11.pdf. Accessed 20 September 2021.

Butaev, M. 2018. Единение ингушей в протесте: как оно было? [Unity of Ingush in protest: how was it?], *RIA Derbent*, 6 October.

Calhoun, C. 1997. *Nationalism*. Buckingham: Open University Press.

Calhoun, C. 2007 *Nations Matter: Culture, History, and the Cosmopolitan Dream*. London and New York: Routledge.

Caucasian Knot. 10 March 2004. Сдача в плен Магомеда Ханбиева – результат спецоперации, сопровождавшейся захватом заложников [The surrender of Magomed Khanbiev is the result of a special operation, accompanied by the taking of hostages].

Caucasian Knot. 19 August 2006. Министр финансов Ингушетии обвиняется в хищении крупной суммы денег [Finance Minister of Ingushetia accused of embezzling a large sum of money].

Caucasian Knot. 31 October 2008. О досрочном прекращении полномочий президента Республики Ингушетия [On the early termination of the powers of the president of the Republic of Ingushetia].

Caucasian Knot. 15 December 2011. Оппозиция подала в духовный суд заявление на главу Ингушетии и председателя избиркома республики [Opposition filed an application to the spiritual court against the head of Ingushetia and the chairman of the republic's election commission].

Caucasian Knot. 16 December 2011. Мехк-Кхел [Mehk-Khel].

Caucasian Knot. 23 February 2012. Вопросы от РОД РИ «Мехк-кхел», предложенные главе республики Ингушетия Евкурову Ю.Б. в целях достижения общественного консенсуса [Questions from the ROD RI 'Mekhk-khel', proposed to the head of the Republic of Ingushetia Yevkurov Y.B. in order to achieve public consensus].

Caucasian Knot. 13 June 2012. Евкуров об оппозиции и о себе [Yevkurov about the opposition and about himself] [online]. YouTube. https://www.youtube.com/watch?v=ce1HIXACqRc. Accessed 18 August 2021.

Caucasian Knot. 20 August 2014. Счетная палата РФ обнаружила в Ингушетии растраты на 1,3 млрд бюджетных рублей [The Accounts Chamber of the Russian Federation found 1.3 billion roubles wasted in Ingushetia's budget].

Caucasian Knot. 28 September 2018. Территориальные споры между Ингушетией и Чечней [Territorial disputes between Ingushetia and Chechnya].

Caucasian Knot. 4 October 2018a. Евкуров подписал закон о границе с Чечней [Yevkurov signed a law on the border with Chechnya].

Caucasian Knot. 8 October 2018b. Неравноценный обмен Ингушетии с Чечней: анализ картографов [Unequal exchange of Ingushetia with Chechnya: analysis of cartographers].

Caucasian Knot. 21 December. 2018. Пользователи соцсетей раскритиковали слова Кадырова после резонансного ДТП [Social media users criticized the words of Kadyrov after a resonant traffic accident].

Caucasian Knot. 26 March 2019. Тысячи людей собрались на акцию протеста в Магасе [Thousands of people gathered for a protest in Magas].

Caucasian Knot. 25 July 2019. Из оппозиции до застенок СИЗО – путь опального Магомеда Хазбиева [From the opposition to the basement of SIZO – the path of the disgraced Magomed Khazbiev].

Caucasian Knot. 1 December 2019. Назначение зятя Кадырова начальником управления МВД вызвало скепсис в Чечне [The appointment of Kadyrov's son-in-law as the head of the Ministry of Internal Affairs caused scepticism in Chechnya].

Caucasian Knot. 30 March 2020. Телесюжет с покаянием сына гадалки вызвал возмущение в Чечне [TV report airing repentance of a fortune-teller's son sparked outrage in Chechnya].

Caucasian Knot. 26 July 2021. Протесты в Ингушетии: хроника передела границы с Чечней [Protests in Ingushetia: Chronicle of the redistribution of the border with Chechnya].

Cherkasov, A. 2004. Почему сдался Магомет Хамбиев [Why did Magomed Khambiev surrender], *Polit*, 11 March.

ChGTRK 'Grozny'. 2015. Духовные управления Чечни и Ингушетии договорились о совместной борьбе с экстремизмом [Spiritual administrations of Chechnya and Ingushetia agreed to fight against extremism together] [online]. YouTube. https://www.youtube.com/watch?v=erpyaJ0FecA. Accessed 18 August 2021.

Coleman, J. 1966. Foundations for a theory of collective decisions, *American Journal of Sociology*, 71(6): 615–627.

Collins, K. 2006. *Clan Politics and Regime Transition in Central Asia*. Cambridge: Cambridge University Press.

Committee to Protect Journalists. 2009. Russian TV crew threatened, forced to leave Ingushetia, *Refworld*, 15 October. https://www.refworld.org/publisher,CPJ,4b25fc07c,0.html

Connerton, P. 1989. *How Societies Remember*. Cambridge: Cambridge University Press.

Constitution of the Chechen Republic. 1992. Grozny. https://Chechen-government.com/конституция-чеченской-республики-ич/. Accessed 3 July 2021.

Dahl, R. 1971. *Polyarchy: Participation and Opposition*. New Haven, CT: Yale University Press.

Dahrendorf, R. 1967. *The Modern Social Conflict*. Berkeley: University of California Press.

Dakhilgov, Sh. 1991. *Proiskhozdenie Ingushskih familij* [The origins of Ingush families]. Grozny: 'Kniga'.

Dement'eva, I 1994. *Vojna i mir Prigorodnogo Rayona* [War and peace of the Prigorodny District]. Moscow: Khabra.

Dettmering, C. 2005. Reassessing Chechen and Ingush (Wainakh) clan structures in the 19th century, *Central Asian Survey*, 24 (4): 469–489.

Doklad parlamentskoj komissii o rassledovanii situatsii v Vedenskom rajone Chechenskoj Respubliki. Report of the Parliamentary Commission for investigation of the situation in Vedensky region of the Chechen Republic. March 1993. Grozny: Archives of the Parliament of the Chechen Republic. Private archive.

Dorofeev, V. 1998. Chechenskie rodovye priznaki [Chechen birthmarks], *Vlast* 24 (276), 30 June.

Dudaev, Dzh. 1993. *A Thorny Path to Freedom*. Vilnius.

Dudaeva, A. 2005. One million first. Ultra. Kultura. https://royallib.com/book/dudaeva_alla/million_perviy.html

Dunlop, J. 1998. *Russia Confronts Chechnya: Roots of a Separatist Conflict*. Cambridge: Cambridge University Press.

Durkheim, E. (1933) 1964. *The Division of Labor*. New York: Free Press.

Dzagaurov, G. 1925. *Pereselenie gortsev v Turtsiyu* [Resettlement of the mountaineers to Turkey]. Rostov-on-Don: Sevkavkazkniga.
Eisenstadt, S. 1974. *Post-Traditional Societies*. New York: W. W. Norton.
Eisenstadt, S. 1995. *Power, Trust and Meaning*. Chicago: Chicago University Press.
Eisenstadt, S. (ed.). 2002. *Multiple Modernities*. New Brunswick, NJ: Transaction Publishers.
Eisenstadt, S. and Roniger, L. 1984. *Patrons, Clients and Friends, Interpersonal Relations and Structure of Trust in Society*. Cambridge: Cambridge University Press.
EnemyOpsBelNews+. 2013. Рамзан Кадыров и чеченский спецназ в условиях ночного леса [Ramzan Kadyrov and the Chechen special forces under conditions of a forest at night] [online]. YouTube. https://www.youtube.com/watch?v=QxHomwMcT4c
EnemyOpsBelNews+. 2015. Спецназ Рамзана Кадырова – лучший на планете [Ramzan Kadyrov's special forces are the best on the planet] [online]. YouTube. https://www.youtube.com/watch?v=8SJuIS959Ws
Etnografia narodov Kavkaza, Issledovaniya i materialy. 1961. [Ethnography of peoples of Caucasus]. Moscow: Nauka.
Evans-Pritchard, E. 1940. *The Nuer: A Description of the Modes of Livelihood and Political Institutions of a Nilotic People*. Oxford: Clarendon Press.
Евгений Argunov Live. 2017. (Гудермес) Учебный центр сил специального назначения 2017! [(Gudermes) Special Forces Training Center 2017!] [online]. https://www.youtube.com/watch?v=Z2dWr9L_Pyw
Имамы Ингушетии требуют 1,7 млрд с правительства России [Imams of Ingushetia demand 1.7 billion from the Russian government]. 2018. *Otkritiye Media*, 8 November.
Fortanga Org. 2019a. Раскрыт очередной обман Евкурова [Another deception from Yevkurov revealed]. YouTube. https://www.youtube.com/watch?v=RQYiGSh0PIg. Accessed 18 August 2021.
Fortanga Org. 2019b. Коррупционное разоблачение от Бараха Чемурзиева и Ахмеда Погорова [Corruption exposure from Barakh Chemurziev and Akhmed Pogorov.] YouTube. https://www.youtube.com/watch?v=m19XWJRH630. Accessed 18 August 2021.
Fortanga Org. 2019c. Завод по производству стеклотары. Очередной выкидыш ФЦП «Социально-экономическое развитие Ингушетии» [Factory for the production of glass containers. Another miscarriage of the Federal Target Program 'Social and Economic Development of Ingushetia']. YouTube. https://www.youtube.com/watch?v=dOyIifXDULk. Accessed 18 August 2021.
Fortes, M. 1953. The structure of unilineal descent groups, *American Anthropologist*, 55(1): 17–41.
Fortes, M. 1969. *Kinship and the Social Order: The Legacy of Lewis Henry Morgan*. London: Routledge & Kegan Paul.
Freedom House, 6 February 2020. 'Russia: Authorities Must Condemn, Investigate Attack on Human Rights Defenders in Chechnya'.
Furman, D. (ed.). 1999. *Chechnya i Rossiya: obschestva i gosudarstva* [*Chechnya and Russia: societies and states*]. Moscow: Polnform-Talburi. http://www.sakharov-museum.ru/chr/ Accessed 25 March 2008.
Gadlo, A. 1979. *Etnicheskaya istoriya Severnogo Kavkaza 4–10 vv* [Ethnic history of the North Caucasus 4th to 10th centuries]. Leningrad: Publishing house of Leningrad University.
Gadzhiev, K. 2016. Правозащитники назвали отказ от 'мягкой силы' причиной нестабильности на Северном Кавказе [Human rights activists called the rejection of 'soft power' the cause of instability in the North Caucasus], Caucasian Knot, 8 June.

Gaev, S., Khadisov, M. and Chagaev, T. 1994. *Khajbakh: sledstvie prodolzhaetsya* [Khajbakh: investigations continue]. Grozny: 'Kniga'.

Gakaev, Dz. 1999. Put' k Chechenskoj Revolutsii [The Road to the Chechen Revolution], in N. Furman (ed.), *Chechnya and Russia: Societies and States*. http://www.sakharov-center.ru/chr/chrus08_1.htm. Accessed 25 March 2008.

Gall, C. and dw Waal, T. 1997. *Chechnya: A Small Victorious War*. London: Pan.

Gammer, M. 1998. *Shamil, Musulmanskoje soprotivlenie tsarizmu, Zavoevanie Dagestana i Chechni* [Shamil, Muslim resistance to the Tsar, invasion of Dagestan and Chechnya]. Moscow: Kron-Press.

Gantemirova, G. 1981. Involvement of Chechen-Ingushetia into the economic system if Russia (second half of 19th century), Summary of the dissertation for the candidate of historical science degree.

Geertz, C. 1973. *The Interpretation of Cultures*. London: Fontana.

Geertz, C. 1994. Primordial and civic ties, in J. Hutchinson and A. Smith (eds), *Nationalism*. New York: Oxford University Press, 29–34.

Gellner, E. 1983. *Nations and Nationalism*. Ithaca, NY: Cornell University Press.

Gellner, E. 1987. *The Concept of Kinship and Other Essays*. Oxford: Basil Blackwell.

Gellner, E. and Waterbury, J. (eds). 1977. *Patrons and Clients in Mediterranean Societies*. London: Duckworth.

Gelman, V. 2016. The vicious circle of post-Soviet neopatrimonialism, *Russia, Post-Soviet Affairs*, 32 (5): 455–473.

Granovetter, M. 1973. The strength of weak ties, *American Journal of Sociology*, 78(6): 1360–1380.

Grebenshikov, P. (ed). 1977. *Checheno-Ingushskaya ASSR. 1917–1977* [Checheno-Ingush ASSR 1917–1977, Collection of Statistics]. Grozny: Chechen-Ingush Publishing House.

Grishina Yu. 6 August 2012. Кадыров и Евкуров не поделили террористов. [Kadyrov and Yevkurov could not share terrorists]. Nezavisimaya. https://www.ng.ru/regions/2012-08-06/1_conflict.html. Accessed 29 September 2021.

Gritsenko, N. 1971. *Klassovaya i anti-kolonialnaya borba krest'yan Checheno-Ingushetii na rubezhe 19–20 vekov* [Class and anti-colonial wars of peasants of Chechen-Ingushetia at the turn of the 19–20th centuries]. Grozny: Chechen-Ingush Publishing House.

Gutseriev, M. 1997. *Svobodnie ekonomicheskie zony (opyt, problemy, perspektivy)* [Free economic zones: experience, problems, perspectives]. Moscow: Otkrytyi mir.

Gutseriev, M. 1998. Formirovanie i razvitie zon ekonomicheskogo blagopriyatstvovaniya (metodologiya i praktika) [Formation and development of zones of economic favourability (methodology and practice)], Dissertation summary, Dr.hab. in economics, Moscow.

The Guardian. 11 August 2009. Chechen aid worker and husband found dead in car boot.

Halbwachs, M. (1926) 1950. *The Collective Memory*. New York: Harper Colophon.

Hale, H. 2014. *Patronal Politics: Eurasian Regime Dynamics in Comparative Perspective*. Cambridge: Cambridge University Press.

Harris, C. 1990. *Kinship*. Minneapolis: University of Minnesota Press.

Helmke, G. and Levitsky, S. 2004. Informal institutions and comparative politics: A research agenda, *Perspectives on Politics*, 2(4): 725–740.

Hicken, A. 2011. Clientelism. *Annual Review of Political Science*, 14: 289–310.

Hille, Ch. 2020. *Clans and Democratization: Chechnya, Albania, Afghanistan and Iraq*. Boston: Brill.

Homans, G. 1961. *Social Behavior: Its Elementary Forms*. New York: Harcourt, Brace and World.

Human Right Center 'Memorial'. 1 July 2008. Ингушетия: 2007 год. Куда дальше? [Ingushetia: 2007. Where to go from here?]. https://memohrc.org/ru/reports/Ingushetiya-2007-god-kuda-dalshe

Human Right Center 'Memorial'. 2009. 'Statement on the death of Maksharip Aushev'. https://memohrc.org/ru/announcements/ob-ubiystve-maksharipa-ausheva-zayavlenie

Human Rights Center 'Memorial'. 26 October 2011. Макшарип Аушев: "На месте некогда спокойной Ингушетии образовалась кровавая карта" [Maksharip Aushev: "A bloody map has formed in the place of the once calm Ingushetia"]. http://old.memo.ru/d/96946.html

Human Rights Center 'Memorial'. 2014. Бюллетень Правозащитного центра «Мемориал». Ситуация в зоне конфликта на Северном Кавказе: оценка правозащитников Зима 2013 – 2014 гг. [*Bulletin of the Human Rights Center 'Memorial'. Situation in the conflict zone in the North Caucasus: an assessment of human rights defenders, winter 2013–2014*] (2013/2014). https://memohrc.org/ru/specials/byulleten-pravozashchitnogo-centra-memorial-situaciya-v-zone-konflikta-na-severnom-kavkaze. Accessed 20 September 2021.

Human Rights Center Memorial. 26 June 2015. «Мемориал» о конфликте вокруг Насыр-Кортской мечети в Ингушетии и его разрешении ['Memorial' on the conflict over the Nasyr-Kort mosque in Ingushetia and its resolution]. https://memohrc.org/ru/news/memorial-o-konflikte-vokrug-nasyr-kortskoy-mecheti-v-Ingushetii-i-ego-razreshenii. Accessed 20 September 2021.

Human Rights Center Memorial. 2019. Ингушетия-Чечня: границы, конфликт, протесты, репрессии [Ingushetia-Chechnya: borders, conflict, protests, repressions]. https://memohrc.org/ru/special-projects/Ingushetiya-Chechnya-granicy-konflikt-protesty. Accessed 20 September 2021.

Human Rights Center Memorial. 27 March 2020. Суд ликвидировал «Совет тейпов ингушского народа» [The court has liquidated 'Council of teips of the Ingush people']. Accessed 20 September 2021.

Human Rights Center Memorial. 8 April 2021. «И мирный протест должен быть наказан» ['And peaceful protest must be punished']. https://memohrc.org/ru/monitorings/i-mirnyy-protest-dolzhen-byt-nakazan. Accessed 20 September 2021.

Human Rights Watch. 28 August 2018. Russia: Chechen Leader Threatens Human Rights Defenders.

Human Rights Watch. 31 May 2019. Россия: Угрозы в адрес активистов, которые помогают пострадавшим от преследований ЛГБТ в Чечне [Russia: Threats against activists who help victims of LGBT persecution in Chechnya].

Human Rights Watch. 7 June 2021. Russia: Protect human rights defenders in Chechnya.

Human Rights Watch. 8 May 2019. Russia: New anti-gay crackdown in Chechnya.

Huntington, S. 1984. Will more countries become democratic?, *Political Science Quarterly*, 99(Summer): 193–218.

Huntington, S. 1991. *The Third Wave: Democratization in the Late Twentieth Century*. Norman: University of Oklahoma.

Huntington, S. 1991/1992. How countries democratize, *Political Science Quarterly*, 106(4): 579–616.

Imams Alims of Ingushetia. 2015. Обращение муфтия Исы-хаджи Хамхоева 8. 06.15 [Address of Mufti Isa-Khadzhi Khamkhoev 8. 06.15] [online]. YouTube. https://www.youtube.com/watch?v=nfSzXp7JTtA&t=206s. Accessed 18 August 2021.

Imams Alims of Ingushetia [Имамы Алимы Ингушетии]. 2018. [Сегодня 27 мая в ДЦМ РИ прошла встреча с участием имамов, тамадов, турков (старейшин сел) населенных пунктов РИ.][Today, on May 27, a meeting with the participation of imams, toastmasters, Turks (village elders) of the settlements of the Republic of Ingushetia was held at the Center for Medical Education of the Republic of Ingushetia]. [VK]. 27 May. https://vk.com/search?c%5Bq%5D=%D0%BC%D0%B5%D1%87%D0%B5%D1%82%D1%8C%20%D0%BC%D0%B0%D0%B3%D0%B0%D1%81&c%5Bsection%5D=auto&w=wall-86608608_1047. Accessed 18 August 2021.

Ingushetia TV. 2018a. Евкуров дал пояснение по соглашению о границе. [Yevkurov gave an explanation on the border agreement]. [online]. https://www.youtube.com/watch?v=TIFIXevw4tU. Accessed 18 August 2021.

Ingushetia TV. 2018b. Мнение общественности о границе между Ингушетией и Чечней. [Public opinion on the border between Ingushetia and Chechnya]. [online]. https://www.youtube.com/watch?v=XcWFefBUXU8. Accessed 18 August 2021.

Ingushskaya gosudarstvennost. Normativno-pravovie akty novejshej istorii. Ingush statehood. Normative-legal acts of contemporary history. 1997. Office of Permanent Representative of Republic Ingushetia with the president of the Russian Federation, Moscow and Nazran.

In // Line. 2018. Ахмед Погоров – о коррупции Евкурова в Ингушетии [Akhmed Pogorov on Yevkurov's corruption in Ingushetia] [online]. YouTube. https://www.youtube.com/watch?v=417vACoAiog. Accessed 18 August 2021.

INKavkaz. 2015. Конфликт в Насыр-Кортской мечети. Хьамзат Чумаков. [Conflict in the Nasyr-Kort mosque. Khamzat Chumakov] [online]. YouTube. https://www.youtube.com/watch?v=wn_bR6-F28A. Accessed 18 August 2021.

Inkels, A. and Smith, D. 1974. *Becoming Modern: Individual Change in Developing Countries*. Cambridge, MA: Harvard University Press.

International Crisis Group (ICG). 2012. *The North Caucasus: The Challenges of Integration (I), Ethnicity and Conflict*. https://www.crisisgroup.org/europe-central-asia/caucasus/north-caucasus/north-caucasus-challenges-integration-i-ethnicity-and-conflict

International Helsinki Federation for Human Rights. 2005. *In a Climate of Fear: 'Political Process' and Parliamentary Elections in Chechnya*. November. https://www.ecoi.net/en/document/1413514.html

Isakova, G.K. and Jalilova, M.M. 2018. Особенности Российского Федерализма В Системе Государственного Управления [Features of Russian federalism in the public administration system], *Economics and Enterprise*, 4(93): 278–281.

Ингушетия тонет в коррупции [Ingushetia is drowning in corruption]. 2019. *Bezformata*, 11 January.

Isaev, S. 1998. Prisoedinenie Chechni k Rossii, Agrarnaya politika tsarisma and narodnie dvizheniya v krae v 19 veke [The annexation of Chechnya to Russia, agrarian politics of tsarism and peoples movements in the region in the 19th century], Dissertation abstract for degree of *candidat* of history, Moscow.

Isaeva, T. 1977. 'Feodalnie vladenia a na territorii Checheno-Ingushetii v XVII veke', *Voprosi istorii Checheno-Ingushetii (dorevolutsionnij period)* [Feudal relations on the territory of Chechen-Ingushetia in the 17th century]. Grozny.

Ivanenkov, N. 1910. *Gornie Chechentsy* [*Mountainous Chechens*], *Tersky sbornik*, Vladikavkaz Issue, 7, 1–58.

Имя Зелимхана Мацуева навечно занесено в списки СОБР Управления Росгвардии по Чеченской Республике [The name of Zelimkhan Matsuev is forever entered into the lists of the SOBR of the Rosgvardia Directorate for the Chechen Republic]. 2020. *Grozny.tv*, 17 July.

Kadyrov Ramzan [@Lord_095]. 2020. [Indebted to Daudov] [Instagram]. 23 April.

Kadyrov, Ramzan. 2021. [Student government election]. [VK]. 17 February.
Kaloy Akhilgov [@akaloy]. 21 July 2021. https://twitter.com/akaloy/status/1417840768761405446. Accessed 18 August 2021.
Kapferer, B. 1969. Norms and the manipulation of relationships in a work context, in J.C. Mitchell (ed.), *Social Networks in Urban Situations*. Manchester: Manchester University Press.
Kara-Murza, V. 2018. Чечено-ингушское размежевание [Chechen-Ingush demarcation], *Radio Svaboda*, 27 September.
Karl, T. 1990. Dilemmas of democratization in Latina America, *Comparative Politics*, 23(1): 1–21.
Katz, E. and Lazarfeld, P.F. 1955. *Personal Influence*. New York: Free Press.
Kavkazskaya Khronika (Grozny) № 17. 1998. July.
Kazharov, V. 1992. *Adygskaia Khasa*. Nalchik: Fond Adygi
Khamchiev, S. 2002. Vybor puti [*Choice of the path*]. http://www.Ingushetia.org/article/59.html. Accessed 24 January 2008.
Khamzat Chumakov. 2017. 5 июня 2015 года Насыр-Корт. 2 года со дня провокации в Насыр-Кортской мечети. [5 June 2015 Nasyr-Kort. 2 years from the day of the provocation in the Nasyr-Kort mosque] [online]. YouTube. https://www.youtube.com/watch?v=C_Evs4sJ0mg. Accessed 18 August 2021.
Ханбиев Магомед Ильманович [Khanbiev Magomed Ilmanovich]. 2013. Parliament of the Chechen Republic. https://parlamentchr.ru/deputatskij-korpus/hanbiev-magomed-ilmanovich.html
Khizraev, S. 1992. Ne gotovim li mi chernuyu polosu v svoej istorii? [Aren't we preparing a new dark period in our history], *Ichkeria*, 6 August.
Khoury, Ph. and Kostiner, J. 1991. *Tribes and State Formation in the Middle East*. London: I.B. Tauris.
Kiefer, T. 1968. Institutionalized friendship and warfare among the Tausug of Jolo, *Ethnology* 7(3): 225–244.
Kodzoev, N. 2002. *Istoriya Ingushskogo naroda s drevnejshih vremen do kontsa 19 veka* [History of the Ingush people from ancient times until the end of the 19th century]. Magas: Izdatelstvo 'Serdalo'.
Kolosov, L. 1964. From the history of development of capitalist relations in Chechen-Ingushetia in the epoch of Imperialism (in Russian), *Izvestiya ЧИНИИИЯЛ*, 4(1). Grozny.
Kommersant. 19 June 2020. Экс-премьер Ингушетии попался на молоке [Former Prime Minister of Ingushetia caught on milk].
Kommersant. 30 July 2020. В братстве нашли террористов. Последователей Батала-хаджи Белхороева обвинили в преступлениях террористической направленности [Terrorist were found in a brotherhood. Followers of Batal-Khadzhi Belkhoroev were accused of terrorism-related crimes].
Kostoeva, M. 2019. Необходимо было разобраться [It was necessary to resolve], *Ingushetia Gialgiachye*, 13 November.
Kosven, M. 1964. *Patronymiya i ee rol v istorii obshestva* [*Patronymiya* and its role in the history of society]. Moscow: Nauka.
Kosven, M. and Khashaeva Kh. (eds). 1958. *Istoriya, geografiya i etnografiya Dagestana v 18–19 vv Arkhivnie materialy* [History, geography and ethnography of Dagestan in the 18–19th centuries, Archive materials]. Moscow: ИВЛ.
Kovalskaya, G. 1996. 'General v teni Kavkaza' [General in the shadow of the Caucasus], *Itogi*, 27 August.

Kozlov, V. 1999. *Massoviye besporyadki v SSSR pri Khushcheve and Brezhneve* [Mass disorders in the USSR during Khushchev and Brezhnev]. Novosibirsk: Sibirskii khonograf.
Kozlov, V. and Kozlova, M. 2004. Wainakh exile, *Ogonek*, December 2004.
Krupnov, E. 1960. *Ancient History of the Northern Caucasus*. Moscow: Publishing House of the Academy of Sciences of USSR.
Krupnov, E. 1961. *O chem govoriat pamiatniki materialnoj kultury ChIASSR* [What do monuments of material culture of the Checheno-Ingush Autonomous Soviet Socialist Republic tell us]. Grozny: Chechen-Ingush Publishing House.
Krupnov, E. 1971. *Srednevekovaya Ingushetia* [Medieval Ingushetia]. Moscow: Nauka.
Kulchik, Yu. 1994. Some aspects of Chechen crisis: teip – religious factor of society as a political factor, *IGPI. Political monitoring*. http://www.igpi.ru/monitoring/1047645476//1994/1294/20.html
Kuper, A. 2004. Lineage theory: A critical retrospect, in R. Parkin and L. Stone (eds), *Kinship and Family: An Anthropological Reader*. Oxford: Blackwell, pp. 79–96.
Kusheva, E. 1963. *Narody Severnogo Kavkaza i ikh sviazi s Rossiej* [Peoples of the North Caucasus and their links to Russia]. Moscow: Academy of Sciences of USSR.
Kusheva, E. and Usmanov, M. 1978. *K voprosu ob obshestvennom stroe vajnakhov*. СЭ № 6.
Kuznetsova, A. 2005. Ethnopolitical processes in the Chechen-Ingush ASSR in 1957–1990: consequences of the deportation and the main aspects of rehabilitation of Chechens and Ingush. Dissertation for candidacy of *kandidat nauk*. http://annyku.narod.ru/disser.htm. Accessed January 2009.
Landa J.T. 1994. *Trust, Ethnicity and Identity*. Ann Arbor: University of Michigan Press.
Laruelle, M. 2012. Discussing neopatrimonialism and patronal presidentialism in the Central Asian context, *Demokratizatsiya: The Journal of Post-Soviet Democratization*, 20(4): 301–324.
Laudaev, U. 1872. Chechenskoje plemia, *Svedeniya o Kazkazskih gortsah*, Tiflis, Vipusk, VI http://oldcancer.narod.ru/caucasus/Laudaev.htm. Accessed 17 November 2008.
Leach, E. 1962. *Pul Eliya, a Village in Ceylon: A Study of Land Tenure and Kinship*. Cambridge: Cambridge University Press.
Ledeneva, A. 1998. *Russia's Economy of Favors: Blat, Networking, and Informal Exchange*. Cambridge: Cambridge University Press.
Ledeneva, A. 2006. *How Russia Really Works: The Informal Practices that Shaped Post-Soviet Politics and Business*. Ithaca, NY: Cornell University Press.
Lenta. 31 October 2008. 'Ингушская оппозиция согласилась сотрудничать с временным президентом республики [Ingush opposition agreed to cooperate with the interim president of the republic].
Lenta. 10 July 2020. Раскрыты подробности задержания ФСБ депутата парламента Ингушетии [Details of the detainment of Ingush MP by EFS have been made public].
Leontovich, F. 1883. *Adaty kavkazskih gortsev* [Adats of the Caucasian mountaineers]. Odessa: V2.
Lerner, D. 1958. The passing of traditional society, in T.J. Roberts and A.B. Hite (eds), *From Modernization to Globalization*. Oxford: Blackwell, 119–133.
Lévi-Strauss, C. 1969. *The Elementary Structures of Kinship*. Boston: Beacon Press.
Lieven, A. 1998. *Chechnya: Tombstone of Russian Power*. New Haven, CT: Yale University Press.
Lijphart, A. 1969. Consociational democracy, *World Politics* 21(2): 207–225.

Lin, N., Ensel, W. and Vaughn, J. 1981. Social resources, strength of ties and occupational tatus attainment, *American Social Science Review*, 46(4): 393–405.
Linz, J. 1990. Transitions to democracy, *Washington Monthly*, 13(3): 143–164.
Lomnitz, L. 1977. *Networks and Marginality: Life in a Mexican Shantytown*. New York: Academic Press.
Lukin, O. 2009. *Presidential and Parliamentary Elections in Chechnya 1997*, 29 January 2007 Prague Watchdog. http://www.voinenet.ru/index.php?aid=9977. Accessed 10 September 2009.
Luong, P. 2002. *Institutional Change and Political Continuity in Post-Soviet Central Asia*. Cambridge: Cambridge University Press.
Madaeva, Z. 1988. *Sotsialno-kulturnie izmemenia v selskih rayonah Checheno-Ingushetii na primere Shalinskogo rayona* [Social-cultural changes in rural regions of Chechen-Ingushetia: the example of Shalinky District]. Grozny: Checheno-Ingushskoje kniznoe izdatelstvo.
Maine, H. 1861. *Ancient Law*. www.avalon.law.yale.edu/19th_century/mainea01asp. Accessed 10 September 2009.
Mainwaring, S. 1992. Transitions to democracy and democratic consolidation: Theoretical and comparative issues, in S. Mainwaring, G. O'Donnell and S. Valenzuela (eds), *Issues in Democratic Consolidation*. Notre Dame, IN: University of Notre-Dame Press, 294–341.
Malashenko, A. and Trenin, D. 2004. *Russia's Restless Frontier: The Chechnya Factor in Post-Soviet Russia*. Washington DC: Carnegie Endowment for International Peace.
Malinowski, B. 1930. 17. Kinship. *Man*, 30, 19–29. https://doi.org/10.2307/2789869.
Malsagov, R. 2007. Investitsionnaya politika depressivnogo regiona [na primere Respubliki Ingushetia]. Aftoreferat na soiskanie uchenoj stepeni kandidata ekonomicheskih nauk [Investment policy of a depressed region (case study of Ingushetia)]. Dissertation abstract for degree of *cand. econ.*, Krasnodar.
Mamakaev, M. 1973. *Chechenskii teip v period ego razlozhenia* [The Chechen teip in the period of its disintegration]. Grozny: Checheno-Ingushskoe kniznoe izdanie.
Mann, M. 1992. *States, War and Capitalism*. Oxford: Wiley-Blackwell.
Mann, M. 1993. *The Sources of Social Power*. Cambridge: Cambridge University Press.
Mann, M. 1995. The autonomous power of the state, in M.E. Olsen and M.N. Marger (eds), *Power in Modern States*. Boulder, CO: Westview Press, 37–48.
Marr, N. 1912. K istorii peredvizhenya yaficheskih narodov s Yuga i s Severa Kavkaza [On the history of movement of Japhethite peoples from the South and the North of the Caucasus]. Sankt-Peterburg: Izvestiya imperatorskoj akademii nauk.
Martin, T. 2001. *The Affirmative Action Empire: Nations and Nationalism in the Soviet Union, 1923–1939*. Ithaca, NY: Cornell University Press
Martirosian, G. 1933. *Istoriya Ingushii* [History of Ingushiya]. Ordzhonikidze: Ingush national publishing house 'Serdalo'.
Marx, K. 1845. *The German Ideology*. http://www.marxists.org/archive/marx/works/1845/german-ideology/. Accessed 5 August 2009.
Marx, K. 1852. *The Eighteenth of Brumaire of Louis Bonaparte*. http://www.marxists.org/archive/marx/works/1852/18th-brumaire/. Accessed 5 August 2009.
Mashkin, S. and Sergeev, N. 2006. Пусть Делимханов сдаст наградное оружие на экспертизу [Let Delimkhanov hand over the premium weapon for inspection], *Kommersant*, 23 November.
McClelland, D. 1961. *The Achieving Society*. Cambridge, MA: Harvard University Press.
McLennan, J. (1865)1998. *Primitive Marriage*. London: Routledge/Thoemmes Press.

Министр строительства Ингушетии задержан по подозрению в мошенничестве [Ingushetia's Minister of Construction detained on suspicion of fraud]. 2017. *Kommersant*, 3 February.

Mezhdunarodnij Institut Gumanitarno-Politicheskih Issledovanij. *Politicheskij monitoring. Chechenskaya* [Political Monitoring Chechen Republic Ichkeria (Muzaev T.)]
June 1998. http://www.igpi.ru/monitoring/1047645476/jun1998/Chechen.html
July 1998. http://www.igpi.ru/monitoring/1047645476/1998/0798/20.html
August 1998. http://www.igpi.ru/monitoring/1047645476/1998/0898/20.html
November 1998. http://www.igpi.ru/monitoring/1047645476/1998/1198/20.html
December 1998. http://www.igpi.ru/monitoring/1047645476/1998/1298/20.html
January 1999. http://www.igpi.ru/monitoring/1047645476/jan1999/Chechnya0199.htm
April 1999. http://www.igpi.ru/monitoring/1047645476/1999/0499/20.html
June 1999. http://www.igpi.ru/monitoring/1047645476/jun2000/Chechen.html
July 1999. http://www.igpi.ru/monitoring/1047645476/1999/0799/20.html
February 1999. http://www.igpi.ru/monitoring/1047645476/1999/0299/20.html
March 1999. http://www.igpi.ru/monitoring/1047645476/1999/0399/20.html
May 1999. http://www.igpi.ru/monitoring/1047645476/1999/0599/20.html

Migdal, J.S. 1987. Strong states, weak states: Power and accommodation, in M. Weiner and S.P. Huntington (eds), *Understanding Political Development*. Boston, Toronto: Little, Brown & Co., 391–434.

Migdal, J. 1988. *Strong Societies and Weak States: State-Society Relations and State Capabilities in the Third World*. Princeton, NJ: Princeton University Press.

Migdal, J. 2004. *Boundaries and Belonging, States and Societies in the Struggle to Shape Identities and Local Practices*. Cambridge: Cambridge University Press.

Migdal, J., Kohli, A. and Shue, V. (eds). 1994. *State Power and Social Forces, Domination and Transformation in the Third World*. Cambridge: Cambridge University Press.

Milashina, E. 2016. Бесстрашный суд [Fearless judgement], *Novaya Gazeta*, 11 October.

Milashina, E. 2017. Недавнее покушение на Кадырова [The recent assassination attempt on Kadyrov], *Novaya Gazeta*, 29 January.

Milashina, E. 2021. «Я служил в чеченской полиции и не хотел убивать людей» ['I served in the Chechen police and did not want to kill people'], *Novaya Gazeta*, 15 March.

Millionervideo. 2014. Рамзан Кадыров - КЛЯТВА верности Родине и Президенту! [Ramzan Kadyrov – Oath to of allegiance to the Motherland and the president] [online]. YouTube. https://www.youtube.com/watch?v=JgdBgozvLWk

Misztal, B. 2003. *Theories of Social Remembering*. Maidenhead: Open University Press.

Morgan, L. (1871) 1997. *Systems of Consanguinity and Affinity of the Human Family*. Lincoln: University of Nebraska Press.

Mostashari, F. 2006. *On the Religious Frontier: Tsarist Russia and Islam in the Caucasus*. London: I.B. Tauris.

MsOnlysee. 2013. Рамзан Кадыров: подготовка чеченского спецназа под руководством Даниила Мартынова [Ramzan Kadyrov: training of Chechen special forces under the leadership of Daniil Martynov] [online]. YouTube. https://www.youtube.com/watch?v=PpQPzTGqZbI

Muradov, M. 2004. «Я докладывал Кадырову, что в его окружение внедряются боевики» ['I reported to Kadyrov that militants were infiltrating his entourage'], *Kommersant*, 25 May.

Muradov, M. 2009. Ингушетией займутся тейп-менеджеры [Teip managers to take care of Ingushetia], *Kommersant*, 15 October.

Muradov, M. and Chernykh, A. 2020. Chief Mufti of Ingushetia died of coronovirus. *Kommersant*, 12 April. https://www.kommersant.ru/doc/4320594

Musrailov, 1998. *Bejbulat Tajmiev, voin i diplomat* [Bejbulat Takmiev, a warrior and diplomat], *Almanach 'Chechenets'* № 4.

Muzaev, T. 1997. *Chechenskaya respublika Ichkeria. Politicheskij monitorin* [Chechen Republic Ichkeria. Political monitoring]. http://www.igpi.ru/monitoring/1047645476/oct_97/Chechen.html. Accessed 25 August 2009.

Muzaev, T. 2004. *Aslan Maskhadov. Politicheskaya Biografiya* [Aslan Maskhadov: A political biography]. http://kavkaz-forum.ru/dossier/3279.html. Accessed 9 March 2009.

Muzaev, T. 2007. *Soyuz gortsev. Russkaya revolutsiya i narody Severnogo Kavkaza 1917–Mart 1918* [The union of mountaineers. The Russian Revolution and the peoples of the North Caucasus 1917–March 1918]. Moscow: 'Patria'.

Naimark, N. 2001. *Fires of Hatred: Ethnic Cleansing in Twentieth-Century Europe*. Cambridge, MA: Harvard University Press.

Needham, R. 1960. Discussion: Descent systems and ideal language, *Philosophy of Science* 27(1), 96–101.

Новое правительство Ингушетии полностью сформировано [Ingushetia's new government is fully formed]. 2018. Press Service of the Government of the Republic of Ingushetia, 21 August.

Novikova A. and Dachaeva, C. 2009. *Schetnaya palata poditozhila nasledie Murata Zyazikova* [Counting Chamber made a summary of the heritage of Zyazikov's rule], *Gazeta*, 21 Mayù.

Nutwood. N. 2009. Generals of the Caucasian politics, *Wild West*, 30 December.

О заключении мирового соглашения [On the conclusion of an amicable agreement]. 2017. Department of the Ministry of Justice of the Russian Federation for the Republic of Ingushetia, 14 September.

Открытую в Ингушетии в 2018 году школу закрыли из-за предаварийного состояния [A school opened in Ingushetia in 2018 was closed due to its pre-emergency condition]. 2019. *Tass*, 15 November.

Обнародованные Погоровым факты коррупции предвосхитили расследования силовиков [Facts of corruption promulgated by Pogorov anticipated in the investigations by security officials]. 2021. *Fortanga*, 3 March.

Obrashenie predsedatelia sledstvennogo komiteta Chechenskoj Respubliki S.M. Khasanova k predsedatelu parlamenta Chechenskoj Respubliki Yu. Soslambekovu [Appeal of Chair of the Investigating Committee of the Chechen Republic S.M. Khasanov to the Chair of Parliament of the Chechen Republic Yu. Soslambekov]. 7 May 1993. Archive of Chechen Parliament.

Отправлен в отставку президент Ингушетии Мурат Зязиков [President of Ingushetia Murat Zyazikov dismissed]. 2008. *Echo Moskvi*, 31 October.

Official website of the Republic of Ingushetia. 2016. Юнус-Бек Евкуров провел встречу с религиозными деятелями республики [Yunus-Bek Yevkurov met with religious leaders of the republic] [online]. YouTube. https://www.youtube.com/watch?v=E2AjKBDrrg8. Accessed 18 August 2021.

Orlov, O. and Cherkasov, A. 1998. *Rossija-Chechnya: Tsep oshibok i prestuplenij* [Russia and Chechnya: A chain of mistakes and crimes]. Moscow: Zveniya.

Parkin, R. and Stone, L. 2004. *Kinship and Family: An Anthropological Reader*. Oxford: Blackwell.
Parliament. 1999. № 2, April 12.
Patiev, Ya. 2007. *Khronika istorii Ingushkogo naroda s drevnejshih vremen do nashih dnej* [Chronicle of history of the Ingush people from ancient times to our days]. Makhachkala: Lotus.
Pierson, C. 1996. *The Modern State*. London: Routledge.
Почти все топ-чиновники Ингушетии избежали реального наказания за коррупцию [Almost all top officials in Ingushetia escaped any real punishment for corruption]. 2020. *Fortanga*, 16 August.
Pokhititel inostrantsv ushl ot suda. No ne ot puli spetsnaza. Kommersant № 80, 12 May 2001.
Polian, P. 2003. *Chechnya mezhdu grazdanskoj i otechestvennimi vojnami- sovetizatsiya po vajnakhski (1922–1941)* [Chechnya between civil and patriotic wars: Sovietization, Wajnakh style (1922–1941)]. Radio Free Europe 'Chechnya and Imperial Power' cycle, 20 July 2003. http://www.Svoboda.org/programs/TD/2003/TD.072003.asp. Accessed 25 February 2009.
Protokol o namereniah [*The Protocol on the Intentions (of official delegations of the Ingush Republics and North Osetian Soviet Socialist Republic)*]. Kislovodsk, 24 January 1993. *Severanaja Osetia*, 27 January 1993.
Правительство республики проанализирует обращения граждан о состоянии социальных объектов в регионе [The government of the republic will analyse the appeals of citizens about the state of social facilities in the region]. 2021. Press Service of the Government of the Republic of Ingushetia, 27 April. https://Ingushetia.ru/news/pravitelstvo_respubliki_proanaliziruet_obrashcheniya_grazhdan_o_sostoyanii_sotsialnykh_obektov_v_reg/
Postanovlenie parlamenta Chechenskoj Respubliki 'O provedenii vsenarodnogo golosovania (referenduma) 27 marta 1993 goda' [Resolution of Parliament of the Chechen Republic 'On carrying out a nation-wide voting (referendum) on 27 March 1993'] # 266 of 16 February 1993 (in Russian), Archives of the Chechen Parliament.
Postanovlenie parlamenta Chechenskoj Respubliki # 308 'O date provedeniya i voprosah vinosimih na vsenarodnoe golosovanie (referendum)' [Resolution of Parliament of the Chechen Republic # 308 'On the date and questions brought for the all-nation voting (referendum)']. 22 April 1993. Archives of the Chechen Parliament.
Postanovlenie kabineta ministrov Chechenskoj Respubliki # 389 'O naznachenii Atabaeva M. pervim zamestitelem ministra oborony Chechenskoj Respubliki.' [Resolution of the Cabinet of Ministers of the Chechen Republic # 389 'On appointing Atabaev M. The 1st deputy minister of defence of the Chechen Republic'], signed by Ya. Mamodaev. 19 October 1992, Archives of the Chechen Parliament.
Postanovlenie Konstitutsionnogo suda Chechenskoj Respubliki po delu o proverke konstitutsionnosti Ukaza Prezidenta Ch.R. ot 24 fevralia 1993 goda # 14 'O nalozhenii veto na Postanovlenie Parlamenta Chechenskoj Respubliki ot 16 fevralia 1993 goda' [Resolution of the Constitutional Court of the Chechen Republic 'On the case on checking the compliance of the Decree of the President of the Chechen Republic of 24 February 1993 # 14 'On Vetoing the Resolution of Parliament of the Chechen Republic of 16 February 1992 "On carrying out all-nation voting (referendum)]."' 11 March 1993, Archive of the Chechen Parliament.
Radcliffe-Brown, A. 1935. Patrilineal and matrilineal succession, *Iowa Law Review*, 20(2): 286–303.

Под эгидой Росгвардии создается новый отряд для проведения учебно-тренировочных занятий в районах Арктики [Under the auspices of the Russian Guard, a new detachment is being created to conduct training sessions in the Arctic regions]. 2017. *Grozny-inform*, 21 October.

Поздравление министра ЧР по делам молодежи Исы Ибрагимова с Днём молодежи России [Congratulations to the Minister of the Chechen Republic for Youth Affairs Isa Ibragimov on the Day of the Youth of Russia]. 2018. *Chechnya Sevodnya*, 27 June.

Razvorot. 2006. Обстановка в Чечне. Последствия событий в Кондопоге [Situation in Chechnya. Consequences of events in Kondopoga], *Echo Moskvi*. 21 September.

Reno, W. 2002. 'Mafia troubles, warlord crises', in M.R. Beissinger and C. Young (eds), *Beyond State Crisis? Postcolonial Africa and Post-Soviet Eurasia in Comparative Perspective*. Washington, DC: Woodrow Wilson Center Press, 105–129.

Republic of Ingushetia. Ministry of Internal Affairs. 2018. *Отчет Министра внутренних дел по Республике Ингушетия, 22 Февраль 2018* [Report of the Minister of Internal Affairs for the Republic of Ingushetia, 22 February 2018]. Magas: Ministry of Internal Affairs.

RIA Novosti. 12 May 2016. Более 70 объектов построено в Ингушетии за 5 лет реализации ФЦП развития региона [More than 70 objects were built in Ingushetia in 5 years of implementation of the federal target program for the development of the region].

Robakidze, A. 1973. *Patronimia i narody Kavkaza* [Patronymiya of the peoples of Caucasus]. Moscow: Nauka.

Rostow, W. 1960. *The Stages of Economic Growth: A Non-Communist Manifesto*. Cambridge: Cambridge University Press.

Roy, O. 2000. *The New Central Asia: The Creation of Nations*. New York: NYU Press.

Russell, B. 1938. *Power: A New Social Analysis*. London: Allen & Unwin.

Russian Federation. General Prosecutor's Office. 2021. *Всего зарегистрировано преступлений Январь – июнь 2021* [Total crimes registered January – June 2021] [Ratings]. General Prosecutor's Office.

Russian Federation. Ministry of Property and Land Relations of the Republic of Ingushetia. 2019. *Продажа государственного (муниципального) имущества и имущества госкомпаний 31 Октябрь 2019* [Sale of state (municipal) property and property of state-owned companies 31 October 2019]. Republic of Ingushetia: Ministry of Property and Land Relations.

Рамзан Кадыров покончил с убийцами своего отца [Ramzan Kadyrov ended his father's killers]. 2008. *Izvestiya*, 29 January.

Рамзан Кадыров против судей. Коротко Руководитель Чечни вынудил главу местного Верховного суда уйти в отставку [Ramzan Kadyrov against judges. In short, the Head of Chechnya forced the head of the local Supreme Court to resign]. 2016. *Meduza*, 16 May.

Rustow, D. 1970. Transitions to democracy: Toward a dynamic model, *Comparative Politics*, 2(3): 337–363.

Sack, P., Middleton, J. and Tait D. (eds). 1958. *Tribes without Rulers: Studies in African Segmentary System*. London: Routledge & Kegan Paul.

Said, E. 1978. *Orientalism*. New York: Random House.

Schatz, E. 2004. *Modern Clan Politics: The Power of 'Blood' in Kazakhstan and Beyond*. Seattle: University of Washington Press.

Schneider, D. 1984. *A Critique of the Study of Kinship*. Ann Arbor: University of Michigan Press.

Schweitzer, P. 2000. *Dividends of Kinship: Meanings and Uses of Social Relatedness*. London and New York: Routledge.

Следствие по делу об убийстве главы Центра 'Э'по Ингушетии завершили [The investigation into the murder of the head of the 'E' Center for Ingushetia has been completed]. 2021. *Tass*, 23 March.

Shils, E. 1957. Primordial, personal, sacred and civil ties, *British Journal of Sociology*, 8: 130–145.

Shin, D. 1994. On the wave of democratization: A synthesis and evaluation of recent theory and research, *World Politics*, 47(1): 135–170.

Shnirelman, V. 2007. *Byt alanami. Intellektuali i politika na Severnom Kavkaze v 20 veke* [To be Alans. Intellectuals and politics in the North Caucasus in the 20th century]. Moscow: Novoye literaturnoe obozrenie.

Simmel, G. 1950. *The Sociology of Georg Simmel*. New York: Free Press.

Simon, G. 1991. *Nationalism and Policy towards Nationalities in the Soviet Union*, trans. K. Forster and O. Forster. New York: Routledge.

Skitsky, B. 1959. K voprosu o feodalnih otnosheniyah v istorii Ingushskogo naroda [To the question of feudal relations in the history of the Ingush people], *Izvestiya Checheno-Ingushskogo NIIYaL*, 1 (1), Grozny.

Smeets, Rieks H. and Wesselink E. 1995. *Chechnya one year of war*, A Pax Christi International Report, 11 December. http://www.georgia.fi/Caucasus/ich_rap1.html. Accessed 20 September 2009.

Smith, A. 1986. *The Ethnic Origins of Nations*. Oxford: Basil Blackwell.

Smith, A. 1995. *Nations and Nationalism in a Global Era*. Cambridge: Polity.

Smith, S. 1998. *Allah Mountains: Politics and War in the Russian Caucasus*. London: I.B. Tauris.

Sovet tiepov Republic of Ingushetia [2019]. Срочно. Совещание в Совете тейпов сегодня 5. 12.2019г [Urgently. Meeting at the Council of Teips today 5.12.2019] [online]. YouTube. Accessed 18 August 2021. https://www.youtube.com/watch?app=desktop&v=XyE4KaKy5zU&feature=share

Soyuz nerushimih [Union of inviolable]. *Nezavisimaya gazeta*, 29 April 2001.

Souleimanov, E.A. and Aliyev, H. 2017. *How Socio-Cultural Codes Shaped Violent Mobilization and Pro-Insurgent Support in the Chechen Wars*. London: Palgrave Macmillan.

Startsev, Ya. 2005. 'Informal' institutions and practices: Objects to explore and methods to use for comparative research. *Perspectives on European Politics and Society*, 6(2), 331–351.

Stepan, A. 1986. 'Paths toward Re-democratization', in G. O'Donnell, P. Schmitter and L. Whitehead (eds), *Transitions from Authoritarian Rule*. Baltimore, MD: Johns Hopkins University Press, 64–84.

Sultan, M. 2003. The quest for peace in Chechnya: the relevance of Pakistan's Tribal Areas experience. *Central Asian Survey*, 22(4): 437–457.

СОВМЕСТНОЕ ЗАЯВЛЕНИЕ: В десятую годовщину убийства Натальи Эстемировой правозащитные организации требуют правосудия [Joint statement: On the tenth anniversary of the murder of Natalya Estemirova, human rights organizations demand justice]. 2019. *Human Rights Watch*, 15 July.

Tatriev, M. 1996. My ne nakhlebniki, my prosto nashli sposob kak vyzhit [We are not free-riders, we have simply found a way to survive], *Serdalo*, 12 March № 11.

Tilly, C. 1975. *The Formation of National States in Western Europe*. Princeton, NJ: Princeton University Press.

Tilly, C. 2005. *Trust and Rule*. Cambridge: Cambridge University Press.
Tishkov, V. 1995. Чеченский кризис. Аналитическое обозрение [Chechen Crisis Analytical Review], vol. 8. Moscow. Center for comprehensive social research and marketing.
Tishkov, V. 1996. Osetino-Ingushskij konflikt, *Serdalo*, 35, 21 August.
Tishkov, V. (ed.). 1998. *Mezhetnicheskie otnosheniya i konflikty v postsovetskih gosudarstvah. Ezhegodnij doklad Seti etnologicheskogo monitoringa i rannego preduprezhdeniya konfliktov* [Inter-ethnic relations and conflicts on the post-Soviet states]. Moscow: Institut Etnologii RAN.
Tishkov, V. 2001. *Obshestvo v vooruzhennom konflikte. Ethnographiya Chechenskoj vojny* [A worn-torn society. Ethnography of the Chechen war]. Moscow: Nauka.
Tishkov, V., with a foreword by M. Gorbachev. 2004. *Life in a War-torn Society: Ethnography of the Chechen War*. Berkeley: University of California Press.
Toriev, B. 2003. *Republic of Ingushetia through Statistics and Expert Analysis (April–May)*. Moscow: IEA RAN.
Три республики Северного Кавказа стали лидерами в России по росту коррупции [Three republics of the North Caucasus become leaders in Russia in the growth of corruption]. 2018. *Regnum*, 5 March.
Trudovie Resursy Checheno-Ingushetii i ikh ratsionalnoe ispolzovanie [Labour resources of Chechen-Ingushetia and their rational use]. 1976. Grozny: Chechen-Ingush Publishing House.
Tumanov, G. 2016. В Чечне ввели «духовно-нравственный паспорт» ['Spiritual and moral passport' introduced in Chechnya], *Kommersant*, 18 February.
Ukaz Prezidenta Chechenskoj Respubliki 'O prekrashenii vseh vyplat v budget Rossijskoj Federatsii i napravlenii ih v budget Chechenskoj Respubliki' [Order of the President of the Chechen Republic 'On ceasing all payments into the budget of the Russian Federation and transferring them into the budget of the Chechen Republic'], 29 January 1992, Archives of the Parliament of the Chechen Republic.
Ukaz Prezidenta Chechenskoj Respubliki 'Ob otmene na territorii Chechenskoj Respubliki 5% naloga s prodazh i 25% naloga s prodazh tovarov povishennogo sprosa' [Decree of the President of the Chechen Republic 'On abolishing 5% sales tax on the territory of the Chechen Republic and 25% taxes from sale of goods of high demand'] of 16 December 1991, Archives of the Chechen Parliament.
Ukaz Prezidenta Chechenskoj Respubliki 'Ob uporyadochenii otpravki strategicheskih tovarov za predely Chechenskoj Respubliki zheleznodorozhnim transportom' [Decree of the President of the Chechen Republic 'On ordering strategic goods beyond the Chechen Republic by railroad'] of 4 January 1992, Archives of the Chechen Parliament.
Ukaz Prezidenta Chechenskoj Respubliki 'O nezakonnom zakhvate administrativnih zdanij i pomeshenij' [Decree of the President of the Chechen Republic 'On illegal capture of administrative buildings and premises'] of 8 January 1992, Archives of the Chechen Parliament.
Ukaz Prezidenta Chechenskoj Respubliki 'O priostanovlenii deyatelnosti Sledstvennogo Komiteta Chechenskoj Respubliki' [Decree of the President of the Chechen Republic 'On suspending the activity of Investigating Committee of the Chechen Republic'] of 2 November 1992, Archives of the Chechen Parliament.
Umarova, A. 2016. Замолчать Чечню [To silence Chechnya], *Echo Kavkaz*, 7 January.
«У меня сотни родных по мужской линии» ['I have hundreds of male relatives']. 2020. *Znak*, 13 February.

В Ингушетии намерены перезапустить простаивающие промышленные предприятия [Ingushetia intends to restart idle industrial enterprises]. 2019. *Tass*, 9 September.

В Чечне подведены итоги референдума [The referendum results summed up in Chechnya]. 2007. *RBC*, 27 March.

Владимиров: ВРП Ставрополья к 2030 году превысит 1,5 трлн рублей [Vladimirov: GDP of Stavropol Territory by 2030 will exceed 1.5 trillion roubles]. 2021. *RBK*, 29 July.

Vachagaev, M. 2009. *Interview to Grani TV*, 20 March 2009. http://grani-tv.ru/entries/669/. Accessed 20 March 2009.

Velikovsky, D. 2009. Kavkaz: Obshestvo s ogranichennoj otvetstvennost'yu [The Caucasus: a society Ltd], *Russkij Reporter*, 24 September.

Vinogradov, V. and Chokaev, K. 1966. *Ancient Evidence on Names and Location of Nakh Tribes*. IChINII, volume VII, issue I, Grozny.

Voprosy istorii klassoobrazovaniya i sotsialnikh dvizhenij v dorevolutsionnoj Checheno-Ingushetii [Issues of history of class formation and social movements in re-revolutionary Chechen-Ingushetia]. 1980. Grozny: Checheno-Ingushskii institut istorii, sotsiologii i filologii.

Ware, R. and Kisriev, E. 2001. Cultures of peace and violence in the Northern Caucasus: The cases of Dagestan and Chechnya. Working paper for the meeting of the International Society of Political Psychology, Cuernavaca, Mexico.

Weber, M. 1930. *The Protestant Ethic and the Spirit of Capitalism*. London: Allen & Unwin.

Weber, M. 1951. *The Religion of India*. New York: Free Press.

Weber, M. 1954. *On Law in Economy and Society*. New York: Free Press.

Weber, M. 1964. *The Theory of Social and Economic Organization*. New York: Free Press.

Weber, M. 1978. *Economy and Society*. Berkeley: University of California Press.

Weber, M. 1995. Power, domination and legitimacy, in M.E. Olsen and N.M. Marger (eds), *Power in Modern Societies*. Boulder, CO: Westview Press, 37–48.

Weiner, M. and Huntington S. (eds). 1987. *Understanding Political Development*. Boston, MA: Little, Brown.

Wilson, J. 1961. The economy of patronage, *Journal of Political Economy*, 69: 4.

Yakovlev, N. 1925. *Ingushi* [The Ingush]. Rostov-on-Don: Publisher 'Krasnii proletarii'.

Yandarbiev, Z. 2001. Islamskij fundamentalism ne opasen [Islamic fundamentalism is not dangerous], *Vrvemia Novostej*, 17 December.

Yandiev, M. 2005. *Zakonodatelnaya vlast RI v sisteme razdeleniya vlastej* [The legislative power in the system of division of powers in the Republic of Ingushetia]. Moscow: Avtoreferat na soiskanie uchenoj stepeni kandidata yuridicheskih nauk.

Yemel'yanova, G. 2002. *Russia and Islam: A Historical Survey*. New York: Palgrave Macmillan.

Yeremenko I. Novikov U. (eds) RAU-University, Russia and Chechnya (1990–1997). 1997. Documents testify.

Yevkurov Ingushetia Meeting of Yunus Bek Yevkurov with congregation of Nasur-Kort mosque before the Friday prayer, Yevkurov Ingushetia. 13 June 2015. https://www.youtube.com/watch?v=WkET4xhlMkQ

Yevkurov, Y. 2012. *Блог Главы Ингушетии* [Blog of the Head of Ingushetia] [online]. 28 July.

Yovloy, U. 2019. Совет тейпов Ингушетии пожаловался на давление властей [Council of Teips of Ingushetia complained about pressure from the authorities], Caucasian Knot, 28 August.

Yuga.ru. 15 March 2019. Чеченский депутат от «Единой России» рассказал о нелюбви к русским и назвал себя сыном Ичкерии [Chechen deputy from 'United Russia' spoke of his dislike of Russians and called himself a son of Ichkeria].

Yuga.ru. 12 February 2020. Кадыров передумал назначать своего 23-летнего племянника главой Совбеза и сделал его министром спорта [Kadyrov changed his mind about appointing his 23-year-old nephew as head of the Security Council and made him Minister of Sports].

Zakayeva, A. and U. Yovloy 2018. Протестующие в Магасе призвали жителей Ингушетии присоединиться к акции [Protesters in Magas urged residents of Ingushetia to join the rally], Caucasian Knot, 4 October.

Zakluchenie Konstitutsionnogo suda Chechenskoj Respubliki 'O sootvetstvii Konstitutsii Chechenskoj Respubliki dejstvij i reshenij visshih dolznostnih lits gosudarstva po ohrane Konstitutsionnogo stroya, prav i svobod Respubliki' [Resolution of the Constitutional Court of the Chechen Republic 'On compliance to the Constitution of the Chechen Republic of actions and decisions by high officials of the state, aimed at protection of the Constitutional order, rights and freedoms of the Republic'], 18 May 1993, Archives of the Chechen Parliament.

Zapodinskaya, E. Chechenskij schit ne spas zakhvachennih zhurnalistov [The Chechen shield has not saved the abducted journalists], *Kommersant* № 90 (1272) of 17 June 1997.

Zaschitnik Otechestva [Defender of the Motherland]. Grozny # 15, October 1997.

Zdravomyslov, A. 1998. *Ossetian-Ingush Conflict: Perspectives of Exiting a Deadlock*. Moscow: ROSSPEN.

Zelkina, A. 2000. *In Quest for God and Freedom: The Sufi Response to the Russian Advance in the North Caucasus*. London: Hurst.

Zheglov, A. and Mashkin, S. 2006. Враг до гроба [Enemy to the grave], *Kommersant*, 20 November.

Zisserman, A. 1879. Двадцать пять лет на Кавказе [Twenty-Five Years in the Caucasus]. Sankt-Peterburg: Izdatelstvo A.S. Suvorina.

Zubarevich, N. April 2018. Отношения центр-регионы: что изменилось за четыре года кризиса? [Relations between center and regions: what has changed in four years of crisis?] Counterpoint. https://www.ponarseurasia.org/kontrapunkt-v11-2018/

Zubov, P. 1835. *Feats of the Russian Warriors in the Caucasian Lands 1800–1834*. St Petersburg: Publishing House of K. Vingeber.

Zulkarnay, I. 2018. Почему Россия вновь скользит от федерализма к унитаризму [Why Russia is again sliding from federalism to unitarianism], *Public Administration Issues*, 5: 116–132.

Index

Abadiev, Idris 75, 160, 166, 170, 173, 195
abduction 76, 100, 139, 162, 179, 186, 195, 211
Abubakarov, Taimaz 96–9, 106, 113, 114
accommodation 6, 7, 51, 120, 176, 216, 232
accountability 177, 198–200, 210, 223
Achaluki 2, 32, 70, 71, 78, 85
Achkhoy-Martan 70, 71
adat 7, 12, 27, 28, 31, 33–5, 37, 40, 43, 45, 53, 74, 76, 168, 200, 228, 229
Adizov, Said-Magomed 110–12
Adyghe 28
affirmative-action 44, 46
agriculture 29, 43, 46, 51–3, 63, 87, 95, 96, 117, 135, 149, 158–60, 191, 195, 197, 225
Akhilgov, Kaloy 204
Akhmadov, Ilyas 127, 133, 137, 139–41, 143, 144
Akhmadov, Khussain 25–8, 58, 63, 92, 95, 102–5, 110–13, 127, 133, 137, 139–41, 143, 144
Akhmadov, Yavus 25–8
Akhmadov and Lanskoy 127, 133, 137, 139–41, 143, 144
Akiev, Batarbek 72, 159
Akiev, Timur 186, 205
Alania Square 198, 199
al-Ghazi-ghuzikumuqi, Jamaladin 36
Alkhan-Kala 59, 70
Alkhanov, Alu 215
Alkhan-Yurt 70
Alkhazurovo 70
Alleroy 69, 71, 73, 108, 142, 149
Altievo 70, 71, 169
amnesty 212, 214
anthropological 5, 13, 15, 66
anthropologist 2, 6, 37, 88
anti-extremism 190, 209
Argun 69, 70, 83, 116, 141, 223

Arsanov, Deni 85
ascriptive ties 13, 18, 121, 145, 151, 223, 233
Aushev, Mussa 48, 73, 74, 77
Aushev, Ruslan 3, 11, 153, 156–66, 170–76, 178, 180, 183, 233, 235
Aushevy 70
authoritarianism 4, 11, 114, 226, 234
Avturkhanov, Umar 115, 116, 118

Barakhoev, Akhmet 198, 200, 201, 205
Barkinkhoy 66, 69, 174
Basaev, Shamil 123, 125–30, 132, 133, 138, 140–4, 147, 149, 150, 215
Batal-Khadzhi vird 84, 88, 189, 208, 209
Baysarov, Movladi 215, 216, 224
Bazaeva, Lipkhan 107
Belkharoev, Batal-Khadzhi 84
Belkharoev, Ibragim 209
Belkharoevy 209
beloshapochniki 50
Benoy 64, 69, 73, 108, 213, 222
Berge, Adolf 31–3, 36, 40
Biltoy 63, 69–71, 107, 108
Bisliev, Abdul-Khalid 109
Bisultanov, Idris 226
Bisultanov, Odes 222
blat 20, 21
Bosoy 70, 72
Bunin, Gleb 102
Busygina, Irina 3, 177, 178
Buzurtanov, Akhmed 185, 190, 192, 194, 200, 208
Buzurtanov, Mukhtar 155, 161, 170, 173

capture 7, 100, 139, 151, 186, 214, 226, 232, 235
Caucasus war 34, 37, 41
ceremonies 54, 74, 77, 78, 84
Chapanovy 32, 70, 78, 85
Cheberloy 32, 70

Chechen-Ingushetia 45, 54, 91–93, 107, 154, 157
Chechenization 211, 228
checks and balances 4, 23, 101, 104, 110, 120, 121, 149, 151, 175, 183, 220, 234, 236
Chemurziev, Barakh 192
Cherkhigov, Adam 226
Cherkhigov, Idris 225
Cherkhigov, Ramzan 225
Cherkzi 65
Chianti 27, 65
Chiri-Yurt 67, 70, 134
Chumakov, Khamzat 188, 198, 199, 202
Clan politics 2, 5, 12, 14, 121, 176, 231–3
cleansing 102, 155, 199, 223
clientelism 6, 20–22, 229
collective memories 55, 56, 58, 199
collectivization 8, 45, 46, 51, 57
Collins, Kathleen 5, 12–14, 17, 121, 231
colonization 6, 26, 27, 41
Commission for rehabilitation of fighters 187, 188, 190
compartmentalization 6, 7, 87, 120, 151, 232
competition 7, 54, 120, 151, 177, 232
complimentary filiation 79
Connerton, Paul 55
Constitutional Court 95, 99–101, 106, 120, 201, 203
coronavirus 77
corruption 1, 6, 21, 22, 162, 173, 174, 180, 181, 183, 191–93, 195, 196, 199, 217, 220, 229, 233, 234
Cossacks 26, 27, 33, 35, 40, 65
Council of Elders 14, 28, 62, 75, 76, 85, 86, 107, 113, 120, 167, 168, 171, 200, 237
Council of Teips 195, 196, 200, 202, 206, 208, 210, 235, 237
counter-insurgency 187
counter-terrorism 151, 186

Dagestan 34, 36, 52, 62, 70, 83, 95, 128, 129, 131, 142, 144, 147, 150, 187, 218, 232
Dattykh 165
dekhoy 79, 81
de-kulakization 8, 45
Delimkhanov, Adam 216, 224, 226
deportation 45–51, 56–8, 64, 72, 74, 75, 80, 86, 91, 102, 153, 231, 234

descent 1, 5–7, 13, 15–18, 26, 49, 63, 64, 66, 68, 69, 72–4, 78, 79, 82, 89, 90, 113, 119, 121, 148, 175, 227–9, 232, 233, 235, 236
Dettmering, Christian 28, 37
Divan 36
Djukti 65
Dolakovo 70, 72, 81, 159, 160
dozal 30, 64
Dudaev, Dzhokhar 58, 64, 71, 83, 91–4, 96–121, 125–7, 129, 140, 141, 145, 148, 150, 157, 158, 175, 176, 232, 234
Dudaeva, Alla 92, 99
Dudaeva, Besira 112
duumvirate 104, 120
Dym 40
Dzeirakh 27
Dzhalka 62

economy 10, 18, 20, 40, 44, 46, 52, 53, 75, 95–7, 99, 100, 104, 113, 114, 117, 119, 123, 128, 132–4, 144, 157, 159–61, 175, 182, 191, 210, 229, 232–4
economy of favours 18, 233
education 2, 10, 19, 43, 44, 50, 53, 75, 87, 89, 95, 97, 98, 102, 103, 113, 114, 117, 120, 124, 127, 132, 135, 136, 145, 150, 157, 162–4, 178, 191, 225
Ekazhevo 2, 70, 71, 80, 153
Eldzharkiev, Ibrahim 84, 209
elite 1, 2, 4, 21, 43, 59, 102, 112, 114, 116–18, 121, 125, 126, 140, 141, 148, 157, 163, 172, 174, 176, 180, 182, 183, 194, 198, 218, 222, 223, 229, 233, 235–7
Elmurzaev, Yusup 117, 146
embezzlement 181, 192, 193, 195, 209
endogamy 49
Evkurov 3, 173, 182
Evloeva, Izabella 194, 199, 201, 206, 207
Evloevy 70, 166, 170, 171, 173
exile 3, 43, 45–51, 54, 56, 57, 59, 92, 102
exogamous 37, 67
Ezhiev, Khizir 217

familia 61, 66–9, 72, 80, 85, 87, 88, 167–9, 173, 174, 206, 207, 233
family 2, 3, 7, 8, 13, 16, 17, 28–31, 33, 40, 43, 46–9, 53–7, 62, 64–9, 72–82, 84, 85, 88, 89, 91, 93, 95, 112, 147, 162, 166–8,

171, 179, 182, 183, 185, 187, 194, 205, 209, 213, 214, 217, 220, 222–8, 233, 234
fear 3, 132, 185, 211, 218, 222, 227, 229
federalism 3, 177, 203
feudalism 27, 28, 31, 41
fictive kinship 13, 17
fieldwork 3, 6, 17, 61, 87, 89, 109, 116, 171, 181
Fortanga media 192–4, 199, 201, 206
Fortes, Meyer 16, 79
fundamentalist 3, 83, 86–9, 124, 129, 131, 132, 139, 141–3, 146, 164, 166, 171, 172

Ga 66
gaar 30, 31, 37, 40, 47, 61, 64, 65, 67–9, 73, 76, 108
Gaev, Salavat 77, 108
Gagiev, Ayub 85, 160, 193
Gakaev, Dzhabrail 26, 91, 114
Galanchozh 70
Galay 67, 68, 70
Gammer, Moshe 33–6
Gamurzievo 2, 70, 71, 80
Gantamirov, Bislan 102, 115–18
Gazdievy 70
Gekhi-Chu 2, 70, 77, 108
Gelaev, Ruslan 126, 128, 140, 141
Gellner, Ernst 16, 17, 66, 93, 119
Gelman, Vladimir 21, 22, 234
genealogy 68
Gorets 215, 216, 224
Granovetter, Mark 19
Groznensky rabochij 92, 128, 132, 134–6, 139, 143, 144, 148
Gruppa Vostok 216
Gruppa Zapad 216
Gudiev, Abukar 67

Hale, Henry 21, 22, 229
healthcare 43, 98, 102, 132, 135, 136, 145, 150, 162, 163, 175, 178, 233

Ibragimov, Turpal-Ali 223
Ichkeria 64, 92, 111, 123, 128, 133, 135, 139, 140, 143, 211, 213, 216, 219
identity 10, 13, 14, 17, 19, 28, 49, 54, 56, 59, 63–5, 89, 106, 107, 109, 124, 131, 156, 171, 199, 210, 220, 231, 232, 234

ideology 4, 6, 21, 50, 65, 90, 93, 112, 114, 121, 124, 146, 148, 150, 153, 169, 172, 220, 229, 232, 235, 236
IDPs 157, 163–6, 178, 179
imamate 9, 35–9, 41, 142
Imam Shamil 34, 35, 38, 41, 64, 95, 110, 142, 201
Imarat Kavkaz 190
impunity 9, 178, 180, 181, 186, 220, 222, 229, 233
indigenous 25, 27, 52, 55, 64, 66, 83, 93, 119, 129, 207, 234, 235
industry 44, 50, 52, 53, 96, 97, 126, 132–5, 137, 144, 145, 157–59, 224, 232
informal institutions 6, 7, 25, 43, 106, 145, 166
informal politics 11, 22, 102, 229
infrastructural power 94, 115, 120, 150, 232, 233
Ingush–Ossetian conflict 55, 102, 156, 162, 180, 181
inner circle 17, 19, 140, 148, 150, 182, 194, 198, 209, 214, 215, 218, 221, 222, 224, 232, 234
insurgency 1, 164, 179, 180, 182, 186, 190, 196, 212, 215, 217, 224
integration 3, 5, 6, 9, 25, 26, 31, 33, 38, 39, 43, 44, 50, 54, 61, 84, 86, 89, 96, 119, 120, 124, 150, 176, 186, 202, 208, 210, 231, 232, 235–7
intellectuals 2, 46, 57, 91, 93, 108, 130, 153, 155, 232
intelligentsia 44, 45, 51, 54, 93, 116, 124
intra-confessional schism 188, 189
Iskhanov, Khusein 98, 99, 106, 121, 141
Islamists 131, 140, 143, 146, 147, 176, 211, 232, 233, 235
Islamization 37, 65, 124, 141, 150
Israilov, Umar 214
Itum-Kali 70

jamaats 130, 131
judiciary 32, 95, 121

Kabardoy 26, 28
Kadyrov, Akhmad 146, 211, 212, 215, 216, 219, 224
Kadyrov, Islam 223
Kadyrov, Khamzat 226
Kadyrov, Khas-Magomed 226

Kadyrov, Ramzan 1, 9, 20, 88, 190, 197, 199, 212–14, 218, 221, 233, 234
Kadyrova, Aymani 219, 225
Kadyrova, Ayshat 225
Kadyrova, Khadizhat 225
Kadyrova, Medni 225
Kadyrova, Zargan 225
Kadyrova, Zulay 225
kadyrovtsy 212, 214
Kan-Kalik, Viktor 109
Karabulak 49, 69–71, 173, 179, 200
Kazakhstan 12, 14, 46–50, 53, 55, 83, 93, 124
Kebedov, Bagautdin 129, 131, 139
Keloy 67, 70, 76
Key 70
khabashism 218
Khadzhi-murid 189, 205, 208, 210
Khadzievy 71
Khajbakh 108
Khakhkhoy 47, 70
Khal-Keloy 50, 67, 70
Khamkhoev, Isa 188–90, 198, 208
Khanbiev, Magomed 127, 213
Khasavyurt Accord 123, 126, 133
Khasiev, Said-Magomed 38, 65, 73, 108, 115, 148, 149
Khattab 129–32, 144, 150
Khautiev, Bagaudin 201
Khel 62, 76, 237
Khulakhoy 174
Kindarov, Baron 110
kinship 1, 2, 5–7, 13–19, 29–31, 49, 51, 54, 64–6, 68, 74, 77–82, 87–90, 112–14, 121, 148, 172, 174, 175, 180, 183, 187, 204, 205, 222, 223, 228, 229, 231, 233–7
Kishiev, Kunta Khadzhi 38, 39, 83–5, 113, 167
Kodzoev, Issa 55, 61, 63, 153
Kodzoev, Nurdin 26, 31, 35, 39, 40, 72, 73, 88
Kodzoevy 71
kolkhoz 45, 46, 111
korchkhoi 67
korenizatsiya 43, 44, 46
Kosven, Mark 28–31
Kotievy 71
krugovaya poruka 20, 22, 182, 233

Kurchaloy 70, 136
kuyan 81, 88
Kuznetsova, Anna 48, 50–53

Laudaev, Umalat 27, 28, 31, 32
law 7, 8, 12, 14, 15, 20, 21, 27, 28, 31–4, 36, 41, 49, 53, 74, 76, 86, 88, 95, 99, 101, 104, 119, 120, 123, 128, 131, 132, 136–9, 143, 146, 153–55, 161, 164, 168, 195, 203, 236
law-enforcement 53, 138, 139, 161, 162, 178, 186, 190, 211, 216
Lebed, Alexander 123
Ledeneva, Alena 20–2, 182, 233
legal pluralism 53, 195
legitimacy 13, 14, 45, 110, 127, 143, 149, 177, 199, 200, 207, 208, 210, 218, 229
Lévi-Strauss, Claude 16
lineage 16, 17, 61, 67, 70–5, 77–9, 82, 109, 169, 171, 173, 200, 207, 227
lustration 138, 143, 146

Magas 69, 76, 158, 161, 165, 181, 189, 195, 197, 199, 201, 203, 208
Malgobek 69, 154, 158, 164, 171, 172, 187, 192, 202
Malinowski, Bronislaw 16
Malsagov, Akhmed 160, 172, 174
Mamakaev, Magomed 29–33, 37, 39, 40
Mamodaev, Yaragi 99, 102, 104
Mann, Michael 8, 94, 115, 120, 150
Mansur, Usurma 27, 38
marginalization 7, 87, 232, 235
Martin, Terry 43, 44
Martirosian, Georgi 25, 27–9, 35, 37
Mashr 61, 193, 200, 201
Maskhadov, Aslan 3, 83, 123, 125–9, 131–4, 137–51, 158, 159, 175, 213, 214, 216, 228, 232, 234
maslat 73
matrilineal 49, 79, 82, 89, 180, 182, 229, 234
Matsuev, Viskhan 225
mazum 36
Mekhk-khel 31, 32, 34, 37, 62, 64, 74, 110–12, 120, 147, 195, 196, 235
Melkhi 83
Memorial, human rights center 2, 151, 178, 183, 186, 197, 204, 205, 213, 218, 220

memory 43, 49, 55–9, 92, 93, 115, 116, 119, 124, 155, 157, 167, 175, 199, 234
Merzhoevy 27, 71, 81
Mesker-Yurt 214
Meskhety 71
Mezhidov, Bektimar 103, 106, 110, 119
Migdal, Joel 7–9, 11, 12, 151
migration 34, 35, 222, 225, 227
Milashina, Elena 217, 222, 223
militias 144, 154
modernization 4–6, 8–10, 13, 21, 43, 45, 54, 59, 119, 157, 158
mold 68, 76–8, 87
Movladi Baysarov 215, 216, 224
mudir 36
mufti 36, 188–90, 211
Muftiyat 172, 188, 189, 200, 202, 208–10, 237
mukhtasibs 36
murid 36, 38, 39, 77, 83, 85, 86, 89, 209, 226, 227
murshid 36, 38
murtazeks 36
Mutsolgov, Magomed 61, 164, 193, 200, 201, 204
Muzaev, Magomed 26, 37, 65, 108, 109, 113
Muzaev, Timur 113, 127, 128, 131, 137, 140, 142, 148
myakhchoy 79
Myalkhi 27

Nadterechny region 51, 70, 83, 113, 115–18, 124, 149
naib 36, 39
naibstvo 36
nakh 25–8, 78, 81
Nalgiev, Ismail 198
Naqshbandi 38, 39, 83–5, 88, 113, 190
Nashkhoy 27, 32, 64, 65, 70, 108
Nasyr-Kort 70, 71, 188, 198, 206
nationalism 45, 92, 93, 119, 131, 146, 218
Naursky region 51, 83, 116, 124
Nazran 2, 33, 35, 39, 59, 69–71, 81, 83, 84, 153, 162, 163, 174, 179, 182, 186, 187, 190, 191, 194, 205, 208
Needham, Rodney 16, 66, 89
negotiations 72, 86, 102, 103, 106, 110, 134, 150, 154, 160, 164, 165, 182

neighbourhood 31, 46, 51, 54, 85, 89, 179, 192, 227
nek 30, 40, 47, 61, 64, 65, 73
nenakhoy 79, 80
neopatrimonialism 18, 21, 22
neo-traditionalism 110, 120
nepotism 20, 21, 23, 88, 110, 149, 151, 173–5, 196, 232, 233, 237
network 2, 5, 6, 13, 14, 18–23, 31, 44, 54, 80, 87–90, 114, 148, 162, 172, 174, 182, 194, 221, 226, 229, 231–4, 237
Nijskho 63, 153, 166
Nizam 35
Nokhcho, Turpal 64
nomenklatura 54, 89, 153
Novaya Gazeta 222, 223
Nozhaj-Yurt 63, 70, 71, 107, 108
Nukhaev, Khoz-Akhmed 147, 148

Opora Ingushetii 197
opposition 23, 49, 83, 84, 86, 91, 106, 108, 114–16, 118–21, 124, 126, 128, 132, 134, 138, 139, 141–8, 151, 160, 175, 181, 183, 185, 187, 190, 192–7, 202, 203, 205, 206, 219, 232, 234, 236
Ortskhoy 32, 83
Ozdoevy 70, 167, 170, 171, 174, 182

paganism 86
Pamyatoy 70, 107
paramilitary 117, 124, 125, 128, 136, 138, 140, 145, 150, 155, 211, 212, 215, 216, 224, 232, 234
patronymia 29, 30
People's front of Chechen-Ingush Republic 91
perpetrators 54, 101, 182, 183
personality cult 218
Pobedinskoye 215, 216
Pogorov, Akhmet 192
Polian, Pavel 44, 45
political prisoner 198, 202, 204, 205
Prigorodny region 48, 51, 69–71, 83, 153–56, 160, 163, 164, 185, 186, 199
primordial 3–6, 121
putsch 92, 110, 154

qadi 36, 40
Qadyri 83, 84, 88, 113

Raduev, Salman 127, 128, 132, 139, 141, 224
referendum 94, 105, 106, 162, 203, 211
regionalism 1, 6, 12, 13, 26, 27, 82, 83, 115, 236
retro-fashion 107, 120, 232
revolution 41, 58, 62, 67, 92, 109–11, 114, 116, 119, 146, 154
Rigkhoy 70
risk 4, 18, 19, 21, 23, 73, 77, 86, 88, 121, 142, 149–51, 176, 221, 236
ritual 49, 76–8, 83, 84, 167, 168, 171, 177, 209, 227
rituals 50, 54, 68, 74, 76–8, 80, 84–9, 171, 209, 232
Robakidze, Aleksey 30
Roshni-Chu 70
rule-making 8, 94, 95
Ruzban 85

sakh 49, 68, 78
Salafism 124, 131, 142, 146, 190, 218
Salgievy 28
Samashki 2, 70, 72, 85, 86
Sampievy 67
SB 212, 214, 215, 223, 224
Schatz, Edward 12–14, 121, 231
Serdalo 158, 159, 161–3, 165, 172–4
Sernovodsk 56, 63, 87
Serzhen-Yurt 130–32
Shakhraj, Sergey 102, 103, 118
Shali 45, 130, 224
sharia 7, 12, 27, 33–7, 40, 43, 45, 53, 76, 86, 113, 128, 129, 131, 136, 137, 139, 141–3, 145, 147, 148, 164, 168, 195, 199, 200, 202, 210
Shatoy 2, 27, 66, 70, 107, 148
Shelkovskoy region 51, 83
shichoy 78
Shnirelman, Victor 26, 27, 57
solidarity 9, 16, 18, 19, 34, 49, 54, 56, 58, 59, 73, 78, 80, 82, 85, 88, 89, 107, 109, 119, 166, 175, 226, 232, 234
Solsa-Khadzi 113
Startsev, Yaroslav 6
state-building 1, 3–5, 7–13, 15, 22, 41, 43, 91, 94, 102, 106, 113, 123, 125, 129, 132, 140, 144–6, 148, 150, 153, 157, 166, 168, 176, 178, 215, 229, 231–6

state-employed 51, 98, 178, 219, 232
state-in-society 11, 12, 151
subnational 1, 3–5, 11, 54, 119, 150, 175, 178, 231–5
Sufism 113, 131, 210

tamada 85, 86, 168
tariqa 38, 39, 51, 61, 83–7, 113, 144, 146, 167, 189, 202, 205, 209, 235
taxes 34–6, 96, 97, 133, 158, 159
teip 2, 3, 14, 15, 27–32, 35, 37, 38, 47–9, 51, 54, 61–75, 77, 78, 82, 84, 85, 87, 89, 106–10, 112, 120, 121, 127, 142, 147–9, 161, 166–71, 173, 174, 182, 183, 195, 196, 202, 204, 207, 208, 210, 222, 227, 231, 232
teip-based 38, 63, 72, 73, 148, 206, 235
Terkjist 113, 117, 149
Tilly, Charles 19, 22, 229, 233, 234
torture 147, 180, 186, 187, 214, 222
tower 28, 70–72, 166–8
traditions 7, 27, 37, 49, 50, 111, 115, 131, 144, 162, 200, 209, 210, 218, 226, 228, 229
trauma 4, 57, 123, 234
trust 3, 4, 18–22, 64, 96, 106, 126, 146, 182, 198, 207, 212, 220, 221, 223, 224, 226, 229, 233, 234, 237
tsa 30
Tsentoroy 213, 214, 217, 223
tsijna nakh 61, 78, 79, 81
tukhum 14, 31, 32, 34, 82, 83, 106, 148
Tumso 65

Udugov, Movladi 126, 128
unemployment 53, 54, 88, 96, 137, 180, 193, 212
uprising 34, 35, 37, 38, 45
Uraza-Bayram 172, 227
urbanization 3, 10, 54
Urus-Martan 69, 70, 83, 108, 113, 115–18, 131, 142, 146, 147
usttsa 79
Uzhakhov, Malsag 200, 202, 206
Uzhakhovy 71

vendetta 73, 82
Vezhery-Yurt 166

vird 50, 51, 54, 77, 83–5, 87, 113, 125, 127, 146, 150, 189, 190, 205, 208, 209, 218, 227
Vismuradov, Abuzaid 224
Vladikavkaz 45, 153–56, 158, 165
Vovnushki 167
vovtkhar 79, 82

Wahhabism 124, 132, 146, 147, 172
Wainakh 49–51, 53, 54, 58, 91, 92
Weber, Max 7–10, 94
weddings 30, 51, 54, 68, 76–8, 80, 82, 86, 168, 199, 205, 209, 210, 227

Yalkhoroy 47
Yamadaevy 224
Yandarbiev, Zelimkhan 105, 123, 125–9, 132, 144
Yandi-Kotar 67, 70
Yarysh-Mardy 129
Yeltsin, Boris 118, 119, 123, 154, 156, 158, 165

Yermolov, Alexei 33, 34, 57
Yevkurov, Yunus-Bek 1, 86, 87, 185–90, 192–9, 201, 203, 205, 206, 208–10, 233
yovkhatar 79
yukyokushverg 79

Zakan-Yurt 70
zakhalsh 79
Zakriev, Sahab 225
Zakriev, Salman 225
Zakriev, Yakub 225
Zamaj-Yurt 2, 70, 71, 107
Zangiev, Vis-Khadzi 50, 51
Zavgaev, Doku 91, 92, 117
Zikrism 39
zikrists 39, 50, 113
ziyarats 218
Znameskoye 116
Zumsoi 65, 66, 70–72, 82
Zyazikov, Murat 3, 170, 177, 178, 180–83, 185, 186, 195, 233

www.ingramcontent.com/pod-product-compliance
Lightning Source LLC
Chambersburg PA
CBHW062122300426
44115CB00012BA/1773